FOOD

Brigid Allen is a cookery writer and historian with strong literary interests. She read History at Somerville College, Oxford in the 1960s, has a doctorate from the University of London, and has worked with archives and manuscripts in Britain and the United States. Her books include several collections of original recipes: *Cooking with Garlic, Ginger and Chillies* (1992), *The Soup Book* (1993), and *The Nut Book* (1994).

FOOD

An Oxford Anthology

Edited by

BRIGID ALLEN

Oxford New York

OXFORD UNIVERSITY PRESS

1995

Oxford University Press, Walton Street, Oxford OX2 6DP
Oxford New York
Athens Auckland Bangkok Bombay
Calcutta Cape Town Dar es Salaam Delhi
Florence Hong Kong Istanbul Karachi
Kuala Lumpur Madras Madrid Melbourne
Mexico City Nairobi Paris Singapore
Taipei Tokyo Toronto
and associated companies in
Berlin Ibadan

Oxford is a trade mark of Oxford University Press

First published 1994
First issued as an Oxford University Press
paperback 1995

British Library Cataloguing in Publication Data
Data available

Library of Congress Cataloging in Publication Data
Food : an Oxford anthology / edited by Brigid Allen.
p. cm. Includes indexes.
1. Food. 2. Cookery. 3. Food habits. I. Allen, Brigid.
TX353.F557 1994 394.1—dc20 93–49408

ISBN 0–19–282504–6

1 3 5 7 9 10 8 6 4 2

Printed in Great Britain
Biddles Ltd
Guildford and King's Lynn

CONTENTS

IV. LAVISHNESS

V. AUSTERITY

VI. FOOD AND THE EMOTIONS

INTRODUCTION

In the changing history of the world, the need for food, and for certain observances bound up with its consumption, has been one of the most constant, major elements in human life. As moral attitudes have altered, whole structures of religious, economic, social, and sexual behaviour have changed with them. Food, like sleep, however, has remained a basic, daily human requirement: more necessary in most climates than clothing or shelter, more immediately assuaging to personal needs than (say) family life, religion, love, or sex. From Homeric times onwards, most social gatherings of any importance have revolved round the dispensation of food and its often required accompaniment or substitute, alcoholic drink. Most religions include or have included some form of ritual sacrament or sacrifice involving food, many of these meant as a direct thanksgiving for present supplies and a propitiation of the forces controlling supplies for the future. The deprivation of food, by means of famine, war, poverty, or neglect, is as terrible an experience today in Africa and other, disturbed parts of the world as it was for the tribesmen of Palestine and Egypt in the last chapters of the Book of Genesis, or for the poor in rural England and Ireland at the time of the corn-shortage and potato blight of the 1840s.

The representation of food in graphic art (for instance, in medieval depictions of cooking and eating, in Brueghel's rustic feasts, or Cézanne's still-lives of fruit), can convey something of the satisfying nature of a life in which good, simple food is in regular supply. The emotional and social resonances connected with food which we find in novels, poetry and drama, biography and autobiography, and diaries and letters, are more various and complicated than those found in graphic art, if in general more casually incidental to the main subject-matter. Pushkin, in *Eugene Onegin*, proudly drew attention to his habit of writing about 'banquets [and] sundry things to eat', and compared himself as he did so with 'godlike Homer'. Fanny Burney's late eighteenth-century heroine Evelina professed herself to be disgusted with young men who were vulgar enough to converse at table about food, and in doing so probably reflected her creator's own feelings. Some novelists, playwrights, and poets have managed to avoid any mention of cooking and eating, or in describing meals have barely indicated the presence of food on the table. It is in Shakespeare's comedies and history plays, not in his great tragedies, that we find the most copious references to food: Petruchio flinging down the joint of mutton in *The Taming of the Shrew*; Mistress Quickly recalling her neighbour's dish of prawns with vinegar in *King Henry IV, Part II*; the triumphantly down-to-earth Falstaff, continually taking metaphors from food and drink; or Hotspur, exclaiming in *King Henry IV, Part I*, that, pursued by a bore, he would

> rather live
> With cheese and garlic in a windmill, far,
> Than feed on cates and have him talk to me
> In any summer-house in Christendom.

Tolstoy, on the other hand, filled his greatest novel, *Anna Karenina*, with references to food, and conveyed the character of its hero, Levin, partly by describing his simple eating-habits in comparison with those of other members of the Russian landowning gentry, and bringing into the narrative from time to time the kind of wholesome foods which Levin most enjoyed when at home in the country.

Understanding people through their food, or satisfying curiosity about individuals' eating-habits, is an activity which certain puritanically minded scholars claim to despise. If, however, we associate food with generosity, pleasure, and the basic texture of life itself, it becomes a matter of more than simply ephemeral interest. Much depends on the approach. The Revd James Woodforde, for example, whose much-quoted, late eighteenth-century diary (omitted from this anthology largely because it is so well known) lists the content of most of the dinners which he ate, and especially of those which he gave to friends and neighbours, is sometimes characterized as 'gluttonous' because of the number of different meat-dishes which appeared together on his table. For a gentleman of his time, however, Woodforde was not conspicuously extravagant with food; and his dispassionate listing of dishes reveals a methodical rather than a greedy disposition. More interesting, from a psychological point of view, are the revelations of diarists, letter-writers, biographers, and autobiographers who have actually considered themselves or their subjects to be greedy: for example, Boswell on Johnson in his declining years, or John Cowper Powys, whose *Autobiography* of 1934 dwells continually on his early gluttony and later, forced abstemiousness.

The chief objects of this anthology are to satisfy curiosity (about what and how people ate, what they felt about food, how they celebrated with it, and how it varied from country to country and region to region), and to provide both pleasure and literary reflection. Its source-material is mainly English and American, from novels, poetry, plays, historical narratives and other documentary sources, biography, diaries, and letters. Some items have been taken from the Bible and the classics; some from well-known European literary works in translation. Nearly all are from published sources; but a few come from unpublished manuscript material, mainly in the Bodleian Library at Oxford and the rich but little-known collection of English letters and diaries in the India Office Records in London.

The arrangement of the anthology is in six main parts. The first part contains two sections, of which the first, 'Food and Character', is devoted to characters in literature as seen through their relationship with food. The second section, 'Eating Habits', contains accounts of the tastes in food and eating-habits of real people, and of households (rather than individuals) in fiction.

In the second part, there are sections dealing with the acquisition, classification and cooking of different kinds of food. These consist of 'Provisioning and Shopping'; 'Food as Gift'; staple foods (bread, butter, meat, fish, vegetables, fruit); 'Food in Season'; 'Home Cooking'; 'Recipes' (four, all in verse); and 'Roughing It'.

The third part, which is about the consumption of food, includes a short general section on 'Meals' and individual sections on breakfast, lunch, tea, and dinner. (Here a certain arbitrariness has been necessary; for although midday dinner still survives among some people in certain areas of Britain, with the same meaning that 'cooked lunch' has for their neighbours, and although 'tea' in one area—particularly the North—has a roughly equivalent meaning to 'supper' in another, most references to meals have been classified by the time of day at which they take place rather than by what they are called by those who eat them.) Other sections contain descriptions of food experienced by travellers in Britain, Continental Europe and the Near East, North America, and India, and by lunchers- and diners-out in various kinds of restaurant.

The fourth part, devoted to ritual, extravagance, and entertainment, contains sections on ceremonial food, parties, and greed, gluttony, and excess. The fifth covers simple and austere food, diets and dieting, hunger and deprivation, school and other institutional food, and unpleasant food generally. The sixth and last part explores the subject of food and the emotions, with sections on food and distress, dream and fantasy food, food and happiness, and food, sensuality, love, and sex.

I

PEOPLE

FOOD AND CHARACTER

Chaucer's vignette of the Franklin, in the General Prologue to the Canterbury Tales, *is a positive and on the whole attractive one. Jovially self-indulgent and generous towards others, he makes the best of his comfortable position in life, and is exacting only towards his cook if meals are late or the sauce insipid. Of all the pilgrims whom Chaucer describes in this Prologue, he characterizes the Franklin by his love of food and hospitality rather than by niceties of physical appearance, behaviour, or dress, so that the expression 'Franklin' in the early eighteenth century acquired the secondary meaning of a particularly generous host. As a well-off landowner, although apparently not of armigerous rank, he seems to have belonged to a higher class than the Prioress with her super-refined table manners and vulgar French; the Wife of Bath with her dressiness and slightly brash sophistication; the Cook with his mere technical competence at producing good dishes; or the randy Summoner with his tags of Latin and his cravings for drink and 'garleek, oynons, and eke leeks'.*

A frankeleyne was in his compaignye.
Whit was his berd as is the dayeseye;
Of his complexioun he was sangwyn.
Wel loved he by the morwe a sop in wyn;
To lyven in delit was evere his wone,
For he was Epicurus owene sone,
That heeld opinioun that pleyn delit
Was verray felicitee parfit.

An householdere, and that a greet, was he;
Seint Julian he was in his contree.
His breed, his ale was alweys after oon;
A better envyned man was nowher noon.
Withoute bake mete was nevere his hous
Of fissh and flessh, and that so plentevous
It snewed in his hous of mete and drynke,
Of alle deyntees that men koude thynke.
After the sondry sesons of the yere,
So chaunged he his mete and his soper.
Ful many a fat partrich hadde he in muwe,
And many a breme and many a luce in stuwe.
Wo was his cook but if his sauce were
Poynaunt and sharp, and redy all his geere.
His table dormant in his halle alway
Stood redy covered al the longe day.
At sessiouns ther was he lord and sire;
Ful oft time he was knyght of the shire.
An anlaas and a gipser al of silk
Heeng at his girdel, whit as morne milk.
A shirreve hadde he been, and a contour.
Was nowher swich a worthy vavasour.

In his company was a franklin [*i.e. a landowner, not of noble rank*]. *His beard was as white as a daisy; his humour was sanguine. He loved bread sopped in wine in the mornings, and was used to living in comfort, since he took after Epicurus, who believed that in comfort was to be found true happiness. He kept open house on a grand scale, like a local St Julian* [*the Hospitaller, the probably mythical patron of hospitality*]. *His bread and ale were always of a uniformly high standard; no man was better stocked with wine than he. His house was never short of supplies of cooked meat and fish, in such quantity that* [*you might say that*] *it snowed food and drink, with all imaginable kinds of delicacies. He adapted his meals to the time of year, always eating what was in season. He had many a plump partridge fattening in the coop, and many a bream and luce* [*pike*] *in the fishpond. It was all up with his cook if the sauce was not tasty and sharp, or if he were behindhand in the kitchen. In his hall a permanent table stood ready laid all day. He presided over the local sessions court and sat in Parliament many times as representative of his county. At his belt, white as morning milk, hung an anlace* [*a short, double-edged dagger*] *and a purse of silk. He had been a shire-reeve and public accountant, and was as worthy a landowner as any.*

Geoffrey Chaucer, *The Canterbury Tales: General Prologue*, *c.*1387

THE PRIORESS

At mete wel ytaught was she with alle:
She leet no morsel from hir lippes falle,
Ne wette hir fyngres in hir sauce depe;
Wel koude she carie a morsel and wel kepe
That no drope ne fille upon hir brest.
In curteisie was set ful muchel hir lest.
Hir over-lippe wiped she so clene
That in hir coppe ther was no ferthyng sene
Of grece, when she dronken hadde hir draughte.
Ful semely after hir mete she raughte.
And sikerly she was of greet desport,
And ful pleasaunt, and amyable of port

* * *

She was so charitable and so pitous
She wolde wepe, if that she saugh a mous
Kaught in a trappe, if it were deed or bledde.
Of smale houndes hadde she that she fedde
With rosted flessh, or milk and wastel-breed.

She was well-trained in table etiquette, and did not let crumbs drop out of her mouth or get her fingers wet by dipping them deep into in her sauce-bowl. She lifted her food up daintily and held it so that nothing spilt down her front. Good manners came naturally to her. She always wiped her upper lip clean so that not a speck of grease showed in her cup after she had drunk. She helped herself politely to food, and was generally pleasant, amusing and kindly in her behaviour. . . . So soft-hearted and tender was she that she would weep if she saw a mouse caught in a trap, whether it was dead or maimed. She had little dogs, and would feed them on roast meat or on the finest bread with milk.

Chaucer, *Canterbury Tales: Prologue*

Like its sister-plays The Merry Wives of Windsor *and* King Henry IV, Part I, *but unlike most of Shakespeare's other plays,* King Henry IV, Part II *wallows cheerfully in vulgarity and silliness, symbolized for the most part by drunkenness and allusions to eating and drinking. Here Mistress Quickly, hostess of a tavern in Eastcheap, is reminding Sir John Falstaff of his proposal of marriage to her.*

HOSTESS. . . . Did not goodwife Keech, the butcher's wife, come in then and call me gossip Quickly? coming in to borrow a mess of vinegar? telling us she had a good dish of prawns; whereby thou didst desire to eat some; whereby I told thee they were ill for a green wound? And didst thou not, when she was gone down stairs, desire me to be no more so familiarity with such poor people; saying that ere long they should call me madam? And didst thou not kiss me and bid me fetch thee thirty shillings? I put thee now to thy book-oath: deny it, if thou canst.

* * * * *

[*At the Tavern, Falstaff drunkenly chaffs Doll Tearsheet.*]

FALSTAFF. Peace, good Doll! do not speak like a death's-head; do not bid me remember mine end.

DOLL. Sirrah, what humour's the prince of?

FALSTAFF. A good shallow young fellow: a' would have made a good pantler, a' would ha' chipped bread well.

DOLL. They say Poins has a good wit.

FALSTAFF. He a good wit? hang him, baboon! his wit's as thick as Tewkesbury mustard; there's no more conceit in him than is in a mallet.

DOLL. Why does the prince love him so, then?

FALSTAFF. Because their legs are both of a bigness; and a' plays quoits well; and eats conger and fennel; and drinks candles' ends for flap-dragons; and rides the wild mare with the boys; and jumps upon joint-stools; and swears with a good grace; and wears his boots very smooth, like unto the sign of the leg . . .

* * * * *

Gloucestershire. A Hall in Justice Shallow's house. Enter Shallow, Falstaff, Bardolph and Page.

SHALLOW. By cock and pie, sir, you shall not away to-night. What, Davy, I say!

FALSTAFF. You must excuse me, Master Robert Shallow.

SHALLOW. I will not excuse you; you shall not be excused; excuses shall not be admitted; there is no excuse shall serve; you shall not be excused. Why, Davy!

Enter Davy [*his servant*].

DAVY. Here, sir.

SHALLOW. Davy, Davy, Davy. Davy, let me see, Davy; let me see, Davy; yea, marry, William cook, bid him come hither. Sir John, you shall not be excused.

DAVY. Marry, sir, thus; those precepts cannot be served: and, again, sir, shall we sow the headland with wheat?

SHALLOW. With red wheat, Davy. But for William cook: are there no young pigeons?

DAVY. Yes, sir. . . .

SHALLOW. . . . Some pigeons, Davy, a couple of short-legged hens, a joint of mutton, and any pretty little tiny kickshaws, tell William cook.

DAVY. Doth the man of war stay all night, sir?

SHALLOW. Yea, Davy. I will use him well: a friend i' the court is better than a penny in purse. Use his men well, Davy, for they are arrant knaves, and will backbite.

* * * * *

Gloucestershire. Shallow's orchard. Enter Falstaff, Shallow, Justice Silence, Davy and the Page.

SHALLOW. Nay, you shall see my orchard, where, in an arbour, we will eat a last year's pippin of my own graffing, with a dish of caraways, and so forth: come, cousin Silence, and then to bed.

FALSTAFF. 'Fore God, you have here a goodly dwelling and a rich.

SHALLOW. Barren, barren, barren; beggars all, beggars all, Sir John: marry, good air. Spread, Davy; spread, Davy; well said, Davy.

FALSTAFF. This Davy serves you for good uses; he is your serving-man and your husband.

SHALLOW. A good varlet, a good varlet, a very good varlet, Sir John: by the mass, I have drunk too much sack at supper: a good varlet. Now sit down, now sit down: come, cousin.

* * * * *

DAVY. There's a dish of leather-coats for you [*to Bardolph*].

SHALLOW. Davy!

DAVY. Your worship! I'll be with you straight [*to Bardolph*]. A cup of wine, sir?

William Shakespeare, 2 Henry IV, II. i, iv; V, i, iii

Pantler: officer of the household in charge of the pantry or bread-room; *chipped bread*: pared the crusts from bread; *flap-dragon*: a party game (also known as Snapdragon) in which participants picked raisins out of a dish of flaming brandy and extinguished them in their mouths; *graffing*: grafting; *caraways*: (probably) sweets flavoured with caraway seeds; *leather-coats*: a type of russet apple with a yellowish, rough skin. (A vehicle for innuendo, possibly of a homosexual kind, from the knowing Davy, whose words contain many more layers of meaning than his master's.)

❧ *Goethe's classic tale of a love-triangle,* The Sorrows of Young Werther, *one of the most powerful early works of the Romantic age in European fiction and poetry, was based on an experience of his own while living in Wetzlar in 1772 at the age of 23. As an apprentice lawyer, new to the town, he made a number of friends, among them Johann Christian Kestner, a hard-working lawyer in his early thirties. Kestner was unofficially engaged to Charlotte Buff, the charming daughter of a widower, who was domesticated enough to look after a family of ten or eleven younger siblings. Goethe fell in love with Charlotte, not knowing her to be engaged, when he called with his partner to take her to a ball at which Kestner would join them later. She was evidently high-spirited, teasing, and even flirtatious towards Goethe; but it was the sight of her at home, as the eternal wife- or mother-figure dispensing bread to her younger brothers and sisters, which made the strongest impression on his heart. For a summer he (Werther), Kestner (Albert) and Charlotte agonized together, before Goethe abandoned Wetzlar for good. In real life he rapidly formed another attachment elsewhere; in the novel, more dramatically, Werther borrowed pistols from Albert and shot himself, to the distress of both Albert and Charlotte, and to the future detriment of many romantic young people who committed suicide believing themselves to be hopelessly in love.*

I had alighted and the maid who came to the gate begged us to wait a moment, Mamselle Lottchen would be with us straightway. I went across the courtyard to the well-built house and, when I had ascended the steps in front and entered at the door, I caught sight of the most charming scene that I have ever witnessed. In the entrance hall there swarmed six children, from two to eleven years of age, round a handsome girl of middle height, who wore a simple white frock with bows on the breast and arms. She was holding a loaf of black bread and cutting a slice for each of the children round her in proportion to its age and appetite, offering it with such an amiable air and each one crying 'Thank you!' so artlessly, after he had stretched his little hands up as high as he could before his slice was cut, and then springing away contentedly with his supper or, if he was of a quieter nature, walking tranquilly towards the gate to see the strangers and the coach in which their Lotte was to drive away.—'I beg your pardon,' she said, 'for giving you the trouble of coming in and making the ladies wait. While I was dressing and making all sorts of arrangements for the house in my absence, I forgot to give the children their supper, and they won't have their bread cut by anyone but me.'

Johann Wolfgang von Goethe, *The Sorrows of Young Werther*, 1774, translated by William Rose, 1929

Werther had a love for Charlotte
Such as words could never utter.
Would you know how first he met her?
She was cutting bread-and-butter.

Charlotte was a married lady
And a moral man was Werther,
And, for all the wealth of Indies,
Would do nothing for to hurt her.

So he sighed and pined and ogled,
And his passion boiled and bubbled,
Till he blew his silly brains out,
And no more was by it troubled.

Charlotte, having seen his body
Borne before her on a shutter,
Like a well-conducted person
Went on cutting bread-and-butter.

William Makepeace Thackeray, 'The Sorrows of Werther', 1855

Fanny Burney's first novel Evelina, *written when she was 25, satirizes the manners of a shallow, rich, heartless society as experienced by the heroine, who tells her story in letters. Among the idle assembly at Bristol hot wells, she has to endure the conversational vulgarity of several foppish young men, who are ill-mannered enough to discuss their tastes in food while eating. Lord Orville, by contrast, whom Evelina admires and who eventually proposes to her, is revealed to share her fastidiousness in this matter.*

After this, the conversation turned wholly upon eating, a subject which was discussed with the utmost delight; and, had I not known they were men of rank and fashion, I should have imagined that Lord Merton, Mr Lovel, and Mr Coverley, had all been professed cooks; for they displayed so much knowledge of sauces and made dishes, and of the various methods of dressing the same things, that I am persuaded they must have given much time, and much study, to make themselves such adepts in this *art*. It would be difficult to determine, whether they were most to be distinguished, as *gluttons*, or *epicures*; for they were, at once, dainty and voracious, understood the right and wrong of every dish, and alike emptied the one and the other. I should have been quite sick of their remarks, had I not been entertained by seeing that Lord Orville, who, I am sure, was equally disgusted, not only read my sentiments, but, by his countenance, communicated to me his own.

Fanny Burney, *Evelina*, 1778

Few passages in Jane Austen's novels are devoted to direct descriptions of, or conversations about, food. For the most part it is taken for granted, as something which polite people have in adequate quantities but do not discuss; and we are made aware of it only in exceptional circumstances, as when Fanny Price in Mansfield Park *revisits her old home and is distressed by the squalor and privation of the eating arrangements, or when her aunt Mrs Norris greedily carries off perquisites from her better-off sister Lady Bertram's kitchen and larder. In* Emma, *however, two inadequate characters are both allowed this preoccupation: the heroine's valetudinarian father, and their futilely chatty village neighbour, the middle-aged Miss Bates.*

[*Emma and her father are entertaining a small group of neighbours to (after-dinner) tea, cards, and late supper.*]

The evening flew away at a very unusual rate; and the supper-table, which always closed such parties, and for which she had been used to sit and watch the due time, was all set out and ready and moved towards the fire before [Emma] was aware. With an alacrity beyond the common impulse of a spirit which was never indifferent to the credit of doing everything well and attentively, with the real good-will of a mind delighted with its own ideas, did she then do all the honours of the meal, and help and recommend the minced chicken and scalloped oysters with an urgency which she knew would be acceptable to the early hours and civil scruples of their guests.

Upon such occasions poor Mr Woodhouse's feelings were in sad warfare. He loved to have the cloth laid, because it had been the fashion of his youth; but his conviction of suppers being very unwholesome made him rather sorry to see anything put upon it; and while his hospitality would have welcomed his visitors to everything, his care for their health made him grieve that they would eat.

Such another small basin of gruel as his own was all that he could, with thorough self-approbation, recommend, though he might constrain himself, while the ladies were comfortably clearing the nicer things, to say: 'Mrs Bates, let me propose your venturing on one of these eggs. An egg boiled very soft is not unwholesome. Serle understands boiling an egg better than anybody. I would not recommend an egg boiled by anyone else; but you need not be afraid—they are very small, you see—one of our small eggs will not hurt you. Miss Bates, let Emma help you to a *little* bit of tart—a *very* little bit. Ours are all apple-tarts. You need not be afraid of unwholesome preserves here. I do not advise the custard. Mrs Goddard, what say you to *half* a glass of wine? A *small* half-glass, put into a tumbler of water? I do not think it could disagree with you.'

* * * * *

[*Emma, shopping, meets Miss Bates, whose niece Jane Fairfax is staying with her.*]

'Then the baked apples came home [from the baker's oven]; Mrs Wallis sent them by her boy; they are extremely civil and obliging to us, the Wallises, always. . . . And it cannot be for the value of our custom now, for what is our consumption of bread, you know? Only three of us. Besides, dear Jane at present—and she really eats nothing—makes such a shocking breakfast, you would be quite frightened if you saw it. I dare not let my mother know how little she eats; so I say one thing, and then I say another, and it passes off. But about the middle of the day she gets hungry, and there is nothing she likes so well as these baked apples, and they are extremely wholesome; for I took the opportunity the other day of asking Mr Perry [the apothecary]; I happened to meet him in the street. Not that I had any doubt before. I have so often heard Mr Woodhouse recommend a baked apple. I believe it is the only way that Mr Woodhouse thinks the fruit thoroughly wholesome. We have apple-dumplings, however, very often. Patty makes an excellent apple-dumpling.

'Indeed they are very delightful apples, and Mrs Wallis does them full justice—only we do not have them baked more than twice, and Mr Woodhouse made us promise to have them done three times; but Miss Woodhouse will be so good as not to mention it. The apples themselves are the very finest sort for baking, beyond a doubt; all from Donwell—some of Mr Knightley's most liberal supply. He sends us a sack every year; and certainly there never was such a keeping apple anywhere as one of his trees—I believe there is two of them. My mother says the orchard was always famous in her younger days.'

Jane Austen, *Emma*, 1816

❧ *Becky Sharp, staying with her schoolfriend Amelia Sedley in London, hopes to captivate Amelia's unprepossessing brother Joseph, who is at home on leave from India.*

Now we have heard how Mrs Sedley had prepared a fine curry for her son, just as he liked it, and in the course of dinner a portion of this dish was offered to Rebecca. 'What is it?' said she, turning an appealing look to Mr Joseph.

'Capital,' said he. His mouth was full of it; his face quite red with the delightful exercise of gobbling. 'Mother, it's as good as my own curries in India.'

'Oh, I must try some, if it is an Indian dish,' said Miss Rebecca. 'I am sure everything must be good that comes from there.'

'Give Miss Sharp some curry, my dear,' said Mr Sedley, laughing.

Rebecca had never tasted the dish before.

'Do you find it as good as everything else from India?' said Mr Sedley.

'Oh, excellent!' said Rebecca, who was suffering tortures with the cayenne pepper.

'Try a chili with it, Miss Sharp,' said Joseph, really interested.

'A chili,' said Rebecca, gasping. 'Oh yes!' She thought a chili was something cool, as its name imported, and was served with some. 'How fresh and green they look!' she said, and put one into her mouth. It was hotter than the curry; flesh and blood could bear it no longer. She laid down her fork. 'Water, for Heaven's sake, water,' she cried. Mr Sedley burst out laughing (he was a coarse man, from the Stock Exchange, where they love all sorts of practical jokes).

'They are real Indian, I assure you,' said he. 'Sambo, give Miss Sharp some water.'

William Makepeace Thackeray, *Vanity Fair*, 1848

❧ *Petya Rostov, the youngest member of the family who are the main protagonists of Tolstoy's novel* War and Peace, *has joined the army as a very junior officer in time for Napoleon's invasion of Russia in 1812. Impetuously generous and foolhardy, he has been forbidden by his general to take part in any enterprise led by Denisov, an old family friend whose detachment he is visiting. Petya, however, is determined to join in the attack which Denisov's guerrilla band are undertaking against the French.*

It was growing dark when Denisov, Petya and the hetman rode up to the forester's hut. In the twilight they could see saddled horses, and Cossacks and hussars rigging up rough shelters in the clearing and kindling a glowing fire in a hollow where the smoke would not be seen by the French. In the entrance of the little watch-house a Cossack with sleeves rolled up was cutting up a sheep. In the hut itself three officers of Denisov's were converting a door into a table-top. Petya pulled off his wet clothes, gave them up to be dried, and at once set to work helping the officers to fix up the dinner-table.

In ten minutes the table was ready, covered with a napkin, and spread with vodka, a flask of rum, white bread, roast mutton and salt.

Sitting at the table with the officers and tearing the fat, savoury mutton with greasy fingers, Petya was in an ecstatic childlike state of melting love for all men and a consequent belief that in the same way they loved him.

* * * * *

'Heavens! I was quite forgetting,' he cried suddenly. 'I have some wonderful raisins with me—you know, those seedless ones. Our new sutler has such first-rate things. I bought ten pounds. I always like sweet things. Will you have some? . . .' And Petya ran out to his Cossack in the passage and returned with baskets containing about five pounds of raisins. 'Help yourselves, gentlemen, help yourselves.'

* * * * *

[*Remembering a captured French drummer-boy who is being held by the detachment as a prisoner, Petya then brings him into the hut and offers him food. That evening he rides off to reconnoitre the French camp with Dolokhov, a fellow-officer of Denisov's; and the following morning, after an ecstatically sleepless night, he joins Dolokhov, Denisov and the Cossacks in their onslaught on the French.*]

The French were making a stand behind a wattle fence in a garden thickly overgrown with bushes, and shooting at the Cossacks clustering in the gateway. Through the smoke as he rode up to the gates Petya caught a glimpse of Dolokhov's pale, greenish face, as he shouted something to his men. 'Go round. Wait for the infantry!' he was yelling, just as Petya appeared.

'Wait? . . . Hurra-a-h! . . .' roared Petya, and without pausing a second threw himself into the fray where the firing and smoke were thickest. A volley rang out, bullets whistled past and landed with a thud. The Cossacks and Dolokhov galloped in at the gates of the yard after Petya. In the dense billowing smoke some of the French flung down their arms and ran out of the bushes to meet the Cossacks, while others fled downhill towards the pond. Petya was tearing round the courtyard, but instead of holding the reins he was waving both arms about in a strange, wild manner, and slipping farther and farther to one side in the saddle. His horse stepped on the ashes of the camp-fire that was smouldering in the morning light, stopped short, and Petya fell heavily to the wet ground. The Cossacks saw his arms and legs jerk rapidly, though his head was quite still. A bullet had pierced his skull.

After parleying with the senior French officer, who came out of the house with a handkerchief tied to his sword to announce that they surrendered, Dolokhov got off his horse and went up to Petya, who lay motionless with outstretched arms.

'Done for!' he said with a frown, and walked to the gate to meet Denisov who was riding towards him.

'Dead?' cried Denisov, recognizing from a distance the unmistakably lifeless attitude—only too familiar to him—in which Petya's body was lying.

'Done for!' repeated Dolokhov, as though the utterance of the words afforded him satisfaction, and he hastened over to the prisoners, who were surrounded by Cossacks who had hurried up. 'We're giving no quarter!' he called out to Denisov.

Denisov did not reply. He rode up to Petya, dismounted, and with trembling hands turned Petya's blood-stained, mud-bespattered face—which had already gone white—towards himself.

'I always like sweet things. Wonderful raisins, take them all,' he recalled Petya's words. And the Cossacks looked round in amazement at the sound, like the howl of a dog, which broke from Denisov as he quickly turned away, walked to the wattle fence and held on to it.

Leo Tolstoy, *War and Peace*, 1869, translated by Rosemary Edmonds, 1957

Mrs Garth at certain hours was always in the kitchen, and this morning she was carrying out several occupations at once there—making her pies at the well-scoured deal table on one side of the room, observing Sally's movements at the oven and dough-tub through an open door, and giving lessons to her youngest boy and girl, who were standing opposite to her with their books and slates before them. A tub and a clothes-horse at the other end of the kitchen indicated an intermittent wash of small things also going on.

Mrs Garth with her sleeves turned above her elbows, deftly handling her pastry—applying her rolling-pin and giving ornamental pinches, while she expounded with grammatical fervour what were the right views about the concord of verbs and pronouns with 'nouns of multitude or signifying many', was a sight agreeably amusing. . . . In her snowy-frilled cap she reminded one of that delightful Frenchwoman whom we have all seen marketing, basket on arm. Looking at the mother, you might hope that the daughter would become like her, which is a prospective advantage equal to a dowry—the mother too often standing behind the daughter like a malignant prophecy—'Such as I am, she will shortly be.'

George Eliot, *Middlemarch*, 1871–2

❧ *Françoise, housekeeper to the family of the fictionalized Marcel, and later to the adult narrator himself, in Proust's great autobiographical novel* À la recherche du temps perdu, *is a character of great, if dwindling, importance in the novel. In this first volume,* Swann's Way, *she is in her element at Combray, a small town in Normandy (in real life Illiers, near Chartres). A composite figure, based on a succession of family servants, Françoise could be said to represent goodness in its simplest, most creative, and most nourishing form. Credulous yet shrewd, instinctively generous, down-to-earth, with a peasant wisdom and understanding of good food, she provides a continuous point of reference for Marcel the narrator in his involvement in the life of aesthetes and rich, amoral socialites in Paris. Unambiguously motherly and feminine, she is a counterweight to all the more elusive, provocative, destructive, and negative female characters in the novel, and a complement to the character of Swann in his own much more complicated representation of human goodness.*

[On Sundays]—and this more than ever from the day on which fine weather definitely set in at Combray—the proud hour of noon, descending from the steeple of Saint-Hilaire from which it blazoned for a moment with the twelve points of its sonorous crown, would long have echoed about our table, beside the 'holy bread,' which too had come in, after church, in its familiar way; and we would still be found seated in front of our Arabian Nights plates, weighed down by the heat of the day, and still more by our heavy meal. For upon the permanent foundation of eggs, cutlets, potatoes, preserves, and biscuits, whose appearance on the table she no longer announced to us, Françoise would add—as the labour of fields and orchards, the harvest of the tides, the luck of the markets, the kindness of neighbours, and her own genius might provide; and so effectively that our bill of fare, like the quatrefoils that were carved on the porches of cathedrals in the thirteenth century, reflected to some extent the march of the seasons and the incidents of human life—a brill, because the fish-woman had guaranteed its freshness; a turkey, because she had seen a beauty in the market at Roussainville-le-Pin; cardoons with marrow, because she had never done them for us in that way before; a roast leg of mutton, because the fresh air made one hungry and there would be plenty of time for it to 'settle down' in the seven hours before dinner; spinach, by way of a change; apricots, because they were still hard to get; gooseberries, because in another fortnight there would be none left; raspberries, which M. Swann had brought specially; cherries, the first to come from the cherry-tree, which had yielded none for the past two years; a cream cheese, of which in those days I was extremely fond; an almond cake, because she had ordered one the evening before; a fancy loaf, because it was our turn to 'offer' the holy bread. And when all these had been eaten, a work composed expressly for ourselves, but dedicated more particularly to my father, who had a fondness for such things, a cream of chocolate, inspired in the mind, created by the hand of Françoise would be laid before us, light and fleeting as an 'occasional piece' of music, into which she had poured the whole of her talent. Anyone who refused to partake of it, saying: 'No, thank you, I have finished; I am not hungry,' would at once have been lowered to the level of the Philistines who, when an artist makes them a present of one of his works, examine its weight and material, whereas what is of value is the creator's intention and his signature. To have left even the tiniest morsel in the dish would have shown as much discourtesy as to rise and leave a concert hall while the 'piece' was still being played, and under the composer's very eyes.

Marcel Proust, *Swann's Way*, 1913, translated by C. K. Scott-Moncrieff, 1922

❧ Clayhanger, *Arnold Bennett's novel of late Victorian life in the Staffordshire Potteries, tells the story of the Clayhanger family: the self-made printer Darius, a parsimonious widower, his son Edwin, and daughters Maggie and Clara. This episode introduces Darius's sister-in-law Clara Hamps, a powerful if unpopular character. Edwin, aged 16, has just left school to join his father's business; the two girls are living at home under the care of a housekeeper, Mrs Nixon. It is six o'clock tea-time.*

Mrs Hamps had splendidly arrived. The atmosphere of the sitting-room was changed. Maggie, smiling, wore her second-best black silk apron. Clara, smiling and laughing, wore a clean long white pinafore. Mrs Nixon, with her dreamy eyes less vacant than usual, greeted Mrs Hamps effusively, and effusively gave humble thanks for kind inquiries after her health. A stranger might have thought that these women were strongly attached to one another by ties of affection and respect. Edwin never understood how his sisters, especially Maggie, could practise such vast and eternal hypocrisy with his aunt. As for him, his aunt acted on him now, as generally, like a tonic. Some effluence from her quickened him. He put away the worry in connexion with his father, and gave himself up to the physical pleasures of tea.

Aunt Clara was a handsome woman. She had been called—but not by men whose manners and code she would have approved—'a damned fine woman'. Her age was about forty, which at that period, in a woman's habit of mind, was the equivalent of about fifty today.

* * * * *

She was a woman of terrific vitality. Her dead sister had been nothing in comparison with her. She had a glorious digestion, and was the envy of her brother-in-law—who suffered much from biliousness—because she could eat with perfect impunity hot buttered toast and raw celery in large quantities. Further, she had independent means, and no children to cause anxieties. Yet she was always, as the phrase went, 'bearing up', or, as another phrase went, 'leaning hard'. . . . Aunt Clara's spiritual life must be imagined as a continual, almost physical leaning on Christ. Nevertheless she never complained, and she was seldom depressed. Her desire, and her achievement, was to be bright, to take everything cheerfully, to look obstinately on the best side of things, and to instil this religion into others.

Thus, when it was announced that father had been called out unexpectedly, leaving an order that they were not to wait for him, she said gaily that they had better be obedient and begin, though it would have been more agreeable to wait for father. And she said how beautiful the tea was, and how beautiful the toast, and how beautiful the strawberry-jam, and how beautiful the pikelets. She would herself pour some hot water into the slop basin, and put a pikelet on a plate thereon, covered, to keep warm for father. She would not hear a word about the toast being a little hard, and when Maggie in her curious quiet way 'stuck her out' that the toast was in fact hard, she said that that precise degree of hardness was the degree which she, for herself, preferred. Then she talked of jams, and mentioned gooseberry-jam, whereupon Clara privately put her tongue out, with the quickness of a snake, to signal to Maggie.

'Ours isn't good this year,' said Maggie.

'I told auntie we weren't so set up with it, a fortnight ago,' said Clara simply, like a little angel.

'Did you, dear?' Mrs Hamps exclaimed, with great surprise, almost with shocked surprise. 'I'm sure it's beautiful. I was quite looking forward to tasting it; quite! I know what your gooseberry-jam is.'

'Would you like to try it now?' Maggie suggested. 'But we've warned you.'

'Oh, I don't want to trouble you *now*. We're all so cosy here. Any time—'

'No trouble, Auntie,' said Clara with her most captivating and innocent smile.

'Well, if you talk about "warning" me, of course I must insist on having some,' said Auntie Clara.

Clara jumped up, passed behind Mrs Hamps, making a contemptuous face at those curls as she did so, and ran gracefully down to the kitchen.

'Here,' she said crossly to Mrs Nixon. 'A pot of that gooseberry, please. A small one will do. She knows it's short of sugar, and so she's determined to try it, just out of spite; and nothing will stop her.'

Clara returned smiling to the tea-table, and Maggie neatly unsealed the jam; and Auntie Clara, with a face beaming with pleasurable anticipation, helped herself circumspectly to a spoonful.

'Beautiful!' she murmured.

'Don't you think it's a bit tart?' Maggie asked.

'Oh no!' protestingly.

'*Don't* you?' asked Clara, with an air of delighted deferential astonishment.

'Oh *no*!' Mrs Hamps repeated. 'It's beautiful!' She did not smack her lips over it, because she would have considered it unladylike to smack her lips, but by less offensive gestures she sought to convey her unbounded pleasure in the jam. 'How much sugar did you put in?' she inquired after a while. 'Half and half?'

'Yes,' said Maggie.

'They do say gooseberries were a tiny bit sour this year, owing to the weather,' said Mrs Hamps reflectively.

Clara kicked Edwin under the table, as it were viciously, but her delightful innocent smile, directed vaguely upon Mrs Hamps, did not relax. Such duplicity passed Edwin's comprehension; it seemed to him purposeless. Yet he could not deny that there might be a certain sting, a certain insinuation, in his auntie's last remark.

Arnold Bennett, *Clayhanger*, 1910

Of the six contrasting voices, three male, three female, whose meditative narrations make up the novel The Waves, *Susan's is the most practical and down-to-earth.*

'I shall have children; I shall have maids in aprons; men with pitchforks; a kitchen where they bring the ailing lambs to warm in baskets, where the hams hang and the onions glisten. I shall be like my mother, silent in a blue apron locking up the cupboards.

'Now I am hungry. I will call my setter. I think of crusts and bread and butter and white plates in a sunny room. I will go back across the fields. I will walk along this grass path with strong, even strides, now swerving to avoid the puddle, now leaping lightly to a clump . . . I return, like a cat or a fox returning, whose fur is grey with rime, whose pads are hardened by the coarse earth. I push through the cabbages, making their leaves squeak and their drops spill. I sit waiting for my father's footsteps as he shuffles down the passage pinching some herb between his fingers. I pour out cup after cup while the unopened flowers hold themselves erect on the table among the pots of jam, the loaves and the butter. We are silent.

'I go then to the cupboard, and take the damp bags of rich sultanas; I lift the heavy flour on to the clean scrubbed kitchen table. I knead; I stretch; I pull, plunging my hands in the warm inwards of the dough. I let the cold water stream fanwise through my fingers. The fire roars; the flies buzz in a circle. All my currants and rices, the silver bags and the blue bags, are locked again in the cupboard.

The meat is stood in the oven; the bread rises in a soft dome under the clean towel'.

Virginia Woolf, *The Waves*, 1931

❧ *Jesiah Oakroyd, a middle-aged carpenter and joiner from Bruddersford, Yorkshire, has left home to work with a theatrical touring company in the south of England.*

'Pass me up them inch nails, Joe,' said Mr Oakroyd. Then he reflected a minute or two. 'Well, I must say I've seen better cooking i'my time than you get round these parts. That's because you're out o'Yorkshire. Down south here t'women doesn't bake and you can't get a curran' teacake or a flat cake or a fatty cake or owt like that. Eh, I'd a right good laugh yesterda'. Woman where I am—Mrs Cullin her name is—she's a widow woman . . . well, Mrs Cullin, she says to me yesterda', she says "Now, Mr Oakroyd, I'm going to give you a treat" she says. "I've a joint of beef for your dinner and you're a Yorkshireman, so I'm going to give you some Yorkshire pudding with it," she says. In comes my dinner—bit o'beef, cabbage, potaters. I looks at it and says "Here, Mrs Cullin, what about that Yorkshire pudding?" I says. "Let's have that first." She stares. "It's here," she says, pointing to t'plate. "What!" I says. "You don't mean this bit o'custard, soft batter stuff, under t'cabbage?" "Yes, I do," she says.

"If that isn't Yorkshire pudding, what is it?" "Nay," I says, "you mustn't ask me, Missis, what it is. All I know is, it's no more Yorkshire pudding ner I am. It's a bit o'custard or pancake, likely enough." And then I tells her about Yorkshire pudding. And tak' notice o'this, Joe, 'cos it'll happen come in handy some time.' Mr Oakroyd paused to relight his pipe, blew out a cloud or two of *Old Salt*, then continued.

' "To begin wi'," I says, "a Yorkshire pudding is eaten by itsen and not mixed up wi' meat and potaters, all in a mush. And it comes straight out o' t'oven," I says, "straight on to t'plate. No waiting," I says, "or you'll spoil it. If you don't put it straight on to t'plate you might as well go and sole your boots with it. And another thing," I says, "you've got to have your oven hot, I do know that. Then if you've mixed right and your oven's hot, pudding'll come out as light as a feather, crisp and brarn, just a top and a bottom, you might say, wi' none o' this custardy stuff in t'middle. Nah d'you see, Missis?" I says. "Nay," she says, "I can't learn about that at my time o'life, and you're letting your dinner get cold wi' talking about your hot ovens," she says. And then we'd a right good laugh together, and I heard her telling her daughter . . . all about it last night.'

J. B. Priestley, *The Good Companions*, 1929

Moses Herzog, a middle-aged New York professor, ruminates on the past and speculates about the nature of Western civilization as he lives through a love-affair, followed by an unsuccessful second marriage, with Madeleine, a Jewish-born convert to Catholicism. Appropriately enough, since memories are often linked with the taste or smell of food, almost every episode in this mainly backward-looking novel contains some reference to food or eating. In this passage, not yet married to Madeleine, their relationship tense with her religious guilt and hostility towards him, he takes her out to breakfast on her way to work after they have spent the night together at her apartment.

'Aren't you coming? What are you doing?' said Madeleine.

Perhaps he was not yet fully awake. Herzog was loitering for a moment near the fish store, arrested by the odor. A thin muscular negro was pitching buckets of ice into the deep window. The fish were packed together, backs arched as if they were swimming in the crushed, smoking ice, bloody bronze, slimy black-green, gray-gold—

the lobsters were crowded to the glass, feelers bent. The morning was warm, gray, damp, fresh, smelling of the river. Pausing on the metal doors of the sidewalk elevator, Moses received the raised pattern of the steel through his thin shoe soles; like Braille. But he did not interpret a message. The fish were arrested, lifelike, in the white, frothing, ground ice. The street was overcast, warm and gray, intimate, unclean, flavored by the polluted river, the sexually stirring brackish tidal odor.

'I can't wait for you, Moses,' said Madeleine, peremptorily over her shoulder.

They went into the restaurant and sat at the yellow formica table.

'What were you dawdling for?'

'Well, my mother came from the Baltic provinces. She loved fish.'

But Madeleine was not to be interested in Mother Herzog, twenty years dead, however mother-bound this nostalgic gentleman's soul might be. Moses, thinking, ruled against himself. He was a fatherly person to Madeleine—he couldn't expect her to consider *his* mother. She was one of the *dead* dead, without effect on the new generation.

* * * * *

Herzog was thinking, however, how she found the strength to spoil her children. She certainly spoiled me. Once, at nightfall, she was pulling me on the sled, over crusty ice, the tiny glitter of snow, perhaps four o'clock of a short day in January. Near the grocery we met an old baba in a shawl who said, 'Why are you pulling him daughter!' Mama, dark under the eyes. Her slender cold face. She was breathing hard. She wore the torn seal coat and a red pointed wool cap and button boots. Clusters of dry fish hung in the shop, a rancid sugar smell, cheese, soap—a terrible dust of nutrition came from the open door. The bell on a coil of wire was bobbing, ringing. . . .

Saul Bellow, *Herzog*, 1961

Iris Murdoch's hero is a retired theatrical director, living alone in the country.

It is after lunch and I shall now describe the house. For lunch, I may say, I ate and greatly enjoyed the following: anchovy paste on hot buttered toast, then baked beans and kidney beans with chopped celery, tomatoes, lemon juice and olive oil. (Really good olive oil is essential, the kind with a taste, I have brought a supply from London.) Green peppers would have been a happy addition only the village shop (about two miles pleasant walk) could not provide them. . . . Then bananas and cream with white sugar. Bananas should be cut, *never* mashed, and the cream should be thin. Then hard water biscuits with New Zealand butter and Wensleydale cheese. Of course I never touch foreign cheeses. Our cheeses are the best in the world. With this feast I drank most of a bottle of Muscadet out of my modest 'cellar'. I ate and drank slowly as one should (cook fast, eat slowly) and without distractions such as (thank heavens) conversation or reading. Indeed eating is so pleasant that one should even try to suppress thought.

* * * * *

Food is a profound subject and one, incidentally, about which no writer lies. I wonder whence I derived my felicitous gastronomic intelligence? A thrifty childhood gave me a horror of wasted food. I thoroughly enjoyed the modest fare we had at home. My mother was a 'good plain cook', but she lacked the inspired simplicity which is for me the essence of good eating. I think my illumination came, like that of St Augustine, from a disgust with excesses. When I was a young director I was idiotic and conventional enough to think that I had to entertain people at well-known restaurants. It gradually became clear to me that guzzling large quantities of expensive, pretentious, often mediocre food in public places was not only immoral, unhealthy and unaesthetic, but also unpleasurable. Later my guests were offered simple joys *chez moi*. What is more delicious than fresh hot buttered toast, with or without the addition of bloater paste? Or plain boiled onions with a little cold corned beef if desired? And well-made porridge with brown sugar and cream is a dish fit for a king. Even then some people, so sadly corrupt was their taste, took my intelligent hedonism for an affected eccentricity, a mere gimmick. . . . And some were actually offended.

Iris Murdoch, *The Sea, The Sea*, 1978

EATING HABITS

Michel Eyquem, Sieur de Montaigne (1533–91), wrote this account of himself in his mid-fifties, in the most autobiographical of his Essais. *It appeared in 1588 as part of a fourth, expanded edition of the first two books of* Essais, *originally published in 1580.*

I hardly ever chuse my dish at table, but fall to of the next at hand, and unwillingly change my dish. A confusion of meats, and a clutter of dishes displeases me as much as any thing whatever. I am easily satisfied with few dishes, and am an enemy to the opinion of Favorinus, that in a feast they must snatch from you the meat you like, and set another plate of another sort before you, and that it's a pitiful supper, if you do not sate your guests with the rumps of several fowls, and that the beccafico only deserves to be all eaten. I usually eat salt-meats, and yet I love bread that has no salt in it; and my baker never sends up other to my table, contrary to the custom of the country. In my infancy, what they had most to correct in me, was the refusal of things that children commonly best love, as sugar, sweet meats and March panes. My governour contended with this aversion to delicate meats as a kind of nicety, and indeed 'tis nothing else but a difficulty of taste in any thing it applys itself unto. Whoever shall cure a child of an obstinate aversion to brown bread, bacon or garlick, will cure him of all kind of delicacy.

* * * * *

They whose concern it is to have a care of me, may very easily hinder me from eating any thing they think will do me harm; for in such things I never covet nor miss any thing I do not see: but withal, if it once comes in my sight, 'tis in vain to perswade me to forbear, so that when I design to fast, I must be parted from those that eat suppers, and must have only so much given to me, as is required for a regular collation; for if I sit down to table, I forget my resolution. When I order my cook to alter the manner of dressing any dish of meat, all my family know what it means, that my stomach is out of order, and that I shall scarce touch it: I love to have all meats that will endure it very little boyl'd or roasted, and love them mightily mortified, and even stinking in many. Nothing but hardness offends me, of any other quality I am as patient and indifferent as any man, I have known; so that contrary to the common humour, even in fish, it oft happens, that I find them both too fresh and too firm: not for want of teeth, which I ever had good, even to excellence, and that age does but now begin to threaten at this time of my life. I have ever been us'd every morning to rub them with a napkin, and before and after dinner.

* * * * *

I am not very fond either of sallets, or fruits, except melons. My father hated all sorts of sawces, and I love them all. Eating too much hurts me, but for the quality of what I eat, I do not yet certainly know that any sort of meat disagrees with my stomach; neither have I observed that either full-moon or decrease, spring or autumn, are hurtful to me. We have in us motions that are inconstant, and for which no reason can be given. For example, I found radishes first grateful to my stomach, since that nauseous, and now at present grateful again. In several other things likewise I find my stomach and appetite to vary after the same manner. I have chang'd and chang'd again from white to claret, from claret to white. I am a great lover of fish, and consequently make my fasts feasts, and my feasts fasts; and I believe what some people say, that it is more easie of digestion than flesh. As I make a conscience of eating flesh upon fish-days, so does my taste make a conscience of mixing fish and flesh, the difference between them seems to me to be too great to do so. From my youth I have us'd sometimes to be out of the way at supper, either to sharpen my appetite against the next morning (for as Epicurus fasted and made lean meals to accustom his pleasure to make shift without abundance, I on the contrary do it to prepare my pleasure to make better and more chearful use of abundance) or else I fasted to preserve my vigour for the service of some action of body or mind; or to cure my sick stomach, and for want of fit company.

'On Experience', *The Essays of Michael, Sieur de Montaigne . . . made English by Charles Cotton, Esq*., 1700

Beccafico: blackcap, garden warbler; a small bird usually eaten in one or two mouthfuls.

GREAT EUROPEANS

Frederick the Great, King of Prussia, who died in 1786, was especially fond of *polenta*, a kind of barley-cake [*sic*] ground up and roasted. This monarch vied with his friend Voltaire in his love of coffee.

* * * * *

Paul I, Emperor of Russia, who was assassinated on the night of 11–12 March 1801, had a passion for duck-liver pâté. He gave the credit for this to a Polish refugee who managed to send him one of these pâtés every week from Toulouse, their freshness remaining unaffected by the journey.

* * * * *

Kant, the prince of German philosophers, who died in 1804, was not at all refined in his tastes; he took great pleasure in a purée of lentils, in a purée of parsnips cooked with pork fat; in a pudding of pork fat, Pomeranian style; in a pudding of dried peas with pigs' trotters, and in dried fruit baked in the oven. Kant considered three hours the right length of time in which to enjoy these various dishes, sitting down to eat at one o'clock and applying himself in a truly philosophical manner to this serious business until he rose at four.

P. G. Philomneste (Gabriel Peignot), *Le Livre des singularités*, 1841

❧ *The poet Shelley is, with the dramatist George Bernard Shaw, probably the best-known British vegetarian.*

The common fruit of stalls, and oranges and apples, were always welcome to Shelley; he would crunch the latter as heartily as a schoolboy. Vegetables, and especially salads, and pies and puddings, were acceptable: his beverage consisted of copious and frequent draughts of cold water, but tea was ever grateful, cup after cup, and coffee. Wine was taken with singular moderation, commonly diluted largely with water, and for a long period he would abstain from it altogether; he avoided the use of spirits almost invariably, and even in the most minute portions.

Like all persons of simple tastes, he retained his sweet tooth; he would greedily eat cakes, gingerbread and sugar; honey, preserved or stewed fruit, with bread, were his favourite delicacies, these he thankfully and joyfully received from others, but he rarely sought for them, or provided them for himself. The restraint and protracted duration of a convivial meal were intolerable; he was seldom able to keep his seat during the brief period assigned to a family dinner.

Thomas Jefferson Hogg, *The Life of Percy Bysshe Shelley*, 1858

❧ *John Pintard was born in 1759 of a Huguenot family in New York. After his parents' deaths he was partly brought up by an uncle, Lewis Pintard, at New Rochelle, New York, then very much a French colony in miniature. He became a businessman and founder of the New-York Historical*

Society; a New York patriot, who was always inclined to look back fondly at the 'good old days' before the American Revolution. As Secretary of the Mutual Insurance Society he lived with his family at 52 Wall Street, overcoming the ignominy of an early failure which had involved him in exile at Newark, New Jersey and in a year spent in Newark Jail. After his beloved elder daughter's marriage to a resident of New Orleans he hardly saw her again; but he wrote to her constantly, often on his favourite subjects, food and cooking.

4 November 1820.

In old times in my good uncle's family, and I suppose every other, there were stated days for every dish, salt fish on Saturday, roast Turkey Sunday, the remainder of Saturday's salt, or dumb fish, hashed up with vegetables & warmed in the frying pan for Monday, Roast beef Wednesday, pease porridge & sausages on Thursday, Apple dumplings Friday, Pancakes Tuesday. This was pretty much the winter course, and always [beef] Alamode on Saturday in summer, which was served up cold on Sunday to prevent cooking, or else veal forced meat ball pie. Hasty pudding all winter long for supper, & buckwheat cakes, which came into vogue just before the revol[utionar]y war, for breakfast. In Philadelphia this article is or used to be considered such a treat, as to be served up for tea in large domestic parties, where they are always prepared the size of the griddle, and cut into quarters. Thus you have the courses of old fashion good feeding when abundance of the best was afforded at a very cheap rate. I have heard my good old uncle say that an excellent dinner of the best of the market could be provided within the compass of a single dollar, and that there were not many persons who could afford to give so extravagant a dinner!

Letters from John Pintard to his daughter Eliza Noel Pintard Davidson, 1816–1833, edited by Dorothy C. Barck, New-York Historical Society, 1937–40

❧ *Benjamin Franklin (1706–90) was born in Milk Street, Boston, Massachusetts, the fifteenth child and youngest son of Josiah Franklin, a tallow chandler, formerly a dyer, who had emigrated from England in 1682. Franklin claimed to remember, in his early childhood, all seventeen of his father's children (seven by his first wife, who had come with him from England, and ten by the second, Abiah Folger) sitting round the family dining-table together. The Franklins were Protestant and conscientiously literate, with nonconformist inclinations; and although Ben's father removed him from grammar school to help with his business when he was 10, the children's education continued at home.*

I suppose you may like to know what kind of a man my father was. . . . At his table he liked to have, as often as he could, some sensible friend or neighbour to converse with, and always took care to start some ingenious or useful topic for discourse which might tend to improve the minds of his children. By this means he turned our attention to what was good, just, and prudent in the conduct of life; and little or no notice was ever taken of what related to the victuals on the table—whether it was well or ill dressed, in or out of season, of good or bad flavour, preferable or inferior to this or that other thing of the kind; so that I was brought up in such a perfect inattention to those matters as to be quite indifferent what kind of food was set before me, and so unobservant of it, that to this day I can scarce tell a few hours after dinner of what dishes it consisted. This has been a great convenience to me in travelling, where my companions have been sometimes very unhappy for want of a suitable gratification of their more delicate, because better instructed, tastes and appetites.

Benjamin Franklin, *Autobiography*, 1791

DR JOHNSON

At supper this night he talked of good eating with uncommon satisfaction. 'Some people (said he) have a foolish way of not minding, or pretending not to mind, what they eat. For my part, I mind my belly very studiously, and very carefully; for I look upon it, that he who does not mind his belly, will hardly mind any thing else.' . . . Yet I have heard him, upon other occasions, talk with great contempt of people who were anxious to gratify their palates; and the 206th number of his Rambler is a masterly essay against gulosity. His practice, indeed, I must acknowledge, may be considered as casting the balance of his different opinions upon this subject; for I never knew any man who relished good eating more than he did. When at table, he was totally absorbed in the business of the moment; his looks seemed rivetted to his plate; nor would he, unless when in very high company, say one word, or even pay the least attention to what was said by others, till he had satisfied his appetite: which was so fierce, and indulged with such intenseness, that while in the act of eating, the veins of his forehead swelled, and generally a strong perspiration was visible. To those whose sensations were delicate, this could not but be disgusting; and it was doubtless not very suitable to the character of a philosopher, who should be distinguished by self-command. But it must be owned, that Johnson, though he could be rigidly *abstemious*, was not a *temperate* man either in eating or drinking. He could refrain, but he could not use moderately. He told me, that he had fasted two days without inconvenience, and that he had never been hungry but once. They who beheld with wonder how much he eat upon all occasions, when his dinner was to his taste, could not easily conceive what he must have meant by hunger; and not only was he remarkable for the extraordinary quantity which he eat, but he was, or affected to be, a man of very nice discernment in the science of cookery. He used to descant critically on the dishes which had been at table where he had dined or supped, and to recollect very minutely what he had liked. . . . When invited to dine, even with an intimate friend, he was not pleased if something better than a plain dinner was not prepared for him. I have heard him say on such an occasion, 'This was a good dinner enough, to be sure: but it was not a dinner to *ask* a man to.' On the other hand, he was wont to express, with great glee, his satisfaction when he had been entertained quite to his mind. One day when he had dined with his neighbour and landlord, in Bolt-court, Mr Allen, the printer, whose old housekeeper had studied his taste in every thing, he pronounced this eulogy: 'Sir, we could not have had a better dinner, had there been a *Synod of Cooks*.'

James Boswell, *The Life of Samuel Johnson, LL.D*, 1791

❧ *Norman Douglas had lived on Capri, and had described it in* Siren Land, *before the First World War. His autobiographical volume,* Alone, *recalls his footloose existence in Italy during that war, after failing to gain civilian employment in any British government department.*

The railway station at Rome has put on a new face. Blown to the winds is that old dignity and sense of leisure. . . . That restaurant, for example—one of those few for which a man in olden days of peace would desert his own tavern in the town—how changed! The fare has deteriorated beyond recognition. Where are those succulent joints and ragoûts, the aromatic wine, the snow-white macaroni, the café-au-lait with genuine butter and genuine honey?

War-time!

Conversed awhile with an Englishman at my side, who was gleefully devouring lumps of a particular something which I would not have liked to touch with tongs.

'I don't care what I eat,' he remarked.

So it seemed.

I don't care what I eat: what a confession to make! Is it not the same thing as saying, I don't care whether I am dirty or clean? When others tell me this, I regard it as a pose, or a poor joke. This person was manifestly sincere in his profession of faith. He did not care what he ate. He looked it. Were I afflicted with this particular ailment, this attenuated form of *coprophagia*, I should try to keep the hideous secret to myself. It is nothing to boast of. A man owes something to those traditions of our race which have helped to raise us above the level of the brute. Good taste in viands has been painfully acquired; it is a sacred trust. Beware of gross feeders. They are a menace to their fellow-creatures. Will they not act, on occasion, even as they feed? Assuredly they will. Everybody acts as he feeds.

Norman Douglas, *Alone*, 1921

❧ *Thomas de Quincey argued that certain objects stood in the way of giving up addictive substances such as alcohol: among them, the British way with food.*

Rudest of barbarous devices is English cookery, and not much in advance of the primitive Chinese step—a fact which it would not be worth while to lament were it not for the sake of the poor trembling deserter from the banners of intoxication, who is thus, and by no other cause, so often thrown back beneath the yoke which he had abjured. Past counting are the victims of alcohol that, having by vast efforts emancipated themselves for a season, are violently forced into relapsing by the nervous irritations of demoniac cookery. . . . Let us glance at three articles of diet, beyond all comparison of most ordinary occurrence—viz, potatoes, bread, and butcher's meat. The art of preparing potatoes for *human* use is utterly unknown, except in certain provinces of our empire and amongst certain sections of the labouring class. In our great cities—London, Edinburgh, &c., the sort of things which you see offered at table under the name and reputation of potatoes are such that, if you could suppose the company to be composed of Centaurs and Lapithae, or any other quarrelsome people, it would become necessary for the police to interfere. The potato of cities is a very dangerous missile, and, if thrown with an accurate aim by an angry hand, will fracture any known skull. In volume and constituency it is very like a paving stone [i.e. a cobblestone]; only that, I should say, the paving stone had the advantage in point of tenderness; and upon this horrid basis, which youthful ostriches would repent of swallowing, the trembling, palpitating invalid, fresh from the scourging of alcohol, is requested to build the superstructure of his dinner. The proverb says that three flittings are as bad as a fire; and on that model I conceive that three potatoes, as they are found at the majority of British dinner tables, would be equal, in principle of ruin, to two glasses of vitriol. The same savage ignorance appears, and only not so often, in the bread of this island. Myriads of families eat it in that early state of sponge which bread assumes during the process of baking; but less than sixty hours will not fit this dangerous article of human diet to be eaten; and those who are acquainted with the works of Parmentier, or Count Rumford, or other learned investigators of bread and of the baker's art, must be aware that this quality of sponginess (though quite equal to the ruin of the digestive organs) is but one in a legion of vices to which the article is liable. A German of much research wrote a book on the conceivable faults in a pair of shoes, which he found to be about six hundred and sixty-six,—many of them, as he observed, requiring a very delicate process of study to find out; whereas the possible faults in bread, which are not less in number, being also, I conceive, about equal to the number of the beast, require no study at all for the detection—they publish themselves through all varieties of misery. But the perfection of barbarism, as regards our insular cookery, is reserved for animal food . . . Our insular sheep, for instance, are so far superior to any which the Continent produces that the present Prussian minister at our court is in the habit of questioning a man's right to talk of mutton as anything beyond a great idea, unless he can prove a residence in Great Britain. One sole case he cites of a dinner on the Elbe where a particular leg of mutton really struck him as rivalling any which he had known in

England. The mystery seemed inexplicable; but, upon inquiry, it turned out to be an importation from Leith. Yet this incomparable article, to produce which the skills of the feeder must co-operate with the peculiar bounty of Nature, calls forth the most dangerous refinements of barbarism in its cookery. A Frenchman requires, as the primary qualification of flesh meat, that it should be tender. We English universally, but especially the Scots, treat that quality with indifference or with bare toleration. What *we*, what *nous autres les barbares*, require is that it should be fresh,—that is, recently killed (in which state it cannot be digestible except by a crocodile, or perhaps here and there a leopard); and we present it at table in a transition state of leather, demanding the teeth of a tiger to rend it in pieces, and the stomach of a tiger to digest it.

Thomas de Quincey, 'National Temperance Movements', 1845

Chinese step: see pp. 82–4, below

Lobbin Clout:

Leek to the *Welch*, to *Dutchmen Butter*'s dear,
Of *Irish* Swains *Potatoe* is the Chear;
Oats for their Feasts the *Scottish* Shepherds grind,
Sweet *Turnips* are the Food of *Blouzelind*.
While she loves *Turnips*, *Butter* I'll despise,
Nor *Leeks* nor *Oatmeal* nor *Potatoe* prize.

Cuddy:

In good *Roast Beef* my Landlord sticks his Knife,
The *Capon* fat delights his dainty Wife,
Pudding our Parson eats, the Squire loves *Hare*,
But *White-pot* thick is my Buxoma's Fare.
While she loves *White-pot*, *Capon* ne'er shall be,
Nor *Hare*, nor *Beef*, nor *Pudding*, Food for me.

John Gay, 'The Shepherd's Week', 1714

A satire on contemporary pastoral poems describing the loves of shepherds and shepherdesses.

❧ *The narrator and her friend Miss Matty have gone to dinner with an old-fashioned farmer, Thomas Holbrook, who in his youth proposed to Miss Matty and (to her subsequent regret) was turned down by her as being insufficiently gentlemanly to marry a clergyman's daughter. Both are now middle-aged and confirmed in their single state.*

We found that dinner was nearly ready in the kitchen—for so I suppose the room ought to be called, as there were oak dressers and cupboards all round, all over by the side of the fireplace, and only a small Turkey carpet in the middle of the flag floor. The room might easily have been made into a handsome dark oak dining-parlour by removing the oven and a few other appurtenances of the kitchen, which were evidently never used, the real cooking-place being at some distance.

* * * * *

We had pudding before meat; and I thought Mr Holbrook was going to make some apology for his old-fashioned ways, for he began—

'I don't know whether you like new-fangled ways.'

'Oh, not at all!' said Miss Matty.

'No more do I,' said he. 'My housekeeper *will* have these in her new fashion; or else I tell her that, when I was a young man, we used to keep strictly to my father's rule, "No broth, no ball; no ball, no beef;" and always began dinner with broth. Then we had suet puddings, boiled in the broth with the beef; and then the meat itself. If we did not sup our broth, we had no ball, which we liked a deal better; and the beef came last of all, and only those had it who had done justice to the broth and the ball. Now folks begin with sweet things, and turn their dinners topsy-turvy.'

Elizabeth Gaskell, *Cranford*, 1851–3

❧ *Turgenev wrote his last novel,* Virgin Soil, *in the 1870s. Its theme is the revolutionary youth of the decade, to whom the antiquated Subotchevs form a touching contrast, representing, in their old-fashioned innocence, a surviving corner of late eighteenth-century Russia.*

Fomishka and Fimishka, otherwise Foma Lavrentievitch and Efimia Pavlovna Subotchev, belonged to one of the oldest and purest branches of the Russian nobility, and were considered to be the oldest inhabitants in the town of S. They married when very young and settled, a long time ago, in the little wooden ancestral house at the very end of the town. Time seemed to have stood still for them, and nothing 'modern' ever crossed the boundaries of their 'oasis'. . . . The Subotchevs' house was filled with domestics and menials just as in days gone by. The old man-servant Kalliopitch, clad in a jacket of extraordinarily stout cloth with a stand-up collar and small steel buttons, announced, in a sing-song voice, 'Dinner is on the table,' and stood dozing behind his mistress's chair as in days of old. The sideboard was in his charge, and so were all the groceries and pickles. To the question, had he not heard of the emancipation [of the serfs], he invariably replied: 'How can one take notice of every idle piece of gossip? To be sure the Turks were emancipated, but such a dreadful thing had not happened to him, thank the Lord!' A girl, Pufka, was kept in the house for entertainment, and the old nurse Vassilievna used to come in during dinner with a dark kerchief on her head, and would relate all the news in her deep voice.

* * * * *

The Subotchevs dined exactly at twelve o'clock and ate only old-fashioned dishes: curd fritters, pickled cabbage, soups, fruit jellies, minced chicken with saffron, stews, custards, and honey. They took an after-dinner nap for an hour, not longer, and on waking up would sit opposite one another again, drinking bilberry wine or an effervescent drink called 'forty-minds,' which nearly always squirted out of the bottle, affording them great amusement, much to the disgust of Kalliopitch, who had to wipe up the mess afterwards. He grumbled at the cook and housekeeper as if they had invented this dreadful drink on purpose. 'What pleasure does it give one?' he asked; 'it only spoils the furniture.' Then the old people again read something, or got the dwarf Pufka to entertain them, or sang old-fashioned duets. . . . Or, if need be, they played at cards, always the same old games, cribbage, écarté, or double dummy whist. Then the samovar made its appearance. The only concession they made to the spirit of the age was to drink tea in the evening, though they always considered it an indulgence, and were convinced that the nation was deteriorating, owing to the use of this 'Chinese herb.' On the whole, they refrained from criticising modern times or from exulting their own. They had lived like this all their lives, but that others might live in a different and even better way they were quite willing to admit, so long as they were not compelled to conform to it. At seven o'clock Kalliopitch produced the inevitable supper of cold hash, and at nine the high striped feather-bed received their rotund little bodies in its soft embrace.

Ivan Turgenev, *Virgin Soil*, 1877, translated by Rochelle S. Townsend, 1911

❧ *John Galsworthy's* The Forsyte Saga *begins in 1886, with the first generation of male Londoners in the family (Jolyon, James, Swithin, Roger, Nicholas, and Timothy) mainly in retirement from business and living on investment incomes. Several of the second generation are married, with or without children. Swithin, the retired land agent, a bachelor of 75 living in Hyde Park Mansions, is giving a dinner for twelve members of the family, on which these observations are based.*

Family dinners of the Forsytes observe certain traditions. There are, for instance, no *hors d'œuvres*. The reason for this is unknown. Theory among the younger members traces it to the disgraceful price of oysters; it is more probably due to a desire to come to the point, to a good practical sense deciding at once that *hors d'œuvres* are poor things. The Jameses alone, unable to withstand a custom almost universal in Park Lane, are now and then unfaithful.

A silent, almost morose inattention to each other succeeds to the subsidence into their seats, lasting well into the first entrée, but interspersed with remarks.

* * * * *

With the second glass of champagne, a kind of hum makes itself heard, which, when divested of casual accessories and resolved into its primal element, is found to be James telling a story, and this goes on for a long time, encroaching sometimes even upon what must be universally recognised as the crowning point of a Forsyte feast—'the saddle of mutton'.

No Forsyte has given a dinner without providing a saddle of mutton. There is something in its succulent solidity which makes it suitable to people 'of a certain position'. It is nourishing and—tasty; the sort of thing a man remembers eating. It has a past and a future, like a deposit paid into a bank; and it is something that can be argued about.

Each branch of the family tenaciously held to a particular locality—old Jolyon swearing by Dartmoor, James by Welsh, Swithin by Southdown, Nicholas maintaining that people might sneer, but there was nothing like New Zealand. As for Roger, the 'original' of the brothers, he had been obliged to invent a locality of his own, and with an ingenuity worthy of a man who had devised a new profession for his sons, he had discovered a shop where they sold German; on being remonstrated with, he had proved his point by producing a butcher's bill, which showed that he had paid more than any of the others. It was on this occasion that old Jolyon, turning to June [his granddaughter], had said in one of his bursts of philosophy:

'You may depend upon it, they're a cranky lot, the Forsytes—and you'll find it out, as you grow older!'

Timothy alone held apart, for though he ate saddle of mutton heartily, he was, he said, afraid of it.

To anyone interested psychologically in Forsytes, this great saddle-of-mutton trait is of prime importance; not only does it illustrate their tenacity, both collectively and as individuals, but it marks them as belonging in fibre and instincts to that great class which believes in nourishment and flavour, and yields to no sentimental craving for beauty.

Younger members of the family indeed would have done without a joint altogether, preferring guinea-fowl, or lobster salad—something which appealed to the imagination, and had less nourishment—but these were females; or, if not, had been corrupted by their wives, or by mothers, who having been forced to eat saddle of mutton throughout their married lives, had passed a secret hostility towards it into the fibre of their sons.

John Galsworthy, *The Forsyte Saga: The Man of Property*, 1906, Part I

❧ Look Homeward, Angel *is Thomas Wolfe's first novel, set mainly in Tennessee in the 1890s. Eugene Gant, who strongly resembles Wolfe himself, is the youngest child of Oliver Gant, a wild, restlessly demanding character, and his impossible wife Eliza, who, as a lodging-house keeper separated from her husband, comes to dominate the later part of the book. At this stage, in Eugene's early childhood, it is the father who dominates; and the family are still together, in a financially precarious state but with no hint of self-denial.*

They fed stupendously. Eugene began to observe the food and the seasons. In the autumn, they barrelled huge frosty apples in the cellar. Gant bought whole hogs from the butcher, returning home early to salt them, wearing a long work-apron and rolling his sleeves half-way up his lean hairy arms. Smoked bacons hung in the pantry, the great bins were full of flour, the dark recessed shelves groaned with preserved cherries, peaches, plums, quinces, apples, pears. All that he touched waxed in rich pungent life: his Spring gardens, wrought in the black wet earth below the fruit trees, flourished in huge crinkled lettuces that wrenched cleanly from the soil with small black clots stuck to their crisp stocks; fat red radishes; heavy tomatoes. The rich plums lay bursted on the grass; his huge cherry trees oozed with heavy gum jewels; his apple trees bent with thick green clusters. The earth was spermy for him like a big woman.

Spring was full of cool dewy mornings, spurting winds, and storms of intoxicating blossoms, and in this enchantment Eugene first felt the mixed lonely ache of the seasons.

In the morning they rose in a house pungent with breakfast cookery, and they sat at a smoking table loaded with brains and eggs, ham, hot biscuit, fried apples seething in their gummed spirits, honey, golden butter, fried steak, scalding coffee. Or there were stacked batter-cakes, rum-coloured molasses, fragrant brown sausages, a bowl of wet cherries, plums, fat juicy bacon, jam. At the mid-day meal they ate heavily: a huge hot roast of beef, fat buttered lima-beans, tender corn smoking on the cob, thick red slabs of sliced tomatoes, rough savory spinach, hot yellow corn-bread, flaky biscuits, a deep-dish peach and apple cobbler spiced with cinnamon, tender cabbage, deep glass dishes piled with preserved fruits—cherries, pears, peaches. At night they might eat fried steak, hot squares of grits fried in egg and butter, pork chops, fish, young fried chicken.

For the Thanksgiving and Christmas feasts four heavy turkeys were bought and fattened for weeks: Eugene fed them with cans of shelled corn several times a day, but he could not bear to be present at their executions, because by that time their cheerful excited gobbles made echoes in his heart. Eliza baked for weeks in advance: the whole energy of the family focussed upon the great ritual of the feast. A day or two before, the auxiliary dainties arrived in piled grocers' boxes—the magic of strange foods and fruits was added to familiar fare: there were glossed sticky dates, cold rich figs, cramped belly to belly in small boxes, dusty raisins, mixed nuts—the almond, pecan, the meaty nigger-toe, the walnuts, sacks of assorted candies, piles of yellow Florida oranges, tangerines, sharp, acrid, nostalgic odours.

Seated before a roast or a fowl, Gant began a heavy clangour on his steel and carving knife, distributing thereafter Gargantuan portions to each plate. Eugene feasted from a high chair by his father's side, filled his distended belly until it was drum-tight, and was permitted to stop eating by his watchful sire only when his stomach was impregnable to the heavy prod of Gant's big finger. 'There's a soft place there,' he would roar, and he would cover the scoured plate of his infant son with another heavy slab of beef. That their machinery withstood this hammer-handed treatment was a tribute to their vitality and Eliza's cookery.

Gant ate ravenously and without caution. He was immoderately fond of fish, and he invariably choked upon a bone while eating it. This happened hundreds of times, but each time he would look up suddenly with a howl of agony and terror, groaning and crying out strongly, while half a dozen hands pounded violently on his back.

'Merciful God!' he would gasp finally. 'I thought I was done for that time.'

'I'll vow, Mr Gant,' Eliza was vexed. 'Why on earth don't you watch what you're doing? If you didn't eat so fast you wouldn't always get choked.'

The children, staring, but relieved, settled slowly back in their places.

He had a Dutch love of abundance: again and again he described the great stored barns, the groaning plenty of the Pennsylvanians.

On his journey to California, he had been charmed in New Orleans by the cheapness and profusion of tropical fruits: a peddler offered him a great bunch of bananas for twenty-five cents, and Gant had taken them at once, wondering desperately later, as they moved across the continent, why, and what he was going to do with them.

Thomas Wolfe, *Look Homeward, Angel*, 1930

After service in the First World War, Gerald Brenan left England for Spain in 1919 and settled in a remote village in Andalusia.

Many people at Yegen had a neurosis about eating. Quite a number of women of the poorer sort seemed to feel an antipathy for food and would rather be offered a cup of coffee than a good meal.

Others were ashamed of being seen to eat and, if compelled to do so in public, would sit in a corner with their backs to the room. I once knew a family of well-to-do people, of partly gipsy descent, each of whom cooked his own food and ate it at a separate table, with his back to the others. One must expect such feelings to arise in a country where for many people food is scarce and any sort of eating an act of daring and extravagance. Old women in particular developed the sort of prudery about it that in other countries they develop about sex.

The general rule, except among the rich, was for the head of the family to eat first by himself. For this he did not draw up to a dining-room table, but had a *mesilla* or little low table placed in oriental style in front of him. His children eat on the ground, squatting in a circle round a pot or frying-pan, while the women of the house took their food last and in a hurried, scrappy manner. Sometimes, however, there would be several grown men in a family, and then they eat out of a common dish placed on a table between them. This was the custom too in ventas and posadas and whenever parties of friends went off to the fields for a festive picnic. According to the novelist, Juan Valera, the Andalusian upper classes always ate in this way down to the middle of the nineteenth century. Naturally, as I have already said, there was an etiquette about this. Everyone selected his segment and ate till the partition separating it from his neighbours' had become thin. Those who had delicate tastes then laid down their spoon, leaving it to the coarsest appetites to eat right through.

Gerald Brenan, *South From Granada*, 1957

Professor Richard Hoggart grew up in the 1920s in two of the poorest areas of Leeds, supported first by his mother, then by his grandmother, with payments from the Public Assistance Board. His father had died when he was very young.

I have always assumed that [our mother], not [her husband], was the organizer. Certainly, our pattern of eating recalls yet again the need for skilful management, usually by the wife and whether or not the husband was alive. I do not remember ever seeing a joint of meat on the table; but that would have been true of most of our near neighbours. Even families with a regular breadwinner would usually have a joint only at Sunday dinnertime and that would have been likely to be the cheap Argentinian beef. . . . Chicken was still expensive, still something talked about as special, a café meal for those who ever managed that, or the laid-on lunch for a workers' outing. The only solid meat I recall was a bit of rabbit occasionally.

Other than that, stews, minces, porridge, bread and margarine, dripping; and the first biscuits tasted, through someone's kindness, at five or six years old. But cocoa, cheap jam (blackberry-and-apple was the staple, much as apricot jam is today in hotel breakfasts right across East and West Europe). Cheap tinned condensed milk spread on bread was a very special treat, its cloying, gooey sweetness a certain hit with children. The cheapest condensed milk was very sweet indeed, very grittily sugary; another staple in many households. In Hunslet later, I met a peculiarly rich and yellow ice-cream which children loved. One day I found by accident the place where it was made; a broken-down backshed which the Public Health inspector should have closed long before. In it we saw the Italian proprietor, before he shooed us away, ladling can after can of cheap condensed milk into his machine.

Richard Hoggart, *A Local Habitation* (*Life and Times, Volume I: 1918–40*), 1988

❧ *V. S. Naipaul grew up in Trinidad as a member of an educated Indian family, and grandson of a Hindu indentured labourer who had emigrated to the West Indies from Uttar Pradesh.*

I came of a family that abounded with pundits. But I had been born an unbeliever. I took no pleasure in religious ceremonies. They were too long, and the food came only at the end. I did not understand the language—it was as if our elders assumed that our understanding would be instinctive—and no one explained the prayers or the ritual. . . . What, then, survived of Hinduism in me? Perhaps I had received a certain supporting philosophy. I cannot say; my uncle often put it to me that my denial was an admissible form of Hinduism. Examining myself, I found only [a] sense of the difference of people . . . a vaguer sense of caste, and a horror of the unclean.

It still horrifies me that people should put out food for animals on plates that they themselves use; as it horrified me at school to see boys sharing Popsicles and Palates, local iced lollies; as it horrifies me to see women sipping from ladles with which they stir their pots. This was more than difference; this was the uncleanliness we had to guard against. From all food restrictions sweets were, curiously, exempt. We bought cassava pone from street stalls; but black pudding and souse, favourite street-corner and sports-ground dishes of the Negro proletariat, were regarded by us with fascinated horror. This might suggest that our food remained what it always had been. But this was not so. It is not easy to understand just how communication occurred, but we were steadily adopting the food styles of others: the Portuguese stew of tomatoes and onions, in which almost anything might be done, the Negro way with yams, plantains, breadfruit and bananas. Everything we adopted became our own; the outside was still to be dreaded, and my prejudices were so strong that when I left Trinidad, shortly before my eighteenth birthday, I had eaten in restaurants only three times. The day of my swift transportation to New York was a day of misery. I spent a frightened, hungry day in that city; and on the ship to Southampton I ate mainly the sweets, which encouraged the steward to say when I tipped him, 'The others made pigs of themselves. But you sure do like ice cream.'

V. S. Naipaul, *An Area of Darkness*, 1964

II

FOODSTUFFS AND COOKING

PROVISIONING AND SHOPPING

Decree of the Privy Council for Scotland, 19 April, 1550.

Item, inlikwise hevand respect to the gret and exorbitant derth of the wyld mete of this realme, and for putting of ordour heirto and remaid hereof, it is divisit and ordanit that all wyld mete be sauld of the preces following. That is to say, in primis, cran and swan to be sauld every ane of thame for v*s*. Item, the wild guyse of the gret bynd, ij*s*. Item, the claik, quynk, and rutt for xviij*d*. Item, the pertrik, viij*d*. Item, the plover and small murfoul, v*d*. Item, the blak cok, and the gray hen, vj*d*. Item the powttis the dosoen, xij*d*. Item, the quhawip, vj*d*. Item, the cunyng, xij*d*. Item, the leprioun, ij*d*. Item, wyd cokis, iiij*d*. Item, ane desain of laverokis and uthair small bredis, ilk desoun, iiij*d*. Item, snype, quelye every ane of thame, ij*d*.—under the pane of baith to the sellar byair of escheting of all thair gudis, takking and punissing of thair personis, at my Lord Governour will. Item, it is divisit and ordenit that nane heron, duke, drake or ony fule ar of revar be slane in ony maner of sort bot be halkis alanerly, under the pane of confiscatioun of all thair gudis and punissing of thair persons at my Lord Governour will.

Similarly, with respect to the great and exorbitant shortage of wild meat in this kingdom, and to remedy this, it is devised and ordained that all wild meat shall be sold at the following prices. That is to say, first of all, crane and swan to be sold for 5s. each. The large-sized wild geese, 2s. The barnacle goose, greylag goose and brent goose for 18d. The partridge, 8d. The plover and small moorfowl, 5d. The blackcock and the grey hen, 6d. Young game-birds, 12d. a dozen. The larger curlew, 6d. The rabbit, 12d. The hare, 2d. Woodcocks, 4d. A dozen larks or other small birds, 4d. a dozen. Snipe, 2d. each. With a penalty to both seller and buyer that their goods shall be seized and their persons punished at my Lord Governor's pleasure. It is also devised and ordained that no heron, duck, drake or any fowl or river-bird shall be killed by any means except by hawking alone, under pain of confiscation of their goods and punishment to their persons at my Lord Governor's pleasure.

Register of the Privy Council for Scotland, Volume I, 1545–69

Next to the market places that I spake of stonde meate markettes, whether be brought not onlye all sortes of herbes, and the fruites of trees with breade, but also fishe, and all maner of iiii footed beastes, and wilde foule that be mans meate. But first the fylthynes and ordure therof is clene washed awaye in the runnynge ryver, without the cytie, in places appoynted, mete for the same purpose. From thence the beastes brought in kylled, and cleane wasshed by the handes of their bondemen. For they permytte not their frie citezens to accustome there selfes to the killing of beastes; through the use whereof they thinke that clemencie, the genteleste affection of our nature, doth by litle and litle decaye and peryshe.

The Utopia of Sir Thomas More . . . in English from the First Edition of Ralph Robyson's Translation in 1551, edited by J. H. Lupton, B. D., 1895

As the editor of this translation pointed out, More's description of an ideal state in which slaughterhouses drained directly into rivers showed him to be by no means in advance of the ideas about public hygiene which prevailed at his time.

CLOWN. . . . Let me see; what am I to buy for our sheep-shearing feast? Three pounds of sugar; five pounds of currants; rice—what will this sister of mine do with rice? But my father hath made her mistress of the feast, and she lays it on. She hath made me four and twenty nosegays for the shearers, three-man song-men all, and very good ones; but they are most of them means and bases; but one puritan among them, and he sings psalms to hornpipes. I must have saffron to colour the warden pies; mace; dates, none, that's out of my note; nutmegs, seven; a race or two of ginger, but that I may beg; four pound of prunes, and as many of raisins o'the sun.

William Shakespeare, *The Winter's Tale*, IV. iii

Warden pies: spiced fruit pies made with warden pears, a kind of baking pear; *race*: a 'hand' or whole rhizome of ginger.

❧ *A more elaborate version, dated c.1619, of the (almost contemporary) rustic's shopping-list in* The Winter's Tale, *from the household accounts of Lord William Howard's steward at Naworth Castle, Cumberland.*

Bought of Mr Hall at St Luke's fair by my wyfe:

A quarter of *c* of reysons solis		xvi *s*	iii *d*
c of fine currants		lii *s*	
140 *li* of powder suger, at 13 *d*	vii *li*	xi *s*	viii *d*
One pound of mace and cloves	½ *li*	xii *s*	
ii *li* of licorace			xii *d*
One *l* of anyseeds			x *d*
ii *li* of large cynomom		vii *s*	iiii *d*
x *li* of jurden [*Jordan*] allmonds, at 16 *d*		xiii *s*	iiii *d*
12 *li* of case pepper at 2 *s* 4 *d*		xxviii *s*	
One loafe of suger of xiii li, xi ounces		xvii *s*	ii *d*
viii *li* of large ginger		viii *s*	
One pound of case nutmeggs		iiii *s*	
One gallon of olives		viii *s*	
6 *li* of cappers [*capers*]		viii *s*	
2 *li* d. of wett sucket [*sweets*]		iii *s*	ix *d*
One pound of candied ginger		iiii *s*	
2 barrells for olives and sucketts			ix *d*
saffron			xii *d*

Nutmeggs	xxii *d*
Sanders [*Indian wood for dyeing jellies*]	vi *d*

Selections from the Household Books of the Lord William Howard of Naworth Castle, Surtees Society, 1878

Reysons solis: raisins of the sun; *c*: hundredweight (112 lbs); *l*[*iber*], pl. *l*[*ibr*]*i*: pound(s).

LONDON MARKETS

Experienc'd Men, inur'd to City Ways,
Need not the *Calendar* to count their Days.
When through the Town, with slow and solemn Air,
Led by the Nostril, walks the muzled Bear;
Behind him moves, majestically dull,
The pride of *Hockley-hole*, the surly Bull;
Learn hence the Periods of the Week to name,
Mondays and *Thursdays* are the Days of Game.

When fishy Stalls with double Store are laid;
The golden-belly'd Carp, the broad-finn'd Maid,
Red-speckled Trouts, the Salmon's silver Joul,
The jointed Lobster, and unscaly Soale,
And luscious 'Scallops, to allure the Tastes
Of rigid Zealots to delicious Fasts;
Wednesdays and *Fridays* you'll observe from hence,
Days, when our Sires were doom'd to Abstinence.

* * *

Successive Crys the Seasons Change declare,
And mark the Monthly Progress of the Year.
Hark, how the Streets with treble Voices ring,
To sell the bounteous Product of the Spring!
Sweet-smelling Flow'rs, and Elder's early Bud,
With Nettle's tender Shoots, to cleanse the Blood:
And when *June*'s Thunder cools the sultry Skies,
Ev'n *Sundays* are prophan'd by Mackrell Cries.

Wallnuts, the *Fruit'rer*'s Hand, in Autumn, stain,
Blue Plumbs, and juicy Pears augment his Gain;
Next Oranges the longing Boys entice,
To trust their Copper-Fortunes to the Dice.

John Gay, 'Trivia, or the Art of Walking the Streets of London', 1716

Hockley-hole: between Clerkenwell and the City of London; *maid*: a kind of shad, or the young of the skate and thornback; *Wednesdays and Fridays*: traditional days of abstinence from meat in the Roman Catholic Church; *Oranges . . . Dice*: possibly a reference to raffling oranges on Shrove Tuesday, before giving up both fruit and gaming for Lent.

❧ *The following letters were written by the widowed Elizabeth Purefoy (1672–1765) and her son Henry (1697–1762), both of Shalstone Manor, Buckinghamshire, between Brackley and Buckingham, just west of Stowe. The way of life that they illustrate is typical of the eighteenth-century English gentry, who, when in the country, often devoted a great deal of energy to procuring certain essential delicacies from London or elsewhere. Most groceries (tea, coffee, sugar, rice, dried fruit, spices) now no longer came from travelling dealers at the local fair, but were ordered from London merchants in the City, St Paul's Churchyard, or Fleet Street, who sent them to the country by carrier's cart. Fish could be a problem, especially in areas such as Oxfordshire and Buckinghamshire which were far away from the sea and where the rivers yielded only coarse fishing. Elizabeth Purefoy, however (who had been born into the Hertfordshire family of Fish), clearly did not intend to keep to the prevailing all-meat diet of her neighbourhood, whatever the practical difficulties of doing otherwise might be.*

E.P. to James Fisher, fishmonger of Newgate, London, 20 April 1737.

I desire Mr ffisher to send mee every week as much ffish as will come to *3s* or *3s 6d* a week, except it be such weeks as you can send mackerell—then send them & no other ffish. The town of Buckingham has been so aflicted with ye small pox wee have had no communication there till now, & what sea fish we have had have [come] from Oxford.

Same to same, 29 May 1737.

I was in hopes by this time Mr ffisher would have sent some mackerell according to my order, but since none are come the weather is now so exceeding hot that what ffish you sent last week stank & could not be eat, so I desire you would not send any more fish till further orders.

E.P. to Thomas Robotham, the family's London agent [*an innkeeper in Islington and husband of one of their former servants*], *12 March 1739.*

We . . . received your kind present of a codling & oysters; the codling was very good, but the Oysters, half of them were black as Ink and the other half was poisoned with the stench, for they were all of a ffroth & your ffishmonger should give you your money again. Wee return you hearty thanks for them. Pray send no more this year for I believe there are none good. . . . I should not have wrote till I had sent you some Hog Puddings but too Day the Dogs chopt on a lusty Hare which is the only one save one that we have had since you was here. I desire your acceptance thereof carriage paid this day.

Same to same, 23 May 1747.

I received your pickled salmon, the pot of anchovies, & six Sevill oranges which were all very good & wee return you thanks for them. The salmon was very good but jumbled into peices & the liquor all run out. . . . I have sent you with your butter a stone Bottle which I desire you to get filled with the very best sallet oyll & sent as soon as may be.

E.P. to Mr Wilson [of Wilson & Thornhill, grocers, successively of Fleet Street and St Paul's Churchyard, London], 6 February 1747.

Mr Willson

I desire you will send mee
One pound of the best Bohea Tea
Half a pound of the best green Tea
Two pounds of the best Coffeeberries
A quarter of a pound of nutmegs
Two ounces of mace
A quarter of an hundred of the best treble refined Loaf sugar
A quarter of an hundred of Household sugar about 6 pence a pound
Half a quarter of an hundred of Poland starch
Half a quarter of an hundred of Rice

Send these by ye Buckingham carrier . . . send your Bill with them & [I] will order you payment. The last Bohea Tea was so ordinary I could not drink it, my neighbours had as good for six shillings a pound. The last hundredweight of Raisins you sent were so bad they spoiled the Liquor they were made on. I hope you will send no more bad Goods, I have had no reason to complain till now, tho' I have dealt at y[ou]r shop these forty years.

H.P. to Benjamin Rose of Deddington, Oxfordshire, 25 September 1751.

Mr Rose

I understand from the People of Astrop that you sell pickled mushrooms, so desire a line or two from you to let mee know the price you sell'em at, & whether by the Quart bottle or in a Pan & when you will have any ready for sale.

Direct yours to mee to be left at Mr Blencow's an ironmonger at Brackley, which will oblige.

Purefoy Letters, 1735–1753, edited by G. Eland FSA, 1931

Astrop, near King's Sutton, Banbury, contains St Rumbold's Well, a chalybeate spring popular in the early eighteenth century for its supposed medicinal properties. In the Purefoys' time it was a flourishing spa where the local gentry met and held parties, especially in late August and September once the harvests were in and (incidentally) at the beginning of the mushroom season.

❧ Beppo *is set in Venice. Byron's advice to the English traveller to equip himself with sauces from the Strand, where the best-known shops for exotic condiments, Peck's and Burgess's, in his day had the title of Italian warehouses, thus contains an element of a 'coals to Newcastle' joke.*

This feast is named the Carnival, which being
Interpreted, implies 'farewell to flesh':
So call'd, because the name and thing agreeing,
Through Lent they live on fish both salt and fresh.
But why they usher Lent with so much glee in,
Is more than I can tell, although I guess
'Tis as we take a glass with friends at parting,
In the Stage-Coach or Packet, just at starting.

And thus they bid farewell to carnal dishes,
And solid meats, and highly spiced ragouts,
To live for forty days on ill-dressed fishes,
Because they have no sauces to their stews;
A thing which causes many 'poohs' and 'pishes',
And several oaths (which would not suit the Muse),
From travellers accustom'd from a boy
To eat their salmon, at the least, with soy;

And therefore humbly I would recommend
'The curious in fish-sauce', before they cross
The sea, to bid their cook, or wife, or friend,
Walk or ride to the Strand, and buy in gross
(Or if set out beforehand, these may send
By any means least liable to loss),
Ketchup, Soy, Chili-vinegar, and Harvey,
Or by the Lord! a Lent will well nigh starve ye.

George Gordon Noel Byron, Lord Byron, *Beppo*, 1819

❧ *Italian warehouses, stocking Parmesan cheese, olive oil, anchovies, and vermicelli, had existed sporadically in London since the very early eighteenth century. By Byron's day, however, they had multiplied, and were fashionable places to shop not only for specifically Italian goods but for the made-up sauces, ketchups, pickles, and spices without which the sophisticated English palate readily became jaded.*

Trade Card [*c.*1800–20] of

Peck's Italian Warehouse

N°. 175 Strand

LONDON

AMBROSE PECK'S TEA

GROCERY & FOREIGN FRUIT WAREHOUSE

OILS, PICKLES &C.

[RECTO]

Lucca Oil · Vegetable Essences · Parmesan Cheese
Mushroom Ketchup · India Soy · Cavioe · Covatch
Espagnole Sauce · Quin Sauce · Compleat Boxes of Rich Fish Sauces
Sauce Piquant · Sauce Royal · Harvey's Sauce · Cherokee Sauce
Walnut Ketchup · Essence Anchovies · Lemon Pickle
Wax and Sperm: Soaps · Candles · Starch & Blues · Curry Powders
Capers · Olives · Vinegar · Pickles · Basket Salt · Salt Petre
Salt Prunella

[VERSO]

Isinglass · Vermacelli · Lemon & Peel · Muscatells
French Prunelle · Turkey Figs · Almonds · Morells · Alspice
Ginger · Cinamon · Nutmeg · Mace · Sugars · Peppers
Cocoa Shells · Preserv'd Ginger · Tamarinds · Curious Teas
H[arts] H[orn] Shavings · Arrow Root · Sage & Sage Powder
Macaroni · Tapioca · Truffles · Pistatia Nutts · Prune du Roy
Prune de la Reine · Imperials · Best Chocolate · Portugal
Plumbs · Various Honeys · Dry Fruits · Brandy Fruits
Kyan Pepper

Bodleian Library, Oxford, John Johnson Collection of Printed Ephemera, *Grocers*

❧ *Ford Madox Ford (1873–1939), the novelist, had eloped with his first wife Elsie Martindale in 1894, and spent most of the next ten years living as a struggling writer on Romney Marsh, then a remote area just inland from the Kent and Sussex coast.*

About twenty-five years ago I wanted some mushroom catsup. Bonnington was in [*sic*] a scattered, little-populated village of the south of England. The village stood on what had formerly been common land; running all down the side of a range of hills. But this common land had been long since squatted on, so that it was a maze of little hawthorn hedges surrounding little closes. Each close had a few old apple- or cherry-trees, a patch of potato ground, a cabbage patch, a few rows of scarlet runners, a few plants of monthly roses, a few plants of marjoram, fennel, borage or thyme. And in each little patch there stood a small dwelling. Mostly these were the original squatters' huts built of mud, whitewashed outside and crowned with old thatched roofs on which there grew grasses, house-leeks, or even irises. There were a great many of these houses beneath the September sunshine and it was all a maze of the small green hedges.

I had been up to the shop in search of my catsup, but though they sold everything from boots and straw hats to darning needles, bacon, haricot beans, oatmeal and British wines they had no catsup. I was wandering desultorily homewards among the small green hedges down hill, looking at the distant sea seven miles away over the marsh. Just beyond a little hedge I saw a woman digging potatoes in the dry, hot ground. She looked up as I passed and said:

'Hullo, Measter!'

I answered: 'Hullo, Missus!' and I was passing on when it occurred to me to ask her whether she knew anyone who sold catsup. She answered: 'Naw! Aw doan't knaw no one!'

I walked on a little further and then sat down on a stile for half an hour or so; enjoying the pleasant weather and taking a read in the country paper which I had bought in the shop. Then I saw the large, stalwart old woman coming along the stony path carrying two great trugs of the potatoes that she had dug up. I had to get down from the stile to let her pass. And then seeing that she was going my way, that she was evidently oldish and was probably tired, I took the potato trugs from her and carried them. She strode along in front of me between the hedges. She wore an immense pair of men's hob-nailed boots that dragged along the stones of the causeway with metallic sounds, an immense shawl of wool that had been beaten by the weather until it was of a dull liver colour, an immense skirt that had once been of lilac cotton print, but was now a rusty brown, and an immense straw hat that had been given to her by someone as worn out and that had cost twopence when new. Her face was as large, as round and much the same colour as a copper warming-pan.

Her mouth was immense and quite toothless except for one large fang, and as she smiled cheerfully all the time her great gums were always to be seen. Her shoulders were immense and moved with the roll and heave of those of a great bullock. This was the wisest and upon the whole the most estimable human being that I ever knew at all well. Her hands were enormous and stained a deep blackish green over their original copper colour by the hops that it was her profession to tie.

* * * * *

I delivered up her trugs to her at her garden gate and she said to me with a cheerful nod:—'Well I'll do the same for you mate, when you come to be my age.' . . . But before I was come to the end of the hedge her voice was calling out after me:

'Measter! Dun you really want ketchup?'

I replied that I really did.

She said:

'Old Meary Spratt up by Hungry Hall wheer ye see me diggin'—she makes ketchup.'

I asked her why she had not told me before and she answered,

'Well, ye see the Quality do be asking foolish questions, I thought ye didn't really want to know.'

I learnt afterwards it wasn't only the dislike of being asked foolish questions. In Meary Walker's long, wise life she had experienced one thing—that no man with a collar and tie is to be trusted. . . . She didn't know that the making of catsup was not illegal. She had heard that many of her poor neighbours had been fined heavily for selling bottles of home-made sloe-gin or mead. She had refused to answer, out of a sense of automatic caution for fear she should get poor old Meary Spratt into trouble.

But next morning she turned up at my cottage carrying two bottles of Meary Spratt's catsup in an old basket covered with a cloth.

Ford Madox Ford, *Return to Yesterday*, 1931

❧ Lark Rise, *a thinly disguised childhood autobiography, tells the story of Laura growing up with her family in a poor North Oxfordshire hamlet in the 1870s and 1880s.*

Callers made a pleasant diversion in the hamlet women's day, and there were more of these than might have been expected. The first to arrive on Monday morning was old Jerry Parish with his cartload of fish and fruit. As he served some of the big houses on his round, Jerry carried quite a large stock; but the only goods he took round to the doors at Lark Rise were a box of bloaters and a basket of small, sour oranges. The bloaters were sold at a penny each and the oranges at three a penny. Even at these prices they were luxuries; but, as it was still only Monday and a few coppers might remain in a few purses, the women felt at liberty to crowd round his cart to examine and criticize his wares, even if they bought nothing.

Two or three of them would be tempted to buy a bloater for their midday meal; but it had to be a soft-roed one, for, in nearly every house there were children under school age at home; so the bloater had to be shared, and the soft roes spread upon bread for the smallest ones.

'Lor' blime me!' Jerry used to say. 'Never knowed such a lot in me life for soft roes. Good job I ain't a soft-roed 'un or I should've got aten up meself before now.' And he pinched the bloaters between his great red fingers, pretending to consider the matter with his head on one side, then declared each separate fish had the softest of soft roes, whether it had or not. 'Oozin', simply oozin' with goodness, I tell ye!' and oozing it certainly was when released from his grip. 'But what's the good of one bloater amongst the lot of ye? Tell ye what I'll do,' he would urge. 'I'll put ye in these three whoppers for tuppence ha'penny.'

It was no good. The twopence-halfpenny was never forthcoming; even the penny could so ill be spared that the purchaser often felt selfish and greedy after she had parted with it; but, after a morning at the washtub, she needed a treat so badly, and a bloater made a tasty change from her usually monotonous diet.

* * * * *

It was on Jerry's cart tomatoes first appeared in the hamlet. They had not long been introduced into this country and were slowly making their way into favour. The fruit was flatter in shape than now and deeply grooved and indented from the stem, giving it an almost starlike appearance. There were bright yellow ones, too, as well as the scarlet; but, after a few years, the yellow ones disappeared from the market and the red ones became rounder and smoother, as we see them now.

At first sight, the basket of red and yellow fruit attracted Laura's colour-loving eye. 'What are those?' she asked old Jerry.

'Love-apples, me dear. Love-apples, they be; though some

hignorant folks be a callin' 'em tommytoes. But you don't want any o' they—nasty sour things, they be, as only gentry can eat. You have a nice sweet orange wi' your penny.' But Laura felt she must taste the love-apples and insisted upon having one.

Such daring created quite a sensation among the onlookers. 'Don't 'ee go tryin' to eat it, now,' one woman urged. 'It'll only make 'ee sick. I know because I had one of the nasty horrid things at our Minnie's.' And nasty, horrid things tomatoes remained in the popular estimation for years; though most people to-day would prefer them as they were then, with the real tomato flavour pronounced, to the watery insipidity of our larger, smoother tomato.

Flora Thompson, *Lark Rise*, 1939

SATURDAY MARKET

Linked up with my memories of Clapham Common is the memory of Lavender Hill on a Saturday night, myself in a little wooden 'push-cart', the string shopping-bag hanging over the handles. Saturday nights had a peculiar flavour of their own, because of the flares on the street-stalls, red as fire against the night-dark sky. The crowds were more dense, too, which was an added excitement. This fascination of street-stalls, and the flavour of a marketing street on a Saturday night, have remained with me. Now, as then, I find a curious excitement in the dark tide of humanity, the yellow glare of lights from the shop-fronts, the warm smell of people pressed close together, the dark fire of the market, bunches of wallflowers stacked on barrows, the earthy, country scent of them, the pungent smell of oranges, and the great glowing blaze of their colour, the bunches of grapes, white and black, suspended like Japanese lanterns from the awnings, the white nakedness of scrubbed celery heads gleaming wantonly in the flicker and shadow, the rhythmic rows of shining apples, and the subtle, acid aroma of them. . . . And the black-shawled gipsy-looking women who sold these things, they and their rough men-folk with the scarves about their necks instead of collars and ties, and brass ear-rings to their ears, gipsy people, infinitely romantic. . . .

All along Lavender Hill they would be ranged, and between them and the pavement stalls put out by the shops themselves, and dark press of people intent on their marketing, hands clutching string-bags and baskets, eyes searching, hands picking over a piece of meat here, a pair of kippers there, pinching the hard green cheeks of cooking apples, delving ruthlessly into green vegetable interiors for their hearts, shopkeepers and costers shouting prices, a din of traffic and shouting, a confusion of movement, colour, shadow, flares . . . and myself of it yet safe from the crush of it, excitingly, being pushed through it all, like a small, dexterously manipulated ship on a dark sea, in my little chair on wheels. Something deliciously dangerous to my child-mind, too, about the wind-blown flares forever threatening the awnings, dipping towards them and then away again, tantalizingly . . . and with it all a great busyness, expertly slick twisting of brown paper bags, cabbages and beetroots wrapped in newspaper, potatoes shot briskly into whatever receptacle was handy, as often as not into the well at the bottom of a perambulator. . . . Fascination of the string-bag which reveals all our purchases growing fuller and fuller like a fishing net heavy with a big catch, and then a bunch of wallflowers, perhaps, stuck in at the top, and then going home, turning our backs on the lights and the busyness and the excitement, turning into dark empty streets, and the scent of wet wallflowers going with us under the starriness. . . . And then coming in at last to the tall old house with its musty smell of closed rooms never adequately aired, and of all the meals ever cooked in it, and a little of the piddled prams left always in the hall . . . and mounting the steep dark stairs, blundering a little as we go, for my mother clings to the heavy bag, and I cling to her skirts . . . and coming finally into our own part of the house, and the little room with the green cloth on the table, and the canary covered up for the night, and the kitchen range shining . . . a room mysterious with the blue-grey dimness of the turned-down gas, somehow removed from everydayness in this strange hard twilight, and a little frightening.

Ethel Mannin, *Confessions and Impressions*, 1936

❧ *Nella Last was a 50-year-old housewife in the Lancashire shipbuilding town of Barrow-in-Furness, with a husband at home and two sons of military age, when she began to keep her wartime diary for the Mass Observation organization. During the war years Nella worked in a WVS (Women's Voluntary Service) Centre, and later in a WVS canteen for defence workers, soldiers, sailors, and others. Her love of food and pleasure in generous cooking permeate the whole of the diary.*

Friday, 8 November, 1940.

It's the custom for fish and fruit shops in Barrow to print their special lines on the outside window with a small brush dipped in whitening: '*SPECIAL*! RABBITS. CRABS.' The better-class shops *never* do, and I was really amused by one such shop today, for on both windows—it's on a corner—was printed neatly and in extra large letters:

NO EGGS

NO LEMONS

NO ONIONS

NO LEEKS

NO PAPER BAGS

I wondered how many times Mrs Jones had had to say those words before, in exasperation, she printed them on the window. The fishmonger's shop was quite nicely stocked—especially with rabbits. I got one and paid *1s. 8d.* Considering the time of year, I thought they were an indifferent sample—I like to see pale pink flesh and the kidneys sunk in creamy fat. I hunted well through the furry rows, and did not feel so suited with what I got finally.

Saturday, 22 March, 1941.

There were closed stalls everywhere in the market today, and those big showy ones, with their tons of sweet biscuits and cheap nasty sweets, have either all gone or else had one tiny space open between shutters. No eggs, fowls or golden butter on the country women's stalls, no little glasses of 'rum butter', golden honey or glowing, home-made orange marmalade, no toffee or candy made on the farm from fresh butter, no glasses of cream or tiny luscious pots of cream cheese. The fishermen's carts and stall had no flukes or plaice, no pile of sweet 'picked' shrimps or baskets of glistening shelled ones—gun practice in the Bay had stopped all that. No shy clumps of pansies and daisies, cuddled up in the folds of newspapers to shelter them from the cold wind. Only muddy-looking—and *far* too small—cockles and pieces of most unpleasant-looking beetroot, which looked as if mangels had been boiled instead. There were no rows of furry rabbits or strings of sea-birds. . . . I wandered about with a sadness in my heart. I loved the market and the joyous spirit there—a meet-a-friend-and-have-a-chat, even when there was no money for bargains. Now, grim-faced women queue and push—and hurry off to another queue when served.

Wednesday, 7 May, 1941.

We decided to go out early after lunch—that I'd shop and then we would go to the pictures. I've a real love and talent for shopping. I am not a 'telephone shopper', and I don't really like my butcher to 'send what he can'. I got veal and mutton for a pie. I'd have preferred beef and mutton, but it should be all right: a veal jelly-bone, with enough meat on it to make a little bowl of potted meat, and a shank-end mutton bone for a stock-pot—all for 2*s.* 1*d.*, so I've still 11*d.* left for when Cliff [her favourite son, on short leave from the Army] goes back. I had put 6d. worth of cress seeds on some felt for my chicks, but it's been grand for salads—with chopped carrots and beets—and our Cliff could eat salads at every meal. There will be enough for the chicks, too, and I've planted a little more to come on later. Lettuce were from 1*s.* 2*d.* to 1*s.* 7*d.* today, and not as good value as my scrap of cress, costing 1*d.* at most. I'm *stubborn*—I'll not buy things I think are too highly priced, or queue for them. I firmly believe women are to blame for high prices. If they would not buy, say, salmon at 8*s.* 6*d.* a pound, next week it would be cheaper. My butcher laughs at me—says I shop like a French woman who demands the best even if it costs less. I understand what he means for I'll order brisket in preference to sirloin, pot-roast it till it's like chicken, or steam and press it and have good, soft, butter-like fat for cooking—at half the price of sirloin which, after eating once hot, is apt to be rather dreary.

Tuesday, 28 April, 1942.

The present rationing has been a farce. Those who have wanted to be greedy have got more than their share. . . . Much as I dislike coupons and chits, I think it's the only fair way to stop overlapping and grabbing. Eggs are another muddle, for people register with an egg and butter dealer, but get eggs with their grocery list, too! I was a bit surprised at my sister-in-law's outlook yesterday. Several times, she spoke as if to get more than she was entitled to was a *grand* game. I said, 'But Beat, if you take someone else's share, they will have to do without.' She said, 'Nonsense—there is plenty of food about. There must be, or else a place could not get it in such quantities. It's only a matter of organising properly.' I did not want to upset her, and start her nerves off and make her cross, so I did not press the point—much as I would have liked to.

Nella Last's War: A Mother's Diary 1939–45, edited by Richard Broad and Suzie Fleming, 1981

FOOD AS GIFT

❧ *Mr Crawley, the incumbent of Hogglestock, a poor, brick-making parish in an ill-favoured corner of Barsetshire, is learned, difficult, proud, and wretchedly ill-paid. Through his wife, who has been befriended by Lady Lufton of Framley Court, the kind-hearted patroness of a neighbouring parish, occasional offerings come into the household to make life easier for her and her surviving children. Mr Crawley, however, is stubbornly opposed to the idea of accepting any form of charity. Now Mrs Robarts, wife of Lady Lufton's protégé Mark Robarts, the vicar of Framley, and her sister-in-law Lucy have come to call on the Crawleys, secretly bearing gifts.*

Mrs Crawley . . . was sitting with one baby in her lap while she was rocking another who lay in a cradle at her feet. Mr Crawley, in the meanwhile, had risen from his seat with his finger between the leaves of an old grammar out of which he had been teaching the children. The whole Crawley family was thus before them when Mrs Robarts and Lucy entered the sitting-room. 'This is my sister-in-law, Lucy,' said Mrs Robarts. 'Pray don't move now, Mrs Crawley; or if you do, let me take baby.' And she put out her arms and took the infant into them, making him quite at home there; for she had work of this kind of her own, at home, which she by no means neglected, though the attendance of nurses was more plentiful with her than at Hogglestock. Mrs Crawley did get up, and told Lucy that she was glad to see her, and Mr Crawley came forward, grammar in hand, looking humble and meek. Could we have looked into the innermost spirit of him and his life's partner, we should have seen that mixed with the pride of his poverty there was some feeling of disgrace that he was poor, but that with her, regarding this matter, there was neither pride nor shame. The realities of life had become so stern to her that the outward aspects of them were as nothing. She would have liked a new gown because it would have been useful; but it would have been nothing to her if all the county knew that the one in which she went to church had been turned three times. It galled him, however, to think that he and his were so poorly dressed. 'I am afraid you can hardly find a chair, Miss Robarts,' said Mr Crawley.

* * * * *

And then Lucy began petting the little boy, and by degrees slipped a small bag of gingerbread-nuts out of her muff into his hands. She had not the patience necessary for waiting, as had her sister-in-law. The boy took the bag, peeped into it, and then looked up into her face.

'What is that, Bob?' said Mr Crawley.

'Gingerbread,' faltered Bobby, feeling that a sin had been committed, though, probably, feeling also that he himself could hardly as yet be accounted deeply guilty.

'Miss Robarts,' said the father, 'we are very much obliged to you; but our children are hardly used to such things.'

'I am a lady with a weak mind, Mr Crawley, and always carry things of this sort about with me when I go to visit children; so you must forgive me, and allow your little boy to accept them.'

'Oh, certainly. Bob, my child, give the bag to your mamma, and she will let you and Grace have them, one at a time.' And then the bag in a solemn manner was carried over to their mother, who, taking it from her son's hands, laid it high on a bookshelf.

'And not one now?' said Lucy Robarts, very piteously. 'Don't be so hard, Mr Crawley,—not upon them, but upon me. May I not learn whether they are good of their kind?'

'I am sure they are very good; but I think their mamma will prefer their being put by for the present.' This was very discouraging to Lucy. If one small bag of gingerbread-nuts created so great a difficulty, how was she to dispose of the pot of guava jelly and box of bon-bons, which were still in her muff; or how distribute the packet of oranges with which the pony carriage was laden? And there was jelly for the sick child, and chicken broth, which was, indeed, another jelly; and, to tell the truth openly, there was also a joint of fresh pork and a basket of eggs from the Framley parsonage farmyard, which Mrs Robarts was to introduce, should she find herself capable of doing so; but which would certainly be cast out with utter scorn by Mr Crawley, if tendered in his immediate presence. There had also been a suggestion as to adding two or three bottles of port; but the courage of the ladies had failed them on that head, and the wine was not now added to their difficulties. Lucy found it very difficult to keep up a conversation with Mr Crawley—the more so, as Mrs Robarts and Mrs Crawley presently withdrew into a bedroom, taking the two younger children with them. 'How unlucky,' thought Lucy, 'that she has not got my muff with her!' But the muff lay in her lap, ponderous with its rich enclosures.

Anthony Trollope, *Framley Parsonage*, 1861

❧ *Laurence Sterne (1713–68) was vicar of Sutton-in-the-Forest, North Yorkshire from 1738 until 1759. An incurable flirt, he drove his wife mad with his 'small, quiet' attentions to other women. Catherine Fourmantel, a Frenchwoman, was living with her mother in York, where she appeared in 1759 to sing at the Assembly Rooms.*

To Catherine Fourmantel, Thursday [*1759*].
My dear Kitty,

I have sent you a Pot of Sweetmeats, and a Pot of Honey, neither of them, half so sweet as yourself—but don't be vain upon this,—or presume to grow Sour, ûpon this Character of Sweetness I give You; for if you do I shall send You a pot of Pickles (by way of contrarys) to sweeten you up, & bring you to yourself again—whatever Changes happen to you, believe me that I am unalterably Yours.

The Letters of Laurence Sterne, edited by Lewis Perry Curtis, 1935

❧ *Brilliana, Lady Harley was the wife of Sir Robert Harley, Master of the Mint and a prominent Parliamentarian during the reign of Charles I. Her son (Sir) Edward (1624–1700) went up to Magdalen Hall, Oxford at the usual age for an undergraduate, 14, and survived the Civil War as a General of Horse for Herefordshire and Radnorshire. Lady Harley died in 1643 during the Royalist siege of her home, Brampton Bryan, which fell to the besiegers the following year.*

[*30 November 1638.*] Deare Ned, if you would have any thinge, send me word; or if I thought a coold pye, or such a thinge, would be of any plesure to you, I would send it to you. But your father says you care not for it, and Mrs Pirson tells me, when her sonne was at Oxford, and shee sent him such thinges, he prayed her that shee would not.

[*8 February 1638/39.*] I purpos, if it pleas God, to remember you with some of Bromton [i.e. Brampton] dyet, against Lent. I wisch, you may not eate too much fisch. I know you like it; but I thinke it is not so good for you.

[*15 February 1638/39.*] I have sent you by the carrier a box, derected to you, in which is a turky pie and 6 pyes, such as my lord, your grandfather, did love. I hope to remember you againe in lent. . . . I have sent your tutor a box of dryed plumes, the box is derected to you; tell him it is a Lenten token.

[*19 April 1638/39.*] I have sent you a pigon pye; and much good may it doo you when you eate it.

[*10 May 1638/39.*] I have made a pye to send you; it is a kide pye. I beleeve you have not that meate ordinaryly at Oxford; one halfe of the pye is seasned with one kind of seasening, and the other with another. I thinke to send it by this carrier.

[*5 July 1639.*] Your father has divers times sence you went asked for strawbery butter, and in memory of you this day I made Hacklet make some. I wisch you a disch of it.

[*1 November 1639.*] I have sent you by this carrier a loyne of veale backed, if the cooke have doun his part it is well.

[*20 February 1639/40.*] I have sent you a gammon of backen by this carrier, and a Lenten tocken of dried sweetmeats for your tutor . . . if I had bine well I had sent you a larger provition for Lent. . . . The dried appells are for you.

[*28 February 1639/40.*] I hope you will find out some way not to keep a strickt Lent, for I am confident it is not good for you. . . . I have sent you by this carrier a turkey pye, but I doubt that it is not a very good one, it is so littell.

25 April [*1639/40.*] I have sent you by Loocker some violet cakes [a seasonal delicacy, decorated with crystallized spring violets]. Deare Ned, be carefull of your self, especially be watchfull over your hart.

Letters of the Lady Brilliana Harley, wife of Sir Robert Harley of Brampton Bryan, Knight of the Bath, with introduction and notes by Thomas Taylor Lewis A. M., Camden Society, 1854

❧ *A. L. Rowse (b. 1903) spent a period doing historical research in Germany, as a Fellow of All Souls College, Oxford, between the two World Wars.*

One morning wasted [in Munich] made me very cross. My mother had sent me a food-parcel. This had been held up in the German bureaucratic manner in the *Postzollamt*, to pay excise on it. I was summoned to claim it, and with difficulty ran the building down; when I got there, it was huge and I had to traipse all over the place to find Room 1103—there duly was my parcel, upon which I had to pay. When I opened it, there was a package of Cornish buns, baked three weeks ago, hard as bricks. I was so furious, I threw them out of the window, and sent home a rocket—they didn't make that mistake again. I know as well as the next man that they had done it 'with the best intentions', etc.; what maddened me was one more reminder of the ignorance of my working-class people, and people have no business to be so ignorant.

A. L. Rowse, *A Cornishman Abroad*, 1976

BREAD

A THANKSGIVING

Lord, Thou hast given me a cell
  wherein to dwell;
And little house, whose humble Roof
  is weather-proof;
Under the sparres of which I lie
  Both soft and drie;
Where Thou my chamber for to ward
  Hast set a Guard
Of harmless thoughts, to watch and keep
  Me, while I sleep.
Low is my porch, as is my Fate,
  Both void of state;
And yet the threshold of my doore
Is worn by th'poore
  Who thither come, and freely get
Good words, or meat:
Like as my Parlour, so my Hall
  And Kitchin's small;
A little Butterie, and therein
  A little Byn,
Which keeps my little loafe of Bread
  Unchipt, unflead.

Robert Herrick, 'A Thanksgiving to God, for his House', (1647)

Unchipt: uncut; *unflead*: unflayed (i.e. not skinned or de-crusted); unflawed (i.e. uncracked); or perhaps 'untouched by flies', the best reason for keeping bread in a bin in warm weather.

❧ *Richard Ligon wrote his account of Barbados in the early 1650s, after his return from that island to England and while a prisoner in the Upper Bench Prison. Here, he lamented, he was 'deprived of both light and lonelinesse', which made it impossible for him to illustrate his book in full colour and minute graphic detail as he would have wished. The book was dedicated to Brian Duppa, Bishop of Salisbury, who had encouraged Ligon to set down his impressions of the island where he had so unluckily failed to recover his lost fortunes.*

Bread, which is accounted the staffe, or main supporter of mans life, has not here that full taste it has in *England*; but yet they account it nourishing and strengthening. It is made of the root of a small tree or shrub, which they call *cassavie*; the manner of his growth I will let alone, till I come to speak of Trees and Plants in generall.

His root only, which we are now to consider, (because our bread is made of it) is large and round, like the body of a small Still or retort; and as we gather it we grow sticks that grow neerest to it, of the same tree, which we put into the ground, and they grow. And as we gather, we plant. This root, before it come to be eaten, suffers a strange conversion; for, being an absolute poyson when 'tis gathered, by good ordering, comes to be wholesome and nourishing; and the manner of doing it, is this: They wash the outside of the root clean, and lean it against a Wheel, whose sole is about a foot broad, and covered with Latine, made rough like a large Grater. The Wheel to be turned about with a foot, as a Cutler turnes his Wheel. And as it grates the root, it falls down in a large Trough, which is the receiver appointed for that purpose. This root thus grated, is as rank poyson, as can be made by the art of an Apothecary, of the most venomous simples he can put together: but being put into a strong piece of double Canvas, or Sackcloth, and prest hard, that all the juice be squeezed out, and then opened upon a cloath, and dried in the Sun, 'tis ready to make bread. And thus 'tis done.

They have a piece of iron, which I guesse is cast round, the diameter of which is about twenty inches, a little hollowed in the middle, not unlike the mould that the Spectacle makers grinde their glasses on, but not so much concave as that; about halfe an inch thick at the brim or verge, but thicker towards the middle, with three feet like a pot, about six inches high, that fire may be underneath. To such a temper they heat this Pone (as they call it) to bake, but not to burn. When 'tis made thus hot, the *Indians*, whom we trust to make it, because they are best acquainted with it, cast the meal upon the Pone, the whole breadth of it, and put it down with their hands, and it will presently stick together: And when they think that side almost enough, with a thing like a Battledore, they turn the other; and so turn and re-turn it so often, till it be enough, which is presently done. So they lay this Cake upon a flat board, and make another, and so another, till they have made enough for the whole Family. This bread they made, when we came first there, as thick as a pancake; but after that, they grew to a higher degree of curiosity, and made it as thin as a wafer, and yet purely white and crispe, as a new made wafer. Salt they never use in it, which I wonder at; for the bread being tastelesse of it selfe, they should give it some little seasoning. There is no way it eats so well as in milk, and there it tasts like Almonds. They offer to make Pie-crust, but very few attain to the skill of that; for, as you work it up with your hand, or roll it out with a roller, it will always crackle and chop, so that it will not be raised to hold any liquor, neither with, nor without, butter or eggs.

But after many tryalls, and as often failings, at last, I learnt the secret of an *Indian* woman, who shew'd me the right way of it, and that was, by searsing it very fine (and it will fall out as fine, as the finest wheat-flower in *England*) if not finer. Yet, this is not all the secret, for this will not cure the cracking. But this is the main skill of the businesse: Set water on the fire in a skillet, and put to it as much of this fine flower, as will temper it to the thicknesse of starch or pap; and let it boyl a little, keeping it stirring with a slice; and mix this with the masse of flower you mean to make into pye-crust, which being very well mingled, and wrought together, you may add what cost you will of butter and eggs, and it will rise and stand neere as well as our past[e] in England.

But those that have not Cows, & cannot make butter upon the place, but must make use of such as is brought from *England* or *Holland*, were better leave it out, & be content to eat their pie-crust drie. Yet I make a main difference, between butter that is brought from either of those places, in respect of the times it is brought. For, if a ship set out from *England* in *November*, and that ship arrive at the Barbadoes at the middle, or neere the end of *December*, when the Sun is at the farthest distance, the butter may come thither in very good condition; and being set in cool places, may retain the taste for a while: But, if the Ship set out in Spring or Summer, that brings this butter, it is not then to be endured, it is so restie and loathsome. Nor can Cheese be brought from thence without spoyle, at that time of the year, except you put it in oyle. Neither are Candles to be brought, for the whole barrell will stick together in one lump, and stinck so profoundly, that neither Rats nor mice will come neer them, much lesse eat of them. For which reason, the Planters, who are much troubled with this annoyance . . . burn for the most part wax lights, which they make themselves, of wax they fetch from *Africa* . . . there being no Bees in the *Barbadoes*.

But I am too apt to flie out in extravagant digressions; for, the thing I went to speak of, was bread only, and the severall kinds of it; and having said as much of the bread of *Cassavie* as I know, I will give you one word of another kinde of bread they make, which is a mixt sort of bread, and is made of the flower of *Mayes* and *Cassavie* mixt together; for the *Maies* it selfe will make no bread, it is so extream heavy and lumpish: But these two being mixt, they make it into large Cakes, two inches thick; and that, in my opinion, tasts the likest to English bread of any.

But the Negres use the *Mayes* another way, which is, toasting the ears of it at the fire, and so eating it warm off the eare. And we have a way to feed our Christian servants with this *Maies*, which is, by pounding it in a large Morter, and boyling it in water, to the thicknesse of a mess of Frumentie; and so put in a Tray such a quantity, as will serve a messe of seven or eight people; give it them cold, and scarce afford them salt with it. This we call *Lob-lollie*. But the Negres, when they come to be fed with this, are much discontented, and crie out, *O! O! no more Lob-lob*.

Richard Ligon, *A True & Exact History of the Island of Barbados*, 1657

Cassavie: *Manihot utilissima*, manioc or cassava, a plant native to South America; *latine*: latten (tin-plate, or any metal made in thin sheets); *searsing*: sieving; *frumentie*: frumenty, 'a dish made with hulled wheat boiled in milk, and seasoned with cinnamon, sugar etc.' (OED). Made with maize flour and water, poured out into a tray and left to set, this dish must have closely resembled the Italian polenta (which, however, needs some form of seasoning, at the very least of salt).

❧ *Celia Fiennes (1662–1741) was the unmarried daughter of Colonel Nathaniel Fiennes, a leading Parliamentarian, and granddaughter of 'Old Subtlety', William Fiennes, the Puritan 8th Baron and 1st Viscount Saye and Sele of Broughton Castle, near Banbury. Between her early twenties and early forties she made several journeys through various parts of England, in the tradition of enquiry continued by her contemporary Daniel Defoe (whose* Tour through the Whole Island of Great Britain *appeared in 1724–7) and, a century or more after her, by John Byng (Lord Torrington) and William Cobbett. Her descriptive narrative, mainly written in 1703, has become a major source for English social history. This visit to the Lake District took place on her 'Great Journey' of 1698, from London to the North of England and back by way of Devon and Cornwall.*

Here [in the Lake District] it was I saw ye oat Clap Bread made. They mix their flour with water, so soft as to rowle it in their hands into a ball, and then they have a board made round and something hollow in the middle riseing by degrees all round to the Edge a little higher, but so little as one would take it to be only a board warp'd, this is to Cast out the Cake thinn and so they Clap it round and drive it to ye Edge in a Due proportion till drove as thinn as a paper and still they Clap it and drive it round, and then they have a plaite [plate] of jron same size with their Clap board, and so shove off the Cake on it and so set it on Coales and bake it; when Enough on one side they slide it off and put the other side; if their jron plaite is smooth and they take Care their Coales or Embers are not too hot but just to make it Looke yellow, it will bake and be as Crisp and pleasant to Eate as any thing you Can jmagine; but as we say of all sorts of bread there is a vast deal of difference in what is housewifely made and what is ill made, so that if its well mixed and Rowled up and but a little flour on the outside which will drye on and make it mealy is a very good sort of food. This is the sort of bread they use in all these Countrys, and in Scotland they breake into their milk or broth or Else sup that up and bite of their bread between while they spread butter on it and Eate it with their meate. They have no other Sort of bread unless at market towns and that is scarce to be had unless the market dayes, soe they make their Cake and Eate it presently for its not soe good if 2 or 3 dayes old. It made me reflect on the description made in Scripture of their Kneeding Cakes and bakeing them on the hearth whenever they had Company Come to their houses, and I Cannot but thinke it was after this maner they made their bread in ye old tymes especially those Eastern Countryes where their bread might be soone dry'd and spoil'd.

Through England On a Side Saddle in the time of William and Mary, being the Diary of Celia Fiennes, 1888

Clapboard: hence the building term for a board thinner at one edge than at the other (shiplap, weatherboarding) used for cladding outer walls, especially in North America.

OATS AND WHEAT

GLENSHEALS [Invernessshire] . . . We had, by the direction of the officers at Fort *Augustus*, taken bread for ourselves, and tobacco for those Highlanders who might show us any kindness. We were now at a place where we could obtain milk, but must have wanted bread if we had not brought it. The people of this valley did not appear to know any English, and our guides now became doubly necessary as interpreters. A woman, whose hut was distinguished by greater spaciousness and better architecture, brought out some pails of milk. The villagers gathered about us in considerable numbers, I believe without any evil intention, but with a very savage wildness of aspect and manner. When our meal was over, Mr *Boswell* sliced the bread, and divided it amongst them, as he supposed them never to have tasted a wheaten loaf before.

*　*　*　*　*

CORIATACHAN IN SKY . . . Their native bread is made of oats, or barley. Of oatmeal they spread very thin cakes, coarse and hard, to which unaccustomed palates are not easily reconciled. The barley cakes are thicker and softer; I begin to eat them without unwillingness; the blackness of their colour raises some dislike, but the taste is not disagreeable. In most houses there is wheat flower, with which we were sure to be treated, if we staid long enough to have it kneaded and baked. As neither yeast nor leaven are used among them, their bread of every kind is unfermented. They make only cakes, and never mould a loaf.

Samuel Johnson, *A Journey to the Western Islands of Scotland*, 1775

❧ The Expedition of Humphry Clinker, *Smollett's last and pleasantest novel, describes a journey round England and Scotland, narrated in a series of letters written by the chief protagonist, Colonel Bramble. On their travels, Bramble's party attract an eccentric Scotsman, Captain Obadiah Lismahago, whose argument with Bramble forms the subject of this letter.*

After some recollection, 'Well, captain (said I) you have argued stoutly for the importance of your own country: for my part, I have such a regard for our fellow-subjects of North-Britain, that I should be glad to see the day, when your peasants can afford to give all their oats to their cattle, hogs, and poultry, and indulge themselves with good wheaten loaves, instead of such poor, unpalatable and inflammatory diet.' Here again I brought myself into a premunire with the disputatious Caledonian. He said, he hoped he should never see the common people lifted out of that sphere for which they were intended by nature and the course of things; that they might have some reason to complain of their bread, if it were mixed, like that of Norway, with saw-dust and fish-bones; but that oatmeal was, he apprehended, as nourishing and salutary as wheat-flour, and the Scots in general thought it at least as savoury. He affirmed, that a mouse, which, in the article of self-preservation, might be supposed to act from infallible instinct, would always prefer oats to wheat, as appeared from experience; for, in a place where there was a parcel of each, that animal had never begun to feed on the latter till all the oats were consumed: for their nutritive quality, he appealed to the hale, robust constitutions of the people who lived chiefly upon oatmeal; and instead of being inflammatory, he asserted, that it was a cooling sub-acid, balsamic and mucilaginous; insomuch, that in all inflammatory distempers, recourse was had to water-gruel, and flummery made of oatmeal.

Tobias Smollett, *The Expedition of Humphry Clinker*, 1771

'Thee an' me, lass, is Robsons—oat-cake folk, while they's pie-crust.'

Elizabeth Gaskell, *Sylvia's Lovers*, 1863–4

Oats. A grain, which in England is generally given to horses, but in Scotland supports the people.

Samuel Johnson, *Dictionary of the English Language*, 1755

I saw here, for the first time [at Lichfield, Johnson's birthplace], *oat ale*; and oat cakes, not hard as in Scotland, but soft like a Yorkshire cake, were served at breakfast. It was pleasant to me to find, that '*Oats*,' the '*food of horses*,' were so much used as the *food of the people* in Dr Johnson's own town. He expatiated in praise of Lichfield and its inhabitants, who, he said, were 'the most sober, decent people in England, the genteelest in proportion to their wealth, and spoke the purest English'.

Boswell, *The Life of Samuel Johnson*

Johnson and Boswell visited Lichfield together in 1776. The soft, leavened oatcakes found there by Boswell, to his evident delight, are still produced slightly farther north, in the Potteries area of North Staffordshire and in parts of Derbyshire, where they are eaten as a traditional accompaniment to a cooked breakfast.

SHELLEY

Bread became his chief sustenance when his regimen attained to that austerity which afterwards distinguished it. He could have lived on bread alone without repining. When he was walking in London with an acquaintance, he would suddenly run into a baker's shop, purchase a supply, and breaking a loaf, he would offer half of it to his companion.

'Do you know', he said to me one day, with much surprise, 'that such an one does not like bread? Did you ever know a person who disliked bread?' and he told me that a friend had repulsed such an offer.

I explained to him that the individual in question probably had no objection to bread in a moderate quantity, at a proper time and with the usual adjuncts, and was only unwilling to devour two or three pounds of dry bread in the streets, and at an early hour.

Shelley had no such scruple; his pockets were generally well-stored with bread. A circle upon the carpet, clearly defined by an ample verge of crumbs, often marked the place where he had long sat at his studies, his face nearly in contact with his book, greedily devouring bread at intervals amidst his profound abstractions. For the most part he took no condiment; sometimes, however, he ate with his bread the common raisins which are used in making puddings, and these he would buy at little mean shops.

Hogg, *The Life of Percy Bysshe Shelley*

❧ *Henry David Thoreau's celebrated period of (near) self-sufficiency, in the woods surrounding Walden Pond, near Concord, Massachusetts, took place in 1845–7 when he was in his late twenties. Eliminating trivia and material detail from his life, Thoreau devoted himself to contemplating nature and to depending as closely as possible on the products of the country immediately around him.*

Bread I at first made of pure Indian meal and salt, genuine hoe-cakes, which I baked before my fire out of doors on a shingle or the end of a stick of timber sawed off in building my house; but it was wont to get smoked and to have a piny flavour. I tried flour also; but have at last found a mixture of rye and Indian meal most convenient and agreeable. In cold weather it was no little amusement to bake several small loaves of this in succession, tending and turning them as carefully as an Egyptian his hatching eggs. They were a real cereal fruit which I ripened, and they had to my senses a fragrance like that of other noble fruits, which I kept in as long as possible by wrapping them in cloths. I made a study of the ancient and indispensable art of bread-making, consulting such authorities as offered, going back to the primitive days and first invention of the unleavened kind, when from the wildness of nuts and meats men first reached the refinement of this diet, and travelling gradually down in my studies through that accidental souring of the dough which, it is supposed, taught the leavening process, and through the various fermentations thereafter, till I came to 'good, sweet, wholesome bread', the staff of life. Leaven, which some deem the soul of bread, the *spiritus* which fills its cellular tissue, which is religiously preserved like the vestal fire,—some precious bottleful, I suppose, first brought over in the *Mayflower*, did the business for America, and its influence is still rising, swelling, spreading in cerealian billows over the land,—this seed I regularly and faithfully procured from the village, till at length one morning I forgot the rules and scalded my yeast; by which accident I discovered that even this was not indispensable,—for my discoveries were not by the synthetic but analytic process,—and I have gladly omitted it since, though most housewives earnestly assure me that safe and wholesome bread without yeast might not be, and elderly people prophesied a speedy decay of the vital forces. Yet I find it not to be an essential ingredient, and after going without it for a year am still in the land of the living; and I am glad to escape the trivialness of carrying a bottleful in my pocket, which would sometimes pop and discharge its contents to my discomfiture.

* * * * *

Every New Englander might easily raise all his own bread-stuffs in this land of rye and Indian corn, and not depend on distant and fluctuating markets for them. Yet so far are we from simplicity and independence that, in Concord, fresh and sweet meal is rarely sold in the shops, and hominy and corn in a still coarser form are hardly used by any. For the most part the farmer gives his cattle and hogs the grain of his own producing, and buys flour, which is at least no more than wholesome, at a greater cost, at the store. I saw that I could easily raise my bushel or two of rye and Indian corn, for the former will grow on the poorest land, and the latter does not require the best, and grind them in a hand-mill, and so do without rice and pork.

Henry David Thoreau, *Walden, or Life in the Woods*, 1854

❧ *Sylvester Graham, originator of graham flour and the graham cracker, was a highly influential advocate of healthy eating in the United States, and an early promoter of unadulterated, vitamin-rich, wholemeal bread.*

Some eight or nine years since, I spent several months in the delightful village of Belvidere, on the banks of the Delaware, in Pennsylvania. While there, I enjoyed for a number of weeks the kind hospitality of S— S—, Esq., a lawyer, and a gentleman of great moral excellence. Mrs S. was born and brought up, I believe, in Philadelphia. . . . She usually kept three female domestics, who, by her kind maternal deportment towards them, were warmly attached to her. . . . Yet . . . Mrs S. invariably made the family bread with her own hands. Regularly as the baking day came, she went into the kitchen and took her stand beside the bread trough, and mixed and kneaded the dough, and put it in its proper place for rising, and, in due time, moulded it into the loaf and baked it.

Do you always make your bread, madam? I inquired one day, as she returned from the performance of that task. 'Invariably,' she replied: 'that is a duty I trust no other person to do for me.'

But cannot your domestics make good bread? I asked. 'I have excellent domestics,' answered Mrs S., 'and they can, perhaps, make as good bread as I can; for they have been with me several years, and I have taken pains to learn them how to do my work; and they are exceedingly faithful and affectionate, and are always willing to do all they can to please me; but they cannot feel for my husband and children as I do, and therefore they cannot feel that interest which I do, in always having such bread as my husband and children will love and enjoy. Besides, if it were certain their care and vigilance and success in bread-making would be always equal to mine, yet it is wholly uncertain how long they will remain with me. Various circumstances may take place, which may cause them to leave me, and bring me into dependence upon those who know not how to make good bread; and therefore I choose to keep my own hand in. But, apart from all other considerations, there is a pleasure resulting from the performance of this duty, which richly rewards me for all the labor of it. When my bread is made and brought upon the table, and I see my husband and children eat and enjoy it, and hear them speak of its excellence, it affords me much satisfaction, and I am glad to know that I have contributed so much to their health and happiness; for, while my bread is so good that they prefer it to anything else upon the table, there is little danger of their indulging, to any injurious extent, in those articles of food which are less favorable to their health.'

I need not say that this lady invariably had excellent bread upon her table. But instances of this kind are, I regret to say, extremely rare, even in christian communities.

Sylvester Graham, *A Treatise on Bread, and Bread-Making*, 1837

Lady (lei.di), s[*u*]*b*[*stantive*]. [O[ld] E[nglish] *hláefdíge* w[ea]k fem[inine]; f[rom] *hláf* LOAF + root *dig-* to knead . . .]

Shorter Oxford English Dictionary

THE BENEFACTIONS OF MISS O'FLANNIGAN

To begin with Bread, which nature did not intend to play humble squire to a baron of beef or to be buried in pompous napkins as stiff as a bishop's mitre; I am not speaking of rolls, nor yet of those pitiful squares of spongy dough which figure at the left-hand side of dinner forks as a matter of custom; I am speaking of Bread—the staff of life, the nourishment of all mankind.

Miss O'Flannigan [a food reform worker] often makes her dinner—and, mark you, she is a hard worker and the picture of health—with just two slices of this Bread and a glass of milk. But, as I say, this is real Bread.

* * * * *

Its constituents are these:

Half a pound of wholemeal flour.
Half a pound of white flour.
One teaspoonful of salt.

Ditto sugar.
Ditto cream of tartar.
Ditto carbonate of soda.
Half a pint of milk.

And the way to make it:

Mix all together; turn on a board sprinkled with flour; knead lightly until there is a smooth side underneath; place, smooth side up, on a greased baking-dish, and bake for about three-quarters of an hour.

A hollow sound responding to a tap of the finger on the bottom of the loaf will announce to you that oven heat has done its work.

* * * * *

This bread, with the best butter on top of it, is a meal in itself, and one slice of it goes far to support body and refresh mind. Two slices of it are really enough for a farm labourer. It is not such bread as the bakers of England take round to the houses of the poor, which grows hard and sour when it is stale, which only blows-out and never pleases, and which drives more men to the public-house than any other cause under heaven. No; it is not such a masquerading bread as that, not such a travesty of nature's staff of life, not such a spongy, cringing, doughy and alumy libel on God's good gift to men as all that. It is bread which has a rich taste, which is like a biscuit in the crust and better than a cake in the crumb; it is bread which will give your children strong bones, vigorous teeth, and sound digestions. It is bread you look forward to.

And this is not a digression.

Bread *must* play an important part in the simple life. If you want to cut down the butcher's bill and the fishmonger's bill, you must provide a bread which is something more than a thumbnail appanage to animal flesh. You must come to think of it as the *pièce de résistance*, and to regard it not only as indubitable food, but as the best food.

Take care of the bread, and the joints will look after themselves.

Life Without Servants, or, The Re-Discovery of Domestic Happiness, by A Survivor, 1916

Almost everyone agrees about the excellence of Spanish bread. The loaf is very close textured, but it has a taste and sweetness like no other bread in the world. This, I imagine, is because the grain is entirely ripe before being harvested. Besides loaves we had *roscos*, or rolls made in the form of rings, and *tortas*, which are flat cakes made with wheat flour, sugar and oil. The poor, and sometimes the rich too, ate maize bread, and in the mountain farms they ate black bread made of rye. For shepherds it had the advantage of not going stale.

There are some curious customs about bread which were strictly observed in my village, and indeed through the whole of Andalusia. Before cutting a new loaf it was proper to make the sign of the cross over it with a knife. If a loaf or *rosca* fell to the ground, the person who picked it up would kiss it and say, 'Es pan de Dios' ('It's God's bread'). Children were never allowed to strike it or treat it roughly or crumble it on the table, and it was considered shocking to offer even stale crusts to a dog. When once I jabbed my knife into a loaf I was reproved and told that I was 'stabbing the face of Christ'. Bread was, in fact, sacred, and this, according to Dr Americo Castro, is not, as one would suppose, a derivation from the cult of the Sacrament but a notion borrowed from the Arabs. Butter, on the other hand, was unknown. *Manteca* meant either lard or rancid dripping worked up with garlic and eaten by workmen in the coast towns with bread. This is explained by the fact that we had no milch cows. Even in the north of Spain there are said to have been none till the Flemish influence at the time of Charles V brought them in, and it is only in recent years that they have been kept in Andalusia. In the nineteenth century the wealthy families of Malaga used to import barrels of salted butter from Hamburg, and on that account they became known as *la gente de la manteca*, or 'the butter folk'. It was a luxury that set a stamp on one's social position, like having a car today.

Brenan, *South From Granada*

BUTTER

DIRECTIONS FOR SUCH AS DESIRE TO BE DAIRY-MAIDS

Those who would endeavour to gain the Esteem and Reputation of good Dairy-Maids, must be careful that all their Vessels be scalded well, and kept very clean, that they Milk their Cattle in due time, for the Kine by Custom will expect it though you neglect, which will tend much to their detriment.

The hours and times most approved, and commonly used for

Milking are in the Spring and Summer time, between five and six in the Morning, and between six and seven in the Evening: And in the Winter between seven and eight in the Morning, and four and five in the Evening.

In the next place you must be careful that you do not waste your Cream by giving it away to liquorish Persons.

You must keep certain days for your Churning, and be sure to make up your Butter neatly and cleanly, washing it well from the Butter-Milk and then Salt it well.

You must be careful to make your Cheeses good and tender by well ordering of them and see that your Hogs have the Whey, and that it be not given away to Gossiping and idle People, who live meerly upon what they can get from Servants.

That you provide your winter Butter and Cheese in Summer, as in May: And when your Rowings come in, be sparing of your fire and do not Lavish away your Milk, Butter, or Cheese.

If you have any Fowls to fat, look to them that it may be for your Credit and not your shame, when they are brought to Table.

When you milk the Cattle, stroke them well, and in the Summer time save these strokings by themselves, to put into your Morning Milk Cheese.

I look upon it to be altogether needless, for to give you any Directions for the making of Butter or Cheese, since there are very few, (especially in the Country) that can be ignorant thereof: I shall only say, that the best time to put up Butter of Winter, is in the Month of *May*, for then the Air is most temperate, and the Butter will take Salt best. However it may be done at any time between May and September.

Hannah Wolley, *The Compleat Servantmaid; or, the Young Maiden's Tutor*, 1685

Rowings: (probably) roughings, i.e. aftermath or second crop of hay; *stroke*: to draw the last milk from the cow by squeezing the teats.

❧ *Thomas Turner (1729–93) was a mercer of East Hoathly, Sussex. His very detailed, spiritually self-probing diary, much concerned with eating, drinking, and the after-effects caused by over-indulgence, covers the period of his not entirely happy first marriage and his widowerhood, ending with his second marriage in 1765.*

Sun. 17. Oct. [1756].

About 9 o'clock my wife, self and nephew set out upon a horse borrowed of Fran Smith to see Mr Hill of Little Horsted where we arrived about 10.30 and found ourselves disappointed of going to church as we had proposed, my uncle being already gone to church. We dined at my uncle's in company with my mother and brother (who came to Horsted Church and so came home with my uncle) on a leg of very ordinary ewe mutton half boiled, very good turnips, but spoiled by almost swimming in butter, a fine large pig roasted, and the rind as tough as any cowhide (and it seemed as if it had been basted with a mixture of flour, butter and ashes), and sauce which looked like what is vomited up by sucking children, a butter pond pudding, and that justly called, for there was almost but enough in it to have drowned the pig, had it been alive.

The Diary of Thomas Turner, 1754–1765, edited by David Vaisey, 1984

Pond pudding: a Sussex sweet dish, consisting of a suet pudding boiled with a lemon, butter and sugar inside it. The 'pond' of sugary, buttery, lemon-flavoured sauce pours out of the pudding when it is first cut. (See Jane Grigson, *English Food*, 1974.)

[*John Pintard to his daughter Eliza Davidson, New York, 21 September 1826.*]

I have just seen your tub of butter nicely packed in a half barrel of salt. It will be sent aboard the Lavinia this morning, I hope in time to go in the run. Stickler says that it comes from one of the best dairies in Orange County & equal in quantity to what he sent us this morning which was a nosegay. We have 2 small covered tubs holding 6 lbs each, one of which is received every Thursday morning & the empty one returned. The butter comes from Mr Ellison's dairy near Newburgh & is superior in quality. Thus the trouble of tasting & rejecting in the market is saved & it comes cheaper by 3d a lb. It astonishes one to see the immense quantity of butter that comes weekly to this city from Orange, Dutchess & Westchester Counties, besides all Long Island. Butter is the great staple article for breakfast & tea among all classes. The idea of restraining children from a liberal use of good fresh butter is exploded, & they almost live upon bread & butter in this city.

Letters from John Pintard to his Daughter

❧ *Harriet Beecher Stowe triumphantly toured the British Isles and visited Germany and Switzerland in 1853, after the overwhelming first success of her anti-slavery novel,* Uncle Tom's Cabin. *Ten years later, at home in Hartford, Connecticut in the third year of the Civil War, she began to write 'House and Home Papers' for the* Atlantic Monthly, *to support her newly retired husband and unmarried daughters, and to help distract herself and her readers from the harrowing events of the war.*

Next to Bread comes *Butter*—on which we have to say, that when we remember what butter is in civilized Europe, and compare it with what it is in America, we wonder at the forebearance and lenity of travellers in their strictures on our national commissariat.

Butter, in England, France and Italy, is simply solidified cream, with all the sweetness of the cream in its taste, freshly churned each day, and unadulterated by salt. At the present moment, when salt is five cents a pound and butter fifty, we Americans are paying, I should judge from the taste, for about one pound of salt to every ten of butter, and those of us who have eaten the butter of England and France do so with rueful recollections.

* * * * *

America must, I think, have the credit of manufacturing and putting into market more bad butter than all that is made in all the rest of the world together. The varieties of bad tastes and smells which prevail in it are quite a study. This has a cheesy taste, that a mouldy; this is flavoured with cabbage, and that again with turnip, and another has the strong, sharp savour of animal fat.

* * * * *

A matter for despair as regards bad butter is that at the tables where it is used it stands sentinel at the door to bar your way to every other kind of food. You turn from your dreadful half-slice of bread, which fills your mouth with bitterness, to your beef-steak, which proves virulent with the same poison; you think to take refuge in vegetable diet, and find the butter in the string-beans, and polluting the innocence of early peas—it is in the corn, in the succotash, in the squash—the beets swim in it, the onions have it poured over them. Hungry and miserable, you think to solace yourself at the dessert—but the pastry is cursed, the cake is acrid with the same plague. You are ready to howl with despair, and your misery is great upon you—especially if this is a table where you have taken board for three months with your delicate wife and four small children. Your case is dreadful; and it is hopeless, because long usage and habit have rendered your host perfectly incapable of discovering what is the matter. 'Don't you like the butter, Sir? I assure you I paid an extra price for it, and it's the very best in the market. I looked over as many as a hundred tubs, and picked out this one.'

Christopher Crowfield (Harriet Beecher Stowe), *House and Home Papers*, 1865

Norman Douglas, travelling in Italy during the First World War, arrived at Levanto in Tuscany, where he was allowed to stay for a week in a hotel.

No butter for breakfast.

The landlord, on being summoned, avowed that to serve crude butter on his premises involved a flagrant breach of war-time regulations. The condiment could not be used save for kitchen purposes, and then only on certain days of the week; he was liable to heavy penalties if it became known that one of his guests . . . However, since he assumed me to be a prudent person, he would undertake to supply a due allowance to-morrow and thenceforward, though never in the public dining-room; never, never in the dining-room!

That is the charm of Italy, I said to myself. These folks are reasonable and gifted with imagination. They make laws to shadow forth an ideal state of things and to display their good intentions towards the community at large; laws which have no sting for the exceptional type of man who can evade them—the sage, the millionaire, and the friend of the family. Never in the dining-room. Why, of course not. Catch me breakfasting in any dining-room.

Was it possible? There, at luncheon in the dining-room, while devouring those miserable macaroni made with war-time flour, I beheld an over-tall young Florentine lieutenant shamelessly engulfing huge slices of what looked uncommonly like genuine butter, a miniature mountain of which stood on a platter before him, and overtopped all the other viands. I could hardly believe my eyes. How about those regulations? Pointing to this golden hillock, I inquired softly:

'From the cow?'

'From the cow.'

He enjoyed a special dispensation, he declared—he need not bribe. Returned from Albania with shattered health, he had been sent hither to recuperate. He required not only butter, but meat on meatless days, as well as a great deal of rest; he was badly run down. And eggs, raw eggs, drinking eggs; ten a day, he vows, is his minimum. Enviable convalescent!

Douglas, *Alone*

MEAT

❧ *Petruchio and Katharina, the temperamental protagonists of* The Taming of the Shrew, *are newly married. They arrive at Petruchio's country house, where the servants have prepared supper.*

PETRUCHIO. Come, Kate, sit down; I know you have a stomach.
Will you give thanks, sweet Kate; or else shall I?
What's this? mutton?
FIRST SERVANT. Ay.
PETRUCHIO. Who brought it?
PETER. I.
PETRUCHIO. 'Tis burnt; and so is all the meat.
What dogs are these! Where is the rascal cook?
How durst you, villains, bring it from the dresser,
And serve it thus to me that love it not?
There, take it to you, trenches, cups, and all.
[*Throws the meat, &c. about the stage*
You heedless joltheads and unmannered slaves!
What, do you grumble? I'll be with you straight.
KATHARINA. I pray you, husband, be not so disquiet:
The meat was well, if you were so contented.
PETRUCHIO. I tell thee, Kate, 'twas burnt and dried away;
And I expressly am forbid to touch it,
For it engenders choler, planteth anger;
And better 'twere that both of us did fast,
Since, of ourselves, ourselves are choleric,

Than feed it with such over-roasted flesh.
Be patient; tomorrow 't shall be mended,
And, for this night, we'll fast for company:
Come, I will bring thee to thy bridal chamber.

* * * * *

Enter Katharina and Grumio

GRUMIO. No, no, forsooth; I dare not for my life.
KATHARINA. The more my wrong, the more his spite appears:
What, did he marry me to famish me?
Beggars, that come unto my father's door,
Upon entreaty have a present alms;
If not, elsewhere they meet with charity:
But I, who never knew how to entreat,
Nor never needed that I should entreat,
Am starved for meat, giddy for lack of sleep;
With oaths kept waking, and with brawling fed:
And that which spites me more than all these wants,
He does it under name of perfect love;
As who should say, if I should sleep or eat,
'Twere deadly sickness, or else present death.
I prithee go and get me some repast;
I care not what, so it be wholesome food.
GRUMIO. What say you to a neat's foot?
KATHARINA. 'Tis passing good: I prithee let me have it.
GRUMIO. I fear it is too choleric a meat.
How say you to a fat tripe finely broil'd?
KATHARINA. I like it well: good Grumio, fetch it me.
GRUMIO. I cannot tell; I fear 'tis choleric.
What say you to a piece of beef and mustard?
KATHARINA. A dish that I do love to feed upon
GRUMIO. Ay, but the mustard is too hot a little.
KATHARINA. Why then, the beef, and let the mustard rest.
GRUMIO. Nay then, I will not: you shall have the mustard
Or else you get no beef of Grumio.
KATHARINA. Then both, or one, or anything thou wilt.
GRUMIO. Why then, the mustard without the beef.
KATHARINA. Go, get thee gone, thou false deluding slave,
[*Beats him*
That feed'st me with the very name of meat:

Sorrow on thee and all the pack of you
That triumph thus upon my misery!
Go, get thee gone, I say.

William Shakespeare, *The Taming of the Shrew*, IV. i, iii

Diet . . . consists in meat and drink, and causes melancholy, as it offends in substance, that is, quantity, quality, or the like. . . . I will briefly touch what kind of meats engender this humour, through their several species, and which are to be avoided. How they alter and change the matter, spirits first, and after humours, by which we are preserved, and the constitution of our body, Fernelius and the others will shew you. I hasten to the thing itself: and first of such a diet as offends in substance.

Beef, a strong and hearty meat (cold in the first degree, dry in the second, saith Galen) is condemned by him, and all succeeding authors, to breed melancholy blood: good for such as are sound, and of a strong constitution, for labouring men, if ordered aright, corned, young, of an ox (for all gelded meats in every species are held best) or if old, such as have been tired out with labour, are preferred. Aubanus & Sabellicus commend Portugal beef to be the most savoury, best and easiest of digestion; we commend ours: but all is rejected and unfit for such as lead a resty life, any ways inclined to Melancholy, or dry of complexion; such, Galen thinks, are easily seized with melancholy diseases.

Pork of all meats is most nutritive in his own nature, but altogether unfit for such as live at ease, are any ways unsound of body or mind: too moist, full of humours, and therefore saith Savanarola, naught for queasy stomacks, in so much, that frequent use of it may breed a quartan ague.

Savanarola discommends goat's flesh, and so doth Bruerinus, calling it a filthy beast, and rammish; and therefore supposeth it will breed rank and filthy substance: yet kid, such as are young and tender, Isaac accepts, Bruerinus, and Galen.

Hart, and red deer, hath an evil name, it yields gross nutriment; a strong and great grained meat, next unto a horse. Which although some countries eat as Tartars, and they of China, yet Galen condemns. Young foals are commonly eaten in Spain as red deer, and to furnish their navies, about Malaga especially, often used; but such meats ask long baking, or seething, to qualify them, and yet all will not serve.

All venison is melancholy, and begets bad blood; a pleasant meat: in great esteem with us, (for we have more Parks in England than there are in all Europe besides), in our solemn feasts. 'Tis somewhat better hunted than otherwise, and well prepared by cookery; but generally bad, and seldom to be used.

Hare, a black meat, melancholy, and hard of digestion; it breeds *incubus*, often eaten, and causeth fearful dreams; so doth all venison, and is condemned by a jury of physicians. Mizaldus and some others say that hare is a merry meat, and that it will make one fair, as Martial's epigram testifies to Gellia, but this is by the way, because of the good sport it makes, merry company, and good discourse, that is commonly at the eating of it, and not otherwise to be understood.

Conies are of the nature of hares. Magninus compares them to beef, pig, and goat, yet young rabbits by all men are approved to be good.

Generally, all such meats as are hard of digestion breed melancholy. Aretaeus reckons up heads and feet, bowels, brains, entrails, marrow, fat, blood, skins, and those inward parts, as heart, lungs, liver, spleen, &c. They are rejected by Isaac, Magninus, Bruerinus, Savanarola.

Robert Burton, *The Anatomy of Melancholy*, 1621

DIRECTIONS FOR CARVING

I shall in the first place acquaint you with those proper Terms that are used by the curious in the Art of Carving.

In cutting up small birds it is proper to say thigh them, as thigh that Woodcock, thigh that Pigeon: but as to others say, mince that Plover, wing that Quail, and wing that Partridge, allay that Pheasant, untack that Curlew, unjoint that Bittern, disfigure that Peacock, display that Crane, dismember that Heron, unbrace that Mallard, frust that Chicken, spoil that Hen, sawce that Capon, lift that Swan, reer that Goose, tire that Egg: As to the Flesh of Beasts, unlace that Coney, break that Deer, leach that Brawn: for Fish, chine that Salmon, string that Lamprey, splat that Pike, sawce that Plaice, and sawce that Tench, splay that Bream; side that Haddock, tush that

Barbel, culpon that Trout, transom that Eel, tranch that Sturgeon, tame that Crab, barb that Lobster, &c.

Wolley, *The Compleat Servantmaid*

❧ *At Gryll Grange, an old-fashioned country house, several guests are at dinner with Mr Gryll and his nieces. An old friend of Mr Gryll, Mr MacBorrowdale, exclaims delightedly when a large sirloin of beef appears in front of his host.*

MR MACBORROWDALE. You are a man of taste, Mr Gryll. That is a handsomer ornament of a dinner-table than clusters of nosegays, and all sorts of uneatable decorations. I detest and abominate the idea of a Siberian dinner, where you just look on fiddle-faddles, while your dinner is behind a screen, and you are served with rations like a pauper.

THE REVEREND DOCTOR OPIMIAN. I quite agree with Mr MacBorrowdale. I like to see my dinner. And herein I rejoice to have Addison at my side; for I remember a paper, in which he objects to having roast beef placed on a sideboard. Even in his day it had been displaced to make way for some incomprehensible French dishes, in which he could find nothing to eat. I do not know what he would have said to its being placed altogether out of sight. Still there is something to be said on the other side. There is hardly one gentleman in twenty who knows how to carve; and as to ladies, though they did know once on a time, they do not now. What can be more pitiful than the right-hand man of the lady of the house, awkward enough in himself, with the dish twisted round to him in the most awkward possible position, digging in unutterable mortification for a joint which he cannot find, and wishing the unanatomisable *volaille* behind a Russian screen with the footmen?

MR MACBORROWDALE. I still like to see the *volaille*. It might be put on table with its joints divided.

MR GRYLL. As that turkey-poult is, Mr MacBorrowdale; which gives my niece no trouble; but the precaution is not necessary with such a right-hand man as Lord Curryfin, who carves to perfection.

MR MACBORROWDALE. Your arrangements are perfect. At the last of these Siberian dinners at which I had the misfortune to be present, I had offered me, for two of my rations, the tail of a mullet and the drum-stick of a fowl. Men who carve behind screens ought to pass a competitive examination before a jury of gastronomers. Men who carve at table are drilled by degrees into something like tolerable operators by the mere shame of the public process.

Thomas Love Peacock, *Gryll Grange*, 1860

Siberian dinner: an allusion to the newly introduced fashion for *service à la Russe*. Instead of a few large courses, each consisting of many different dishes which were carved or divided at the table, grand dinners now consisted of a succession of small courses, the food for each of which was usually brought to the table by servants and carried round for each guest to help himself. Hence the proliferation of epergnes and other decorations, replacing the dishes which had previously been symmetrically laid out along the centre of the dinner-table; *Addison*: a quotation from *Tatler* No. 148. 'I was now in great hunger and confusion, when I thought I smelled the agreeable savour of roast beef; but could not tell from which dish it arose, though I did not question but it lay disguised in one of them. Upon turning my head I saw a noble sirloin on the side-table, smoking in the most delicious manner. I had recourse to it more than once, and could not see without some indignation that substantial English dish banished in so ignominious a manner, to make way for French kickshaws.' Joseph Addison (1672–1719) contributed to Richard Steele's *Tatler* in 1709–11, before the two collaborated to produce the *Spectator*; *volaille*: fowl.

CRACKLING

Mankind, says a Chinese manuscript . . . for the first seventy thousand ages ate their meat raw, clawing or biting it from the living animal, just as they do in Abyssinia to this day. This period is not obscurely hinted at by their great Confucius in the second chapter of his Mundane Mutations, where he designates a kind of Golden Age by the term Cho-Fang, literally the Cook's holiday. The manuscript goes on to say that the art of roasting, or rather broiling (which I take to be the elder brother) was accidentally discovered in the manner following. The swine-herd, Ho-ti, having gone out into the woods one morning, as his manner was, to collect mast for his hogs, left his cottage in the care of his eldest son Bo-bo, a great lubberly boy, who being fond of playing with fire, as younkers of his age commonly are, let some sparks escape into a bundle of straw, which kindling quickly, spread the conflagration over every part of their poor mansion, till it was reduced to ashes. Together with the cottage (a sorry antediluvian make-shift of a building, you may think it), what was of much more importance, a fine litter of new-farrowed pigs, no less than nine in number, perished. China pigs have been esteemed a luxury all over the East from the remotest periods that we read of. Bo-bo was in utmost consternation, as you may think, not so much for the sake of the tenement, which his father and he could easily build up again with a few dry branches, and the labour of an hour or two, at any time, as for the loss of the pigs. While he was thinking what he should say to his father, and wringing his hands over the smoking remnants of one of those untimely sufferers, an odour assailed his nostrils, unlike any scent which he had before experienced. What could it proceed from?—not from the burnt cottage—he had smelt that smell before—indeed this was by no means the first accident of the kind which had occurred through the negligence of this unlucky young fire-brand. Much less did it resemble that of any known herb, weed, or flower. A premonitory moistening at the same time overflowed his nether lip. He knew not what to think. He next stepped down to feel the pig, if there were any signs of life in it. He burnt his fingers, and to cool them he applied them in his booby fashion to his mouth. Some of the crums of the scorched skin had come away in his fingers, and for the first time in his life (in the world's life indeed, for no man before him had known it) he tasted—*crackling!* Again he felt and fumbled at the pig. It did not burn him so much now, still he licked his fingers from a sort of habit. The truth at length broke into his slow understanding, that it was the pig that smelt so, and the pig that tasted so delicious; and, surrendering himself up to the newborn pleasure, he fell to tearing up whole handfuls of the scorched skin with the flesh next to it, and was cramming it down his throat in his beastly fashion, when his sire entered amid the smoking rafters, armed with retributory cudgel, and finding how affairs stood, began to rain blows upon the young rogue's shoulders, as thick as hailstones, which Bo-bo heeded not any more than if they had been flies. The tickling pleasure, which he experienced in his lower regions, had rendered him quite callous to any inconveniences he might feel in those remote quarters. His father might lay on, but he could not beat him from his pig, till he had fairly made an end of it, when, becoming a little more sensible of his situation, something like the following dialogue ensued.

'You graceless whelp, what have you got there devouring? Is it not enough that you have burnt me down three houses with your dog's tricks, and be hanged to you, but you must be eating fire, and I know not what—what have you got there, I say?'

'O, father, the pig, the pig, do come and taste how nicely the burnt pig eats.'

* * * * *

There is no flavour comparable, I will contend, to that of the crisp, tawny, well-watched, not over-roasted, *crackling*, as it is well called—the very teeth are invited to their share of the pleasure at this banquet in overcoming the coy, brittle resistance—with the adhesive oleaginous—O call it not fat—but an indefinable sweetness growing up to it—the tender blossoming of fat—fat cropped in the bud—taken in the shoot—in the first innocence—the cream and quintessence of the child-pig's yet pure food—the lean, no lean, but a kind of animal manna—or rather, fat and lean, (if it must be so) so blended and running into each other, that both together make one ambrosian result, or common substance.

* * * * *

Pig—let me speak his praise—is no less provocative of the appetite, than he is satisfactory to the criticalness of the censorious palate. The strong man may batten on him, and the weakling refuseth not his mild juices.

* * * * *

His sauce should be considered. Decidedly, a few bread crumbs, done up with his liver and brains, and a dash of mild sage. But, banish, dear Mrs Cook, I beseech you, the whole onion tribe. Barbecue your whole hogs to your palate, steep them in shalots, stuff them out with plantations of the rank and guilty garlic; you cannot poison them, or make them stronger than they are—but consider, he is a weakling—a flower.

Charles Lamb, 'A Dissertation upon Roast Pig', *Essays of Elia*, 1823

William Hickey (?1749–1830) was an attorney who practised for some years among the British in Calcutta. His racily garrulous Memoirs, *covering the period from his birth until 1809, remained unpublished until 1913–25. In them he depicted the cheerful amorality of Calcutta society, with kept women, adultery, prostitution, greed, heavy drinking, gambling, and corruption, before the onset of the cleaning-up process in private and public which made the mid-nineteenth-century Raj the respectable institution that it became.*

Mr Nathaniel Penry Rees . . . was the son of Doctor Rees, the learned Dissenting Minister, and Editor or Composer of the Encyclopaedia, but Penry had not profited from his respectable and worthy precepts or example, being a sad profligate fellow. . . . [In Bengal] he was attacked with a dysentery which though unusually slow in its progress, continued to harass him, and would not yield to any medicine. After being reduced to an absolute skeleton by the disease, the Physicians admitted his case was hopeless, at least that they could do nothing more but as an only remaining chance of recovery, they recommended change of climate and trial of the sea air. He therefore resolved to make the experiment . . . [and] engaged a passage for himself and his elegant companion on board a ship called the *Althea*. . . . Still, however, and notwithstanding all the care of his friends, he gradually and visibly sunk, becoming weaker and weaker, so much so that within five days' sail of the Island of St Helena he had not strength enough left to raise himself in his bed, his death being hourly expected, of which circumstance he was himself perfectly aware.

*   *   *   *   *

While in this melancholy state of bodily infirmity, the chief officer went into his cabin to ask how he was, and in the course of conversation with Miss Rivers [Rees's mistress], mentioned that an uncommonly fine fat sheep had been killed that morning. Rees, who had been attentively listening to what passed, the moment the officer left the cabin, sent a message to the Captain requesting immediately to see him. Captain Roberts, imagining his dying passenger had something of importance relative to his private affairs to communicate, instantly obeyed the summons, when upon entering the invalid's cabin, he with much earnestness addressed him thus: 'My dear Roberts, I understand you have this morning killed a remarkably fine Bengal sheep. Now, as you must very well know, that I cannot hold out many hours longer, and no evil can therefore ensue from a compliance with my request, do, my good fellow, gratify me with a mutton chop, for upon my soul I am cursed hungry.'

Captain Roberts, a good deal surprized at the oddity of the request, felt at a loss what to say, but upon Rees's repeating it with a strong, firm voice, he answered 'certainly, my dear Rees, if you insist upon it, you shall have a chop, but permit me to suggest that a boiled chicken or a little weak broth would be better suited for you.' 'Psha! Damn your broth and your boiled chicken,' replied Rees. 'I desire no such execrable stuff, and as to being better for me, that is all cudree fal lal, sheer nonsense. I am dished beyond redemption, completely done up at the least for this world; by this hour tomorrow, instead of my tongue running as it does at present, a dozen hungry sharks will be nibbling at the wooden case in which I presume your humanity will induce you to enclose my bag of bones, anxious to scrape a leg or an arm and gobble up guts if they can find any.' The mutton chops were accordingly dressed and sent to his bedside. He eat two with as much apparent pleasure and appetite as ever man did, though so debilitated he could not sit upright without a person on each side to support him. Having finished his meal, he cordially thanked Captain Roberts, shook him affectionately by the hand, and said, 'You have done all that was possible for me, God bless you. Good-bye to you, my worthy fellow. . . .' In three hours afterwards, he drew his last breath.

Memoirs of William Hickey, Volume IV, 1790–1809, edited by Alfred Spencer, 1925

❧ *Becky Sharp has begun life as governess to two small daughters of the parsimonious landowner Sir Pitt Crawley. In a letter to her best friend Amelia Sedley, she describes, in highly satirical terms, her first dinner with the family at King's Crawley.*

'My lady is served,' says the Butler in black, in an immense white shirt-frill, that looked as if it had been one of the Queen Elizabeth's ruffs depicted in the hall; and so, taking Mr Crawley's arm, she [Lady Crawley] led the way to the dining-room, whither I followed with my little pupils in each hand.

Sir Pitt was already in the room with a silver jug. He had just been to the cellar, and was in full dress too—that is, he had taken his gaiters off, and showed his little dumpy legs in black worsted stockings. The sideboard was covered with glistening old plate—old cups, both gold and silver; old salvers and cruet-stands, like Rundell and Bridge's shop. Everything on the table was in silver too, and two footmen, with red hair and canary-coloured liveries, stood on either side of the sideboard.

Mr Crawley said a long grace, and Sir Pitt said Amen, and the great silver dish-covers were removed.

'What have we for dinner, Betsy?' said the Baronet.

'Mutton broth, I believe, Sir Pitt,' answered Lady Crawley.

'*Mouton aux navets*,' added the Butler gravely (pronounce, if you please, moutongonavvy); 'and the soup is *potage de mouton à l'écossaise*.

The side-dishes contain *pommes de terre au naturel*, and *chou-fleur à l'eau*.'

'Mutton's mutton,' said the Baronet, 'and a devilish good thing. What *ship* was it, Horrocks, and when did you kill?'

'One of the black-faced Scotch, Sir Pitt; we killed on Thursday.'

'Who took any?'

'Steel, of Mudbury, took the saddle and two legs, Sir Pitt; but he says the last was too young and confounded woolly, Sir Pitt.'

'Will you take some *potage*, Miss ah—Miss Blunt?' said Mr Crawley.

'Capital Scotch broth, my dear,' said Sir Pitt, 'though they call it by a French name.'

'I believe it is the custom, sir, in decent society,' said Mr Crawley haughtily, 'to call the dish as I have called it;' and it was served to us on silver soup-plates by the footmen in the canary coats, with the *mouton aux navets*. Then 'ale and water' were brought, and served to us young ladies in wine-glasses. I am not a judge of ale, but I can say with a clear conscience I prefer water.

While we were enjoying our repast, Sir Pitt took occasion to ask what had become of the shoulders of the mutton.

'I believe they were eaten in the servants' hall,' said my lady humbly.

'They was, my lady,' said Horrocks; 'and precious little else we get there neither.'

Sir Pitt burst into a horse-laugh, and continued his conversation with Mr Horrocks. 'That there little pig of the Kent sow's breed must be uncommon fat now.'

'It's not quite busting, Sir Pitt,' said the Butler with the gravest air, at which Sir Pitt, and with him the young ladies this time, began to laugh violently.

'Miss Crawley, Miss Rose Crawley,' said Mr Crawley, 'Your laughter strikes me as being exceedingly out of place.'

'Never mind, my lord,' said the Baronet, 'we'll try the porker on Saturday. Kill un on Saturday morning, John Horrocks. Miss Sharp adores pork, don't you, Miss Sharp?'

Thackeray, *Vanity Fair*

❧ *Frank Buckland (1826–80), naturalist, was the son of William Buckland, geologist and clergyman, a canon of Christ Church, Oxford 1825–45 and Dean of Westminster 1845–56. The Buckland household in Christ Church was eccentric even by Oxford standards for the number of caged and loose animals which it contained; and as an undergraduate of the college Frank kept a bear (until detected), a monkey, an eagle, and a jackal in his rooms, together with various snakes, marmots, guinea-pigs, and dormice. Throughout his life he was particularly keen on experimenting with unusual animals as food: a process known in his day as 'acclimatization'*

At his father's table at Christ Church the viands were varied. A horse belonging to his brother-in-law having been shot, Dr Buckland had the tongue pickled and served up at a large luncheon party, and the guests enjoyed it much, until told what they had eaten.

Alligator was a rare delicacy . . . but puppies were occasionally, and mice frequently eaten. So also at the Deanery, hedgehogs, tortoise, potted ostrich, and occasionally rats, frogs, and snails were served up for the delectation of favoured guests. 'Party at the Deanery,' one guest notes; 'tripe for dinner; don't like crocodile for breakfast.'

* * * * *

'On January 21, 1859, I had the good fortune,' [Frank] wrote, 'to be invited to a dinner, which will, I trust, hereafter form the date of an epoch in natural history; I mean the now celebrated eland dinner, when, for the first time, the freshly killed haunch of this African antelope was placed on the table of the London Tavern. The savoury smell of the roasted beast seemed to have pervaded the naturalist world, for a goodly company were assembled, all eager for the experiment. At the head of the table sat Professor Owen himself, his scalpel turned into a carving knife, and his gustatory apparatus in full working order. It was, indeed, a zoological dinner to which each of the four points of the compass had sent its contribution. We had a large pike from the East; American partridges shot but a few days ago in the dense woods of the Transatlantic West; a wild goose, probably a young bean goose, from the North; and an eland from the South. The assembled company ardent lovers of Nature and all her works: most of them distinguished in their individual departments. The gastronomic trial over, we next enjoyed an intellectual treat in hearing from the professor his satisfaction at having been present at a new epoch in natural history. He put forth the benefits which would accrue to us by naturalising animals from foreign parts, animals good for food as well as ornamental to the parks.'

* * * * *

On February 6, 1868, a dinner of horse-flesh was given at the Langham Hotel, as an experiment of the value of that article of food, which is said to be now rather extensively used in Paris. The guests were many, scientific and intellectual, but, according to Frank Buckland, the pleasures of the table were social rather than gastronomic, 'A very pleasant party at our end of the table, but the meat simply horrible.'

'*February 7.*—Very seedy indeed; partly effects of horse, partly of a very bad cold; felt very queer all day.'

The flavour of the meat, though served in various ways, he described as resembling the aroma of a horse in a perspiration.

'In the middle of the dinner I stood up to watch the countenances of the people eating, and I devoutly wished I had had the talent of a Hogarth to be able to record the various expressions. Instead of "men's beards wagging," there seemed to be a dubious and inquisitive cast spread over the features of most who were present. Many, indeed, reminded me of the attitude of a person about to take a pill and draught; not a rush at the food, but a "one, two, three!" expression about them, coupled not infrequently by calling in the aid of the olfactory powers, reminding one of the short and doubtful sniff, that a domestic puss not over-hungry takes of a bit of bread and butter. The bolder experimenters gulped down the meat, and instantly followed it with a draught of champagne, then came another mouthful, and then, as we say, *fiat haustus ut antea* [let it be drunk off as before].'

The condition of the animals slaughtered may affect the flavour of the meat: on another occasion Frank Buckland and Mr Bartlett experimented with prime steaks of horse and beef, and were unable to distinguish between them; yet few would eat horseflesh willingly. A suggestion was made to the Home Office, by Frank Buckland, that if prisoners were fed on horseflesh the prisons would soon be empty. Tenderness for the criminal class has prevented its adoption.

George Bompas, *Life of Frank Buckland*, n.d.

Everett Wharton, an ambitious young man, and his friend Ferdinand Lopez have been discussing their political and business prospects while dining at the Progress Club (*i.e. the Reform Club in thin disguise*).

'I fear you are too far gone' [said Wharton] 'to abandon the idea of making a fortune.'

'I *would* abandon it to-morrow if I could come into a fortune ready-made. A man must at any rate eat.'

'Yes;—he must eat. But I am not quite sure,' said Wharton, thoughtfully, 'that he need think about what he eats.'

'Unless the beef is sent up without horse radish!' It had happened that when the two men sat down to their dinner the insufficient quantity of that vegetable supplied by the steward of the club had been all consumed, and Wharton had complained of the grievance.

'A man has a right to that for which he has paid,' said Wharton with mock solemnity, 'and if he passes over laches of that nature without observation he does an injury to humanity at large. I'm not going to be caught in a trap, you know, because, I like horse radish with my beef.'

Anthony Trollope, *The Prime Minister*, 1876

BŒUF À LA MODE

Before leaving the house [my father] said to my mother: 'See that you have a good dinner for us to-night; you remember, I'm bringing de Norpois back with me.' My mother had not forgotten. And all that day, and overnight, Françoise, rejoicing in the opportunity to devote herself to that art of the kitchen,—of which she was indeed a past-master, stimulated, moreover, by the prospect of having a new guest to feed, the consciousness that she would have to compose, by methods known to her alone, a dish of beef in jelly, had been living in the effervescence of creation; since she attached the utmost importance to the intrinsic quality of the materials which were to enter into the fabric of her work, she had gone herself to the Halles to procure the best cuts of rump-steak, shin of beef, calves' feet, as Michelangelo passed eight months in the mountains of Carrara choosing the most perfect blocks of marble for the monument of Julius II.—Françoise expended on these comings and goings so much ardour that Mama, at the sight of her flaming cheeks, was alarmed lest our old servant should make herself ill with overwork, like the sculptor of the Tombs of the Medici in the quarries of Pietrasanta. And overnight Françoise had sent to be cooked in the baker's oven, shielded with breadcrumbs, like a block of pink marble packed in sawdust, what she called a 'Nev'-York ham'. Believing the language to be less rich than it actually was in words, and her own ears less trustworthy, the first time she had heard anyone mention York ham she had thought, no doubt—feeling it to be hardly conceivable that the dictionary should be so prodigal as to include at once a 'York' and a 'New York'—that she had misheard what was said, and that the ham was really called by the name already familiar to her. And so, ever since, the word York was preceded in her ears, or before her eyes when she read it in an advertisement, by the affix 'New' which she pronounced 'Nev' '. And it was with the most perfect faith that she would say to her kitchen-maid: 'Go and fetch me a ham from Olida's. Madame told me especially to get a Nev'-York.'

* * * * *

The cold beef, spiced with carrots, made its appearance, couched by the Michelangelo of our kitchen upon enormous crystals of jelly, like transparent blocks of quartz.

'You have a chef of the first order, Madame,' said M. de Norpois, 'and that is no small matter. I myself, who have had, when abroad, to maintain a certain style in housekeeping, I know how difficult it often is to find a perfect master-cook. But this is a positive banquet that you have set before us!'

And indeed Françoise, in the excitement of her ambition to make a success, for so distinguished a guest, of a dinner the preparation of which had been obstructed by difficulties worthy of her powers, had given herself such trouble as she no longer took when we were alone, and had recaptured her incomparable Combray manner.

'That is a thing you can't get in a chophouse,—in the best of them, I mean; a spiced beef in which the jelly does not taste of glue and the beef has caught the flavour of the carrots; it is admirable! Allow me to come again,' he went on, making a sign to shew that he wanted more of the jelly. 'I should be interested to see how your Vatel managed a dish of a quite different kind; I should like, for instance, to see him tackle a *bœuf Stroganoff*.'

Marcel Proust, *Within a Budding Grove*, 1919, Volume I, translated by C. K. Scott Moncrieff, 1924

❧ *The novel* Dog Years *is set in Kashubia, a rural area of West Prussia near Danzig, before the Second World War. The narrator and his cousin Tulla are children. When her deaf-mute younger brother is accidentally drowned, Tulla retreats into the kennel of the family's dog, Harras, and refuses to come out.*

On the second dog-kennel day

a Tuesday, Harras no longer had to tug when August Pokriefke wanted to renew the shavings. Tulla began to take food, that is, she ate with Harras out of his dish, after Harras had dragged a boneless chunk of dog meat into the kennel and whetted her appetite by nuzzling the cold meat with his nose.

Now this dog meat really wasn't bad. Usually it was stringy cow meat and was cooked in large quantities on our kitchen stove, always in the same nut-brown enamel pot. We had all of us, Tulla and her brothers and myself as well, eaten this meat in our bare hands, without bread to push it down. It tasted best when cold and hard. We cut it into cubes with our pocket knives. It was cooked twice a week and was compact, gray-brown, traversed by pale-blue little veins, sinews, and sweating strips of fat. It smelled sweetish soapy forbidden. Long after gulping down the marbled cubes of meat—often while playing we had both pockets full of them—our palates were still deadened and tallowy. We even spoke differently after we had eaten of those meat cubes: our speech became palatal metamorphosed four-legged: we barked at each other. We preferred this dish to many that were served at the family board. We called it dog meat. When it wasn't cow meat, it was never anything worse than horse meat or the mutton from a forced slaughtering. My mother threw coarse-grained salt—a handful—into the enamel pot, piled up the foot-long tatters of meat in the boiling salt water, let the water boil up again for a moment, put in marjoram, because marjoram is supposed to be good for a dog's sense of smell, turned the gas down, covered the pot, didn't touch it for a whole hour; for that was the time required by cow-horse-sheep meat to turn into the dog meat which Harras and we ate and which, thanks to the marjoram cooked with it, provided us all, Harras and the rest of us, with sensitive olfactories. It was a Koshnavian recipe. Between Osterwick and Schlangenthin they said: Marjoram is good for your looks. Marjoram makes money go further. Against Devil and hell strew marjoram over the threshold. The squat long-haired Koshnavian sheep dogs were celebrated for their marjoram-favored keenness of smell.

Rarely, when there was no meat displayed on the low-price counter, the pot was filled with innards: knotted fatty beef hearts, pissy, because unsoaked, pig's kidneys, also small lamb kidneys which my mother had to detach from a finger-thick coat of fat lined with crackling parchment: the kidneys went into the dog pot, the suet was rendered in a cast-iron frying pan and used in the family cooking, because mutton suet wards off tuberculosis. Sometimes, too, a piece of dark spleen, halfway between purple and violet, went into the pot, or a chunk of sinewy beef liver. But because lung took longer to cook, required a larger cooking pot, and when you come right down to it doesn't yield much meat, it almost never went into the enamel pot, in actual fact only during the summer meat shortages brought on by the cattle plague that sometimes came to Kashubia as well as Koshnavia. We never ate the boiled innards. Only Tulla, unbeknownst to the grownups, but before our eyes as we looked on with a tightening of the throat, took long avid gulps of the brownish-gray broth in which the coagulated excretion of the kidneys floated sleetlike and mingled with blackish marjoram to form islands.

On the fourth dog-kennel day

. . . I brought her . . . a bowlful of heart, kidney, spleen, and liver broth. The broth in the bowl was cold, for Tulla preferred to drink her broth cold. A layer of fat, a mixture of beef tallow and mutton tallow, covered the bowl like an icecap. The cloudy liquid emerged only at the edges, and drops of it rolled over the layer of tallow.

* * * * *

Cupping the bowl in her right hand, which rests on the ground, [Tulla] slowly guides her mouth and the edge of the bowl together. She laps, sips, wastes nothing. In one breath, without removing the bowl from her lips, Tulla drinks the fatless spleen-heart-kidney-liver broth with all its granular delicacies and surprises, with the tiny bits of cartilage at the bottom, with Koshnavian marjoram and coagulated urea. Tulla drinks to the dregs: her chin raises the bowl. . . . Skinny, sinewy and pale, Tulla's childlike neck labors until the bowl lies on top of her face and she is able to lift her hand from the bowl and move it away between the bottom of the bowl and the side-slipping sun. The overturned bowl conceals the screwed-up eyes, the crusty nostrils, the mouth that has had enough.

Günter Grass, *Dog Years*, 1963, translated by Ralph Manheim 1965

❧ *Jean Rennie worked as a housemaid, kitchen-maid, and scullery-maid for a succession of wealthy families between 1924 and 1940. Here she is working in the kitchen of a ducal family in Scotland. The belief that game should be well hung to the point of rottenness is no longer the article of faith that it was before the days of universal refrigeration.*

[The Chef] used to come in with the game or rabbits in his hands, throw them on the floor, and say, casually, 'To-morrow,' or 'Dinner,' or 'Now.'

And I would leave them, or start them straight away, according to the above instructions, and how my work was progressing.

This Sunday morning, early in the year, he had brought the two pheasants in and thrown them on the floor and said, 'To-night.'

I put them on my table, and went to get some old newspapers to take the feathers, taking a few feathers off the breast first.

I'd noticed they looked rather bloated about the necks, and they had certainly hung quite a few days.

When I got back, *those pheasants had moved!*

Gingerly, I pulled at those feathers on the neck, and the skin came away in my hands . . .

Certainly I had seen maggots before, had even enjoyed throwing them on the hot stove and watching them wriggle before they were swept into the flames.

But this teeming, crawly heap of obscene life was something I'd never seen before, or since.

The entire neck, from head to crop, was moving—even in the bird's mouth. The whole area of the back and tail end and legs was a filthy mass of these heaving dirty monstrosities, some about an inch long.

* * * * *

I gasped: 'Chef!—those pheasants! They're horrible—they're walking—they *moved!* I can't touch them—they're absolutely *walking!*'

He raised his eyebrows and his eyes twinkled.

He picked up his sharp little knife and rubbed it on the steel which he wore at his side from his belt, as he walked in front of me to the scullery where the horrible things lay.

'Well,' he said conversationally, 'it is a nice Sunday morning, perhaps they like a little walk, yes?'

With about two slashes on each bird, he cut away the breasts, cleanly and decisively.

'There,' he said, as he threw the bodies on my paper, 'put them out—I've got all I want,' and away he went, with the four little pheasant breasts in his hand.

Hastily I smothered the horrors in lots of newspaper and put them out to be collected by the old man who tended the garden boilers, and incinerator, and laundry fires, and things like that.

Yes, I was learning fast!

Jean Rennie, *Every Other Sunday: The Autobiography of a Kitchenmaid*, 1955

FISH

❧ *Celia Fiennes tasted potted char on the same visit to Westmorland, in 1698, as that on which she reported seeing oat clapbread made. Char,* salmo salvelinus, *a small, cold-water fish of the trout variety, was a Lake District delicacy popular all over England in the potted form which made it transportable. Poached, skinned, and boned, the fish were placed in earthenware pots, covered in melted butter and heated for a time in an oven, then left so that the butter congealed. It was characteristic of Celia Fiennes's enquiring nature to wish to see the lake from which the char were caught, even though this lay out of her way.*

At the Kings arms [in Kendal], one Mrs Rowlandson, she does pott up the Charr ffish the best of any in the Country. I was Curious to have some and so bespoke some of her, and also was as Curious to see the great water [Windermere] which is the only place that ffish is to be found in, and so went from Kendall . . . 6 miles thro' narrow Lanes.

* * * * *

[The largest island on Lake Windermere] did not Looke to be so bigg at ye shore, but takeing boat I went on it and found it as large and very good Barley and oates and grass. The water is very Cleer and full of good ffish, but ye Charr ffish being out of season Could not Easily be taken, so I saw none alive but of other ffish I had a very good supper. The season of the Char ffish is between Michaelmas and Christmas; at that tyme I have had of them, which they pott with sweete spices. They are as big as a small trout, Rather slenderer and ye skinn full of spotts, some Red Like the finns of a perch, and the inside flesh Looks as Red as any salmon if they are in season; their taste is very rich and fatt tho' not so strong or Clogging as the Lamprys are, but its as fatt and rich a food.

The Diary of Celia Fiennes

[*Weymouth, Dorset, 29 August 1782.*]

The fish market is poorly serv'd; and fine and foolish people keep it at a high price, by bidding against each other; and thinking lavishness gentility.—I purchas'd my fish at early morning; and now begin to judge the prices; viz, large soles at 1s. 6d. the pair, mackarel at three half pence or two pence each, pipers one shilling, dories one, and 2 shillings, red mullets ditto. crab two pence the pound; which is by no means cheap, at this distance from the Metropolis, and on a sea coast.—Should smuggling subside, I shall hope that fishing would commence and [be] encourag'd by premiums. Were I an inhabitant of a sea situation, I could wish to keep a boat and nets with some neighbours, and not to depend upon the idleness, and insolence, of the fishermen.

My life now begins to be arranged in a regular way: I rise at six o'clock, buy fish, read news papers, walk the beach, visit my horse; at nine o'clock return to breakfast; ride at ten, dine at four; in the evening walk beach again till the [Assembly] rooms begin, cards till ten o'clock; light supper, bed.

[*2 September.*]

At the fish market, buy crabs, prawns, and red mullets; then walk'd the parade, and the beach, where I saw a large conger eel, that was lately caught, and a turbot just spear'd of eighteen pounds weight; turbots of this size are struck by a three forked spear, and bleed excessively which renders their flesh firmer and whiter; (tho' this size is too large and coarse;) they are discover'd at the bottom of the water by the glitter of their eyes.

The Torrington Diaries, Containing the Tours Through England and Wales of the Hon John Byng (later fifth Viscount Torrington) Between the Years 1781 and 1794, edited by C. Bruyn Andrews, 1936, Volume I

The scene is a dinner-party at Crotchet Castle, a rich businessman's villa on the Thames; the dialogue, the kind of learned or pseudo-learned symposium which is characteristic of Peacock's novels. The chief participants are two of the Crotchets' guests, an erudite clergyman, the Revd Dr Folliott, and a Scottish political economist, Mr Mac Quedy.

THE REV DR FOLLIOTT. Here is a very fine salmon before me: and May is the very *point nommé* to have salmon in perfection. There is a fine turbot close by, and there is much to be said in his behalf; but salmon in May is the king of fish.

MR CROTCHET. That salmon before you, doctor, was caught in the Thames this morning.

THE REV DR FOLLIOTT. *Παπαπαί!* Rarity of rarities! A Thames salmon caught this morning. Now, Mr Mac Quedy, even in fish your Modern Athens must yield. *Cedite Graii*.

MR MAC QUEDY. Eh! sir, on its own ground, your Thames salmon has two virtues over all others: first, that it is fresh; and, second, that it is rare; for I understand you do not take half a dozen in a year.

THE REV DR FOLLIOTT. In some years, sir, not one. Mud, filth, gas dregs, lock-weirs, and the march of mind, developed in the form of poaching, have ruined the fishery. But when we do catch a salmon, happy the man to whom he falls.

MR MAC QUEDY. I confess, sir, this is excellent; but I cannot see why it should be better than a Tweed salmon at Kelso.

THE REV DR FOLLIOTT. Sir, I will take a glass of Hock with you.

MR MAC QUEDY. With all my heart, sir. There are several varieties of the salmon genus: but the common salmon, the *salmo salar*, is only one species, one and the same every where, just like the human mind. Locality and education make all the difference.

THE REV DR FOLLIOTT. Education! Well, sir, I have no doubt schools for all are just as fit for the species *salmo salar* as for the genus *homo*. But you must allow, that the specimen before us has finished his education in a manner that does honour to his college. However, I doubt that the *salmo salar* is only one species, that is to say, precisely alike in all localities. I hold that every river has its own breed, with essential differences; in flavour especially. And as for the human mind, I deny that it is the same in all men. I hold that there is every variety of natural capacity from the idiot to Newton and Shakespeare; the mass of mankind, midway between these extremes, being blockheads of different degrees; education leaving them pretty nearly as it found them, with this single difference, that it gives a fixed direction to their stupidity, a sort of incurable wry neck to the thing they call their understanding. So one nose points always east, and another always west, and each is ready to swear that it points due north.

MR CROTCHET. If that be the point of truth, very few intellectual noses point due north.

MR MAC QUEDY. Only those that point to the Modern Athens.

THE REV DR FOLLIOTT. Where all native noses point southward.

MR MAC QUEDY. Eh, sir, northward for wisdom, and southward for profit.

MR CROTCHET, JUN. Champagne, doctor?

THE REV DR FOLLIOTT. Most willingly. But you will permit my drinking it while it sparkles. I hold it a heresy to let it deaden in my hand, while the glass of my *compotator* is being filled on the opposite side of the table. By the bye, captain, you remember a passage in Athenaeus, where he cites Menander on the subject of fish sauce. . . . The science of fish sauce, Mr Mac Quedy, is by no means brought to perfection; a fine field of discovery still lies open in that line.

MR MAC QUEDY. Nay, sir, beyond lobster sauce, I take it, ye cannot go.

THE REV DR FOLLIOTT. In their line, I grant you, oyster and lobster sauce are the pillars of Hercules. But I speak of the cruet sauces, where the quintessence of the sapid is condensed in a phial. I can taste in my mind's palate a combination, which, if I could give it reality, I would christen with the name of my college, and hand it down to posterity as a seat of learning indeed.

Thomas Love Peacock, *Crotchet Castle*, 1831

Παπαπαί! : 'Good gracious!'; *Cedite Graii*: 'Yield, Greeks'; *Modern Athens*: Edinburgh; *cruet sauces*: commercial fish sauces were extremely popular by the early nineteenth century.

❧ *Abraham Hayward's* The Art of Dining *(1852) reflects the solemn preoccupation of many moneyed early Victorians with how and what they ate. Cookery writing, in the sense of publishing volumes of recipes, was at that time an occupation for both men and women. Eliza Acton's* Modern Cookery . . . for Private Families *had appeared in 1845; Mrs Beeton's* Household Management *appeared in serial form in 1859–61, and in book form in 1861. Well-known chefs such as Alexis Soyer and Charles-Elmé Francatelli also published volumes of recipes during the 1850s and early 1860s. It was predominantly clubmen such as Hayward, however, used to eating out in exclusively masculine company in London clubs and chophouses or the more expensive Paris restaurants, who made a genre of the theoretical literature of dining. This lasted, in book or essay-form, from the early Victorian to the Edwardian period, sometimes extending its range to cover the art of entertaining (or being entertained) at home, but rarely concerning itself with the practicalities of cooking.*

Fish richly merits a book to itself; but we must confine ourselves to a limited number of hints. Our first relates to the prevalent method of serving, which is wrong. The fish should never be covered up, or it will suffer fatally from the condensation of the steam. Moreover, the practice of putting boiled and fried fish on the same dish cannot be too much reprobated; and covering hot fish with cold green parsley is abominable. Sometimes one sees all these barbarities committed at once; and the removal of the cover exhibits boiled and fried fish, both covered with parsley; the fried fish deprived of all its crispness from contact with the boiled, and both made sodden by the fall of the condensed steam from the cover: so the only merit the fish has is being hot, which it might have just as well if it followed instead of accompanying the soup. . . . Of sauces, Dutch sauce is applicable to all white-fleshed fish, except perhaps cod, when oyster sauce may be allowed. There is little mystery in the composition of oyster sauce; but lobster sauce is not so generally understood. The Christchurch and Severn salmon are decidedly the best in England; for the Thames salmon may now almost be considered extinct. The salmon at Killarney, broiled, toasted, or roasted on arbutus skewers, is a thing apart, and unfortunately inimitable. . . . London is principally supplied with eels from Holland; and whole cargoes are daily sent up the river to be eaten as Thames eels at Richmond, Eel-pie Island, &c. Pope's well-known line—

> The Kennet swift, for silver eels renown'd,

were enough to bring poetical authority into discredit. The Kennet is a slow river; there are no eels at all in the upper part, and those in the lower part are too large. The silver eel, from a running stream with a gravelly bottom, may be eaten in perfection at Salisbury, Anderton, or Overton. He is best spatch-cocked. The best lampreys and lamperns are from Worcester.

The late Duke of Portland was in the habit of going to Weymouth during the summer months for the sake of the red mullet which formerly abounded there. The largest used to be had for three-pence or four-pence apiece; but he has been known to give two guineas for one weighing a pound and a half. His Grace's custom was to put all the livers together into a butter-boat, to avoid the chances of inequality; very properly considering that, to be helped to a mullet in the condition of an East Indian nabob, would be too severe a shock for the nerves or spirits of any man. The mullet have now nearly deserted Weymouth for the coast of Cornwall, whither we recommend the connoisseur to repair in the dog-days, taking care to pay his respects to the dories of Plymouth on the way . . . There are epicures who combine these luxuries, eating the flesh of the dory with the liver of the mullet; but though the flesh of the mullet be poor, it is exactly adapted to the sauce which nature has provided for it, and we consequently denounce all combinations of this description to be heterodox.

Abraham Hayward, *The Art of Dining; or Gastronomy and Gastronomers*, 1852

The Ballad of Bouillabaisse

A street there is in Paris famous,
For which no rhyme our language yields,
Rue Neuve des Petits Champs its name is—
The New Street of the Little Fields;
And here's an inn, not rich and splendid,
But still in comfortable case,
The which in youth I oft attended
To eat a bowl of Bouillabaisse.

This Bouillabaisse a noble dish is—
A sort of soup, or broth, or brew,
Or hotchpotch of all sorts of fishes,
That Greenwich never could outdo;
Green herbs, red peppers, mussels, saffern,
Soles, onions, garlic, roach, and dace,
All these you eat at Terré's tavern,
In that one dish of Bouillabaisse.

Indeed, a rich and savoury stew 'tis;
And true philosophers, methinks,
Who love all sorts of natural beauties,
Should love good victuals and good drinks.
And Cordelier or Benedictine
Might gladly, sure, his lot embrace,
Nor find a fast-day too afflicting
Which served him up a Bouillabaisse.

William Makepeace Thackeray, 'The Ballad of Bouillabaisse', 1849

❧ Siren Land *is Norman Douglas's classic description of life on Capri and in nearby parts of the Italian mainland* c.1910.

'Can you supply me with something to eat, fair Costanza?'

'How not? Whatever you command'

Whatever you command. Fairy-like bubbles of Southern politeness which, when pricked, evaporate—as a friend of mine used to say—into indifferent maccheroni.

* * * * *

'We have a fish soup, *guarracini* and *scorfani* and *aguglie* and *toteri* and—'

Take breath, gentle maiden, the while I explain to the patient reader the ingredients of the diabolical preparation known as '*zuppa di pesce*'. The *guarracino*, for instance, is a pitch-black marine monstrosity, one to two *inches* long, a mere blot, with an Old Red Sandstone profile and insufferable manners, whose sole recommendation is that its name is derived from *korakinos* (korax = a raven; but who can live on Greek roots?) As to the *scorfano*, its name is unquestionably onomatopoetic, to suggest the spitting-out of bones; the only difference, from a culinary point of view, between the *scorfano* and a toad being that the latter has twice as much meat on it. The *aguglia*, again, is all tail and proboscis; the very nightmare of a fish—as thin as a lead pencil. Who would believe that for this miserable sea-worm with verdigris-tinted spine, which an ordinary person would not thank you for setting on his table, the inhabitants of Siren land fought like fiends; the blood of their noblest was shed in defence of privileges artfully wheedled out of Anjou and Aragonese kings defining the *ius quoddam pescandi vulgariter dictum sopra le aguglie*; that a certain tract of sea was known as the 'aguglie water' and owned, up to the days of Murat, by a single family who defended it with guns and man-traps? And everybody knows the *totero* or squid, an animated ink-bag of perverse leanings, which swims backwards because all other creatures go forwards and whose india-rubber flesh might be useful for deluding hunger on desert islands, since, like American gum, you can chew it for months but never get it down.

These, and such as they, float about in a lukewarm brew of rancid oil and garlic, together with a few of last week's bread-crusts, decaying sea-shells and onion-peels, to give it an air of consistency.

* * * * *

How unfavourably this hotch-potch compares with the Marseillese bouillabaisse! But what can be expected, considering its ingredients? Green and golden scales, and dorsal fins embellished with elaborate rococo designs, will satisfy neither a hungry man nor an epicure, and if Neapolitans pay untold sums for the showy Mediterranean sea-spawn, it only proves that they eat with their eyes, like children who prefer tawdry sweets to good ones. They have colour and shape, these fish of the inland sea, but not taste; their flesh is either flabby and slimy and full of bones in unauthorised places, or else they have no flesh at all—heads like Burmese dragons but no bodies attached to them; or bodies of flattened construction on the *magnum in parvo* principle, allowing of barely room for a sheet of paper between their skin and ribs; or a finless serpentine framework, with long slit eyes that leer at you while you endeavour to scratch a morsel off the reptilian anatomy.

There is not a cod, or turbot, or whiting, or salmon, or herring in the two thousand miles between Gibraltar and Jerusalem; or if there is, it never comes out; its haddocks (haddocks, indeed!) taste as if they had fed on mouldy sea-weed and died from the effects of it; its lobsters have no claws; its oysters are bearded like pards; and as for its soles—I have yet to see one that measures more than five inches round the waist. The fact is, there is hardly a fish in the Mediterranean worth eating and therefore *ex nihilo nihil fit*. Bouillabaisse is only good because cooked by the French, who, if they cared to try, could produce an excellent and nutritious substitute out of cigar-stumps and empty matchboxes. But even as a Turk is furious with a tender chicken because it cheats him out of the pleasure of masticating, so the Neapolitan would throw a boneless *zuppa di pesce* out of the window: the spitting and sputtering is half the fun.

Norman Douglas, *Siren Land*, 1911

ius ... aguglie: 'a certain right to fish, as they say in the vernacular, over the aguglie'; *Murat*: Joachim Murat (1767–1815), created King of Naples by Napoleon in 1808.

VEGETABLES

MELANCHOLY

Among herbs to be eaten, I find gourds, cowcumbers, coleworts, melons, disallowed, but especially cabbage. It causeth troublesome dreams, and sends up black vapours to the brain. Galen of all herbs condemns cabbage; and Isaac, it brings heaviness to the soul. Some are of opinion that all raw herbs and sallets breed melancholy blood, except bugloss and lettuce. Crato speaks against all herbs and worts, except borage, bugloss, fennel, parsley, dill, balm, succory. Magninus all herbs are simply evil to feed on (as he thinks). So did that scoffing Cook in Plautus hold.

Like other cooks I do not supper dress
That put whole meadows into a platter,
And make no better of their guests than beeves,
With herbs and grass to feed them fatter.

Our Italians and Spaniards do make a whole dinner of herbs and sallets, which our said Plautus calls garden suppers, Horace bloodless suppers, by which means, as he follows it,

Their lives, that eat such herbs, must needs be short,
And 'tis a fearful thing for to report,
That men should feed on such a kind of meat,
Which very juments would refuse to eat.

Burton, *Anatomy of Melancholy*

Succory: chicory; *Horace*: a mistake for Ovid; *juments*: yoke-beasts, beasts of burden.

MAKING A SALAD

I am not ambitious of being thought an excellent *Cook*, or of those who set up, and value themselves, for their skill in *Sauces*; such as was *Mithacus* a *Culinary Philosopher*, and other *Eruditae Gulae* [gastronomes]; who read Lectures of *Hautgouts*, like the *Archestratus* in *Athenaeus*: Tho' after what we find the *Heroes* did of old, and see them chining out the slaughter'd *Ox*, dressing the Meat, and do the Offices of both *Cook* and *Butcher* (for so Homer represents *Achilles* himself, and the rest of the illustrious *Greeks*) I say, after this, let none reproach our *Sallet-Dresser*, or disdain so clean, innocent, sweet, and Natural a Quality; compar'd with the Shambles Filth and *Nidor* [stink], Blood and Cruelty; whilst all the World were *Eaters*, and *Composers* of *Sallets* in its best and brightest Age . . .

The Ingredients therefore gather'd and proportion'd, as above; Let the *Endive* have all its out-side Leaves stripp'd off, slicing *in* the White: In like manner the *Sellery* is also to have the hollow green

Stem or Stalk trimm'd and divided; slicing-in the blanched Part, and cutting the Root into four equal Parts.

Lettuces, *Cresses*, *Radish*, &c . . . must be exquisitely pick'd, cleans'd, wash'd, and put into the Strainer; swing'd, and shaken gently, and, if you please, separately, or all together; Because some like not so well the *Blanch'd* and Bitter Herbs, if eaten with the rest: Others mingle *Endive*, *Succory* and *Rampions*, without distinction, and generally eat *Sellery* by it self, as also Sweet *Fennel*.

From *April* till *September* (and during all the Hot *Months*) may *Guinny-Pepper* and *Horse-Radish* be left out; and therefore we only mention them in the Dressing, which should be in this manner.

Your *Herbs* being handsomly parcell'd, and spread on a clean Napkin before you, are to be mingl'd together in one of the Earthen glaz'd Dishes. Then, for the *Oxoleon*; take of clear, and perfectly good *Oyl-Olive*, three Parts; of sharpest *Vinegar* (sweetest of all *Condiments*), *Limon*, or Juice of *Orange*, one Part; and therein let steep some Slices of *Horse-Radish*, with a little *Salt*; Some in a separate *Vinegar*, gently bruise a *Pod* of *Guinny-Pepper*, straining both the *Vinegars* apart, to make Use of Either or One alone, or of both, as they best like; then add as much *Tewkesbury*, or other dry *Mustard* grated, as will lie upon an Half-Crown Piece: Beat, and mingle all these very well together; but pour not on the *Oyl* and *Vinegar*, 'till immediately before the *Sallet* is ready to be eaten. And then with the *Yolk* of two new-laid *Eggs* (boyl'd and prepar'd, as before is taught) squash, and bruise them all into mash with a Spoon; and lastly, pour it all upon the Herbs, stirring, and mingling them 'till they are well and thoroughly imbib'd; not forgetting the Sprinklings of *Aromaticks*, and such flowers, as we have already mentioned, if you think fit, and garnishing the Dish with the thin Slices of *Horse-Radish*, *Red Beet*, *Berberries*, &c.

John Evelyn, *Acetaria. A Discourse of Sallets*, 1699

Homer: especially *Iliad*, Book IX; *rampion*: a kind of bell-flower, *campanula rapunculus*, naturalized on sandy soil, with a white, tuberous root which was used in salad; *Guinny-Pepper, Guinea pepper*: cayenne pepper; *oxoleon*: an oil and vinegar dressing (from the Greek *oxos*, vinegar, and Latin *oleum*, oil).

'Palestine soup!' said the Reverend Doctor Opimian, dining with his friend Squire Gryll; 'a curiously complicated misnomer. We have an excellent old vegetable, the artichoke, of which we eat the head; we have another of subsequent introduction, of which we eat the root, and which we also call artichoke, because it resembles the first in flavour, although, *me judice* [in my opinion], a very inferior affair. This last is a species of the helianthus, or sunflower genus of the *Syngenesia frustranea* class of plants. It is therefore a girasol, or turn-to-the-sun. From this girasol we have made Jerusalem, and from the Jerusalem artichoke we make Palestine soup.'

MR GRYLL. A very good thing, Doctor.

THE REVEREND DOCTOR OPIMIAN. A very good thing; but a palpable misnomer.

Peacock, *Gryll Grange*

❧ *Joyce Conyngham Green, who had worked in the theatre before the Second World War, spent the war years living in a Hertfordshire village with her husband.* Salmagundi *is an amalgam of wartime diary and meditation on the seasons, with much reference to folklore and country customs, English literature and drama, and seasonal (as well as austerity) food.*

MAY EIGHT

> Your mother has vitamins again rather badly; we eat little but carrots, generally raw.
>
> JOHN GALSWORTHY, *The Silver Spoon*

Without having vitamins at all badly we eat little but raw carrots plus shredded raw cabbage, because there is nothing else here. Offal, poultry, game, rabbits, have all entirely vanished these four years, and fish is seldom obtainable. Mercifully we have always had a light salad-and-coffee lunch, so compulsory almost-vegetarianism has not hit us as hard as it has our two-meat-meals-a-day friends. But now that vegetables have disappeared as well, with the exception of spring cabbage, cooked beetroot, and potatoes, we are on the point of starvation.

And what spring cabbage! About four edible leaves in each cabbage to a great mass of tough outside greenery which is about as chewable, cooked, as deck-chair canvas, and not, I should think, as flavoursome. As they are sold by the pound, it is quite costly to get enough 'inside' for one salad or cooked dish; and the amount of waste has to be seen to be believed. I feel quite worn out and blighted just coping with the washing of cabbage.

It is no exaggeration to say that from Friday's, Saturday's, and Sunday's salads alone there was: (*a*) an outsize enamel bucket full of outside leaves to give to Mrs Convallaria's hens; (*b*) a ditto shopping-basket ditto ditto; (*c*) a large basin of not-quite-so-far outside leaves (Saturday's); (*d*) a large pile on the scullery window-sill of ditto (Sunday's), the two latter for Dee to look over in the faint hope that fresh eyes, so to speak, might discover some that were cookable; (*e*) one very small basin of reasonably tender just-outside-the-heart—heart, huh!—that could be cooked, and, what is more important, *eaten* when cooked.

All of these were quite apart from salad leaves and one molehill of outside which I had 'souped' before the sight of mountains of more or less unusable cabbage had begun to unnerve me entirely; and two large bucketfuls which had previously gone up to Mrs Convallaria. Cee swore he could smell the huge pile of decaying relics of Monday's, Tuesday's, Wednesday's, and Thursday's salads which had had to be dumped on the compost heap in despair—after all, we have some war-work to do apart from rushing unwanted and unemployable brassica about—not only all over the garden, but all over the village as well, as well.

A dreadful belief is arising in our bosoms that our house is becoming—like the Tite Barnacles'—a sort of bottle, only instead of being filled 'with concentrated provisions and extract of Sink from the pantry' it is pervaded by the effluvia of ancient and modern cabbage, and that when the stopper is taken out, i.e. the front door is opened, a great gust of *Brassica oleracea capitata* will burst into the face of the waiting visitor.

Joyce Conyngham Green, *Salmagundi*, 1947

Tite Barnacles: characters in Charles Dickens's *Little Dorrit*.

❧ *Avocado pears have been widely available in England since the late 1950s or early 1960s. Two letters to* The Times, *11 May 1989, contribute to a debate about their use.*

[*From Mr J. R. Colclough.*]
Sir, Ned Sherrin's doubts (Review, April 22) as to the veracity of the records of avocado consumption are not, I feel, well founded.

Except during the war years there has certainly been some importation of avocados throughout the present century.

In 1912 the Pacific Steam Navigation Co's boat, on which I returned to England from Chile, loaded at Valparaiso a deck cargo of 20 or 30 crates. I was told that these contained unripe avocados which would ripen during our progress through the tropics but which (I was warned in case I might escape parental control and make an attack on them) would not be fit to eat for some weeks after they were landed at Liverpool.

However, the ship's stores contained an adequate supply of ripe avocados, which were always on the menu as hors-d'œuvre and sometimes as sorbets.

In London avocados seemed unobtainable, though once or twice we managed to get some at Shearns, the vegetarian restaurant and greengrocers in Tottenham Court Road.

My mother mentioned this to the proprietor of the grocers in Coptic Street, opposite the British Museum, who specialised in South American produce and from whom we used to buy Huasco honey and palm syrup.

He immediately produced half-a-dozen from his store-room, explaining that he supplied them in bulk to the South American embassies for their banquets and dinners.

From 1914 to 1927 avocados were unobtainable in London but they were available in Paris from 1919 onwards and during school holidays I was often sent to Félix Potin's in the Boulevard Haussmann to purchase some. Potin's had them at all times, regardless of season, evidently having suppliers both in the northern and southern hemispheres.

In 1927 the Chilean Government induced Poupart's of Covent Garden to promote the sale of Chilean fruit, which they did with little success, except in the case of avocados, which remained readily available until the outbreak of war.

In the years immediately following the war they were from time to time on sale at the fruiterers at the top of Leather Lane, Holborn. Since the entry of the Israeli producers into the market in 1950 there have always been plenty of them about, and at all times of the year.

I am, Sir, yours faithfully, J. R. Colclough.

[*From Mr J. S. Champion.*]

Sir, In paying tribute to the versatility of the avocado pear your recent correspondents (May 1, 4) appear to have overlooked its military applications.

When I was employed in the Colonial Secretariat in Entebbe 30 years ago, there was a fruitful avocado tree in our garden, windfalls from which provided an arsenal of ammunition for the rival gangs in which our own children and those of our colleagues used to play their games.

Indeed the gang based on the other side of our garden fence was fittingly known and respected as the Mighty Pear-Balls.

The over-ripe, rotten avocado pear is singularly well adapted for use as a projectile in juvenile gang warfare. It is not lethal; it is exactly the right size and weight for throwing; its large stone provides the requisite solidity and mass; and in the event of a direct hit its explosive potential is spectacularly satisfying.

Yours faithfully, John Champion.

FRUIT

THE TREE OF KNOWLEDGE

To whom the guileful Tempter thus reply'd.
Empress of this fair World, resplendent *Eve,*
Easie to mee it is to tell thee all
What thou commandst, and right thou shouldst be obeyd:
I was at first as other Beasts that graze
The trodden Herb, of abject thoughts and low,
As was my food, nor aught but food discern'd
Or Sex, and apprehended nothing High:
Till on a day roaving the field, I chanc'd
A goodly Tree farr distant to behold
Loaden with fruit of fairest colours mixt,
Ruddie and Gold: I nearer drew to gaze;
When from the boughs a savorie odour blown,
Grateful to appetite, more pleas'd my sense
Then smell of sweetest Fenel, or the Teats
Of Ewe or Goat dropping with Milk at Eevn,
Unsuckt of Lamb or Kid, that tend thir play.
To satisfie the sharp desire I had
Of tasting those fair Apples, I resolv'd
Not to deferr; hunger and thirst at once,
Powerful perswaders, quickn'd at the scent
Of that alluring fruit, urg'd me so keen.

About the mossie Trunk I wound me soon,
For high from ground the branches would require
Thy utmost reach or *Adams*: Round the Tree
All other Beasts that saw, with like desire
Longing and envying stood, but could not reach.
Amid the Tree now got, where plenty hung
Tempting so nigh, to eat and pluck my fill
I spar'd not, for such pleasure till that hour
At Feed or Fountain never had I found.
Sated at length, ere long I might perceave
Strange alteration in me, to degree
Of Reason in my inward Powers, and Speech
Wanted not long, though to this shape retain'd.
Thenceforth to Speculation high or deep
I turned my thoughts, and with capacious mind
Considerd all things visible in Heav'n,
Or Earth, or Middle, all things fair and good.

John Milton, *Paradise Lost*, 1667, Book IX

THE GARDENER'S ALMANAC

[September] *Fruits* in *Prime*, or yet lasting.

APPLES

The *Belle-bonne*, the *William*, Summer *Pear-Main*, *Lording-Apple*, *Pear-apple*, *Quince-apple*, *Red-greening ribb'd*, Bloody Pepin, Harvey, Violet-apple, &c.

PEARS

Hamden's Bergamot (first ripe), Summer *Bon-Chrestien*, *Norwich*, *Black Worcester* (baking), *Greenfield*, *Orange*, *Bergamot*, the *Queen* Hedge-pear, *Lewis-pear* (to dry excellent), *Frith-pear*, *Arundel-pear* (also to bake), *Brunswick-pear*, Butter pear, Winter *Poppering*, *Bing's-pear*, *Bishop's pear* (baking), *Diego*, *Emperour's-pear*, *Cluster-pear*, *Messire Jean*, *Rowling-pear*, *Balsam-pear*, *Bezy d'Hery*, Pear Evelyn, &c.

PEACHES, &C.

Violet Peach, *Admirable*, *Purple* Peach, *Malacoton*, and some others, if the year prove backwards.

Almonds, &c.
Quinces.
Figs, perfectly ripe.
Little *Blue Grape*, *Muscadine-Grape*, *Frontiniac*, *Parsly*, great *Blue Grape*, the *Verjuice-grape* excellent for Sauce, &c.
Barberries, &c.
Melons, as yet.

John Evelyn, *Kalendarium Hortense; or, the Gard'ner's Almanac*, 1699

FRUIT IN THE ANCIENT WORLD

It would be almost impossible to enumerate all the articles, either of the animal or the vegetable reign, which were successively imported into Europe, from Asia and Egypt; but it will not be unworthy of the dignity, and much less of the utility, of an historical work, slightly to touch on a few of the principal heads. 1. Almost all the flowers, the herbs, and the fruits, that grow in our European gardens, are of foreign extraction, which, in many cases, is betrayed even by their names: the apple was a native of Italy, and when the Romans had tasted the richer flavour of the apricot, the peach, the pomegranate, the citron, and the orange, they contented themselves with applying to all these new fruits the common denomination of apple, discriminating them from each other by the additional epithet of their country. 2. In the time of Homer, the vine grew wild in the island of Sicily, and most probably in the adjacent continent; but it was not improved by the skill, nor did it afford a liquor grateful to the taste, of the savage inhabitants. A thousand years afterwards, Italy could boast that, that of the fourscore most generous and celebrated wines, more than two-thirds were produced from her soil. The blessing was soon communicated to the Narbonnese province of Gaul; but so intense was the cold to the north of the Cevennes, that, in the time of Strabo, it was thought impossible to ripen the grapes in those parts of Gaul. This difficulty, however, was gradually vanquished; and there is some reason to believe, that the vineyards of Burgundy are as old as the age of the Antonines [AD 98–180]. The olive, in the western world, followed the progress of peace, of which it was considered a symbol. Two centuries after the foundation of Rome, both Italy and Africa were strangers to the useful plant; it was naturalised in those countries; and at length carried into the heart of Spain and Gaul. The timid errors of the ancients, that it required a certain degree of heat, and could only flourish in the neighbourhood of the sea, were insensibly exploded by industry and experience.

Edward Gibbon, *Decline and Fall of the Roman Empire*, 1776–88, Volume I

Where the remote *Bermudas* ride
In th'Oceans bosome unespy'd,
From a small Boat, that row'd along,
The listning Winds receiv'd this Song.
What should we do but sing his Praise
That led us through the watry Maze,
Unto an Isle so long unknown,
And yet far kinder than our own?
Where he the huge Sea-Monsters wracks,
That lift the Deep upon their Backs.
He lands us on a grassy Stage;
Safe from the Storms, and Prelat's rage.
He gave us this eternal Spring,
Which here enamells every thing;
And sends the Fowls to us in care,
On daily Visits through the Air.
He hangs in Shades the Orange bright,
Like golden Lamps in a green Night,
And does in the Pomgranates close,
Jewels more rich than *Ormus* shows.
He makes the Figs our mouth to meet;
And throws the Melons at our feet.
But Apples plants of such a price,
No Tree could ever bear them twice.

Andrew Marvell, 'Bermudas', *c.*1653

Apples: pineapples, propagated annually by suckering.

❧ *Richard Ligon compiled his account of Barbados with a painter's eye for form and colour. Pineapples were virtually unknown in England at the time of the Protectorate, when Ligon wrote his* History *in prison, and remained scarce, imported luxuries from the Restoration until the early to*

mid-eighteenth century, when a fashion began in England among those who could afford to do so for constructing 'pineries' of dung and tan-bark roofed over with glass.

Now to close up all that can be said of fruit [in Barbados], I must name the Pine, for in that single name, all that is excellent in a superlative degree, for beauty and taste, is summarily included; and if it were here to speak for it selfe, it would save me much labour, and do it selfe much right. 'Tis true, that it takes up double the time that the Plantine does, in bringing forth the fruit; for 'tis a full year before it be ripe; but when it comes to be eaten, nothing of rare taste can be thought on that is not there; nor is it imaginable, that so full a Harmony of tastes can be raised, out of so many parts, and all distinguishable. . . . There are two sorts of Pines, the King and Queen Pine: the Queen is farre more delicate, and has her colours of all greens, with their shadowes intermixt, with faint Carnations, but most of all frost upon green, and Sea greens. The King Pine, has for the most part, all sorts of yellows, with their shadows intermixt with grass greens, and is commonly the larger Pine. I have seen some of them fourteen inches long, and sixe inches in the diametre; they never grow to be above four foot high, but the most of them having heavy bodies, and slender stalks, leane down and rest upon the ground. . . . When we gather them, we leave some of the stalk to take hold by; and when we come to eat them, we first cut off the crown, and send that out to be planted; and then with a knife, pare off the rinde, which is so beautifull, as it grieves us to rob the fruit of such an ornament; nor do we do it, but to enjoy the pretious substance it contains; like a Thiefe, that breaks a beautifull Cabinet, which he would forbear to do, but for the treasure he expects to finde within. The rinde being taken off, we lay the fruit in a dish, and cut it in slices, halfe an inch thick; and as the knife goes in, there issues out of the pores of the fruit, a liquor, cleer as Rock-water, neer about six spoonfulls, which is eaten with a spoon; and as you taste it, you finde it in a high degree delicious, but so milde, as you can distinguish no taste at all; but when you bite a piece of the fruit, it is so violently sharp, as you would think it would fetch all the skin off your mouth; but, before your tongue have made a second triall upon your palat, you shall perceive such a sweetnesse to follow, as perfectly to cure that vigorous sharpnesse; and between these two extreams, of sharp and sweet, lies the relish and flaver of all fruits that are excellent; and those tastes will change and flow so fast upon your palat, as your fancy can hardly keep way with them, to distinguish the one from the other: and this at least to a tenth examination, for so long the Eccho will last. This fruit within, is neer of the colour of an Abricot not full ripe, and eates crisp and short as that does; but it is full of pores, and those of such formes and colours, as 'tis a very beautifull sight to look on, and invites the appetite beyond measure. Of this fruit you may eat plentifully, without any danger of surfeting. I have had many thoughts, about how this fruit might be brought into *England*, but cannot satisfie myself in any; preserv'd it cannot be, whole; for, the rinde is so firm and tough, as no sugar can enter in; and if you divide it in pieces, (the fruit being full of pores) all the pure taste will boyle out. 'Tis true, that the *Dutch* preserve them at *Pernambock*, and send them home; but they are such as are young, and their rinde soft and tender: But those never came to their full taste, nor can we know by the taste of them, what the others are. From the *Bermudoes*, some have been brought hither in their full ripenesse and perfection, where there has been a quick passage, and the fruites taken in the nick of time; but that happens very seldome. But, that they should be brought from the *Barbadoes*, is impossible, by reason of severall Climates between. We brought in the ship seventeen of severall growths, but all rotten, before we came halfe the way.

Ligon, *History of the Island of Barbados*

❧ *John Evelyn referred, in his diary for 1661, to seeing King Charles II eating a Queen pineapple from Barbados. The first of these (he added) had been sent to Cromwell 'four years since', perhaps as a result of the appearance of Ligon's* History. *Here he tastes a King pine at the royal table.*

19th [August 1668].

I saw the magnificent entry of the French Ambassador Colbert, received in the Banqueting House. I had never seen a richer coach than that which he came in to Whitehall. Standing by his Majesty at dinner in the presence, there was of that rare fruit called the King-pine, growing in Barbadoes and the West Indies; the first of them I had ever seen. His Majesty having cut it up, was pleased to give me a piece off his own plate to taste of; but, in my opinion, it falls short of those ravishing varieties of deliciousness described in Captain

Ligon's History, and others; but possibly it might be, or certainly was, much impaired in coming so far; it has yet a grateful acidity, but tastes more like the quince and melon than of any other fruit he mentions.

The Diary of John Evelyn, edited by William Bray, 1907, Volume II

❧ *By the middle of the eighteenth century, thanks largely to the efforts of the Dutch-born merchant Sir Matthew Decker (1679–1749) and his gardener at Richmond, Henry Telende, pineapples were being raised by skilled gardeners in the kitchen gardens of the English upper classes. There was as yet no profit to be made in importing them; and William Stukeley, the diarist, tasted one for the first time in his fifties, at a great Norfolk country house.*

2 Sep[tember 1741].

I visited Sir R[obert] Walpole at Houghton. we eat a pine apple, a most delicious mixture of a pomegranate, a melon, a quince and most other fine fruits.

William Stukeley, MS Diary for 1741

❧ *The poet, describing an English summer day, imagines himself in the Tropics.*

Bear me, Pomona! to thy citron groves;
To where the lemon and the piercing lime,
With the deep orange glowing through the green,
Their lighter glories blend. Lay me reclined
Beneath the spreading tamarind, that shakes,
Fanned by the breeze, its fever-cooling fruit.
Deep in the night the massy locust sheds
Quench my hot limbs; or lead me through the maze,
Embowering endless, of the Indian fig;
Or, thrown at gayer ease on some fair brow,
Let me behold, by breezy murmurs cooled,
Broad o'er my head the verdant cedar wave,
And high palmettos lift their graceful shade.
Oh, stretched amid these orchards of the sun,

Give me to drain the cocoa's milky bowl,
And from the palm to draw its freshening wine!
More bounteous far than all the frantic juice
Which Bacchus pours. Nor, on its slender twigs
Low-bending, be the full pomegranate scorned;
Nor, creeping through the woods, the gelid race
Of berries. Oft in humble station dwells
Unboastful worth, above fastidious pomp.
Witness, thou best Anana, thou the pride
Of vegetable life, beyond whate'er
The poets imaged in the golden age:
Quick let me strip thee of thy tufty coat,
Spread thy ambrosial stores, and feed with Jove!

James Thomson, 'The Seasons: Summer', 1730

'the massy locust sheds': i.e. the massed fruit shed by the locust (probably the carob tree, *Ceratonia siliqua*, a leguminous tree with pods containing sweet, pulpy divisions between the seeds, used to make a syrup and, more recently, a chocolate-substitute). The use of 'locust-tree' for another leguminous plant, *Robinia pseudacacia*, seems to have come after this; *anana*: pineapple.

The Duchess of Malfi, a widow at the court of her brother Ferdinand, Duke of Calabria, has secretly married Antonio, her steward, in defiance of her brother's prohibition against her marrying again. Bosola, a court spy, suspects her of being pregnant.

BOSOLA. I observe our Duchess
Is sick a-days, she pukes, her stomach seethes,
The fins of her eyelids look most teeming blue,
She wanes i'th'cheek, and waxes fat i'th'flank;
And, contrary to our Italian fashion,
Wears a loose-bodied gown: there's somewhat in't.
I have a trick, may chance discover it,
A pretty one; I have bought some apricocks,
The first our spring yields

* * * * *

BOSOLA. I have a present for your Grace.
DUCHESS. For me sir?

BOSOLA. Apricocks, Madam.
DUCHESS. O sir, where are they?
I have heard of none to-year.
BOSOLA [*aside*]. Good, her colour rises.
DUCHESS. Indeed I thank you: they are wondrous fair ones.
What an unskilful fellow is our gardener!
We shall have none this month.
BOSOLA. Will not your Grace pare them?
DUCHESS. No, they taste of musk, methinks; indeed they do.
BOSOLA. I know not: yet I wish your Grace had par'd 'em.
DUCHESS. Why?
BOSOLA. I forgot to tell you the knave gard'ner,
Only to raise his profit by them the sooner,
Did ripen them in horse-dung.
DUCHESS. O you jest.
[*to Antonio*] You shall judge: pray taste one.
ANTONIO. Indeed Madam,
I do not love the fruit.
DUCHESS. Sir, you are loth
To rob us of our dainties: 'tis a delicate fruit,
They say they are restorative?
BOSOLA. 'Tis a pretty art
This grafting.
DUCHESS. 'Tis so: a bett'ring of nature.
BOSOLA. To make a pippin grow upon a crab,
A damson on a black-thorn: [*aside*] How greedily she eats them!
A whirlwind strike off these bawd farthingales,
For, but for that, and the loose-bodied gown,
I should have discover'd apparently
The young springal cutting a caper in her belly.
DUCHESS. I thank you Bosola: they were right good ones,
If they do not make me sick.
ANTONIO. How now Madam?
DUCHESS. This green fruit and my stomach are not friends.
How they swell me!
BOSOLA [*aside*]. Nay, you are too much swell'd already.
DUCHESS. O, I am in an extreme cold sweat!
BOSOLA. I am very sorry.
[*Exit*
DUCHESS. Lights to my chamber! O, good Antonio,

I fear I am undone.

[*Exit Duchess*

DELIO. Lights, there, lights!
ANTONIO. O my most trusty Delio, we are lost:
I fear she's fall'n in labour: and there's left
No time for her remove.

John Webster, *The Duchess of Malfi*, 1623, II. i

❧ *A conversation at dinner at Mansfield Park between the grasping, resentful Mrs Norris (widow of the former rector of Mansfield, and sister-in-law of Sir Thomas Bertram of Mansfield Park) and the incumbent of the Parsonage, Dr Grant and his wife. Moor Park apricots had been highly esteemed since they were first raised* c.*1760 at Moor Park in Hertfordshire, an early eighteenth century mansion (now on the outskirts of north-west London) with grounds laid out by Capability Brown. Apricots of any kind are notoriously difficult to ripen in the English climate, needing light, fertile soil, much sun, and training against a south-facing wall.*

[*Mrs Norris*:] 'If dear Sir Thomas were here, he could tell you what improvements we made; and a great deal more would have been done, but for poor Mr Norris's state of health. . . . We were always doing something as it was. It was only a spring twelvemonth before Mr Norris's death, that we put in the apricot against the stable wall, which is now grown such a noble tree, and getting to such perfection, sir,' addressing herself then to Dr Grant.

'The tree thrives well, beyond a doubt, madam,' replied Dr Grant. 'The soil is good; and I never pass it without regretting that the fruit should be so little worth the trouble of gathering.'

'Sir, it is a moor park, we bought it as a moor park, and it cost us—that is, it was a present from Sir Thomas, but I saw the bill, and I know it cost seven shillings, and was charged as a moor park.'

'You were imposed on, madam,' replied Dr Grant; 'these potatoes have as much the flavour of a moor park apricot, as the fruit from that tree. It is an insipid fruit at the best; but a good apricot is eatable, which none from my garden are.'

'The truth is, ma'am,' said Mrs Grant, pretending to whisper across the table to Mrs Norris, 'that Dr Grant hardly knows what the natural taste of our apricot is; he is scarcely ever indulged with one, for it is so valuable a fruit, with a little assistance, and ours is such a remarkably large, fair sort, that what with early tarts and preserves, my cook contrives to get them all.'

Mrs Norris, who had begun to redden, was appeased, and, for a little whiie, other subjects took place of the improvements of Sotherton. Dr Grant and Mrs Norris were seldom good friends; their acquaintance had begun in dilapidations, and their habits were totally dissimilar.

Jane Austen, *Mansfield Park*, 1814

❧ *Reginald Heber was Bishop of Calcutta from 1822 until his premature death at Trichinopoly at the age of 43 in 1826.*

June 10 [1824].

Of the fruits which this season offers, the finest are leeches [lychees] and mangoes: the first is really very fine, being a sort of plum, with the flavour of a Frontigniac grape. The second is a noble fruit in point of size, being as large as a man's two fists; its flavour is not unlike an apricot, more or less smeared in turpentine. It would not, I think, be popular in England, but in India it may pass for very good, particularly when the terebinthian flavour does not predominate. When not quite ripe it makes an excellent tart.

Reginald Heber, *Narrative of a Journey through the Upper Provinces of India from Calcutta to Bombay, 1824–1825, by the late Right Rev. Reginald Heber, DD*, 1849, Volume I

Very excellent Indian mangoes . . . may be purchased at the Italian warehouses, and to many tastes will be more acceptable than any English pickle.

Eliza Acton, *Modern Cookery . . . for Private Families*, 1845

❧ *The narrator is staying at Cranford with Miss Matilda Jenkyns, a middle-aged spinster of set habits and economical ways, whose sister and former companion has recently died.*

Many a domestic rule and regulation had been the subject of plaintive whispered murmurs to me during Miss Jenkyns's life; but now that she was gone, I do not think that even I, who was a favourite, durst have suggested an alteration. To give an instance: we constantly adhered to the forms which were observed, at meal times, in 'my father, the rector's house.' Accordingly, we had always wine and dessert; but the decanters were only filled when there was a party, and what remained was seldom touched, though we had two wine glasses apiece every day after dinner, until the next festive occasion arrived, when the state of the remainder wine was examined into in a family council. The dregs were often given to the poor; but occasionally, when a good deal had been left at the last party (five months ago, it might be), it was added to some of a fresh bottle, brought up from the cellar. I fancy poor Captain Brown did not much like the wine, for I noticed he never finished his first glass, and most military men take several. Then, as to our dessert, Miss Jenkyns used to gather currants and gooseberries for it herself, which I sometimes thought would have tasted better fresh from the trees; but then, as Miss Jenkyns observed, there would have been nothing for dessert in summer-time. As it was, we felt very genteel with our two glasses apiece, and a dish of gooseberries at the top, of currants and biscuits at the sides, and two decanters at the bottom. When oranges came in, a curious proceeding was gone through. Miss Jenkyns did not like to cut the fruit; for, as she observed, the juice all ran out nobody knew where; sucking (only I think she used some more recondite word) was in fact the only way of enjoying oranges; but then there was the unpleasant association with a ceremony frequently gone through by little babies; and so, after dessert, in orange season, Miss Jenkyns and Miss Matty used to rise up, possess themselves each of an orange in silence, and withdraw to the privacy of their own rooms to indulge in sucking oranges.

I had once or twice tried, on such occasions, to prevail on Miss Matty to stay, and had succeeded in her sister's lifetime. I held up a screen, and did not look, and, as she said, she tried not to make the noise very offensive; but now that she was left alone, she seemed quite horrified when I begged her to remain with me in the warm dining-parlour, and enjoy her orange as she liked best. And so it was in everything. Miss Jenkyns's rules were made more stringent than ever, because the framer of them was gone where there could be no appeal.

Gaskell, *Cranford*

[*September 1920*.]

It grew hot. Everywhere the light quivered green-gold. The white soft road unrolled, with plane-trees casting a trembling shade. There were piles of pumpkins and gourds: outside the house the tomatoes were spread in the sun. Blue flowers and red flowers and tufts of deep purple flared in the road-side hedges. A young boy, carrying a branch, stumbled across a yellow field, followed by a brown high-stepping little goat. We bought figs for breakfast, immense thin-skinned ones. They broke in one's fingers and tasted of wine and honey. Why is the northern fig such a chaste fair-haired virgin, such a *soprano*? The melting contraltos sing through the ages.

The Journal of Katherine Mansfield, edited by John Middleton Murry, 1927

ANDALUSIA, *c*.1920

Not far from the kitchen was the store-room, and this was an important place. Every autumn we hung from its ceiling two or three hundred pounds of thick-skinned grapes, which kept fresh till April, though getting sweeter and more shrunken all the time. There would also be several hundred persimmons from two trees that grew in the garden: picked after the first frost, they ripened slowly and were eaten with a spoon when they went soft and squashy. Quinces were also kept there as well as oranges and lemons and apples, and pots of marmalade and cherry jam and green fig jam, which I had taught Maria [the maid] how to make. And there were always one or two of the famous Alpujarra hams, which kept through the summer if they were rubbed every week or two with salt. Then came the vegetables—dried tomatoes and egg plants, cut into slices and laid out on shelves, pimentos hung from the ceiling, jars of home-cured olives and of dried apricots and figs, chick peas and lentils and other sorts of beans in *espuertas* or large frails. And upstairs in the *azotea* were onions, for *olla sin cebolla, es baile sin tamborín*, 'a stew without onions is like a dance without a tabor'. None of these things could be obtained in the shop, but must be stored through the year or bought at a higher price from a neighbour.

Brenan, *South From Granada*

FOOD IN SEASON

❧ Kolokynte, *the Greek word translated here as 'cucumber', usually means pumpkin, squash, or gourd. (Thus Colocynth, the bitter apple or bitter cucumber, is a plant of the gourd family, once used as a purgative medicine.) The translation 'cucumber' implies a summer fruit rather than one which might normally be preserved in the autumn for winter.*

Once, in the season of winter, cucumbers were served to us, and we all wondered, thinking they were fresh, and we recalled what the witty Aristophanes said in *The Seasons* when he praised the fair city of Athens in these lines: '*A* [?the goddess Athena]. You will see, in midwinter, cucumbers, grapes, fruit, wreaths of violets, roses, and lilies—in dust-clouds utterly blinding. The same tradesman sells thrushes, pears, honeycomb, olives, beestings, haggis, celandine, cicadas, embryo-meat. You can see baskets of figs and of myrtle-berries together, covered with snow, and what is more, they sow cucumbers at the same time with turnips, so that nobody knows any longer what time of the year it is. . . . A very great boon, if one may get throughout the year whatever he wants. *B*. A very great evil, rather! For if they couldn't get these things, they wouldn't be so eager for them and spend so much money on them. As for me, I would supply these things for a brief season and then take them away. *A*. I too do that for other cities, but not for Athens. The Athenians enjoy all these things because they revere the gods. *B*. Much good, then, does it do them for revering you, as you say! *A*. Why, how's that? *B*. You have made their city Egypt instead of Athens.' We wondered, as I was saying, that we should be eating cucumbers in the month of January; for they were fresh and had all their native savour. But it so happened that they belonged to the class of things which are compounded by cooks who know how to play these kind of tricks.

Athenaeus, *The Deipnosophists*, with an English translation by Charles Burton Gulick, 1927–41

FEBRUARY TWENTY-TWO.

That was Shrove Tuesday; fritters, pancakes, cock-fighting, and ball-games. In many places there were processions and mummingplays, morris-dancers, musicians, giants, and the town dragon; with the populace dressed up as monks, fools, devils, animals, or kings and queens, as the fancy took it. The frolics have gradually dwindled away until only the pancakes remain; though before the war the pancake bell was still rung in a few parishes, and ball or bottle games were played in others.

It seems curious that the pancake has kept its popularity, while the apple fritter has vanished from Shrove Tuesday, except for one or two districts in the north of England, when a well-made apple fritter is such a delicious sweet. Mrs Glasse, in *The Art of Cookery*, gives a receipt for apple fritters that it is possible to make at the present time:

HASTY FRITTERS—Take a stewpan, put in some butter, and let it be hot; in the meantime, take a pint of all-ale, not bitter, and stir in some flour by degrees in a little of the ale; put in a few currants, or chopped apples, beat them up quick, and drop a large spoonful at a time all over the pan. Take care they don't stick together, and turn them over with an egg-slice, and when they are of a fine brown, lay them in a dish, and throw some sugar over them. Garnish with an orange cut in quarters.

There is an engaging airiness about these directions; 'a fine brown' and 'throw some sugar over them'—it does my heart good to think of throwing sugar about. Another version comes from Massachusetts a hundred years later, from Boston, to be exact:

> The home of the bean and the cod
> Where the Lowells talk to the Cabots
> And the Cabots talk only to God.

BOSTON APPLE FRITTERS—Two cups flour; one cup stewed apples (mushy, or rubbed through a moulinette or colander); half-cupful milk; one egg. Beat all well together. Drop the batter from a spoon into boiling lard, and fry a light brown. Dredge with sugar.

Pancakes, and fritters, and their foreign relations the crêpes (especially Suzette) and cannelonis; single, rolled, piled, savoury, sweet, fruit, wine, liqueur; a succulent rosary to be rolled over the tongue of memory. 'I count thee, every pearl apart.' Peach fritters, apricot, orange, pineapple, and what about rhubarb fritters? Another almost forgotten Victorian sweet, and yet both pleasant and practical when you wish to eke out young and still expensive rhubarb.

RHUBARB FRITTERS—Cut the rhubarb into equal lengths. Dip each piece into a light batter, lift it out with a fork, and plunge it into deep hot fat, and fry. They take about five to six minutes to cook, and the covering should be crisp, dry and a light brown. Pile on a dish and strew with sugar, or serve with a little warm golden syrup. If the rhubarb is ageing, peel it.

A note from Charles Elmé Francatelli, pupil of the celebrated Carême, late *maître d'hôtel* and chief cook to Queen Victoria:

Most novel kinds of frying batters, never before thought of, may be easily prepared by . . . using, instead of water, any kind of white wine, or any sort of liqueur; such as maraschino, kummel, curaçao, brandy, etc.; only, in order to prevent extravagance, bear in mind that one glassful of any kind of liqueur is sufficient, making up the deficiency with tepid water.

It is interesting to find that chefs like Francatelli use water in place of milk in their coating batters; it makes a beautiful, crisp, light batter even with dried eggs, and yet you will not find one ordinary cookery book in a hundred that gives this practical suggestion for wartime use.

Green, *Salmagundi*

Mrs Glasse: Hannah Glasse, *The Art of Cookery Made Plain and Easy* (1747); *Francatelli*: *The Cook's Guide, and Housekeeper's & Butler's Assistant: A Practical Treatise on English and Foreign Cookery in all its Branches* (1861).

The poet John Keats (1795–1821) left London in late June 1819 for the Isle of Wight, then moved six weeks later to Winchester, where he remained, reading, writing, and walking, until October. A year later, far advanced in tuberculosis, he sailed from England to die in Italy.

[*To his sister, Fanny Keats, Winchester, 28 August 1819.*]

The delightful Weather we have had for two months is the highest gratification I could receive—no chill'd red noses—no shivering—but fair atmosphere to think in—a clean towel mark'd with the mangle and a basin of clear Water to drench one's face with ten times a day: no need of much exercise—a Mile a day being quite sufficient. . . . Give me Books, fruit, french wine and fine whether [*sic*] and a little music out of doors, played by somebody I do not know . . . and I can pass a summer very quietly without caring very much about Fat Louis, fat Regent or the Duke of Wellington. . . . I should like now to promenade round you[r] Gardens—apple tasting—pear tasting—plumb judging—apricot nibbling—peach scrunching—Nectarine-sucking and Melon carving. I have also a great feeling for antiquated cherries full of sugar cracks—and a white currant tree kept for company. I admire lolling on a lawn by a water-lilied pond to eat white currants and see gold fish: and go to the Fair in the Evening if I'm good. There is not hope for that—one is sure to get into some mess before evening.

The Letters of John Keats, edited by Maurice Buxton Forman, 1952

Fat Louis: Louis XVIII of France (1755–1824).

AUGUST ONE.

Lammas was another of the four great pagan festivals and witches' sabbats; the Gule of August. In Hertfordshire, Bedfordshire, and Buckinghamshire, the day was celebrated by the countryfolk with a meal of cherry pasties made with the wild black cherries, and this custom has survived for hundreds of years at Princes Risborough, where it was kept up until this war. We, in a humble way, have revived it here, for when we found last year what delicious puddings these cherries made, we recommended them to various friends, with the result that there has been quite an orgy of both puddings and pies. To-day I noticed that Mrs Quant had wild cherries for sale among her vegetables, though a piece of careworn brown paper bore the inscription COOKING CHERRYS in wavering white capitals.

The name Lammas is said to be derived from *hláfmaesse* or loaf-mass, the mass at which the first loaves from the newly harvested grain were blessed. But again, this is one of the pagan feasts of which the origins are lost in time, and veiled by the superimposed ceremonies of the Christians. Probably the frumenty or furmenty pot which welcomed the harvesters also had some esoteric meaning which has long been forgotten, for the frumenty mixture of creed wheat, currants, eggs, spice and milk was a ritual dish on other special days such as Christmas, Easter, Mothering Sunday, and Ash Wednesday. It would be interesting to find out if there was any connection between the eating of *hoboob* by the Mohammedans on the tenth day of the first month of their New Year and the eating of frumenty in England; for *hoboob* according to Lane in his *Modern Egyptians* consists of wheat, raisins, nuts, spice, and honey.

* * * * *

There is a picture by Pieter Brueghel the Elder called 'The Peasant's Bridal' of which I am particularly fond. It shows a feast in a barn round about harvest-time. A crowd of peasants in their best clothes are busy eating, wine and beer are flowing, while the cook and his assistant are busy bringing in more food arranged on a stretcher improvised from a barn door supported on two rough poles. Musicians are playing energetically, though the nearest one, who has not had time to shave, is paying less attention to his medieval bagpipe than to the food on the stretcher, which he is eyeing with some anxiety as if doubtful of its holding out until his job is done and his turn is come. A typical Brueghel child, almost 'bonneted' by a flat scarlet hat ornamented with a long peacock's feather is seated on a loaf in the foreground, very messily engaged with a tilted plate of provender.

* * * * *

My belief is that there is no bridegroom, but that this painting represents the feast of the corn maiden, which was celebrated on the Continent with even more elaborate rites than it was in this country. The 'bride' . . . is really the corn maiden, swelling with overweening speechless conceit at having been chosen for this important role. It is obvious that she is unmarried, as her hair flows over her shoulders from under a small circlet, whereas the other women wear the white cap of the matrons of the period.

* * * * *

All the plates, with two exceptions, are filled with the same flat golden mass which looks remarkably like frumenty, especially as all the guests are using spoons, with the exception of the badly brought up child in the foreground who is licking his fingers. The other two plates contain a white substance which might be milk, cream, or curd cheese; apart from this, the only other food that is visible is bread. Another significant touch, I think, is that the curtain behind the maiden is hung from pitchfork heads instead of ordinary hooks. There is possibly a meaning in the shade of the curtain, which may represent the hoped-for green of the fertile fields after the next wheat-sowing.

Green, *Salmagundi*

AUTUMN PASTORAL

Ye swains, now hasten to the hazel-bank,
Where down yon dale the wildly-winding brook
Falls hoarse from steep to steep. In close array,

Fit for the thickets and the tangling shrub,
Ye virgins, come. For you their latest song
The woodlands raise; the clustering nuts for you
The lover finds amid the secret shade;
And, where they burnish on the topmost bough,
With active vigour crushes down the tree;
Or shakes them ripe from the resigning husk,
A glossy shower, and of an ardent brown
As are the ringlets of Melinda's hair—

* * * * *

Hence from the busy joy-resounding fields,
In cheerful error let us tread the maze
Of Autumn unconfined; and taste, revived,
The breath of orchard big with bending fruit.
Obedient to the breeze and beating ray,
From the deep-loaded bough a mellow shower
Incessant melts away. The juicy pear
Lies in a soft profusion scattered round.
A various sweetness swells the gentle race,
By Nature's all-refining hand prepared,
Of tempered sun, and water, earth, and air,
In ever-changing composition mixed.
Such, falling frequent through the chiller night,
The fragrant stores, the wide-projected heaps
Of apples, which the lusty-handed year
Innumerous o'er the blushing orchard shakes.

* * * * *

And, as I steal along the sunny wall,
Where Autumn basks, with fruit empurpled deep,
My pleasing theme continual prompts my thought—
Presents the downy peach, the shining plum
With a fine bluish mist of animals
Clouded, the ruddy nectarine, and dark
Beneath his ample leaf the luscious fig.

Thomson, 'The Seasons: Autumn'

[*Tonbridge Wells, Kent, 30 August 1823.*]

This is a great *nut* year. I saw them hanging very thick on the way-side during a great part of this day's ride; and they put me in mind of the old saying, 'A great *nut* year is a great *bastard year*.' That is to say, the *succeeding year* is a great year for bastards. I once asked a farmer, who had often been *overseer* of the poor, whether he really thought, that there was any ground for this old saying, or whether he thought it was mere banter? He said, that he was sure that there were *good grounds for it*; and he even cited instances in proof, and mentioned one particular year, when there were four times as many bastards as had ever been born in a year in the parish before; an effect which he ascribed solely to the crop of nuts of the year before. Now, if this be the case, ought not PARSON MALTHUS, LAWYER SCARLETT, and the rest of that tribe, to turn their attention to the nut-trees? The *Vice Society*, too, with that holy man Wilberforce at its head, ought to look out sharp after these mischievous nut-trees. A law to cause them all to be grubbed up, and thrown into the fire, would, certainly, be far less unreasonable than many things which we have seen and heard of.

William Cobbett, *Rural Rides*, 1830

Malthus: The Revd Thomas Robert Malthus (1766–1834), clergyman and political economist, famous for his *Essay on Population* (1798), in which he argued the necessity of periodic checks on population growth (e.g. through war, famine, or disease) to prevent the demand for subsistence outrunning the supply; *Scarlett*: Sir James Scarlett, later 1st Baron Abinger (1769–1844), M.P., member of a committee to enquire into capital punishment in cases of felony; *Wilberforce*: William Wilberforce (1759–1833), philanthropist and founder of the Proclamation Society for suppressing vice.

Laura Ingalls Wilder's The Little House in the Big Woods *is an autobiographical children's classic, describing the life of a family of settlers in the late nineteenth century in American Indian country in Wisconsin. The trilogy continues with* The House at Plum Creek *and* The Little House on the Prairie.

Along the rail fence the sumac held up its dark red cones of berries above bright flame-coloured leaves. Acorns were falling from the oaks, and Laura and Mary made little acorn cups and saucers for the playhouses. Walnuts and hickory nuts were dropping to the ground in the Big Woods, and the squirrels were scampering busily everywhere, gathering their winter's store of nuts and hiding them away in hollow trees.

Laura and Mary went with Ma to gather walnuts and hickory nuts and hazelnuts. They spread them in the sun to dry, then they beat off the dried outer hulls and stored the nuts in the attic for winter.

It was fun to gather the large round walnuts and the smaller hickory nuts, and the little hazelnuts that grew in bunches on the bushes. The soft outer hulls of the walnuts were full of a brown juice that stained their hands, but the hazelnut hulls smelled good and tasted good, too, when Laura used her teeth to pry a nut loose.

Everyone was busy now, for all the garden vegetables must be stored away. Laura and Mary helped, picking up the dusty potatoes after Pa had dug them from the ground, and pulling the long yellow carrots and the round, purple-topped turnips, and they helped Ma cook the pumpkin for pumpkin pies.

With the butcher knife Ma cut the big, orange-coloured pumpkins into halves. She cleaned the seeds out of the centre and cut the pumpkin into long slices, from which she pared the rind. Laura helped her cut the slices into cubes.

Ma put the cubes into the big iron pot on the stove, poured in some water, and then watched while the pumpkin slowly boiled down, all day long. All the water and the juice must be boiled away, and the pumpkin must never burn.

The pumpkin was a thick, dark, good-smelling mass in the kettle. It did not boil like water, but bubbles came up in it and suddenly exploded, leaving holes that closed quickly. Every time a bubble exploded, the rich, hot pumpkin smell came out. Laura stood on a chair and watched the pumpkin for Ma, and stirred it with a wooden paddle. She held the paddle in both hands and stirred carefully, because if the pumpkin burned there wouldn't be any pumpkin pies.

For dinner they ate the stewed pumpkin with their bread. They made it into pretty shapes on their plates. It was a beautiful colour, and smoothed and moulded so prettily with their knives. Ma never allowed them to play with their food at table; they must always eat nicely everything that was set before them, leaving nothing on their plates. But she did let them make the rich, brown, stewed pumpkin into pretty shapes before they ate it.

At other times they had baked Hubbard squash for dinner. The rind was so hard that Ma had to take Pa's axe to cut the squash into pieces. When the pieces were baked in the oven, Laura loved to spread the soft insides with butter and then scoop the yellow flesh from the rind and eat it.

For supper, now, they often had hulled corn and milk. That was good, too. It was so good that Laura could hardly wait for the corn to be ready, after Ma started to hull it. It took two or three days to make hulled corn.

The first day, Ma cleaned and brushed all the ashes out of the cookstove. Then she burned some clean, bright hardwood, and saved its ashes. She put the hardwood ashes in a little cloth bag.

That night Pa brought in some ears of corn with large, plump kernels. He rubbed the ears—shelling off the small, chaffy kernels at their tips. Then he shelled the rest into a large pan, until the pan was full.

Early next day Ma put the shelled corn and the bag of ashes into the big iron kettle. She filled the kettle with water, and kept it boiling a long time. At last the kernels of corn began to swell, and they swelled and swelled until their skins split open and began to peel off.

When every skin was loose and peeling, Ma lugged the heavy kettle outdoors. She filled a clean washtub with cold water from the spring, and she dipped the corn out of the kettle into the tub.

Then she rolled the sleeves of her flowered calico dress above her elbows, and she knelt by the tub. With her hands she rubbed and scrubbed the corn until the hulls came off and floated on top of the water.

Often she poured the water off, and filled the tub again with buckets of water from the spring. She kept on rubbing and scrubbing the corn between her hands, and changing the water, until every hull came off and was washed away.

Ma looked so pretty, with her bare arms plump and white, her cheeks so red and her dark hair smooth and shining, while she scrubbed and rubbed the corn in the clear water.

She never splashed one drop of water on her pretty dress. When at last the corn was done, Ma put all the soft, white kernels in a big jar in the pantry. Then at last, they had hulled corn and milk for supper.

Sometimes they had hulled corn for breakfast, with maple syrup, and sometimes Ma fried the soft kernels in pork dripping. But Laura liked them best with milk.

Wilder, *The Little House in the Big Woods*, 1932

CHRISTMAS IN WARTIME

We had two most welcome gifts. Food, of course. One was a cockerel, the other a tin box containing twenty-nine lemons, sent by a soldier in the Middle East. How we called down blessings on his head as we discussed the rival merits of *lemon pie*, *lemon cheese*, *lemon marmalade*, gin and lemon, lemon juice in our salad dressing, and grated lemon-peel in the stuffing of the cockerel. Even with twenty-nine lemons we had to limit our aspirations, so we finally decided on a *lemon pie*, *lemon marmalade*, and lemon-peel in the stuffing. Then we would see. How lucky it was that the lemons came when we had our extra rations of margarine and sugar. We had to make some *lemon marmalade* because we are perennially short of marmalade. One pound does not spin out for breakfast for three people for a month, spread we never so thin, and our grocer refuses to allow us more. 'Two jams: one mar.' is his stern ruling from which he never departs.

* * * * *

Our Christmas dinner-table looked quite lovely covered with a heavy cream lace cloth, and decorated with a centre-piece of yellow and pink rosebuds mixed with sprays of jessamine in an outsize Victorian celery glass, which is useless for celery as it takes about a dozen heads to even make a showing in it, but which is admirable for flowers. The yellow of the jessamine matched the dinner-service in colour, and the coppery leaves of the roses were a darker shade of the wineglass stems. The all-important item, the food, was very simple. Some home-made cocktail biscuits with a glass of sherry; the cockerel, accompanied by mashed potatoes and own colewort; mince pies; and some Corton '26.

We had our misgivings about the cooking of the cockerel, because we could not spare any fat to baste it, and only two small rashers of bacon were available to cover its large acreage of breast. So we packed it in several layers of greased paper like an especially precious parcel, which indeed it was, and put it in a covered 'baker,' while breathing a special prayer to the patron saint of cooks to watch over it. St Winifred must have obligingly heard us, for to our relief it came out a beautiful brown, neither dry nor steamed, its stuffing delicately flavoured with our own dried tarragon, and a *soupçon* of grated lemon-peel. The colewort was delicious. I wonder it is not grown more, as it has the great merit of keeping its colour and flavour whether it is boiled or steamed, which is rare among cabbagy things.

Green, *Salmagundi*

HOME COOKING

❧ *Lady Mary Wortley Montagu (1689–1762) accompanied her husband, Edward Wortley Montagu, during his two years as Ambassador to Constantinople in 1716–18, and afterwards became a famously outspoken society figure. She is chiefly remembered for having introduced inoculation against smallpox into England (demonstrating its harmless effects on her own children), and for her volumes of posthumously published letters. She lived abroad, without her husband, between 1739 and his death in 1761, settling at Brescia in Northern Italy from 1746 to 1756 before moving to Venice.*

[*To her daughter, Lady Bute, Brescia, 27 November 1749 and 19 June 1751.*]

I have had this morning as much delight in a Walk in the Sun as ever I felt formerly in the crouded Mall [in London] even when I imagin'd I had my share of the admiration of the place, which was generally sour'd before I slept by the Informations of my female Freinds, who seldom fail'd to tell me it was observ'd I had shew'd an inch above my shoe heels, or some other criticism of equal weight, which was construe'd affectation, and utterly destroy'd all the Satisfaction my vanity had given me. I have now no other but in my little Huswifery, which is easily gratify'd in this Country, where (by the help of my receipt Book) I make a very shineing Figure amongst my Neighbours by the Introduction of Custards, Cheescakes and mince'd Pies, which were entirely unknown in these Parts, and are receiv'd with universal applause, and I have reason to beleive will preserve my Memory even to Future ages, particularly by the art of Butter makeing, in which I have so improv'd them that they now make as good as in any part of England.

* * * * *

[*The inhabitants of Brescia proposed in 1751 to erect a statue of Lady Mary in her honour. She intervened, however, just in time to stop the project.*]

This complement was certainly founded on reasons not unlike those that first fram'd Goddesses, I mean being usefull to them, in which I am second to Ceres. If it be true she taught the art of sowing Wheat, it is sure I have learn'd them to make Bread, in which they continu'd in the same Ignorance Misson complains of (as you may see in his Letter from Padua). I have introduc'd French rolls, custards, minc'd Pies, and Plumb pudding, which they are very fond of. 'Tis impossible to bring them to conform to Sillabub, which is so unnatural a mixture in their Eyes, they are even shock'd to see me eat it. But I expect immortality from the Science of Butter makeing, in which they are become so skillfull from my Instructions, I can assure you here is as good as in any part of Great Brittain. I am afraid I have bragg'd of this before, but when you do not answer any part of my Letters I suppose them lost, which exposes you to some repetitions.

The Complete Letters of Lady Mary Wortley Montagu, Volume II, 1721–51, edited by Robert Halsband, 1966

Misson: a late seventeenth-century writer, who complained that the people of the Veneto had no idea of how to make bread; although white and made with flour, it reminded him of earth; *sillabub*: a mixture of wine and cream, sweetened and beaten to a froth.

[*John Pintard to his daughter Eliza Davidson.*]
30 August 1819.

I am happy to inform you that we are at length likely to be domestically comfortable. Nancy the young girl who was with us from Princeton, was taken off, as usual, at an hours notice by her mother. . . . We were destitute of help for a week. Your Sister doing all the work, but we refrained from cooking & lived on rice & milk & chocolate until Saturday, when the weather being cool she roasted a sirloin elegantly. You must know she is an epicure and a good cook.

6 December 1819.

Your sister is a dear good girl, possessed of intrinsic merit as a housekeeper. This summer she made her first essay & has been peculiarly successful in preparing her confectionary. Thro' fear of failure, as she was determined to do all herself, her experiment was on a small scale. . . . She likewise has made, agreeably to our family receipts, Cherry & Raspberry Brandy Noyau & Persico, all to my taste exquisitely fine & superior to any imported, and this entirely herself, as she insisted on preparing compounding & infusing all the ingredients with her own hands. . . . She is equally successful with her pastry & is very fond of the kitchin department, & enjoys the peculiar felicity of not only seeing to a good dish, but relishing it when dressed. Mama however objects, and properly to her exposing herself to the consequences of superintending the kitchin. She carves a Turky, Goose, or duck with the dexterity of a Surgeon.

16 December 1826.

Today Sister prepares her mince meat. 'Shall auld acquaintance be forgot.' Keep up my beloved daughter these little anniversary memorials of the olden times, which serve to revive family customs & the memory of departed friends, and moreover prove that we had hospitable good livers before us. When every thing was cheap & plenty, & less glitter & more substance, good cheer was the universal order of the day, & all vied, not so much in the redundant variety as in the superior excellence of the dishes. Every female was instructed in the art of cooking preserves, & pastry, as well as the more ordinary duties of house keeping. . . . No whole hours, days, weeks & years, wasted in fingering a harpsichord. Perhaps there were not a dozen before 1774, in this city. Dinner hour was genteel & late at 2, tea visits at 4 & home just before candle light. . . . Your dear Sister is determined to be a notable housekeeper. This week she has put up a handsome shoat of 170 lbs. so that we shall have plenty of sausages, head cheese & roasting pieces to treat the younkers.

Letters from John Pintard to his Daughter

Noyau: a liqueur or cordial flavoured with almonds or fruit-kernels; *persico*: peach-kernel cordial.

In seventeenth- and eighteenth-century England, women who could afford to employ domestic servants often kept the daintier preparation of food to do themselves, as an art and source of pleasure, in their own private kitchen or still-room. Salads, fricassés and other delicate chicken dishes, cakes, biscuits, sweets, preserves, and desserts all feature in the manuscript cookery books which they passed down from one generation to another, together with recipes for herbal medicines and home-made wines. By the nineteenth century, few upper- or urban middle-class Englishwomen would admit to knowing anything about cooking. In America, however, there was much less of this kind of social prejudice, as we have seen from John Pintard's account of his younger daughter's enthusiasm in the kitchen. In The Wide, Wide World, *a largely forgotten American classic, the effectively orphaned Ellen Montgomery has arrived in the household of Miss Alice, another unashamed cooking enthusiast.*

She led the way across the hall to the room on the opposite side; a large, well-appointed and spotlessly neat kitchen. Ellen could not help exclaiming at its pleasantness.

'Why, yes—I think it is. I have been in many a parlour that I did not like as well. Beyond this is a lower kitchen where Margery does all her rough work; nothing comes up the steps but the very nicest and daintiest of kitchen matters. Margery, if you will put the kettle on and see to the fire, I will make some of my cakes for tea.'

'I'll do it, Miss Alice; it is not good for you to go so long without eating.'

Alice now rolled up her sleeves above the elbows, and tying a large white apron before her, set about gathering the different things she wanted for her work—to Ellen's great amusement. A white moulding-board was placed upon a table as white; and round it soon grouped the pail of flour, the plate of nice yellow butter, the bowl of cream, sieve, tray, and sundry etceteras. And then, first sifting some flour into the tray, Alice began to throw in the other things, one after another, and toss the whole about with a carelessness that looked as if it would all go wrong, but with a confidence that seemed to say all was going right. Ellen gazed in comical astonishment.

'Did you think cakes were made without hands?' said Alice, laughing at her look. 'You saw me wash mine before I began.'

'O, I am not afraid of that,' said Ellen. 'I am not afraid of your hands.'

'Did you never see your mother do this?' said Alice, who was now turning and rolling about the dough upon the board in a way that seemed to Ellen curious beyond expression.

'No, never,' she said. 'Mamma never kept house, and I never saw anybody do it.'

'Then your aunt does not let you into the mysteries of bread and butter-making?'

'Butter-making? O,' said Ellen with a sigh, 'I have enough of that.'

Alice now applied a smooth wooden roller to the cake, with such quickness and skill, that the lump forthwith lay spread upon the board in a thin even layer, and she next cut it into little round cakes with the edge of a tumbler.

Elizabeth Wetherall, *The Wide, Wide World; Or, the Early History of Ellen Montgomery*, 1852, Volume I

The effervescent Bella Wilfer, who is living grandly with the Boffin family, has come on a visit to her parents and sister Lavinia.

Mr and Mrs Wilfer had seen a full quarter of a hundred more anniversaries of their wedding day than Mr and Mrs Lammle had seen of theirs, but they still celebrated the occasion in the bosom of their family. Not that these celebrations ever resulted in anything particularly agreeable, or that the family was ever disappointed by that circumstance on account of having looked forward to the return of the auspicious day with sanguine anticipations of enjoyment. It was kept morally, rather as a Fast than a Feast, enabling Mrs Wilfer to hold a sombre darkling state, which exhibited that impressive woman in her choicest colours.

* * * * *

The revolving year now bringing the day round in its orderly sequence, Bella arrived in the Boffin chariot to assist in the celebration. It was the family custom when the day recurred, to sacrifice a pair of fowls on the altar of Hymen; and Bella had sent a note beforehand, to intimate that she would be bringing the votive offering with her. So, Bella and the fowls, by the united energies of two horses, two men, four wheels, and a plum-pudding carriage dog with as uncomfortable a collar on as if he had been George the Fourth, were deposited at the door of the parental dwelling. They were there received by Mrs Wilfer in person, whose dignity on this, as on most special occasions, was heightened by a mysterious toothache.

* * * * *

'Now, Ma,' said Bella, reappearing in the kitchen . . . 'you and Lavvy think magnificent me fit for nothing but I intend to prove the contrary. I mean to be Cook today.'

'Hold!' rejoined her majestic mother. 'I cannot permit it. Cook in that dress!'

'As for my dress, Ma,' returned Bella, merrily searching in a dresser-drawer, 'I mean to apron it and towel it all over the front; and as to permission, I mean to do without.'

'*You* cook?' said Mrs Wilfer. '*You*, who never cooked when you were at home?'

'Yes, Ma,' returned Bella; 'that is precisely the state of the case.'

She girded herself with a white apron, and busily with knots and pins contrived a bib to it, coming close and tight under her chin, as if it had caught her round the neck to kiss her. Over this bib her dimples looked delightful, and under it her pretty figure not less so. 'Now, Ma,' said Bella, pushing back her hair from her temples with both hands, 'what's first?'

'First,' returned Mrs Wilfer solemnly, 'if you persist in what I cannot but regard as conduct utterly incompatible with the equipage in which you arrived—'

('Which I do, Ma.')

'First, then, you put the fowls down to the fire.'

'To-be-sure!' cried Bella; 'and flour them, and twirl them round, and there they go!' sending them spinning at a great rate. 'What's next, Ma?'

'Next,' said Mrs Wilfer with a wave of her gloves, expressive of abdication under protest from the culinary throne, 'I would recommend examination of the bacon in the saucepan on the fire, and also of the potatoes by the application of a fork. Preparation of the greens will further become necessary if you persist in this unseemly demeanour.'

'As of course I do, Ma.'

Persisting, Bella gave her attention to one thing and forgot the other, and gave her attention to the other and forgot the third, and remembering the third was distracted by the fourth, and made amends whenever she went wrong by giving the unfortunate fowls an extra spin, which made their chance of ever getting cooked exceedingly doubtful. But it was pleasant cookery too. Meantime Miss Lavinia, oscillating between the kitchen and the opposite room, prepared the dining-table in the latter chamber. This office she (always doing her household spiriting with unwillingness) performed in a startling series of whisks and bumps; laying the table-cloth as if she were raising the wind, putting down the glasses and salt-cellars as if she were knocking at the door, and clashing the knives and forks in a skirmishing manner suggestive of hand-to-hand conflict.

* * * * *

'But what,' said Bella, as she watched the carving of the fowls, 'makes them pink inside, I wonder, Pa! Is it the breed?'

'No, I don't think it's the breed, my dear,' returned Pa. 'I rather think it is because they are not done.'

'They ought to be,' said Bella.

'Yes, I am aware they ought to be, my dear,' rejoined her father, 'but they—ain't.'

So, the gridiron was put in requisition, and the good-tempered cherub [Mr Wilfer], who was often as un-cherubically employed in his own family as if he had been in the employment of some of the Old Masters, undertook to grill the fowls.

Charles Dickens, *Our Mutual Friend*, 1864–5, Book III

Spinning: the Wilfers' modest kitchen evidently contained a spit and gridiron to use over an open fire, but no range or oven.

Kitty has married Constantine Levin, a country landowner, and is pregnant with their first child. Her mother, Princess Shcherbatsky, and her elder sister Dolly Oblonsky are staying with her. Against a background of jam-making (and in French, in order not to be understood by Levin's housekeeper, Agatha Mihaylovna, whom they are supervising), the old princess and her daughters are discussing proposals of marriage. The jam, however, is a matter of almost equal importance, since, as in all Russian country households, this is the main way of conserving the copious but short-lived crops of soft fruit which are the only kind that grow in the cold, northerly climate.

All the women of the household were assembled on the balcony. They always liked to sit there after dinner, but today they had special business there. Besides the sewing of little shirts and the knitting of swaddling bands, on which they were all engaged, today jam was being made there in a way new to Agatha Mihaylovna: without the addition of water to the fruit. Kitty was introducing this new way, which had been employed in her old home; but Agatha Mihaylovna, to whom this work had formerly been entrusted, and who considered that nothing that used to be done in the Levin household could be wrong, had, despite her directions, put water to the strawberry and wild strawberry jam, declaring it to be indispensable. She had been detected doing this, and now the raspberry jam was being made in every one's presence, as Agatha Mihaylovna had to be convinced that without water the jam could turn out well.

Agatha Mihaylovna, with a flushed face and aggrieved expression, her hair ruffled and her thin arms bared to the elbow, was shaking the preserving pan over the brazier with a circular movement, looking dismally at the raspberries and hoping with all her heart that they would harden and not get cooked through. The old Princess, conscious that against her, as chief adviser in the matter of jam boiling, Agatha Mihaylovna's wrath should be directed, tried to look as if she were thinking of other things and was not interested in the raspberries. She talked of other matters, but watched the brazier out of the corner of her eye.

'I always buy dress materials for the maids myself at the sales,' the Princess said, continuing the conversation. 'Is it not time to take the scum off, my dear?' she added, turning to Agatha Mihaylovna. 'It's not at all necessary for you to do it yourself, besides it's hot,' she said, stopping Kitty.

'I will do it,' said Dolly, and she got up and began carefully sliding the spoon over the surface of the bubbling syrup, and now and then, to remove what had stuck to the spoon, she tapped it against a plate already covered with the yellowish pink scum with blood-red streaks of syrup showing beneath it. 'How they'll lick it up at tea-time!' she thought of the children, remembering how she herself, when a child, used to marvel that the grown-ups did not eat the scum—the nicest part.

* * * * *

'Well, I think it is ready now,' said Dolly, dripping syrup from the spoon. 'When it begins to string, it is ready. Boil it up a little longer, Agatha Mihaylovna.'

'Oh, these flies!' cried Agatha Mihaylovna crossly. 'It will come out just the same.'

'Oh, how sweet he is—don't frighten him!' exclaimed Kitty unexpectedly, looking at a sparrow that had settled on a railing, turned a raspberry stalk over, and was pecking at it.

* * * * *

'Well, Agatha Mihaylovna, is the jam done?' asked Levin, smiling at her and wishing to cheer her up. 'Has it turned out well the new way?'

'I suppose so. We'd have thought it overdone.'

'It's better so, Agatha Mihaylovna: it won't ferment, and we have no ice left in the cellar and nowhere to keep it cool,' said Kitty, immediately seeing her husband's intention and addressing the old woman in the same spirit. 'On the other hand, your pickling is such that Mama says she never tasted anything like it!' she added, smiling and putting the old woman's kerchief straight.

Agatha Mihaylovna looked crossly at Kitty.

'You need not comfort me, ma'am. I just look at you and him, and then I feel happy,' she said, and that disrespectful way of speaking of her master as *him* seemed touching to Kitty.

'Come with us and get mushrooms! You will show us the right places.'

Agatha Mihaylovna smiled and shook her head, as much as to say: 'Though I should like to be cross with you, I can't do it.'

'Please follow my advice,' said the old Princess, 'cover the jam with paper soaked in rum, and then it will not get mouldy, even without ice.'

Leo Tolstoy, *Anna Karenina*, 1874–7, translated by Louise and Aylmer Maude, 1912

❧ *Giles Winterborne is an apple-grower and cider-maker, living alone with his servant in a remote Dorset woodland village. Grace, the daughter of Mr Melbury, a timber-merchant who is slightly Giles's social superior, has returned home, refined and marriageable, from boarding-school. Diffidently, Giles has invited the Melbury family to his house, uncertain (as Melbury is himself) whether Grace will condescend to visit him.*

Winterborne, in his modesty, had mentioned no particular hour in his invitation to the Melburys, though he had to the inferior guests; therefore Mr Melbury and his family, expecting no other people, chose their own time, which chanced to be rather early in the afternoon, by reason of the somewhat quicker despatch than usual of the timber-merchant's business that day.

They showed their sense of the unimportance of the occasion by walking quite slowly to the house, as if they were merely out for a ramble, and going to nothing special at all; or at most intending to pay a casual call and take a cup of tea.

At this hour stir and bustle pervaded the interior of Winterborne's domicile from cellar to apple-loft. He had planned an elaborate high tea for six o'clock or thereabouts, and a good roaring supper to come on about eleven. Being a bachelor of rather retiring habits the whole of the preparations devolved upon himself and his trusty man and familiar Robert Creedle, who did everything that required doing, from making Giles's bed to catching moles in his field. He was a survival from the days when Giles's father held the homestead and Giles was a playing boy.

These two, with a certain dilatoriness which appertained to both, were now in the heat of preparation in the bakehouse, expecting nobody before six o'clock. Winterborne was standing in front of the brick oven in his shirt-sleeves, tossing in thorn-sprays, and stirring about the blazing mass with a long-handled, three-pronged Beelzebub kind of fork, the heat shining out upon his streaming face and making his eyes like furnaces; the thorns crackling and sputtering; while Creedle, having ranged the pastry dishes in a row on the table till the oven should be ready, was pressing out the crust of a final apple-pie with a rolling-pin. A great pot boiled on the fire; and through the open door of the back-kitchen a boy was seen seated on the fender, emptying the snuffers and scouring the candle-sticks, a row of the latter standing upside down on the hob to melt out the grease.

Looking up from the rolling-pin Creedle saw passing the window first the timber-merchant, in his second best suit, next Mrs Melbury in her best silk, and behind them Grace in the fashionable attire which [she had] lately brought home with her from the Continent. . . . The eyes of the three had been attracted through the window to the proceedings within by the fierce illumination which the oven threw out upon the operators and their utensils.

'Lord, lord! if they bain't come a'ready!' said Creedle.

'No—hey?' said Giles, looking round aghast; while the boy in the background waved a reeking candlestick in his delight.

As there was no help for it Winterborne hastily rolled down his shirt-sleeves and went to meet them in the doorway.

'My dear Giles, I see we have made a mistake in the time,' said the timber-merchant's wife, her face lengthening with concern.

'Oh, it is not much difference. I hope you'll come in.'

'But this means a regular randyvoo!' Mr Melbury accusingly glanced round and pointed towards the viands in the bakehouse with his stick.

'Well, yes,' said Giles.

'And—not Great Hintock band, and dancing, surely?'

'I told three of 'em they might drop in if they'd nothing else to do,' Giles mildly admitted.

'Now why the name didn't ye tell us afore that 'twas going to be a bouncing kind of thing? How should I know what folk mean if they don't say? Now, shall we come in, or shall we go home, and come back-along in a couple of hours?'

'I hope you'll stay, if you'll be so good as not to mind, now you are here! I shall have it all right and tidy in a very little time. I ought not to have been so backward; but Creedle is rather slow.'

Giles spoke quite anxiously for one of his undemonstrative temperament; for he feared that if the Melburys once were back in their own house they would not be disposed to turn out again.

' 'Tis we ought not to have been so forward; that's what 'tis,' said Mr Melbury testily. 'Don't keep us in here in your best sitting-room; lead on to the bakehouse, man. Now we are here we'll help ye get ready for the rest. Here, miss'es, take off your things, and help him out in his baking, or he won't get done tonight. I'll finish heating the oven, and set you free to go and skiver up them ducks.' His eye had passed with pitiless directness of criticism into yet remoter recesses of Winterborne's awkwardly built premises, where the aforesaid birds were hanging.

'And I'll help finish the tarts,' said Grace cheerfully.

'I don't know about that,' said her father. ' 'Tisn't quite so much in your line as it is in your step-mother's and mine.'

'Of course I couldn't let you, Grace!' said Giles with distress.

'I'll do it, of course,' said Mrs Melbury, taking off her silk train, hanging it up to a nail, carefully rolling back her sleeves, pinning them to her shoulders, and stripping Giles of his apron for her own use.

So Grace pottered idly about while her father and his wife helped on the preparations. A kindly pity of his household management, which Winterborne saw in her eyes whenever he caught them, depressed him much more than her contempt would have done.

Thomas Hardy, *The Woodlanders*, 1887

The action of Ulysses *takes place in Dublin on a single day, 16 June 1904. Leopold Bloom's kitchen rituals (interrupted by his purchase, while the kettle is boiling, of a pork kidney from Dlugacz's butcher's shop) introduce his long, ruminative share in the events of the day.*

Mr Leopold Bloom ate with relish the inner organs of beasts and fowls. He liked thick giblet soup, nutty gizzards, a stuffed roast heart, liver slices fried with crustcrumbs, fried hencod's roes. Most of all he liked grilled mutton kidneys which gave to his palate a fine tang of faintly scented urine.

Kidneys were in his mind as he moved about the kitchen softly, righting her breakfast things on the humpy tray. Gelid light and air were in the kitchen but out of doors gentle summer morning everywhere. Made him feel peckish.

The coals were reddening.

Another slice of bread and butter: three, four: right. She didn't like her plate full. Right. He turned from the tray, lifted the kettle from the hob and set it sideways on the fire. It sat there, dull and squat, its spout stuck out. Cup of tea soon. Good. Mouth dry. The cat walked stiffly round a leg of the table with tail on high.

—Mkgnao!

* * * * *

He listened to her licking lap. Ham and eggs, no. No good eggs with this drouth. Want pure fresh water. Thursday: not a good day either for a mutton kidney at Buckley's. Fried with butter, a shake of pepper. Better a pork kidney at Dlugacz's. While the kettle is boiling.

* * * * *

As he went down the kitchen stairs [his wife] called:

—Poldy!

—What?

—Scald the teapot.

On the boil sure enough: a plume of steam from the spout. He scalded and rinsed out the teapot and put in four full spoons of tea, tilting the kettle then to let water flow in. Having set it to draw, he took off the kettle and crushed the pan flat on the live coals and watched the lump of butter slide and melt. While he unwrapped the kidney the cat mewed hungrily against him. Give her too much meat she won't mouse. Say they won't eat pork. Kosher. Here. He let the bloodsmeared paper fall to her and dropped the kidney amid the sizzling butter sauce. Pepper. He sprinkled it through his fingers, ringwise, from the chipped eggcup.

* * * * *

The tea was drawn. He filled his own moustachecup, sham crown Derby, smiling. Silly Milly's birthday gift. Only five she was then. No wait: four. I gave her the amberoid necklace she broke. Putting pieces of folded brown paper in the letterbox for her. He smiled, pouring.

* * * * *

He prodded a fork into the kidney and slapped it over: then fitted the teapot on the tray. Its hump bumped as he took it up. Everything on it? Bread and butter, four, sugar, spoon, her cream. Yes. He carried it upstairs, his thumb hooked in the teapot handle.

Nudging the door open with his knee he carried the tray in and set it on the chair by the bedhead.

—What a time you were, she said.

James Joyce, *Ulysses*, 1922

❧ *The novelist Ford Madox Ford (1873–1939), after service in the First World War, moved in April 1919 to Red Ford Cottage, a semi-derelict labourer's cottage near Pulborough, Sussex. He was joined there soon afterwards by Stella Bowen, the young Australian artist whom he had met in 1918 after the collapse of his first marriage to Elsie Martindale.* It Was the Nightingale *is one of his many collections of autobiographical sketches, incorporating material (much of it, like this anecdote, lightly fictionalized) from several earlier volumes.*

I have said that the word despair is not to be found in my vocabulary. . . . The immense rusty key grated in the lock of the door of an unknown room. It was a space filled with shadows. The house had been unoccupied for many years: if one had spoken, one would have whispered. The floor was ankle-deep in dry leaves; on the hearth were bushels of twigs dropped by the starlings who had nested in the chimney. I lit a candle and used the last daylight outside in . . . finding more wood and the cast-iron crock. Fortunately the house was bone-dry.

I had my bed and my canvas table up very quickly and then had to face my mutton-neck and shallots. Here there came in the ridiculous omen. It was when I confronted my shallots. A shallot is perhaps the best of all the onion tribe: but shallots are very small things; scores of them lay under my nose. I touched the frontiers of dismay where it borders on the slough of despair. I was at the lowest ebb of my life. It would take me hours and the last of my strength to skin those bulbs. I could not tackle that job.

That really shamed me. One may be poor, friendless, fallen in estate, infinitely alone. But if one goes back on one's arts one loses self-respect, and once one loses that—so I have been told—one is lost indeed. And I knew I should never skin those dwarf onions. I sat on the edge of my bed and faced facts and the fire.

On it, in the crock, the neck of mutton was already browning in butter. Cooking is an art, the first of whose canons is that all stewed meats must first be braised in butter or olive oil, according as your cooking is *au beurre* or *à l'huile*. (The French call the process *rissoler*). The second canon is that a portion at least of your onion matter—onions, garlic, shallots, chives even—must be browned too.

I said to destiny:

'Look here, I will skin and brown nine shallots. . . . But not a single other one.'

So far I had not lost self-respect. The shallots browned. But then I did a thing that I have never done before or since. When the mutton and the rest were nicely *rissoled* and I had added the quota of water and the water had come to the boil, I closed my eyes so that I might not see the deed, and tipped all the rest of the shallots into that crock—skins and all (I *had* washed them).

* * * * *

But the skins came off those shallots and floated in the bubbling on the top of the crock. So, after an hour and three-quarters of waiting I skimmed them off and ate a fair to middling stew and drank half a bottle of port.

Ford Madox Ford, *It Was the Nightingale*, 1934

ENGLISH EXPATRIATES IN THE SOUTH OF FRANCE

Some of my mother's new acquaintances met for a game of cards at the Café de la Marine on Tuesdays and Thursdays, and we were asked to join them. First step was putting dinner forward, these assignations being for a quarter to nine. The *upheaval*, my mother said, like dining out before a dance. To save me another walk down and up the hill, we did our own cooking. She made the soup, potatoes and leeks or potatoes and *cresson*, the ubiquitous good soup of the evening of the urban and suburban French (the peasant's main-dish soup was something else). I made the *œufs-sur-le-plat* in a couple of small round buttered dishes gently till the whites were set pure and creamy with the yolks still perfect, as my father had taught me when I wasn't tall enough to reach the spirit-lamp (now it was *more* tricky on the charcoal-stove but attention—also taught by him—would do it). These were not the fried eggs of the English hotel breakfast: hardened, brown and frizzy at the edges, sputtered fat congealing into tepid grease. Our bi-weekly menu was always the same: small courses in the pattern of the French en famille at night (who ate more, much more, than we did at noon). After our eggs, we had a slice of ham with a green salad lightly dressed, and to end with a cœur-crème with apricot jam.

Sybille Bedford, *Jigsaw*, 1989

RECIPES

SALAD DRESSING

Two boiled potatoes passed through kitchen sieve,
Softness and smoothness to the salad give.
Of mordant mustard add a single spoon,
Distrust the condiment that bites too soon
Yet deem it not, thou man of taste, a fault
To add a double quantity of salt—
Four times the spoon with oil of Lucca crown
And twice, with vinegar procured from Town;
The flavour needs it, and your poet begs
The pounded yellow of two well boiled eggs;
Let onion atoms lurk within the bowl
And, scarce suspected, animate the whole;
And, lastly, in the flavoured compound toss
A magic soupçon of anchovy sauce.
Oh, green and glorious! Oh, herbaceous treat!
'Twould tempt the dying anchorite to eat.
Back to the world he'd turn his fleeting soul,
And plunge his fingers in the salad-bowl.
Serenely full, the epicure would say,
Fate cannot harm me, I have dined today.

Sydney Smith, 'Recipe for Salad', 1840. (See Lady Holland, *Memoir of the Reverend Sydney Smith*, 1855, Volume I)

The Revd Sydney Smith (1771–1845), wit and bon viveur, wrote this recipe for Elizabeth, Lady Holland, wife of Henry Richard Vassal Fox, 3rd Baron Holland, and the centre of the famous Holland House circle of aristocratic Whigs, who prided themselves on their love of good food as much as on their liberal political principles and literary leanings. (The author of the *Memoir*, Smith's daughter Saba, was the wife of a baronet, (Dr) Sir Henry Holland, unrelated to the family at Holland House.)

CURRY

Three pounds of veal my darling girl prepares,
And chops it nicely into little squares;
Five onions next procures the little minx
(The biggest are the best, her Samiwel thinks),
And Epping butter nearly half a pound,
And stews them in a pan until they're brown'd.

What's next my dexterous little girl will do?
She pops the meat into the savoury stew,
With curry-powder table-spoonfuls three,
And milk a pint (the richest that may be),
And, when the dish has stewed for half an hour,
A lemon's ready juice she'll o'er it pour.
Then, bless her! Then she gives the luscious pot
A very gentle boil—and serves quite hot.

PS—Beef, mutton, rabbit, if you wish,
Lobsters, or prawns, or any kind of fish,
Are fit to make a CURRY. 'Tis, when done,
A dish for Emperors to feed upon.

William Makepeace Thackeray, 'Kitchen Melodies—Curry', 1846

'How to make stew in the Pinacate Desert:
Recipe for Locke & Drum'

A. J. Bayless market bent wire roller basket buy up parsnips, onion,
carrot, rutabaga and potato, bell green pepper,
& nine cuts of dark beef shank.
They run there on their legs, that makes beef tasty.

Seven at night in Tucson, get some bisquick for the dumplings.
Have some bacon. Go to Hadley's in the kitchen right beside the
frying steak—Diana on the phone—get a little plastic bag from
Drum—
Fill it up with tarragon and chili; four bay leaves; black pepper
corns and basil; powdered oregano, something free, maybe about
two teaspoon worth of salt.

Now down in Sonora, Pinacate country, build a fire of Ocotillo,
broken twigs and bits of ironwood, in an open ring of lava: rake
some coals aside (and if you're smart) to windward,
keep the other half ablaze for heat and light.

Set Drum's fourteen-inch dutch oven with three legs across the
embers.
Now put in the strips of bacon.
In another pan have all the vegetables cleaned up and peeled and
sliced.
Cut the beef shank up small and set the bone aside.
Throw in the beef shank meat,
And stir it while it fries hot,
lots of ash and sizzle—singe your brow—
Like Locke says almost burn it—then add water from the jeep
can—
add the little bag of herbs—cook it all five minutes more—and
then throw in the pan of all the rest.
Cover it up with big hot lid all heavy, sit and wait, or drink budweiser
beer.
And also mix the dumpling mix aside, some water in some
bisquick,
finally drop that off the spoon into the stew.
And let it cook ten minutes more
and lift the black pot off the fire
to set aside another good ten minutes,
Dish it up and eat it with a spoon, sitting on a poncho in the dark.
13.XII.1964

Gary Snyder, *The Back Country*, 1968

SUMMER PUDDING

Begin with half a pound of raspberries
picked from the deep end of your garden, where the birds
play hopscotch in the draggled fruitnets; add
a quarter of redcurrants; gently seethe in orange juice
fox six or seven minutes with some sugar,
give the pan a ritual shake from time to time, inducing
a marriage of those fine, compatible
tastes; and leave to cool. An open kitchen door invites
whatever breeze will help itself to flavour,
attenuating it downhill across the neighbours' gardens
(be generous!) so summer will surprise them,
an unidentifiable recalled fulfilment haunting

the giant bellflower and the scarlet runners.
Now introduce your strawberries, sliced to let the pallid heartsflesh
transfuse its juices into the mass, transmute
cooled fruit to liquid crystal while you line your bowl with bread
and add the mixture—keeping back some juice—
lid it with bread, cover and weight it, chill it if you like
(as if the winter took a hand) and hoard it,
opus magnum, ripening its secret, edible,
inviolable time. And when you dare
slide your knife around its socket to uncling—a sudden suck—
this gelid Silbury mined with the wealth
of archetypal summer, let it be on one of three
occasions: for a kitchenful of children . . .
or for the friends around your polished table
. . . or for whoever
will join you in your garden when the sun
carries out summer to the edge of dark, and stay to eat
there in the early chill as twilight gels
and owlhoots quiver from the gulf of darkness, where a floodlit
cathedral floats under your eyes, and still
(wreckage of smeared plates and clotted spoons piling the table)
after the lights are killed and the cathedral
vanishes like a switchedoff hologram, remain to plot
the moon's progress across the brimming air
scaled by the nightscented stocks, or with binoculars
arrest the Brownian movement of the stars.

Grevel Lindop, 'Summer Pudding—for Carole Reeves', *Tourists*, 1987

ROUGHING IT

❧ *Trinculo and Stephano, two discreditable characters recently landed on Prospero's island from a shipwreck, have encountered Caliban, Prospero's slave, whom they make drunk.*

CALIBAN. I'll kiss thy foot. I'll swear myself thy subject.
STEPHANO. Come on then. Down, and swear!
TRINCULO. I shall laugh myself to death at this puppy-headed monster. A most scurvy monster! I could find in my heart to beat him—
STEPHANO. Come, kiss.
TRINCULO. But that the poor monster's in drink. An abominable monster!
CALIBAN. I'll show thee the best springs; I'll pluck thee berries;
I'll fish for thee, and get thee wood enough.
A plague upon the tyrant that I serve!
I'll bear him no more sticks, but follow thee,
Thou wondrous man.
TRINCULO. A most ridiculous monster, to make a wonder of a poor drunkard.
CALIBAN. I prithee let me bring thee where crabs grow;
And I with my long nails will dig thee pignuts,
Show thee a jay's nest, and instruct thee how
To snare the nimble marmoset; I'll bring thee
To clust'ring filberts, and sometimes I'll get thee
Young scamels from the rock. Wilt thou go with me?

William Shakespeare, *The Tempest*, II. ii

Crabs: (wild) crab apples; *pignuts*: earth-nuts (tubers of *bunium flexuosum*, a native of Britain), or, just possibly, peanuts (*arachis hypogaea*, originally from South America).

CRUSOE'S ISLAND: COOKING UTENSILS

No Joy at a Thing of so mean a Nature was ever equal to mine, when I found I had made an Earthen Pot which would bear the Fire; and I had hardly Patience to stay till they were cold, before I set one on the Fire again, with some Water in it, to boil me some Meat, which it did admirably well; and with a Piece of a Kid, I made some very good Broth, though I wanted Oatmeal, and several other Ingredients, requisite to make it so good as I would have had it been.

My next Concern was, to get me a Stone Mortar, to stamp or beat some Corn in; for as to the Mill, there was no thought at arriving to the Perfection of Art, with one Pair of Hands. To supply this Want I was at a great Loss; for of all Trades in the World I was as perfectly unqualified for a Stone-cutter, as for any whatever; neither had I any Tools to go about it with. I spent many a Day to find out a great Stone big enough to cut hollow, and make fit for a Mortar, and could find none at all; except what was in the solid Rock, and which I had no way to dig or cut out; nor indeed were the Rocks in the Island of Hardness sufficient, but were all of a sandy crumbling Stone, which neither would bear the Weight of a heavy Pestle, or would break the Corn without filling it with Sand; so after a great deal of Time lost in searching for a Stone, I gave it over, and resolved to look out for a great Block of hard Wood, which I found indeed much easier; and getting one as big as I had Strength to stir, I rounded it, and form'd it in the Out-side with my Axe and Hatchet, and then with the Help of Fire, and infinite Labour, made a hollow Place in it, as the *Indians* in *Brasil* make their *Canoes*. After this, I made a great heavy Pestle or Beater, of the Wood call'd the Ironwood, and this I prepar'd and laid by against I had my next Crop of Corn, when I propos'd to myself, to grind, or rather pound my Corn into Meal to make my Bread.

My next difficulty, was to make a Sieve, or Search, to dress my Meal, and to part it from the Bran, and the Husk, without which I did not see it possible I could have any Bread. . . . At last I did remember that I had among the Seamens Cloaths which were sav'd out of the Ship, some Neckcloths of Callicoe, or Muslin; and with some Pieces of these, I made three small Sieves, but proper enough for the Work; and thus I made shift for some Years.

* * * * *

The baking Part was the next Thing to be consider'd, and how I should make Bread when I came to have Corn; for first I had no Yeast; as to that Part, as there was no supplying the Want, so I did not concern myself much about it; But for an Oven, I was indeed in great Pain, at length I found out an experiment for that also, which was this; I made some Earthen Vessels very broad, but not deep; that is to say, about two Foot Diameter, and not above nine Inches deep; these I burnt in the Fire, as I had done the other, and laid them by; and when I wanted to bake, I made a great Fire upon my Hearth, which I had pav'd with some square Tiles of my own making, and burning also; but I should not call them square.

When the Fire-wood was burnt pretty much into Embers, or live Coals, I drew them forward upon this Hearth so as to cover it all over, and there I let them lye, till the Hearth was very hot, then sweeping away all the Embers, I set down my Loaf, or Loaves, and whelming down the Earthen Pot upon them, drew the Embers all round the Out-side of the Pot, to keep in, and add to the Heat; and thus, as well as in the best Oven in the World, I bak'd my Barley Loaves, and became in little Time a meer Pastry-Cook into the Bargain; for I made myself several Cakes with the Rice, and Puddings; indeed I made no Pies, neither had I any Thing to put into them, supposing I had, except the Flesh either of Fowls or Goats.

Daniel Defoe, *The Life and Strange Surprizing Adventures of Robinson Crusoe, of York, Mariner*, 1719

Five years after Daniel Defoe published Robinson Crusoe, *an English sailor was allegedly abandoned by the Dutch on Ascension Island with 'a Cask of Water two bucketts an frying pan and a Muskett', together with the materials for a tent which he secured against the weather with stones and 'a peas of an old tarpauling'. His MS diary (almost certainly a custom-made forgery) begins on 5 May 1724, the date on which he claimed to have been cast ashore, and subsequently found its way into the possession of the non-juring bishop and fellow of St John's College, Oxford, Richard Rawlinson (1690–1755), a keen collector of diaries, letters, and manuscripts of all kinds.*

Wednesday 9 [May] in the Morning I went to look for the turtil I had kild the day before. I tuck my hachite with me and Cut it up the back it being so large I Could not turn it. I Cut Som of the flesh of the fore Leg and brought it home to my tent and Salted it and put it in the Sun to drye. I began again to build an other bulwarck of Stons about my tent and Secure it from the weather the best I could with the Tarpauling.

Thursday 10 this Morning I tuck 4 or 5 onions a few peas and Calavances and went to the So[uth] Side of the Island to See if I Could find a proper place to Set them in. I Looked very Carefully on the Sand to See if I Could discover the track of aney beast or aney water or aneything Els that might be Sarois to me but found nothing onley a little purslin which I eat as I walked back. when I was half way back [I found] Som Greens but I knew not if thay were good to Eat or no.

Friday 11 I went into the Countray again and found Som rutes Som what [looked] like petatose but Could not think they ware good to Eat. I looked very Carefully for a greater discovery but found nothing. I Set me down being very discontented all most ded with thirst and afterward walked to My tent on the Other Side of the Island. thear is a Sanday bay by the Largest hill. this Evening I boyled Som rice being the first time I was out of order.

Saturday 12. In the Morning boyled Som more and Eaight of it. after I had prayed I went in to the Countray to See if I Could See aney Shiping but to My great Sorrow Could not See aney So Return'd to my tent and walked along the beach but found nothing onley Sum Shels of fish. I keep allways walking a bout that being all the hope I have; then returnd to my tent and read till I was a weary then mended my Cloues. this afternoon I put the onions peas and Callavances in the ground to See if they would produce aney More for as yet I Cante afoard water to boyle aney.

Sunday 13. In the Morning I went to See for Sea fouls eggs but found none. walking back I found a Small turtel Just by my tent; I tuck Som of its Eggs and flesh and boiled it with Som rice for My dinner and buried the remainder in the Sand because it Should not infect me. afterwards I found Som nests of fouls eggs of which I boyled Som and found them very good to Eate. I melted Som of the turtles fat to make oyle and in the night burnt it haveing nothing for a Lamp but a Sasoer.

* * * * *

Sunday 10 with the Last of my water I boyled Som of my Rice haveing but very little of aney thing Else to Eaight but farsting I commit my Sole to God Hoping he will have Marsey on it but not giveing over all hopes while I can walk. I went to the other Side of the Island to Sea for Water I haveing heard thear was a well of water. I walked up and down the hill not Leaveing any place un S[e]arched by me. after fore howers walking I was very thirsted and the heat of the Sun Made my Life a Burden to Me More than I was able to baire but was resolved to prosede as Long as I Could walk and going [to the] anding of the Rockes god of his infinit Marsey Led me to a place whear thear was Som water running out of the Rock. its impossable to Express the great Joy I was in when I fownd it I thought I Should drink till I burst. I set down by it then drank again; I walked to my tent and Carried Som home with me.

MS Diary of a Castaway on Ascension Island

Callavances: pulse, chick-peas.

GYPSIES

I see a column of slow-rising smoke
O'ertop the lofty wood that skirts the wild.
A vagabond and useless tribe there eat
Their miserable meal. A kettle, slung
Between two poles upon a stick transverse,
Receives the morsel—flesh obscene of dog,
Or vermin, or at best of cock purloin'd
From his accustom'd perch. Hard-faring race!
They pick their fuel out of every hedge,
Which, kindled with dry leaves, just saves unquench'd
The spark of life. The sportive wind blows wide
Their fluttering rags, and shows a tawny skin,
The vellum of the pedigree they claim.
Great skill have they in palmistry, and more
To conjure clean away the gold they touch,
Conveying worthless dross into its place;
Loud when they beg, dumb only when they steal.

William Cowper, *The Task*, 1784, Book I, 'The Sofa'

Born in Nizhni Novgorod and orphaned as a child, Maxim Gorky (1868–1936) spent much of his early adulthood wandering through the eastern and southern areas of Russia doing odd jobs for a living. He became a provincial journalist in the 1890s and a best-selling, revolutionary novelist in the early 1900s.

The tramp who remains impressed most vividly on my memory is 'Bashka', a man I came to know during the construction of the Beslan–Petrovsk railway. . . . Taking him to be the 'boss', I made my way to his side and asked whether there was any work for me to do? In a thin, piercing voice he replied:

'I'm not an idiot—I don't work.'

* * * * *

In the sky, across the ravine, the wind was at work, anxiously gathering the clouds together like a flock of sheep. On the side exposed to the sun the rust-coloured shrubs of autumn trembled violently, shaking down their dead leaves. From afar came the sound of blasting; the reverberations thundered among the mountains, and mingled with the crunching of cart-wheels and the regular pounding of hammers as they drove the steel 'needles' into the ore and drilled the deep holes for the charges.

'You want food, I suppose?' the little hunchback asked me. 'They're going to ring the bell for dinner in a minute. What crowds of people like you are roaming about the world! . . .' he grumbled, turning away to spit.

A piercing whistle sounded. It was as though a metallic chord had slashed the air in the ravine, deafening every other sound.

'Off with you,' said the hunchback. With his arms and legs he propelled himself rapidly over the stones, catching at the branches with the dexterity of a monkey, and rolled noiselessly down the slope, in an ugly, huddled mass.

The men dined outside in the open, sitting round the kettles, on stones and wheelbarrows, and eating a hot and salt porridge of millet with lamb. There were six people besides myself at our kettle. The hunchback behaved like a man in authority; having tasted the gruel, he wrinkled up his nose, lifted the spoon threateningly in the direction of an old man in a woman's straw hat, and shouted angrily: 'Too much salt again, you idiot!'

The other five men growled fiercely, and a big, black peasant put in: 'He ought to get a thrashing!'

'Can *you* make gruel?' asked the hunchback, turning to me. 'Really? You're not lying? Let's give him a try,' he suggested, and the rest agreed with him at once.

After dinner the hunchback disappeared in the direction of the camp, while the old cook, a red-faced, good-natured fellow, showed me where the bacon, the grain, the bread and the salt were stored. In a whisper he warned me: 'Don't make any mistake about him. Although he's a cripple, he's a gentleman all right, and a landowner too. He's been a big man in his time, he has. He's got a head on his shoulders, *I* can tell you! He's like a regular master with us! Keeps the accounts and all that. Strict? I should think he was! He's a rare bird, he is!'

An hour later work roared and rumbled once again in the ravine and the men rushed about. I began to wash the kettles and spoons in the brook, built up a wood-pile, hung a kettle with water over it, and started peeling the potatoes.

Maxim Gorky, *Fragments from My Diary*, 1924, translated by Moura Budberg, 1940

❧ *Howard Ruede, a member of a Moravian family from Bethlehem, Pennsylvania, obeyed the classic advice to 'Go West, young man,' and in 1877, at the age of 23, left home for Osborne, Kansas. Here he joined a community of homesteaders of mainly German descent, in which farmers' wives cooked for kitchenfuls of hungry workmen, and, in the absence of alcohol, every meal was accompanied by coffee or a coffee-substitute. After a few months Ruede's father and brothers came out to join him, and the male members of the family began a new life together at Kill Creek, 15 miles from Osborne, in a one-room 'dugout' or 'sod-house' which they constructed from earth and turf.* Sod-House Days *is a collection of Ruede's letters home to Pennsylvania in 1877–8.*

At Landes's, Osborne, Kansas, 13 June 1877.

Most people out here don't drink real coffee because it is too expensive. Green coffee berries sell at anywhere from 40 to 60 cents a pound, and such a price is beyond the means of the average person. Even Arbuckles Ariosa at 35 cents a pound takes too much out of the trade when eggs sell at three to six cents a dozen and butter at six or eight cents a pound. So rye coffee is used a great deal—parched brown or black according to whether the users like a strong or mild drink. To give the beverage a ranker flavor, what is known as 'coffee essence' is used. . . . This essence is a hard, black paste put up in tins holding some two ounces, with a red or yellow wrapper on which is printed in bold black type the figure 5000. What that stands for I never heard; reckon it is a trade mark. Directions for use are also on the wrapper, but I never saw anybody follow 'em. The women folks use 'about so much' for a pot of coffee, and often they have to use the stove-lid lifter, or a hammer, or anything else that is handy to pound it with, to break the hard paste before they can get it out of the tin. It is probably made of bran and molasses. When rye is not used, wheat is sometimes used for coffee, but is considered inferior.

* * * * *

Yesterday [some months later] I tasted a new kind of coffee. Mrs Greenfield ran out of coffee—either the real article or the rye substitute—and there she had a gang of men to be fed, and it wouldn't be supper without coffee, so she set her wits to work, with the result that when we gathered at the table a hot amber-colored drink was poured into the cups and set before us. One after another took a sip, set the cup down and demanded what under the sun it was. The lady smiled, but refused to name it. 'It ain't coffee,' said Charlie, 'of that I am sure, for I know the last was used at noon.' 'If you guess right, I'll tell you,' teasingly retorted his wife. Everybody took a turn, and as is often the case, the last was the lucky winner. He noticed several sacks of millet seed leaning against the side of the room and hazarded 'Millet.' 'Right,' said Lida. 'I thought I'd try it, just to see what it tasted like.' It was the queerest tasting coffee any of us had ever put into his mouth, but it 'went,' or the crowd didn't get any hot drink.

* * * * *

At the Dugout, Kill Creek, Kansas, 22 August 1877.

Hurrah! we moved to the dugout this morning. . . . The dugout looks pretty large; in fact, it is pretty fair sized for a dugout. It is 14 × 16 inside, and nearly 8 feet high in the middle. The sod roof is pretty heavy, but is not thick enough yet. . . . I dug some potatoes out of my patch. Nobody need tell me now that the upland is worth little for raising potatoes, as I got some that weighed over a pound apiece, and would make enough for a meal for two. I took an inventory this morning. . . . Stove, tin wash boiler, 2 iron pots, teakettle, 2 spiders, 3 griddles, 3 bread pans, 2 tin plates, a steamer, coffee pot, coal oil can, gridiron, 4 tincups, wash basin, pepper box, and 2 lb nails for $25.40. . . . Then I got ½ dozen knives and forks, and a dozen spoons, which amounted to $2.35; lamp and chimney, 75¢; bucket, 25¢; salt, 10¢; rice, 25¢; ½ dozen china plates, 85¢; 2 bowls, 24¢; 2 store boxes, $1; sugar, 25¢; soap, 25¢; coffee, 35¢; coal oil, 20¢ . . .

29 August 1877.

Yesterday Heiser went to the mill and brought us 100 lbs flour. Then we went to the woods to cut some [timber] for Greenfield. Worked awhile and then came back. Pa went to see if Mrs Hoot could let us have bread, and while he was gone I tried my hand at biscuits, and succeeded, much to our satisfaction. It was good I made the biscuit, for Pa came back without bread. For supper we had steamed potatoes, hot biscuit, a few roasting ears [of corn] I managed to secure in my patch, and coffee. It was about 9 o'clock when we had supper.

30 August 1877.

Up by sunrise, and after breakfast went to chopping again. We made our breakfast on bread and butter and coffee, but we find that it costs too much to eat light bread. Flour at $3 per cwt. and baking at 5¢ per loaf (40 loaves to the cwt.) makes the bread cost about 12½ cents per loaf, and we eat a loaf at a meal. Now with 3 tincups of flour (about a pound) and a little butter I can make enough biscuit to last three meals—so that we expect to make biscuit a standard. About 10 we quit chopping, and I came home to bake, while Pa went to Hall's, about 2 miles from our place, to try to get eggs. That was the last I saw of him till 2 p.m., when he presented himself with 3 dozen eggs. I don't know which I was most glad to see—him or the eggs. . . . I write this while waiting for the water to boil in order to make coffee. It's getting dark, so I'll quit writing and take a smoke before supper. It is generally 8 or 9 o'clock by the time supper is ready.

Howard Ruede, *Sod-House Days: Letters from a Kansas Homesteader 1877–78*, edited by John Ise, 1937

❧ *Bevis and Mark are living the life of make-believe savages by the Longpond (Coate Reservoir, now on the outskirts of Swindon) in Wiltshire. Bevis, roaming through a fir-wood with his bow and arrows, sees a moor-cock feeding.*

It was about ten yards to the willow which hung over the water, but he could not get any nearer, for there was no more cover beyond the alder—the true savage is never content unless he is close to his game. Bevis grasped the bow firm in his left hand, drew the arrow quick but steadily—not with a jerk—and as the sharp point covered the bird, loosed it. There was a splash and a fluttering and he knew instantly that he had hit. 'Mark! Mark' he shouted, and ran down the bank, heedless of the jagged stones. Mark heard, and came racing through the firs.

'Here's where the arrow went in.'

'Feel how warm he is.'

'Let's eat him.'

'All right. Make a fire.'

Thus the savages gloated over their prey. They went back up the bank and through the firs to the sward.

* * * * *

So they dressed, and then found that Mark had broken a nail, and Bevis had cut his foot with the sharp edge of a fossil shell projecting from one of the stones. But that was a trifle; they could think of nothing but the bird. While they were gathering armfuls of dead sticks from among the trees, they remembered that John Young, who always paunched the rabbits and hares and got everything ready for the kitchen, said coots and moorhens must be skinned, they could not be plucked because of the 'dowl'.

Dowl is the fluff, the tiny featherets no fingers can remove. So after they had carried the wood they had collected to the round hollow in the field beyond the sycamore trees, they took out their knives, and haggled the skin off. They built their fire very skilfully; they had made so many in the Peninsula (for there is nothing so pleasant as making a fire out of doors) that they had learnt exactly how to do it.

* * * * *

Bevis piled on the branches, and when he came back there was a large fire. Then the difficulty was how to cook the bird? If they put it on the ashes, it would burn and be spoiled; if they hung it up, they could not make it twist round and round, and they had no iron pot to boil it; or earthenware pot to drop red-hot stones in, and so heat the water without destroying the vessel. The only thing they could do was to stick it on a stick, and hold it to the fire till it was roasted, one side at a time.

'The harpoon will do,' said Bevis. 'Spit him on it.'

'No,' said Mark; 'the bone will burn and get spoiled—spit him on your arrow.'

'The nail will burn out and spoil my arrow, and I've lost one in the elms. Go and cut a long stick.'

'You ought to go and do it,' said Mark; 'I've done everything this morning.'

'So you have; I'll go,' said Bevis, and away he went to the nut-tree hedge. He soon brought back a straight hazel-rod to which he cut a point, the bird was spitted, and they held it by turns at the fire, sitting on the sward.

* * * * *

'I found these buttons,' said Bevis; 'I had forgotten them.'

He put the little mushrooms, stems upwards, on some embers which had fallen from the main fire. The branches as they burned became white directly, coated over with a film of ash, so that except just in the centre they did not look red, though glowing with heat under the white layer. Even the flames were but just visible in the brilliant sunshine, and were paler in colour than those of the hearth. Now and then the thin column of grey smoke, rising straight up out of the hollow, was puffed aside at its summit by the light air wandering over the field. As the butterflies came over the edge of the hollow into the heated atmosphere, they fluttered up high to escape it.

'I'm sure it's done,' said Mark, drawing the stick away from the fire. The bird was brown and burnt in one place, so they determined to eat it and not spoil it by over-roasting. When Bevis began to carve it with his pocket-knife he found one leg quite raw, the wings were burnt, but there was a part of the breast and the other leg fairly well cooked. These they ate, little pieces at a time, slowly, and in silence, for it was proper to like it. But they did not pick the bones clean.

'No salt,' said Mark, putting down the piece he had in his hand.

'No bread,' said Bevis, flinging the leg away.

'We don't do it right somehow,' said Mark. 'It takes such a long time to learn to be savages.'

'Years,' said Bevis, picking a mushroom from the embers. It burnt his fingers and he had to wait till it was cooler. The mushrooms were better, their cups held some of the juice as they cooked, retaining the sweet flavour. They were so small, they were but a bite each.

Richard Jefferies, *Bevis, the Story of a Boy*, 1882

❧ *In Arthur Ransome's series of adventure stories for children, dating from the 1930s and 1940s, food is presented as a repetitive, fairly crude necessity when cooked by the children for themselves. In the* 'Swallows' *books, the eldest, most domesticated girl, Susan, is for ever opening tins of 'pemmican', or corned beef, and disguising it in various ways or serving it with (to an adult) bizarre accompaniments. Here Dick and Dorothea, who come from a polite, middle-class academic background (and probably know as little about cooking as the Swallows, whose parental background is naval and colonial), are the guests of the 'Death and Glories', local boatbuilders' sons camping on a boat of their own on the Norfolk Broads.*

It grew darker and darker.

'What about a lantern?' said Pete.

'In a minute,' said Bill, who was holding a big tin in a damp rag that kept slipping and letting the heat get at his fingers while he was trying to use the tin-opener.

'You can't see what you're doing,' said Tom.

'Joe, you get the grease off them plates,' said Bill. He had got his tin open and emptied its contents, black and shiny, out on a frying pan.

'Shall I lend you a torch?' said Dick.

'No, thanks,' said Bill and turned his back on the party, taking the frying pan with him into the fo'c'sle.

They heard the striking of a match, which lit up the little fo'c'sle, though Bill's body was in the way and they could not see what he was doing. They heard him strike another, and yet another.

'What's gone wrong, Bill?' said Joe.

'Drat it, there ain't nothing go wrong,' said Bill. 'You wait, can't you.'

Another match flared in the fo'c'sle and went out. Then, after a dark pause, they heard the gobble, gobble of liquid pouring from a bottle.

Another match was lit, and the next moment Bill was coming backwards into the cabin, bearing the Christmas pudding in a sea of blue flames.

'What about that?' said Bill.

'I say,' said Dick.

'It's lovely,' said Dorothea. 'Oughtn't you to slop the flames all over it and get some of it burning on each plate?'

Bill hesitated a moment.

'Better not,' he said. 'Wait till that die down.'

He put the frying pan with the flaming pudding on the table and turned to the lighting of the lantern. The lantern, burning brightly, was hanging from its hook under the cabin roof by the time the sea of flame round the pudding had shrunk, died away, flamed up again and gone out. There was a most decided smell of methylated spirits.

Bill carved his pudding and served it out, a helping each on three plates, and a helping each on the three saucers. He watched anxiously the faces of the visitors.

'That want a lot of sugar,' he said.

People helped themselves to sugar again and again and in the end the helpings of pudding disappeared.

'It did burn beautifully,' said Dorothea.

'That's the way to make it,' said Bill, much relieved. 'That don't fare to light without you have a drop of spirit.'

They washed it down with ginger beer, and finished up with oranges, the juice of which took away the last traces of the methylated, which had hung about in people's mouths in spite of all the sugar. Everybody agreed that it had been a first class feast.

Arthur Ransome, *The Big Six*, 1940

III

EATING AT HOME AND ABROAD

MEALS

The Deipnosophistae *of Athenaeus, a Greek writer who was born at Naucratis in Egypt and lived in the late second and early third centuries* AD, *has been translated as* 'The Dinner-Table Philosophers', 'The Authorities on Banquets', *or, more simply*, 'The Gastronomes'. *It is a miscellaneous, multi-volume work dealing with all aspects of food and cookery, from a literary, historical, and analytical angle rather than as a recipe-book. It therefore complements (but does not refer to the existence of) the now much better-known and more manageable Roman cookery manual of Apicius*, De Re Coquinaria, *a collection of recipes probably compiled during the reign of Tiberius in the first half of the first century* AD. *The distinction, or lack of it, remarked here by Athenaeus between Homeric, Classical, and post-Classical mealtime terminology is, at best, confusing. In Homeric Greek*, ariston *is used to mean 'early meal' or 'breakfast'. Later writers, retaining the sense of* ariston *as 'breakfast', also use the noun* akratisma *('[bread dipped] in pure wine') or the verb* akratizomai *('to drink pure wine') to mean 'breakfast'. By Athenaeus's time* ariston *means 'midday meal', while* akratisma *may still mean 'breakfast', but can also mean a light collation at midday. This gradual overlapping shift in meanings is comparable with the evolution of the French word* déjeuner *(originally meaning 'breakfast') into (midday) dinner.*

In the matter of meals, the heroes of Homer took first the so-called *akratisma*, or breakfast, which he calls *ariston*. This he mentions once in the *Odyssey*: 'Odysseus and the godlike swineherd kindled a fire and prepared breakfast [*ariston*].' And once in the *Iliad*: 'Quickly they set to work and prepared breakfast [*ariston*].' He calls the morning meal *embroma*; we call it *akratismos*, because we eat pieces of bread sopped in unmixed [*akratos*] wine. So Antiphanes retains the Homeric usage: 'While the cook is getting breakfast [*ariston*]', immediately continuing 'Have you time to join me at breakfast [*synkratisasthai*]?' Cantharus also identifies *ariston* and *akratismos*: '*A*. Let us, then, take breakfast here [*akratizometh'*]. —*B*. Not so; we will breakfast at the Isthmus [*aristesomen*].' Aristomenes: 'I'll get a little breakfast [*akratioumai mikron*], a bite or two of bread, and then come back.' But Philemon says that the ancients had four meals, *akratisma*, *ariston*, *hesperisma* ['evening meal'] and *deipnon* ['dinner']. Now the *akratisma* they called *breaking the fast*, the *ariston* ['luncheon'] they called *deipnon*, the evening meal *dorpestos*, the dinner *epidorpis*. In Aeschylus may be found the proper order of these terms, in the verses wherein Palamedes is made to say: 'I appointed captains of divisions and of hundreds over the host, and meals I taught them to distinguish, breakfasts, dinners and suppers third [*arista*, *deipna*, *dorpa*]. The fourth meal is mentioned by Homer in these words: 'Go thou when thou hast supped,' referring to what some call *deilinon*, which comes between our *ariston* ['luncheon'] and *deipnon* ['dinner']. So *ariston*, in Homer, is the meal eaten in the early morning, whereas *deipnon* is the noon meal we to-day call *ariston*, and *dorpon* is the evening meal. Perhaps, also, *deipnon* in Homer is sometimes synonymous with *ariston*; for of the morning meal he somewhere said [*Iliad*, viii. 53–4]: 'They then took their *deipnon*, and after that began to arm for battle;' that is, immediately after sunrise and the *deipnon*, they go forth to fight.

Athenaeus, *The Deipnosophists*

A note to this edition quotes the comment of a scholiast that confusion about Homeric names for meals has remained a long-standing puzzle, not solved by Athenaeus' contribution.

❧ *Thomas Hearne (1678–1735), the diarist, had been an undergraduate at St Edmund Hall, Oxford, and was appointed an assistant Librarian at the Bodleian Library. Forced to resign as a non-juror, he spent the rest of his life writing and editing scholarly works in his old college.*

Feb. 27 (Ashwed.) [1723].

It hath been an old Custom in Oxford for the Scholars of all Houses, on Shrovetuesday, to go to Dinner at 10 Clock (at which time the little Bell call'd Pan-cake Bell rings, or, at least, should ring, at St Marie's [the University Church of St Mary the Virgin]) and [to Supper] at four in the Afternoon, and it was always follow'd in Edmund Hall as long as I have been in Oxford, 'till Yesterday, when they went to dinner at 12 and Supper at six, nor were there any Fritters at Dinner, as there us'd always to be. When laudable old Customs alter, 'tis a Sign Learning dwindles.

Remarks and Collections of Thomas Hearne, Volume VIII, Oxford Historical Society, 1907

❧ *William Tayler, a 30-year-old servant in the household of Mrs Prinsep, a rich widow, in Great Cumberland Street, Mayfair, kept a diary throughout 1837 to improve his handwriting and to 'note down some of the chief things which come under my observation each day'. All Mrs Prinsep's sons were in India, where her husband had also made his fortune; and she lived alone with an unmarried daughter, three resident maidservants, and Tayler. The following entry indicates the vagueness attached to the idea of lunch at a time when it had not yet become an accepted part of every person's day, but when a household of women who indulged in it might create a demand for something similar among their servants. If the Prinseps' maidservants took lunch, this must have been in the form of elevenses, followed by a proper dinner at one o'clock, then by tea and by a late, light supper after their employers had finished eating for the day.*

[January] 22nd.

This being Sunday of course I went to church. I think I will give an account of our liveing during the next week. They breakfast at eight in the kitchen on bread and butter and toast—or anything of the kind if they like to be at the trouble of making it—and tea. All most all servants are obliged to find their own tea and sugar. For my own part I care very little about breakfast at all, therefore I jenerally wait until the breakfast comes down from the parlour at ten o'clock when my apatite has come and I can then git a cup of coco, which I am very fond of, and a rowl or something of the kind. Anyone can have lunch, there it is for them but, as I have breakfast so late, I want no lunch. This day we had for dinner a piece of surloin of beef, roasted; brocoli and potatos and preserved damson pie. We all have tea together at four o'clock with bread and butter and sometimes a cake. At nine o'clock we have supper; this evening it's cold beef and damson pie. We keep plenty of very good table ale in the house and every one can have as much as they like.

[May] 14th.

I said some time agoe I would give an account of the way the people live in the parlour. Now I think I will begin just to give you some idea of it, but as the old Lady and her daughter are quite allone at present, there is not so much cooking for the parlour as there is in general. For the parlour breakfast, they have hot rolls, dry toast, a loaf of fancy bread and a loaf of common and a slice of butter. They have the hot water come up in a hurn that has a place in the middle for a red hot iron which keep the water boiling as long as the iron keep hot. With this, they make their tea themselves. They have chocalate which is something like coffee but of a greasey and much richer nature. This is all they have for breakfast and it's the same every morning. They have it as soon as they are up, which is nine o'clock. It take them about three-quarters of an houre to breakfast.

Lunch at one, the same time we dine in the kitchen. They generally have some cut from ours or have cold meat and some vegitibles. Dinner at six which is considered very early. This day they had two soles fryed with saws [sauce], a leg of mutton, a dish of ox, pullets, potatos, brocolo, rice and a rhubarb tart, a tabiaca pudding, cheese and butter. Has tea at eight o'clock with bread and butter and dry toast; never any supper—it's not fashionable.

[May] 15th.

Breakfast as usual, cold beef and potatos for lunch. For dinner, fish and minced mutton with poarched eggs, curry, which is a kind of hot indian dish, potatos, rice, greens, cheese and butter, beer, sherry and port.

Diary of William Tayler, Footman, 1837, edited by Dorothy Wise, St Marylebone History Society, 1962

❧ *In this essay, Thomas de Quincey examines the gradual movement forward of the ancient Romans' main meal of the day from morning to evening, and compares it with a similar movement in England between the sixteenth and the early nineteenth century.*

[The] revolution as to dinner was the greatest in virtue and value ever accomplished. . . . A nation must be barbarous, neither could it have much intellectual business, which dined in the morning. They could not be at ease in the morning. So much *must* be granted: every day has its separate *quantum*, its dose of anxiety, that could not be digested so soon as noon. . . . In Henry VII's time the Court dined at eleven in the forenoon. But even that hour was considered so shockingly late in the French Court that Louis XII actually had his grey hairs brought down with sorrow to the grave by changing his regular hour of half-past nine for eleven, in gallantry to his young English bride. He fell a victim to late hours in the forenoon. In Cromwell's time they dined at one P.M. One century and a half had carried them on by two hours. Doubtless, old cooks and scullions wondered what the world would come to next. Our French neighbours were in the same predicament. But they far surpassed us in veneration for the meal. They actually dated from it. Dinner constituted the great era of the day. *L'après dîner* is almost the only date which you find in Cardinal de Retz's memoirs of the *Fronde*. Dinner was their *Hegira*—dinner was their *line* in traversing the ocean of the day: they crossed the Equator when they dined.

Our English Revolution came next; it made some little difference, I have heard people say, in Church and State; I daresay it did; like enough, but its great effects were perceived in dinner. People now dined at two. So dined Addison for his last thirty years; so, through his entire life, dined Pope, whose birth was coeval with the Revolution. Precisely as the Rebellion of 1745 arose did people (but, observe, very great people) advance to four P.M. Philosophers, who watch the 'semina rerum,' and the first symptoms of change, had perceived this alteration singing in the upper air like a coming storm some little time before. About the year 1740, Pope complains of Lady Suffolk's dining so late as four. Young people may bear these things, he observed: but, as to himself, now turned fifty, if such doings went on, if Lady Suffolk would adopt such strange hours, he really must absent himself from Marble Hill . . .

The next relay on that line of road, the next repeating frigate, is Cowper in his poem on 'Conversation.' He speaks of four o'clock as still the elegant hour for dinner—the hour for the *lautiores* and the *lepidi homines*. Now, this might be written about 1780, or a little earlier; perhaps, therefore, just one generation after Pope's Lady Suffolk. But then Cowper was living amongst the rural gentry, not in high life; yet, again, Cowper was nearly connected by blood with the eminent Whig house of Cowper, and acknowledged a kinsman.

About twenty-five years after this we may take Oxford as a good exponent of the national advance. . . . Now, in Oxford, about 1804–5, there was a general move in the dinner hour. Those colleges who dined at three, of which there were still several, now began to dine at four: those who had dined at four now translated their hour to five. These continued good general hours till about Waterloo. After that era, six, which had been somewhat of a gala hour, was promoted to the fixed station of dinner-time in ordinary; and there perhaps it will rest through centuries. For a more festal dinner, seven, eight, nine, ten, have all been in requisition since then; but I am not aware of any man's dining later than ten P.M., except in that classic case, recorded by Mr Joseph Miller, of an Irishman who must have dined much later than ten, because his servant protested, when others were enforcing the dignity of their masters by the lateness of their dinner hours, that *his* master invariably dined 'to-morrow'.

Thomas de Quincey, 'The Casuistry of Roman Meals', 1839

Louis XII: an exaggeration. Louis (1462–1515) married, as his third wife, in October 1514, Mary Tudor, sister of Henry VIII of England, and died less than three months later aged 52. Mary was already in love with the Duke of Suffolk, her future husband, and agreed to marry Louis for political reasons with the full intention of marrying Suffolk afterwards. It is unlikely that a change in Louis' dinner-hour did anything to hasten his death, at a respectably late age for the time in which he lived; *hegira*: the flight of Muhammad from Mecca to Medina in 622, determining the beginning of the Muslim era; *lautiores, lepidi homines*: most fashionable people, bon ton.

BREAKFAST

Dr Samuel Johnson (1709–84) travelled with his friend James Boswell through the Highlands and Western Isles of Scotland between August and November 1773. At that time, the simplest English breakfast consisted of bread, butter, and tea, or plain bread and milk; while more elaborate versions included cold meat, bread, butter, and coffee, tea, or chocolate. Orange marmalade was virtually unknown in England; and sweet spreads rarely, if ever, appeared on the breakfast table.

A man of the Hebrides, for of the woman's diet I can give no account, as soon as he appears in the morning, swallows a glass of whisky; yet they are not a drunken race, at least I never was present at much intemperance; but no man is so abstemious as to refuse the morning dram, which they call a *skalk*.

The word *whisky* signifies water, and is applied by way of eminence to *strong water*, or distilled liquor. The spirit drunk in the north is drawn from barley. I never tasted it, except once for experiment at the inn in *Inverary*, where I thought it preferable to any *English* malt brandy. It was strong, but not pungent, and free from the empyrheumatick taste or smell. What was the process I had no opportunity of enquiring, nor do I wish to improve the art of making poison pleasant.

Not long after the dram, may be expected the breakfast, a meal in which the Scots, whether of the lowlands or mountains, must be confessed to excel us. The tea and coffee are accompanied not only with butter, but with honey, conserves and marmalades. If an epicure could remove by a wish, in quest of sensual gratification, wherever he had supped he would breakfast in Scotland.

In the islands, however, they do what I found it not very easy to endure. They pollute the tea-table [at breakfast] by plates piled with large slices of cheshire cheese, which mingles its less grateful odours with the fragrance of the tea.

Johnson, *Journey to the Western Islands*

❧ *An insight into country-house mealtimes before luncheon was introduced as a regular feature of the day. Although written in a spirit of satirical exaggeration, the novel is true to life in its depiction of the kind of breakfast (during the Regency period still mainly cold, with no bacon and fried eggs or sputtering kidneys in chafing-dishes) with which country-house guests used to sustain themselves until dinner in mid- to late afternoon.*

It was an old custom at Headlong Hall to have breakfast ready at eight, and continue it till two; that the various guests might rise at their own hour, breakfast when they came down, and employ the morning as they thought proper; the squire only expecting that they should punctually assemble at dinner. During the whole of this period, the little butler stood sentinel at a side-table near the fire, copiously furnished with all the apparatus of tea, coffee, chocolate, milk, cream, eggs, rolls, toast, muffins, bread, butter, potted beef, cold fowl and partridge, ham, tongue, and anchovy. The Reverend Doctor Gaster found himself rather *queasy* in the morning, therefore preferred breakfasting in bed, on a mug of buttered ale and an anchovy toast. The three philosophers made their appearance at breakfast, and enjoyed *les prémices des dépouilles* [the first-fruits of the spoils]. Mr Foster proposed that, as it was a fine frosty morning, and they were all good pedestrians, they should take a walk to Tremadoc, to see the improvements carrying on in that vicinity. This being readily acceded to, they began their walk.

Thomas Love Peacock, *Headlong Hall*, 1816

❧ *From an epic poem about life among the Lithuanian gentry, politically separated from their fellow-Poles in the Grand Duchy of Warsaw, on the eve of Napoleon's Russian campaign of 1812.*

Then in the quiet deserted house arose first a murmur, then an uproar and merry cries, as in an empty hive when bees fly back into it: that was a sign that the guests had returned from hunting, and that the servants were busying themselves with breakfast.

Through all the rooms there reigned a mighty bustle; they were carrying about knives and forks, plates of food and bottles; the men, just as they had come in, in their green suits, walked about the rooms with plates and glasses, and ate and drank; or, leaning against the window casements, they talked of guns, hounds, and hares. The Chamberlain and his family and the Judge were seated at the table; in a corner the young ladies whispered together; there was no such order as is observed at dinners and suppers. In this old-fashioned Polish household this was a new custom; at breakfasts the Judge, though loth, permitted such disorder, but he did not commend it.

There were likewise different dishes for the ladies and for the gentlemen. Here they carried around trays with an entire coffee service, immense trays, charmingly painted with flowers, and on them fragrant, smoking tin pots, and golden cups of Dresden china, and with each cup a tiny little jug of cream. In no other country is there such coffee as in Poland. In Poland, in a respectable household, a special woman is, by ancient custom, charged with the preparation of coffee. She is called the coffee-maker; she brings from the city, or gets from the river barges, berries of the finest sort, and she knows secret ways of preparing the drink, which is black as coal, transparent as amber, fragrant as mocha, and thick as honey. Everybody knows how necessary for coffee is good cream: in the country this is not hard to get; for the coffee-maker, early in the day, after setting her pots on the fire, visits the dairy, and with her own hands lightly skims the fresh flower of the milk into a separate little jug for each cup, that each of them may be dressed in its separate little cap.

The older ladies had risen early and had already drunk their coffee; now they had made for them a second dish, of warm beer, whitened with cream, in which swam curds cut into little bits.

The gentlemen had their choice of smoked meats; fat half-geese, hams, and slices of tongue—all choice, all cured in home fashion in the chimney with juniper smoke. Finally they brought in stewed beef with gravy as the last course: such was breakfast in the Judge's house.

Adam Mickiewicz, *Pan Tadeusz*, 1834, translated by George Rapall Noyes, 1930

❧ *Phoebe, a young girl, has come to stay with her eccentric elderly relation, Hepzibah, at the House of the Seven Gables* (*in Salem, Massachusetts*).

When Phoebe awoke—which she did with the early twittering of the conjugal couple of robins in the pear tree—she heard movements belowstairs, and, hastening down, found Hepzibah already in the kitchen. She stood by a window, holding a book in close contiguity to her nose, as if with the hope of gaining an olfactory acquaintance with its contents, since her imperfect vision made it not very easy to read them. . . . It was a cookery book, full of innumerable old fashions of English dishes, and illustrated with engravings, which represented the arrangements of the table at such banquets as it might have befitted a nobleman to give in the great hall of his castle. And, amid these rich and potent devices of the culinary art . . . poor Hepzibah was seeking for some nimble little titbit, which, with what skill she had, and such materials as were at hand, she might toss up for breakfast.

Soon, with a deep sigh, she put aside the savory volume, and inquired of Phoebe whether old Speckle, as she called one of the hens, had laid an egg the preceding day. Phoebe ran to see, but returned without the expected treasure in her hand. At that instant, however, the blast of a fish-dealer's conch was heard, announcing his approach along the street. With energetic raps at the shop-window, Hepzibah summoned the man in, and made purchase of what he warranted as the finest mackerel in his cart, and as fat a one as ever he felt with his finger so early in the season. Requesting Phoebe to roast some coffee—which she casually observed was the real Mocha, and so long kept that each of the small berries ought to be worth its weight in gold—the maiden lady heaped fuel into the vast receptacle of the ancient fireplace in such quantity as soon to drive the lingering dusk out of the kitchen. The country girl, willing to give her utmost assistance, proposed to make an Indian cake, after her mother's peculiar method, of easy manufacture, and which she could vouch for as possessing a richness, and, if rightly prepared, a delicacy, unequalled by any other mode of breakfast cake. Hepzibah gladly assenting, the kitchen was soon the scene of savory preparation.

* * * * *

Life, within doors, has few pleasanter prospects than a neatly arranged and well-provisioned breakfast table. We come to it freshly, in the dewy youth of the day, and when our spiritual and sensual elements are in better accord than at a later period; so that the material delights of the morning meal are capable of being fully enjoyed, without any very grievous reproaches, whether gastric or conscientious, for yielding even a trifle overmuch to the animal department of our nature. The thoughts, too, that run around the ring of familiar guests have a piquancy and mirthfulness, and oftentimes a vivid truth, which more rarely find their way into the elaborate intercourse of dinner. Hepzibah's small and ancient table, supported on its slender and graceful legs, and covered with a cloth of the richest damask, looked worthy to be the scene and center of one of the cheerfullest of parties. The vapor of the broiled fish arose like incense from the shrine of a barbarian idol, while the fragrance of the Mocha might have gratified the nostrils of a tutelary Lar, or whatever power has scope over a modern breakfast table. Phoebe's Indian cakes were the sweetest offering of all—in their hue befitting the rustic altars of the innocent and golden age—or, so brightly yellow were they, resembling some of the bread which was changed to glistening gold when Midas tried to eat it. The butter must not be forgotten—butter which Phoebe herself had churned, in her own rural home, and brought it to her cousin as a propitiatory gift—smelling of clover blossoms, and diffusing the charm of pastoral scenery through the dark-panelled parlour.

Nathaniel Hawthorne, *The House of the Seven Gables*, 1851

❧ *Ellen Montgomery, a young girl from New York, has been sent to stay with an unknown aunt up-country while her mother accompanies her dying father to Europe.*

The noise of hissing and sputtering now became quite violent, and the smell of the cooking, to Ellen's fancy, rather too strong to be pleasant. Before a good fire stood Miss Fortune, holding the end of a very long handle by which she was kept in communication with a flat vessel on the fire, in which Ellen soon discovered that all this noisy and odorous cooking was going on.

* * * * *

In a few minutes the pan was removed from the fire, and Miss Fortune went on to take out the brown slices of nicely-fried pork, and arrange them in a deep dish, leaving a small quantity of clear fat in the pan. Ellen, who was greatly interested, and observing every step most attentively, settled in her own mind that certainly this would be thrown away, being fit for nothing but the pigs. But Miss Fortune did not think so, for she darted into some pantry close by, and returning with a cup of cream in her hand emptied it all into the pork fat. Then she ran into the pantry again for a little round tin-box, with a cover full of holes, and shaking this gently over the pan, a fine white shower of flour fell upon the cream. The pan was then replaced on the fire and stirred, and to Ellen's astonishment the whole changed, as if by magic, to a thick, stiff, white froth. It was not till Miss Fortune was carefully pouring this over the fried slices in the dish that Ellen suddenly recollected that breakfast was ready and she was not.

Wetherall, *The Wide, Wide World*

❧ *Fred and Rosamond Vincy have both returned to their parents' comfortable home in Middlemarch: Rosamond from boarding-school, where she has acquired refined tastes and manners, and Fred from university, where he has failed his examinations.*

[The] table often remained covered with the relics of the family breakfast long after Mr Vincy had gone with his second son to the warehouse, and when Miss Morgan was already far on in morning lessons with the younger girls in the school-room. It awaited the family laggard, who found any sort of inconvenience (to others) less disagreeable than getting up when he was called. This was the case one morning of the October in which we have seen Mr Casaubon visiting the Grange; and though the room was a little overheated with the fire, which had sent the spaniel panting to a remote corner, Rosamond, for some reason, continued to sit at her embroidery longer than usual, now and then giving herself a little shake, and laying her work on her knee to contemplate it with an air of hesitating weariness. Her mamma, who had returned from an excursion to the kitchen, sat on the other side of the small work-table with an air of more entire placidity, until, the clock again giving notice that it was going to strike, she looked up from the lace-mending which was occupying her plump fingers and rang the bell.

'Knock at Mr Fred's door again, Pritchard, and tell him it has struck half-past ten.'

* * * * *

'Mamma,' said Rosamond, 'when Fred comes down I wish you would not let him have red herrings. I cannot bear the smell of them all over the house at this hour of the morning.'

'Oh, my dear, you are so hard on your brothers! It is the only fault I have to find with you. You are the sweetest temper in the world, but are so tetchy with your brothers.'

'Not tetchy, mamma; you never hear me speak in an unladylike way.'

'Well, but you want to deny them things.'

'Brothers are so unpleasant.'

* * * * *

'Have you got nothing else for my breakfast, Pritchard?' said Fred, to the servant who brought in coffee and buttered toast; while he walked round the table surveying the ham, potted beef, and other cold remnants, with an air of silent rejection, and polite forbearance from signs of disgust.

'Should you like eggs, sir?'

'Eggs, no! Bring me a grilled bone.'

'Really, Fred,' said Rosamond when the servant had left the room, 'if you must have hot things for breakfast, I wish you would come down earlier. You get up at six o'clock to go out hunting. I cannot understand why you find it so difficult to get up on other mornings.'

'That is your want of understanding. Rosy, I can get up to go hunting because I like it.'

'What would you think of me if I came down two hours after every one else and ordered grilled bone?'

'I should think you were an uncommonly fast young lady,' said Fred, eating his toast with the utmost composure.

'I cannot see why brothers are to make themselves disagreeable, any more than sisters.'

'I don't make myself disagreeable; it is you who find me so. Disagreeable is a word that describes your feelings and not my actions.'

'I think it describes the smell of grilled bone.'

Eliot, *Middlemarch*

❧ *Kester is working on a farm, probably in Mrs Gaskell's native Cheshire.*

They were late in rising the next morning. Kester was long since up, and at his work among the cattle, before he saw the house-door open to admit the fresh, chill morning air; and even then Sylvia brushed softly past, and went about almost on tiptoe. When the porridge was ready, Kester was called to his breakfast, which he took, sitting at the dresser, with the family. A large wooden platter stood in the middle; and each had a bowl of the same material filled with milk. The way was for everyone to dip his pewter spoon into the central dish, and convey as much or as little as he liked at a time of the hot porridge into his pure fresh milk. But, today, Bell told Kester to help himself all at once, and to take his bowl up to the master's room and keep him company. . . . So Kester went up slowly, carrying his over-full basin tenderly, and seated himself on the step leading down into the bed-room (for levels had not been calculated, when the old house was built), facing his master.

Gaskell, *Sylvia's Lovers*

The scarlet and orange light outside the malthouse did not penetrate to its interior, which was, as usual, lighted by a rival glow of similar hue radiating from the hearth.

The maltster, after having lain down in his clothes for a few hours, was now sitting beside a three-legged table, breakfasting off bread and bacon. This was eaten on the plateless system, which is performed by placing a slice of bread upon the table, the meat flat upon the bread, a mustard plaster upon the meat, and a pinch of salt upon the whole, then cutting them vertically downwards with a large pocket-knife till wood is reached, when the severed lump is impaled on the knife, elevated, and sent the proper way of food.

The maltster's lack of teeth appeared not to sensibly diminish his powers as a mill. He had been without them for so many years that toothlessness was felt less to be a defect than hard gums an acquisition. Indeed, he seemed to approach the grave as a hyperbolic curve approaches a straight line—less directly as he got nearer, till it was doubtful if he would ever reach it at all.

In the ashpit was a heap of potatoes roasting, and a boiling pipkin of charred bread, called 'coffee', for the benefit of whomsoever should call, for Warren's was a sort of clubhouse, used as an alternative to the inn.

Thomas Hardy, *Far From the Madding Crowd*, 1874

In the mid-nineteenth century, malthouses were as common as breweries, and existed to provide these with a constant supply of malted barley for brewing beer. The fires which heated the malt-kilns were usually banked up and left smouldering overnight; but a maltster working single-handed might well stay with his fire to keep it going and to make sure that the kilns did not become accidentally overheated.

❧ *Bitter 'Oxford' marmalade in its distinctive, lidless stoneware jars became a regular feature of undergraduate breakfasts from 1874, when Frank Cooper and his wife began to manufacture and sell the product at their family grocery shop, the Italian Warehouse, in High Street, Oxford. All kinds of health-giving properties were attributed to marmalade in the years before the First World War; and Frank Cooper promoted it especially as an energy-giving food for athletes in training. Aesthetes, on the other hand, adopted coffee, rolls, and marmalade as a preferable alternative to the heavy, meaty, masculine breakfasts of the (mainly lunchless) Victorian period.*

§ The Duke of Dorset is in his lodgings opposite the Sheldonian Theatre in Broad Street.

The breakfast things were not yet cleared away. A plate freaked with fine strains of marmalade, an empty toast-rack, a broken roll—these and other things bore witness to a day inaugurated in the right spirit.

Away from them, reclining along his window-seat, was the Duke. Blue spirals rose from his cigarette, nothing in the air to trouble them. From their railing across the road, the Emperors gazed at him.

Max Beerbohm, *Zuleika Dobson*, 1911

§ *Willie Elmhirst went up to Worcester College, Oxford in 1911. In his second term he entertained 'Togger', the college team in the Torpids boat-race, to a customary breakfast.*

Thursday, 22 February 1912.

At 8.15 after keeping Chapel I met Wyatt [his college servant] on the Terrace & he said things were going contrariwise as my table had just broken in half! So they were putting us in the leccer room below. However everything was ready by 8.30 & so were the Togger. . . . We began with porridge, then chicken, omelette, lettuce & watercress, prunes, jam or marmalade & an apple to top up with. Jones wouldn't take the head of the table so I had to. We finished about 9.30 & then they all thanked us profusely. They have the same thing next term when the Eight goes into training.

Willie Elmhirst, *A Freshman's Diary, 1911–1912*, 1969

§ *Charles Ryder, an 'aesthetic' undergraduate in the 1920s, has spent a sleepless night after a disturbing conversation the previous evening.*

It was the last Sunday of term; the last of the [academic] year. As I went to my bath, the quad filled with gowned and surpliced undergraduates drifting from chapel to hall. As I came back they were standing in groups, smoking; Jasper had bicycled in from his digs to be among them.

I walked down the empty Broad to breakfast, as I often did on Sundays, at a tea-shop opposite Balliol. The air was full of bells from the surrounding spires and the sun, casting long shadows across the surrounding spaces, dispelled the fears of night. The tea-shop was hushed as a library; a few solitary men in bedroom-slippers from Balliol and Trinity looked up as I entered, then turned back to their Sunday newspapers. I ate my scrambled eggs and bitter marmalade with the zest which in youth follows a restless night. I lit a cigarette and sat on, while one by one the Balliol and Trinity men paid their bills and shuffled away, slip-slop, across the street to their colleges.

It was nearly eleven when I left, and during my walk I heard the change-ringing cease and, all over the town, give place to the single chime which warned the city that the service was about to start.

Evelyn Waugh, *Brideshead Revisited*, 1945

John, Susan, Titty, and Roger have been captured by Chinese pirates and taken to the home of the English-educated pirate princess, Missee Lee. Their uncle Jim (*Captain Flint*) *has been imprisoned.*

A bell sounded and the amah bustled them out. 'Missee Lee,' she said. 'You belong chow chiu fan . . . bleakfast . . . longside Missee Lee.'

She led the way through the garden to Miss Lee's house and into Miss Lee's Cambridge study.

'Good morning,' said Miss Lee, who was pouring out coffee at the head of a trestle-table that had been put up at one side of the room.

Staring at the table, they said 'Good morning.'

'Gosh!' murmured Roger.

'Sit down, please,' said Miss Lee, and they sat down, three on each side. In the middle of the table was a large jar of Cooper's Oxford marmalade. In front of each of them was a bowl of porridge and from somewhere in the house came a smell of fried ham that made Roger sniff and sniff again.

'Knives and forks,' said Roger.

'And spoons,' said Titty.

'Evellything Camblidge fashion,' said Miss Lee proudly. 'Sugar, please? Please take milk.'

'Jolly good porridge,' said Nancy after her first mouthful. 'Wouldn't Uncle Jim like some. . . .'

For a moment they all thought of Captain Flint, sitting behind bars, doing his best to eat rice with chopsticks. The thought spoilt the taste of the porridge.

'Chinese food is velly wholesome,' said Miss Lee. 'You need not wolly about your Captain Flint. Taicoon Chang will tleat him velly well till he gets his answer from Amelica.'

* * * * *

The smell of fried ham grew suddenly stronger, and men came in, took the empty porridge bowls away and set a plate before each one of them, with fried ham on fried toast with two very little eggs, fried, on top of the ham.

Miss Lee said she was sorry about the size of the eggs. 'Camblidge eggs are bigger. Velly small eggs. Velly small hens.'

'Bantams, I bet,' said Roger.

After the ham and eggs, Miss Lee invited them to take toast and marmalade. 'We always eat Oxford marmalade at Camblidge,' she said. 'Better scholars, better plofessors at Camblidge but better marmalade at Oxford.'

Arthur Ransome, *Missee Lee*, 1941

LUNCH

❧ *Formerly a mid-morning snack or 'nuncheon', taken to fill the gap between an early breakfast and an afternoon dinner, lunch in England became a recognizable meal in its own right early in the nineteenth century, among a small (largely female) section of society, as the dinner-hour among fashionable people progressed, with some fluctuation backwards and forwards, from three, four, or five in the afternoon to the drastically later hour of eight.*

The furtive snack was thriving like some poor foundling who learns that he is the bearer of an honoured name. As early as 1818 luncheon seems to have been served regularly between 1 and 2 o'clock at Bowood, the Lansdownes' place in Wiltshire. Such a habit was unusual; very few of the subjects of George III were anticipating our custom so closely. However, in the very same year that Creevey was supporting 3.45 as 'much the best hour to dine at', in the year 1822 there was appearing, in monthly parts, a work entitled *Real Life in London*. . . . 'Women . . . [this stated] are not quite so irrational as men, in London, for they generally sit down to a substantial lunch about three or four; and if men would do the same, the meal at eight would be relieved of many of its weighty dishes.' To emphasize his point, that luncheon was a fashionable innovation, welcomed by the ladies but despised by the gentlemen, the writer goes on to say that even in those circles where hostesses had their way and dinner was delayed till 8, the gentlemen, rather than fall in with new-fangled notions, would arrive famished and fasting, having eaten practically nothing since breakfast. In these circumstances dinner naturally grew larger and lasted longer than ever, and supper disappeared. The stomachs of men like Creevey, dining one day at 3.45 and another at 8, supping one night and not the next, must have been enviably accommodating.

* * * * *

Thus began a domestic schism which was to last for a long time and has not yet been entirely healed. The day divided into two forms, a man's day and a woman's, and they ran on simultaneously and separate. We will look first at the ladies.

* * * * *

1823 Miss Edgeworth, on her way to visit Sir Walter Scott at Abbotsford, stopped for lunch at Moulinan. 'First course, cold; two roast chickens, better never were; a ham, finer never seen, even at my mother's luncheons; pickled salmon, and cold boiled round. Second course, hot; a large dish of little trout from the river; new potatoes and . . . a dish of mashed potatoes for me; fresh greens, with toast over, and poached eggs. Then, a custard pudding, a gooseberry tart, and plenty of Highland cream—*highly* superior to lowland—and butter, ditto.' For this, she was charged six shillings. On arrival at Abbotsford she passed—she had no choice—into Scott's régime, back into the days of no luncheon, dinner in the middle of the afternoon, late supper, and all the rest of it.

1831 The same lady, being in London, attended a luncheon party of forty people. It was an unusual affair, not only on account of its size but also because a man presided, the Bishop of Llandaff.

1832 (approximately) In one of the early chapters of *Coningsby* two gentlemen, wandering round a large London house, open the door of a room where the ladies are lunching. The hour seems to have been about 2.45. They are invited to join the ladies and, with some apparent hesitation, they do so and are served with chicken pie with truffles, sherry, and 'confectionery'.

The idea of a set luncheon was slow to make its mark in the modest houses of rural districts. At Mrs Reed's (*Jane Eyre*) dinner was over by three. Even so, luncheon is mentioned, but it can hardly have been more than the old-time snack. In *Cranford* nobody, not even the Honourable Mrs Jamieson, ever lunched or could have lunched. One of Miss Mitford's villagers still 'rose at four in winter and summer, breakfasted at six, dined at eleven in the forenoon, supped at five, and was regularly in bed by eight.' She is, of course, presented as a survival, but the reader is clearly meant to be amused, not incredulous, much as we should be today by an old gentleman who persisted in paying afternoon calls in a top hat.

Arnold Palmer, *Movable Feasts. A Reconnaissance of the Origins and Consequences of Fluctuations in Meal-Times with special attention to the introduction of Luncheon and Afternoon Tea*, 1952

Nathaniel Hawthorne (1804–64) was American consul at Liverpool from 1853 until he left for Italy in 1858.

March 6th [1856].

Yesterday I lunched on board Captain Russell's ship the *Princeton*. These daily lunches on shipboard might answer very well the purposes of a dinner; being, in fact, noonday dinners, with soup, roast mutton, mutton chops, and a macaroni pudding—brandy, port and sherry wines. There were three elderly Englishmen at table, with white heads,—which, I think, is oftener the predicament of elderly heads here than in America. One of these was a retired Customs-House officer, and the other two were connected with the shipping in some way. There is a satisfaction in seeing Englishmen eat and drink, they do it so heartily, and, on the whole, so wisely,—trusting so entirely that there is no harm in good beef and mutton, and a reasonable quantity of good liquor; and these three hale old men, who had acted on this wholesome faith so long, were proofs that it is well on earth to live like earthly creatures. In America, what squeamishness, what delicacy, what stomachic apprehension, would there not be among three stomachs of sixty or seventy years' experience! I think this failure of American stomachs is partly due to our ill-usage of our digestive powers, and partly to our want of faith in them.

Passages from the English Note-Books of Nathaniel Hawthorne, 1870, Volume I

Most Oxford and Cambridge colleges lagged behind other English institutions in recognizing the existence of lunch. Until the Second World War, some colleges provided only 'commons' at lunch-time: individual rations of soup, bread and cheese or cold meat, and college-brewed ale, which undergraduates ordered from the buttery and ate alone or with a friend in their rooms. King's College, Cambridge, under the stewardship of an enthusiastically sociable Fellow, Oscar Browning, was among the earliest to institute an informal, communal lunch, offering plain, hot or cold nursery food such as 'white' soup, fish, mince or cold roast meat, and rice pudding or stewed fruit. Here we find ourselves in the ambience of a novel by E. M. Forster rather than in that of Zuleika Dobson *or* Brideshead Revisited; *for it was not (as Browning emphasized) the food which mattered at these meals, but the opportunities for exchanging ideas and making new friends.*

Oscar Browning to Michael Sadler (Steward of Christ Church, Oxford), 12 May 1891.

My dear Sadler,

Our common luncheon in Hall is a great success. Things are ordered à la carte. The usual prices are Soup 6d., Fish or Entrée 6d., made dish 8d., cold meat 3d. or 4d. Vegetables or salad 1d., Pudding 3d. Men order whatever they like but the whole style is simple. There is also a charge of 3d. for bread and waiting which is imposed on Fellows as well as on Undergraduates and is charged to the Buttery account.

2. Members of College entertain out[-of-]College friends at luncheon. The luncheon is served at the tables used for dinner and the most delightful part of the arrangement is that Dons, Undergraduates & their friends all sit together and the conversation is quite general and I may say unrestrained.

3. Men still continue to give luncheon parties in their own rooms, but I imagine there is very little of that kind of entertainment. You must understand that our undergraduates here are as a rule poor, and are simple in their habits of life. I do not expect a man to bring in more than two friends to luncheon at a time although there is no rule.

4. Some men still lunch in their rooms on bread and marmalade for sake of economy and some people I know find that the Hall luncheon is an occasion of expense. I think it saves me personally about £40 a year.

5. The common luncheon has certainly tended to increase the sociability of the College, but I must repeat that the general character of it is as I said before extremely simple.

Believe me, / Ever yours, / Oscar Browning.

Steward's Memorandum Book, 1888–95, Christ Church, Oxford

I once gave a waiter—but a head, head-waiter—advice. He was the incredibly all-knowing, bearded, inscrutable *maître d'hôtel* of the Carlton Grill Room. He positively came to me one day when I was lunching and asked if I could give him advice how to find the house in which Casanova lived in London. . . . He wanted the information for some American clients who were making a pilgrimage to all the places dwelt in by Casanova—and if possible to the very houses.

* * * * *

Later he came back to my table and leaning one hand on the cloth said:

'Why do you ever lunch anywhere else but here? This is the best grill-room in the most famous hotel in the world. It should be good enough for you.' I used the word: 'Expensive.'

He looked down sardonically at my *couvert*.

'Yes,' he said, 'but what do you want with a lunch like that? Half a dozen oysters, that alone is enough for a lunch for a young man like you. But you follow it by *pâté de Périgord* and quails stewed with grapes. And you drink a half Berncastler and a half Pontet Canet 1906. . . . What sort of lunch is that and can you grumble if it costs you the eyes out of your head?'

I said that I was very busy and need sustaining. He said:

'A lunch like that will not sustain you. After it you will be sleepy and your business will be a battle. Do you suppose I could do my work if I lunched like that? No, take my advice. Lunch here every day. We do not ask you to spend enormous sums but to have a good lunch. You will take a chump chop, or a steak, or some kidney or any other thing of the grill. You will have some Stilton or Cheshire cheese, butter and the choice of twelve different sorts of bread and cheese biscuits. You will drink iced water or Perrier or, if you like, a half bottle of our vin ordinaire rouge which I drink myself. It costs one and ninepence. If you have mineral water you will save a shilling. So your lunch will cost you two or three and ninepence. The chop and the cheese cost two shillings. You will have the same seat and the same waiter whom I will choose for you myself. You will tip him fifteen shillings on the first day of every month. You will be troubled by no tiresome suggestions to take more costly food and you will be under no sense of obligation. I have several of the richest and most distinguished men in London among my regular clients and they never spend or tip more.'

Ford, *Return to Yesterday*

❧ *Constantine Levin, a young, liberal-minded landowner, has returned to his country estate after staying in Moscow, where he has unsuccessfully proposed to Kitty Shcherbatsky. Wanting exercise, and having discovered that he enjoys mowing hay with a scythe, he tells his brother Koznyshev that he intends to spend a whole day in the field with the peasants. Throughout the novel, most of the food associated with Levin's way of life is wholesome and simple; but in this incident the shared bread and water has an almost sacramental quality, confirming Levin's commitment to hard work and an understanding of his work-people.*

'It is splendid physical exercise, but you will hardly be able to hold out,' remarked Koznyshev without the least sarcasm.

'I have tried it. At first it seems hard, but one gets drawn into it. I don't think I shall lag behind.'

'Dear me! But tell me, how do the peasants take it? . . . How can you dine with them? It would not be quite the thing to send you claret and roast turkey out there?'

'No; I will just come home at their dinner-time.'

* * * * *

Levin did not notice how time passed. Had he been asked how long he had been mowing he would have answered 'half an hour', although it was nearly noon. As they were about to begin another swath the old man drew Levin's attention to the little boys and girls approaching from all sides along the road and through the long grass, hardly visible above it, carrying jugs of kvas stoppered with rags, and bundles of bread which strained their little arms.

'Look at the midges crawling along!' he said, pointing to the children and glancing at the sun from under his lifted hand. They completed two more swaths and then the old man stopped.

'Come, master! It's dinner-time,' said he with decision. All the mowers on reaching the river went across the swaths to where their coats lay, and where the children who had brought their dinners sat waiting for them. The men who had driven from a distance gathered in the shadow of their carts; those who lived nearer sheltered under the willow growth, on which they hung grass.

Levin sat down beside them; he did not want to go away.

All the peasants' restraint in the presence of the master had vanished. The men began preparing for dinner. Some had a wash. The young lads bathed in the river; others arranged places for their after-dinner rest, unfastened their bags of bread and unstoppered their jugs of kvas. The old man broke some rye bread into a bowl, mashed it with a spoon handle, poured over it some water from his tin, broke more bread into it and salted it, and then, turning to the East, said grace.

'Come, master, have some of my dinner,' said he, kneeling in front of his bowl.

The bread and water was so nice that Levin gave up all intention of going home for lunch. He shared the old man's meal and got into conversation with him about his domestic affairs, taking a lively interest in them and telling him about his own, giving him all the particulars which would interest the old peasant. When the old man got up and, having said grace, lay down beneath the willows with an armful of grass under his head, Levin did the same, regardless of the flies, importunate and persistent in the sunshine, and of the crawling insects that tickled his perspiring face and body. He at once fell asleep.

Tolstoy, *Anna Karenina*, translated by Louise and Aylmer Maude

Kvas: rye beer.

❧ *Ursula Brangwen, a new young teacher in a crowded, alienating school, has befriended a colleague, Maggie Schofield. 'Dinner' in this context means the midday meal (classified here, for convenience, as lunch), which working people earlier this century, especially in the North of England, often took with them to eat reheated, or had delivered to them hot by a member of the family, at the workplace.*

Ursula took her dinner to school, and during the second week ate it in Miss Schofield's room. Standard Three classroom stood by itself and had windows on two sides, looking on to the playground. It was a passionate relief to find such a retreat in the jarring school. For there were pots of chrysanthemums and coloured leaves, and a big jar of berries: there were pretty little pictures on the wall, photogravure reproductions from Greuze, and Reynolds's 'Age of Innocence', giving an air of intimacy.

* * * * *

It was Monday. She had been at school a week and was getting used to the surroundings, though she was still an entire foreigner in herself. She looked forward to having dinner with Maggie. That was the bright spot of the day. Maggie was so strong and remote, walking with slow, sure steps down a hard road, carrying the dream within her. Ursula went through the class teaching as through a meaningless daze.

Her class tumbled out at midday in haphazard fashion. . . . She hurried away to the teachers' room.

Mr Brunt was crouching at the small stove, putting a little rice-pudding into the oven. He rose then, and attentively poked in a small saucepan on the hob with a fork. Then he replaced the saucepan lid.

'Aren't they done?' asked Ursula gaily, breaking in on his tense absorption.

She always kept a bright, blithe manner, and was pleasant to all the teachers. For she felt like a swan among the geese, of superior heritage and belonging. And her pride at being the swan in this ugly school was not yet abated.

'Not yet,' replied Mr Brunt, laconic.

'I wonder if my dish is hot,' she said, bending down at the oven. She half expected him to look for her, but he took no notice. She was hungry and she poked her finger eagerly in the pot to see if her brussels sprouts and potatoes and meat were ready. They were not.

'Don't you think it's rather jolly bringing dinner?' she said to Mr Brunt.

'I don't know as I do,' he said, spreading a serviette on a corner of the table, and not looking at her.

* * * * *

Miss Schofield took her brown dish, and Ursula followed with her own. The cloth was laid in the pleasant Standard Three room, there was a jar with two or three monthly roses on the table.

* * * * *

Maggie Schofield . . . poured out her savoury mess of big golden beans and brown gravy.

'It is vegetarian hot-pot,' said Miss Schofield. 'Would you like to try it?'

'I should love to,' said Ursula.

Her own dinner seemed coarse and ugly beside this savoury, clean dish.

'I've never eaten vegetarian things,' she said. 'But I should think they can be good.'

'I'm not really a vegetarian,' said Maggie. 'I don't like to bring meat to school.'

'No,' said Ursula, 'I don't think I do either.'

And again her soul rang an answer to a new refinement, a new liberty. If all vegetarian things were as nice as this, she would be glad to escape the slight uncleanness of meat.

'How good!' she cried.

'Yes,' said Miss Schofield, and she proceeded to tell her the receipt.

D. H. Lawrence, *The Rainbow*, 1915

❧ *Eugene Gant is now 8 years old, and his parents, while continuing to live in the same town, have separated: his mother to run a boarding-house with new-found habits of parsimony, his father continuing his former way of life, looked after by Eugene's indulgent elder sister Helen.*

Of mornings he stayed at Gant's with Helen, playing ball with Buster Isaacs, a cousin of Max, a plump, jolly little boy who lived next door; summoned later by the rich incense of Helen's boiling fudge. She sent him to the little Jewish grocery down the street for the sour relishes which she liked so well: tabled in mid-morning they ate sour pickles, heavy slabs of ripe tomatoes, coated with thick mayonnaise, amber percolated coffee, fig-newtons and ladyfingers, hot pungent fudge pebbled with walnuts and coated fragrantly with butter, sandwiches of tender bacon and cucumber, iced belchy soft drinks.

Wolfe, *Look Homeward, Angel*

TEA

❧ *'Of late years,' Charlotte Brontë's novel* Shirley *begins, 'an abundant shower of curates has fallen upon the north of England.' In 1811, when this novel begins, there are fewer; but a group of three curates, all close friends, has descended on the Rectory, home of Mr Helstone and his young niece Caroline, where she is already unwillingly entertaining female neighbours. The clergymen, she is told, will stay for* (*high*) *tea.*

Miss Helstone's duties of hostess performed, more anxiously than cheerily, she betook herself to the kitchen, to hold a brief privy-council with Fanny and Eliza about the tea.

'What a lot on 'em!' cried Eliza, who was cook. 'And I put off the baking to-day because I thought there would be bread plenty to fit while morning: we shall never have enow.'

'Are there any tea-cakes?' asked the young mistress.

'Only three and a loaf. I wish these fine folk would stay at home till they're asked'.

'Then,' suggested Caroline, to whom the importance of the emergency gave a certain energy, 'Fanny must run down to Briarfield and buy some muffins and crumpets, and some biscuits: and don't be cross, Eliza, we can't help it now.'

'And which tea-things are we to have?'

'Oh, the best, I suppose: I'll get out the silver service,' and she ran upstairs to the plate-closet, and presently brought down tea-pot, cream-ewer, and sugar-basin.

'And mun we have th'urn?'

'Yes; and now get it ready as quickly as you can, for the sooner we have tea over, the sooner they will go—at least, I hope so.'

*   *   *   *   *

Yorkshire people, in those days, took their tea round the table; sitting well into it, with their knees duly introduced under the mahogany. It was essential to have a multitude of plates of bread and butter, varied in sorts and plentiful in quantity: it was thought proper, too, that on the centre-plate should stand a glass dish of marmalade; among the viands was expected to be found a small assortment of cheesecakes and tarts: if there was also a plate of thin slices of pink ham garnished with green parsley, so much the better.

Eliza, the Rector's cook, fortunately knew her business as provider: she had been put out of humour a little at first, when the invaders came so unexpectedly in such strength; but it appeared that she regained her cheerfulness with action, for in due time the tea was spread forth in handsome style; and neither ham, tarts nor marmalade were wanting among its accompaniments.

Charlotte Brontë, *Shirley*, 1849

❧ *Rachel Ray is the spirited younger daughter of a widow living in a Devon village. Her stern, widowed elder sister, Mrs Prime, lives with them, exerting a repressive influence except when absent on good works.*

There were during the summer months four Dorcas afternoons held weekly in Baslehurst, at all of which Mrs Prime presided. It was her custom to start soon after dinner, so as to reach the working-room by three o'clock, and there she would remain till nine, or as long as the daylight remained. The meeting was held in a sitting-room belonging to Miss Pucker, for the use of which the Institution paid some moderate rent. The other ladies, all belonging to Baslehurst, were accustomed to go home to tea in the middle of their labours; but, as Mrs Prime could not do this because of the distance, she remained with Miss Pucker, paying for such refreshment as she needed. In this way there came to be a great friendship between Mrs Prime and Miss Pucker; or rather, perhaps, Mrs Prime thus obtained the services of a most obedient minister.

Rachel had on various occasions gone with her sister to the Dorcas meetings, and once or twice had remained at Miss Pucker's house, drinking tea there. But this she greatly disliked. She was aware, when she did so, that her sister paid for her, and she thought that Dorothea showed by her behaviour that she was mistress of the entertainment. And then Rachel greatly disliked Miss Pucker. . . . When Rachel had last left Miss Pucker's room she had resolved that she would never again drink tea there. She had not said to herself positively that she would attend no more of the Dorcas meetings;—but as regarded their summer arrangement this resolve against the tea-drinking amounted almost to the same thing.

* * * * *

No word had been said on a subject so wicked and full of vanity, but Mrs Ray knew that her evening meal would be brought in at half-past five in the shape of a little feast,—a feast which would not be spread if Mrs Prime had remained at home. At five o'clock Rachel would slip away and make hot toast, and would run over the Green to Farmer Sturt's wife for a little thick cream, and there would be a batter cake, and so there would be a feast. Rachel was excellent at the preparation of such banquets, knowing how to coax the teapot into a good drawing humour, and being very clever in little comforts; and she would hover about her mother, in a way very delightful to that lady, making the widow feel for a time that there was a gleam of sunshine in the valley of tribulation.

Anthony Trollope, *Rachel Ray*, 1863

❧ *The narrator Marcel, as a boy, has befriended Gilberte Swann, a girl of his own age, whom he visits regularly in Paris.*

On those tea-party days, pulling myself up the staircase step by step, reason and memory already cast off like outer garments, and myself no more now than the sport of the basest reflexes, I would arrive in the zone in which the scent of Mme Swann greeted my nostrils. I felt that I could already behold the majesty of the chocolate cake, encircled by plates heaped with little cakes, and by tiny napkins of grey damask with figures on them, as required by convention but peculiar to the Swanns. But this unalterable and governed whole seemed, like Kant's necessary universe, to depend on a supreme act of free will. For when we were all together in Gilberte's little sitting-room, suddenly she would look at the clock and exclaim:

'I say! It's getting a long time since luncheon, and we aren't having dinner till eight. I feel as if I could eat something. What do you say?'

And she would make us go into the dining-room, as sombre as the interior of an Asiatic Temple painted by Rembrandt, in which an architectural cake, as gracious and sociable as it was imposing, seemed to be enthroned there in any event, in case the fancy seized Gilberte to discrown it of its chocolate battlements and to hew down the steep brown slopes of its ramparts, baked in the oven like the bastions of the palace of Darius. Better still, in proceeding to the demolition of that Babylonitish pastry, Gilberte did not consider only her own hunger; she inquired also after mine, while she extracted for me from the crumbling monument a whole glazed slab jewelled with scarlet fruits, in the oriental style. She asked me even at what o'clock my parents were dining, as if I still knew, as if the disturbance that governed me had allowed to persist the sensation of satiety or of hunger, the notion of dinner or the picture of my family in my empty memory and paralysed stomach. Alas, its paralysis was but momentary. The cakes that I took without noticing them, a time would come when I should have to digest them. But that time was still remote. Meanwhile Gilberte was making 'my' tea. I went on drinking it indefinitely, whereas a single cup would keep me awake for twenty-four hours. Which explains why my mother used always to say: 'What a nuisance it is; he can never go to the Swanns' without coming home ill.' But was I aware even, when I was at the Swanns', that it was tea that I was drinking? Had I known, I should have taken it just the same, for even had I recovered for a moment the sense of the present, that would not have restored to me the memory of the past or the apprehension of the future. My imagination was incapable of reaching to the distant time in which I might have the idea of going to bed, and the need to sleep.

Gilberte's girl friends were not all plunged in that state of intoxication in which it is impossible to make up one's mind. Some of them refused tea! Then Gilberte would say, using a phrase highly fashionable that year: 'I can see that I'm not having much of a success with my tea!' And to destroy more completely any idea of ceremony, she would disarrange the chairs that were drawn up round the table, with: 'We look just like a wedding breakfast. Good lord, what fools servants are!'

She nibbled her cake, perched sideways upon a cross-legged seat placed at an angle to the table. And then, just as though she could have had all those cakes at her disposal without having first asked leave of her mother, when Mme Swann, whose 'day' coincided as a rule with Gilberte's tea-parties, had shewn one of her visitors to the door, and came sweeping in, a moment later, dressed sometimes in blue velvet, more often in a black satin gown draped with white lace, she would say with an air of astonishment: 'I say, that looks good, what you've got there. It makes me quite hungry to see you all eating cake.'

'But, Mamma, do! We invite you!' Gilberte would answer.

Proust, *Within a Budding Grove*, Volume I, translated by C. K. Scott-Moncrieff

❧ *Jean Rennie was born in 1906, the daughter of a Clydeside riveter, and educated at Greenock High School. Unable to take up a scholarship to Glasgow University because of her father's unemployment, she worked in a factory until made redundant at the age of 18, then went into service as third housemaid in a castle in Argyllshire. This passage describes her first meal in the servants' hall: evidently her first experience of 'afternoon tea', rather than the traditional, northern, and working-class high tea which also did the duty of supper.*

Jessie [the second housemaid] took me along to the 'hall'—the servants' hall—where we ate and sat in our leisure time, which was never very long at a stretch. She picked up a hand-bell and rang it furiously, then took me along to the lovely kitchen. She took me to the big kitchen range, all hot and glowing, with three big kettles on it, boiling quietly and cheerfully.

She showed me how to make the tea in a great big teapot, and fill a large jug with hot water. She put them on a tray, and the whole contraption looked as big as herself, as she led me back to the hall. This time the table, laid with a white cloth, was occupied.

Only, at this meal, the cook did not appear. She had a cup of tea taken to her in her room, and only appeared at 6.30, when she started getting the dinner ready.

At the cook's place there were a lot of cups and saucers, milk and sugar, and we each had a small plate and a knife. The table was loaded with cut bread, two large plates of butter, two dishes of jam, a plate of home-made scones, and a large fruit cake. The kind of cake that I had only ever seen at New Year, and we always knew as 'bun'. I watched very closely what the others did, because we always had 'something to our tea' at home, which meant a knife and fork. And I thought, privately, that this was a very poor show for a big house.

But I watched how they put a lump of butter on the side of their plates, then a great spoonful of jam, and they used their own knives to spread the butter thick on the bread, and then thick with jam. So I did the same. There was some talk round the table in which I could not really join because it was mostly about our employer, the owner of this lovely castle and the miles of land around it.

* * * * *

Then we started on the scones, with more butter and jam. And then—I saw for the first time, but not for the last: butter *and* jam, spread thick on the lovely fruit cake—and, to add to my horror, some of it was left on the plates, and, of course, put out to the pigs on the home farm. I nearly choked with anger at the wanton waste. I could remember so many hungry children—and here was good food being contemptuously pushed aside. And I must be allowed to say, here and now, that in all the sixteen years that were to follow,

I never met a single domestic servant, male or female, who was at any time satisfied with the food served to them.

Rennie, *Every Other Sunday*

DINNER

❧ *John Jorrocks, the sporting grocer of Great Coram Street, London, and the Surrey Hunt, is a memorably racy figure of Victorian light literature, continuing the tradition begun by Dickens in* The Pickwick Papers. *Here, with his usual panache, he gives a dinner for his friends at home in Bloomsbury.*

The dining-room was the breadth of the passage narrower than the front drawing-room, and, as Mr Jorrocks truly said, was *raythe*r small,—but, the table being extremely broad, made the room appear less than it was. It was lighted up with spermaceti candles, in silver holders, one at each corner of the table, and there was a lamp in the wall between the red curtained windows, immediately below a brass nail, on which Mr Jorrocks's great hunting-whip and a bunch of boot-garters were hung. Two more candles in the hands of bronze Dianas on the marble mantel-piece, lighted up a coloured copy of Barraud's picture of John Warde, on Blue Ruin; while Mr Ralph Lambton, on his horse Undertaker, with his hounds and men, occupied a frame on the opposite wall. . . . The dinner table was crowded, not covered. There was scarcely a square inch of cloth to be seen on any part. In the centre stood a magnificent finely spun barley-sugar windmill, two feet and a half high, with a spacious sugar foundation, with a cart and horses and two or three millers at the door, and a she-miller working a ball-dress flounce at a lower window.

The whole dinner, first, second, third and fourth course—everything, in fact, except dessert—was on the table, as we sometimes see it at ordinaries or public dinners. Before Mr and Mrs Jorrocks were two great tureens of mock turtle soup, each capable of holding a gallon, and both full up to the brim. Then there were two sorts of fish; turbot and lobster sauce, and a great salmon. A round of boiled beef and an immense piece of roast occupied the rear of these, ready to march on the disappearance of the fish and soup—and behind the walls, formed by the beef of old England, came two dishes of grouse, each dish holding three brace. The side dishes consisted of a calf's head hashed, a leg of mutton, chickens, ducks, and mountains of vegetables; and round the windmill were plum-puddings, tarts, jellies, pies, and puffs.

* * * * *

'Now, gentlemen,' said Mr Jorrocks, casting his eye up the table, as soon as they had all got squeezed and wedged round it, and the dishes were uncovered, '*you see your dinner*, eat whatever you like except the windmill—hope you'll be able to satisfy nature with what's on—would have had more but Mrs J. is so werry fine, she won't stand two joints of the same sort on the table.'

Mrs J. Lauk, John, how can you be so wulgar! Who ever saw two rounds of beef, as you wanted to have. Besides, I'm sure the gentlemen will excuse any little defishency, considering the short notice we have had, and that this is not an elaborate dinner.

Mr Spiers. I'm sure, ma'am, there's no de*fish*ency at all. Indeed, I think there's as much fish as would serve double the number—and I'm sure you look as if you had your soup 'on sale or return,' as we say in the magazine line.

Mr J. Haw! haw! haw! werry good, Mr Spiers. I owe you one. Not bad soup though—had it from Birch's. Let me send you some; and pray lay into it, or I shall think you don't like it. . . . Who's for some salmon—bought at Luckey's—and there's both Tallyho and Tantivy *sarce* to eat with it. Somehow I always fancies I rides harder after eating these sarces with fish.

R. S. Surtees, *Jorrocks's Jaunts and Jollities. The Hunting, Shooting, Racing, Driving, Sailing, Eccentric and Extravagant Exploits of that Renowned Sporting Citizen Mr John Jorrocks*, 1869

Birch's: a renowned eating-place in Cornhill, London, famed for its (usually real) turtle soup.

Edwin Clayhanger, a young man from a narrowly parsimonious background in a Staffordshire potteries town, has been invited by his old schoolfriend Charlie Orgreave to 'a sort of supper at eight' with his large and cheerful family. It is his first evening visit as an adult to any house other than his aunt's; and Charlie's sister Janet has bet her brother a shilling that he will be unable to persuade his friend to come. When Edwin does so, he finds the Orgreaves listening to music and discussing newly acquired

books in a style more lavish and adventurous than anything that he has encountered before. The same generosity is apparent when they sit down to eat.

'Now, father, let's have a bottle of wine, eh?' Charlie vociferously suggested.

Mr Orgreave hesitated: 'You'd better ask your mother.'

'Really, Charlie—' Mrs Orgreave began.

'Oh yes!' Charlie cut her short. 'Right you are, Martha!'

The servant, who had stood waiting for a definite command during this brief conflict of wills, glanced interrogatively at Mrs Orgreave and, perceiving no clear prohibition in her face, departed with a smile to get the wine. She was a servant of sound prestige, and had the inexpressible privilege of smiling on duty. In her time she had fought lively battles of repartee with all the children from Charlie downwards. Janet humoured Martha, and Martha humoured Mrs Orgreave.

The whole family . . . was now gathered in the dining-room, another apartment on whose physiognomy were written in cipher the annals of the vivacious tribe. Here the curtains were drawn, and all the interest of the room centred on the large white gleaming table, about which the members stood or sat under the downward radiance of a chandelier. Beyond the circle illuminated by the shaded chandelier could be discerned dim forms of furniture and of pictures, with a glint of high light here and there on the corner of some gold frame. . . . The table seemed to Edwin to be heaped with food: cold and yet rich remains of bird and beast; a large fruit pie, opened; another intact; some puddings; cheese; sandwiches; raw fruit; at Janet's elbow were cups and saucers and a pot of coffee; a large glass jug of lemonade shone near by; plates, glasses, and cutlery were strewn about irregularly. The effect upon Edwin was one of immense and careless prodigality; it intoxicated him; it made him feel that a grand profuseness was the finest thing in life. In his own home the supper consisted of cheese, bread, and water, save on Sundays, when cold sausages were generally added, to make a feast. But the idea of the price of living as the Orgreaves lived seriously startled the prudence in him. Imagine that expense always persisting day after day, night after night! There were certainly at least four in the family who bought clothes at Shillitoe's, and everybody looked elaborately costly. . . . But equally, they all seemed quite unconscious of their costliness.

Bennett, *Clayhanger*

❧ *Jack Grant, in disgrace in England after expulsion from both public school and agricultural college, has arrived to make a working life for himself with his mother's Australian relations. The family lawyer, Mr George, has met him from the ship and accompanied him to his aunt and uncle's house. 'Tea', the evening meal, is equivalent in this context to dinner.*

'Tea's ready. Tea's ready.'

They trooped into the dining room where a large table was spread. Aunt Matilda seated herself behind the tea-kettle, Mr George sat at the other end, before the pile of plates and the carvers, and the others took their places where they would. Jack modestly sat on Aunt Matilda's left hand, so the tawny Monica at once pounced on the chair opposite.

Entered the Good Plain Cook with a dish covered with a pewter cover, and followed by a small, dark, ugly, quiet girl carrying vegetable dishes.

'That's my niece, Mary, Jack. Lives with Aunt Matilda here, who won't spare her or I'd have her to live with me. Now you know everybody. What's for tea?'

He was dangerously clashing the knife on the steel. Then lifting the cover, he disclosed a young pig roasted in all its glory of gravy. Mary meanwhile had nodded at Jack and looked at him with her big, queer, very black eyes. You might have thought she had native blood. She sat down to serve the vegetables.

'Grace, there's a fly in the milk,' said Aunt Matilda, who was already pouring large cups of tea. Grace seized the milk jug and jerked from the room.

'Do you take milk and sugar, as your dear father used to, John?' asked Aunt Matilda of the youth on her left.

'Call him Bow. Bow's his name out here—John's too stiff and Jack's too common,' exclaimed Mr George, elbows deep in carving.

'Bow'll do for me,' put in Mr Ellis, who said little.

'Mary, is there any mustard?' said Aunt Matilda.

Jack rose vaguely to go and get it, but Aunt Matilda seized him by the arm and pushed him back.

'Sit still. She knows where it is.'

'Monica, come and carry the cups, there's a good girl.'

'Now which end of the pig do you like, Jack?' asked Mr George.

'Matilda, will this do for you?' he held up a piece on his fork. Mary arrived with a ponderous gyrating cruet-stand, which she made place for in the middle of the table.

'What about bread?' said Aunt Matilda. 'I'm sure John eats bread with his meat. Fetch some bread, Grace, for your cousin John.'

'Everybody does it,' thought Jack in despair, as he tried to eat amid the bustle. 'No servants, nothing ever still. On the go all the time.'

D. H. Lawrence and M. L. Skinner, *The Boy in the Bush*, 1924

❧ *Soames and Irene Forsyte, a rich, childless, young couple, are giving dinner to Soames's young cousin June and her fiancé, the architect Philip Bosinney, whom Soames has engaged to design a country house just outside London. Philip and Irene are strongly attracted to one another, as June has just discovered by overhearing a conversation between them. The seven courses, served by Bilson the maid, are clearly a routine dinner for Soames's household: their lightness showing his modernity of taste, as does the fact that the ladies do not retire before the men drink their brandy.*

Dinner began in silence; the women facing one another, and the men.

In silence the soup was finished—excellent, if a little thick, and fish was brought. In silence it was handed.

Bosinney ventured: 'It's the first spring day.'

Irene echoed softly: 'Yes—the first spring day.'

'Spring!' said June: 'there isn't a breath of air!' No one replied.

The fish was taken away, a fine fresh sole from Dover. And Bilson brought champagne, a bottle swathed around the neck with white.

Soames said: 'You'll find it dry.'

Cutlets were handed, each pink-frilled about the legs. They were refused by June, and silence fell.

Soames said: 'You'd better take a cutlet, June; there's nothing coming.'

But June again refused, so they were borne away. And then Irene asked; 'Phil, have you heard my blackbird?'

* * * * *

'Salad, sir?' Spring chicken was removed.

But Soames was speaking: 'The asparagus is very poor. Bosinney, glass of sherry with your sweet? June, you're drinking nothing!'

June said: 'You know I never do. Wine's such horrid stuff!'

An apple charlotte came on a silver dish. And smilingly Irene said: 'The azaleas are wonderful this year!'

To this Bosinney murmured: 'Wonderful! The scent's extraordinary!'

June said: 'How *can* you like the scent? Sugar, please, Bilson.'

Sugar was handed her, and Soames remarked; 'This charlotte's good!'

The charlotte was removed. Long silence followed. Irene, beckoning, said: 'Take out the azaleas, Bilson. Miss June can't bear the scent.'

'No, let it stay,' said June.

Olives from France, with Russian caviare, were placed on little plates. And Soames remarked: 'Why can't we have the Spanish?' But no one answered.

The olives were removed. Lifting her tumbler. June demanded: 'Give me some water, please.' Water was given her. A silver tray was brought, with German plums. There was a lengthy pause. In perfect harmony all were eating them.

* * * * *

Egyptian cigarettes were handed in a silver box. Soames, taking one, remarked: 'What time's your play begin?'

No one replied, and Turkish coffee followed in enamelled cups.

Irene, smiling quietly, said: 'If only—'

'Only what?' said June.

'If only it could always be the spring!'

Brandy was handed; it was pale and old.

Soames said, 'Bosinney, better take some brandy.'

Bosinney took a glass; they all arose.

'You want a cab?' asked Soames.

June answered: 'No. My cloak, please, Bilson.' Her cloak was brought.

Galsworthy, *The Man of Property*, Part II

Major Brendan Archer, mildly dazed after his service in the First World War, has travelled to Co. Wicklow, Ireland to stay as a family guest at the English-run Majestic Hotel, having inadvertently become engaged to Angela, the daughter of the hotel's proprietor, Edward Spencer.

He found the Spencers waiting for him around a dimly lit table above which a faint aura of exasperation seemed to hang. He assumed that they were displeased at being made to wait for him. As soon as he made his appearance Edward picked up a heavy hand-bell and rang it vigorously. This done, he went to a small concealed door in the oak panelling (which the Major took to be a broom cupboard) and whisked it open. An elderly lady stepped out. She was dressed entirely in black except for a white lace cap pinned haphazardly to her faded bundle of grey hair. She was evidently blind, for Edward led her to the table and sat her down before instructing her in deafening tones that Brendan, that was to say the Major, Angela's Major, had come home, home from the war. . . .

'Angela's Major,' she murmured. 'Where is he?'

And the Major was apologized to and led forward to kneel beside the chair while the old lady ran a withered hand over his features. Suddenly she cried petulantly: 'That's not him! That's someone else!' and there was confusion for a moment while old Mrs Rappaport (for the Major had identified her as Angela's widowed grandmother) was shifted into a position suitable for addressing the steaming plate of brown soup in front of her. A silver spoon was put in her hand, a napkin was tied round her neck and, still protesting feebly, she began to siphon up her soup with great rapidity.

Thereafter the meal became lugubrious and interminable, even to the Major who thought that in hospital he had explored the very depths of boredom. Edward and Ripon [his loutish son] were annoyed with one another for some reason and disinclined for conversation. . . . The food was entirely tasteless except for a dish of very salty steamed bacon and cabbage that gave off a vague, wispy odour of humanity. But the Major did not really mind. He was hungry once more and chewed away with a weary ferocity. Indeed, he was light-headed with fatigue and as he chewed his thoughts kept wandering to the bed that awaited him, as a bridegroom throughout a long wedding-feast might contemplate his bride.

In the farthest shadowy reaches of the dining-room a handful of guests dotted here and there at small tables occasionally revealed their presence by a cleared throat or a rattle of silver. But silence collected between the tables in layers like drifts of snow. Once in the course of the meal a brief, querulous argument broke out at the other end of the room; someone complained that his private jar of pickles had been used without his consent (it seemed to be the old man Ripon had described as a 'friend of Parnell' but the Major could not be sure); but then silence returned, and once again the clinking of cutlery.

* * * * *

The meal progressed to some form of apple pudding which the Major, gorged on bacon and cabbage, declined politely. Edward and Ripon maintained their sullen feud. (What the devil was it all about?) Old Mrs Rappaport ate noisily and voraciously. As for Angela, his erstwhile 'fiancée', she seemed to have exhausted herself completely with her afternoon's evocation of the splendours of her youth. Pale and listless, oblivious of her Major's return from the war or of her ritual 'every day I miss you more and more', she toyed with her napkin ring and kept her eyes, unfocused and unseeing, on the sparkling silver crown of the cut-glass salt-cellar in front of her.

When at last it was over (no question of the women retiring while the men drank port; at the Majestic everyone retired together, 'like a platoon under fire', thought the Major sourly), and in the pitch-black corridor of the third floor he felt his hand close over the handle of the door to his room the Major was assailed by an immense sensation of relief and surrender. With a sigh he opened the door.

J. G. Farrell, *Troubles*, 1970

IN BRITAIN

❧ *Celia Fiennes travelled in 1698 on 'My Great Journey to Newcastle and to Cornwall', the most impressive of her tours by coach and on horseback through England. This began in London and took her on a zig-zag route, first to East Anglia, then to Derbyshire, Cheshire, and Wales, then to the Lake District, across to Newcastle and back to Manchester, then southwards through Worcestershire and Gloucestershire as far as Land's End, and finally through the south of England back to London.*

[*Kendal, Westmorland*]. In these Northern Countyes they have only the summer Graine, as barley, oates, peas, beans, and Lentils, noe wheate or Rhye, for they are so cold and late in their yeare they Cannot venture at that sort of tillage, so have none but what they are supply'd out of other Countys adjacent. The Land seemes here in many places very ffertile; they have much Rhye in Lancashire

Yorkshire and Stafford and Shropshire and so Herriford and Worcestershire, which I found very troublesome in my journeys, for they would not own they had any such thing in their bread, but it so disagrees with me as allwayes to make me sick which I found by its Effects when ever I met with any, tho' I did not discern it by the taste; in Suffolke and Norfolke I also met with it—but in these parts [in Westmorland] its altogether the oatbread.

[*St Austell, Cornwall*]. Here was a pretty good dineing roome and Chamber within it, and very neate Country women. My Landlady brought me one of ye west Country tarts this was the first I met with, though I had asked for them in many places in Sommerset and Devonshire; its an apple pye with a Custard all on the top, its ye most acceptable entertainment yt Could be made me. They scald their Creame and milk in most parts of those Countrys and so its a sort of Clouted Creame as we Call it, with a Little sugar and soe put on ye top of ye apple pye. I was much pleased with my supper tho' not with the Custome of the Country which is a universall smoaking, both men women and children have all their pipes of tobacco in their mouths and soe sit round the fire smoaking which was not delightfull to me when I went down to talke with my Landlady for jnformation of any matter and Customs amongst them.

The Diary of Celia Fiennes

John Byng (1743–1813), who succeeded briefly to the title of 5th Viscount Torrington just before he died, was an inveterate traveller for pleasure. Frustrated by his job with the Inland Revenue at Somerset House, and disliking the cramped accommodation and chattering society life of Mayfair which, as a landless gentleman, were all that he could look on as home, he formed the habit of riding on summer tours round England, staying at inns where the food was at best acceptable, at worst appalling. His travel diaries, in scrapbooks containing all kinds of pasted-in ephemera, are written in a relaxed, discursive style, aimed ultimately at publication (a hundred or two hundred years ahead), but more immediately concerned with expressing his feelings and opinions to his wife, with whom his relationship was one of loving, tolerant irritation.

[*Andover, Hampshire, 7 September 1782.*]

I never dined worse, or was in a crosser humour about it; a little miserable stale trout, some raw, rank, mutton chops and some cold hard potatoes. For the sake of hasty gain, innkeepers hire horrid servants, buy bad provisions, and poisonous liquors; wou'd any man dare, with a large capital, to set up a good inn, with the best beds, and wine, he wou'd get a fortune, let him charge ever so highly. I am more and more convinced that fowls are the only things to bespeak at an inn, as every other dish is either ill-dress'd, or the leavings of other companies.

[*Welwyn, Hertfordshire, 29 May 1789.*]

[The weather] clearing up, I continued my slow, and pleasant Route to near Wellwyn, when another Storm hinted to me the White Swan (for it is as convenient in Travelling to know the Stops of the Road, as in Hunting, The Covers, and the right Points.)—Mrs S. Talk'd about mutton chops but I stuck to my demand of cold meat, with a gooseberry tart; and was right, for she instantly produced a cold Tongue, and a cold Fillet of Veal: as for her old fusty tart of last years fruit, I open'd the Lid, and closed it tightly down for the next Comer. No Tricks upon Travellers.

[*Ashbourne, Derbyshire, 16 June 1789.*]

If travellers (Cocknies) expect, when in the country, to revel in fruit, to eat trout, and to purchase venison, they will be sadly mistaken; for fruit is not to be bought, trout are not to be caught; and venison (good) is not even to be had in gentlemen's houses, as they delay, relative to the season, too long e'er they kill deer, and for age, and flavour, never wait long enough, by three years!—

For fruit, for wine, for fish, for venison, for turtle, London is the only mart in the world.—So that tourings and country visitings only serve to whet desire for London quiet and London luxuries. A London gentleman steps into a coffee house, orders venison, and turtle, in the instant; and (if known) a delicious bottle of port, or claret: upon a clean cloth, without form, he dines at the moment of his appetite and walks away at the moment, he is satisfied; neither importun'd by civilities, or harass'd by freedoms; he labours not under obligation, he has not submitted to ridicule, or offended from a want of high breeding.—To these thoughts I am urged, from seeing our inn yard crowded by chaises full of company, going to a grand dinner in this town; there to be overwhelm'd by dress, compliments, hams and fowls, ducks, custards, and trifles; losing their time, their peace, and not improving their politeness.

[*Biggleswade, Bedfordshire, 27 May 1792.*]

I had for dinner at 2 o'clock (the hour of rational and useful appetite) a boil'd fowl, greens, roast beef, Yorkshire pudding, asparagus, tarts, and custards! . . . I ate like a parson, or a farmer (Swift could not decide who was the better eater), and so greedily at first, that I only eyed, and threaten'd, the tarts, and custards. Mark the effect of the country air upon one, who was form'd for a quiet country gentleman; to be idly busied in farming, planting, and gardening, and not to be worried, every morning, by revenue prosecutions, and every evening, by sights, and relations of follies, and fashions.

[*28 May.*]

At 10 o'clock I intended my ride . . . but Mr Repton—the now noted landscape gardener—came in, and delay'd me for ½ an hour: he is a gentleman I have long known, and of so many words that he is not easily shaken off. . . . My dinner (I love to repeat good ones) consisted of spatchcock'd eel, roasted pigeons, a loyn of pork roasted, with tarts, jellies, and custards. Enough for one gentleman?

[*Giggleswick, Yorkshire, 20 June 1792.*]

The bread and butter of this country are bad, and I do wish for the fruit and garden stuff of summer. . . . I had an early dinner of beef steaks, lamb chops, pickled salmon, and tart, and for supper last night, a trout, lamb chops, potted trout, and tart; so that under the article *eating* I have not been over-charged.

[*Llanrhaeadr-ym-Mochnant, Wales, 6 August 1793.*]

Of 3 ale-houses I had to chuse [from] . . . mine—the Coach and Horses—the miserable, was reckon'd the best. Some cart-horses made room for mine; corn was to be had for them, but nothing for myself, but cheese and butter, (these the delights of Welshmen, are worse in Wales than in any county in England);—however, a bustling wench said she would find me some eggs—which she cook'd with slices of bacon.

[*Powis Castle, Wales, 12 August 1793.*]

The present (grandly-descended) peer [Lord Powis] is a mean, silly man, the bubble of his mistress (& of his steward, consequently) who rarely comes here, to sneak about, for a day or two. . . . It is one of the most neglected, sorrowful places I ever saw. . . . One goes over [such] a place in misery, and in satire. A kitchen garden should be an attachment to your house, and stables; what has been here, I know not; the present poor kitchen garden is a mile distant from the house, and is only paled around.

Our ancestry were surrounded by walls—and orchards—which prevented all views; tho they were useful and comfortable, these have all been pull'd down—: No orchards are replanted, and many old fruits are almost lost!! We pique ourselves upon forcing peaches in May,—poor tasteless things—; but the old-fashion'd service—medlar—quince—bullus—and above all the mulberry—& fig—are rooted out! Who has got figs? What is pleasanter in a hot day than standing under a mulberry tree—& regaling upon its fruit? What is become of the small, rough, knotted golden pippin? And of the brown and green Bury pear?—Now these remarks may spring, in some measure, from going selldom upon visits—for when I do—then I have observed these remarks to be just,—and that few gardens can afford apricots sufficient for tarts and puddings.

The Torrington Diaries, Volumes I, IV, II, and III

❧ *Between late June and early August 1818, the poet John Keats and his friend Charles Brown took a walking holiday in the Lake District and Scotland. The first letter quoted here, from Keats to his sister Fanny, contains an early draft of the ballad* Old Meg, *inspired by the moors of Dumfriesshire ('Meg Merrilies' country'), and several versions of the nonsense-rhyme 'There was a naughty boy | a naughty boy was he'.*

John Keats to Fanny Keats, Dumfries/Newton Stewart, 2–4 July 1818.

My dear Fanny I am ashamed of writing you such stuff, nor would I if it were not for being tired after my day's walking, and ready to tumble into bed so fatigued that when I am asleep you might sew my nose to my great toe and trundle me round the town like a Hoop without waking me—Then I get so hungry—a Ham goes but a very little way and fowls are like Larks to me—A Batch of Bread I make no more ado with than a sheet of parliament; and I can eat a Bull's head as easily as I used to do Bull's eyes—I take a whole string of Pork Sausages down as easily as a Pen'orth of Lady's fingers—Oh dear I must soon be contented with an acre or two of oaten cake a hogshead of Milk and a Cloaths basket of Eggs morning noon and night when I get among the Highlanders.

John Keats to his brother Thomas Keats, 'Cairn-something'/Oban, 17–21 July 1818.

July 20th For these two days past we have been so badly accommodated more particularly in coarse food that I have not been at all in cue to write. Last night poor Brown with his feet blistered and scarcely able to walk, after a trudge of 20 miles down the Side of Loch Awe had no supper but Eggs and Oat Cake—we have lost the sight of white bread entirely—Now we had eaten nothing but Eggs all day—about 10 a piece and they had become sickening—. To day we have fared rather better but no oat Cake wanting—we had a small Chicken and even a good bottle of Port but all together the food is too coarse—I feel it a little—another week will break us in. . . . I feel [fell] upon a bit of white Bread to day like a Sparrow—it was very fine—I cannot manage the cursed Oatcake.

Charles Brown to Charles Wentworth Dilke, Sr., Inverness, 7 August 1818.

At last we come wet and weary to the long wished for Inn. What have you for Dinner? 'Truly nothing.' No Eggs? 'We have two.' Any loaf bread? 'No, Sir, but we've nice oat-cakes.' Any bacon? any dried fish? 'No, no, no, Sir!' But you've plenty of Whiskey? 'Oh yes, Sir, plenty of Whiskey!' This is melancholy. Why should so beautiful a Country be poor? Why can't craggy mountains, and granite rocks, bear corn, wine, and oil? These are our misfortunes. . . . But I am well repaid for my sufferings. We came out to endure, and to be gratified with scenery, and lo! we have not been disappointed either way. As for the Oat-cakes, I was once in despair about them. I was not only too dainty, but they absolutely made me sick. With a little gulping, I can manage them now. Mr Keats however is too unwell for fatigue and privation. I am waiting here to see him off in the Smack for London. He caught a violent cold in the Island of Mull, which, far from leaving him, has become worse, and the Physician here thinks him too thin and fevered to proceed on our journey. It is a cruel disappointment. We have been as happy as possible together.

The Letters of John Keats

Parliament: parliament-cake, 'a thin crisp rectangular sheet of gingerbread' (*OED*); ***lady's fingers***: small, elongated biscuits, sponge fingers.

❧ *Joseph Sedley, cowardly, boastful, ostentatious, and greedy, has returned home to England after several years' absence in the Bengal Civil Service. Landing at Southampton, he delays his journey to London, where his elderly father and sister are waiting for him, while he orders new waistcoats of elaborate material and design.*

To make these waistcoats for a man of his size and dignity took at least a day, part of which he employed in hiring a servant to wait upon him and his native, and in instructing the agent who cleared his baggage, his boxes, his books, which he never read; his chests of mangoes, chutney, and curry-powders; his shawls for presents to people whom he didn't know as yet; and the rest of his *Persicos apparatus*.

At length he drove leisurely to London on the third day, and in the new waistcoat—the native, with chattering teeth, shuddering in a shawl on the box by the side of the new European servant; Jos puffing his pipe at intervals within, and looking so majestic that the little boys cried Hooray, and many people thought he must be a Governor General. *He*, I promise, did not decline the obsequious invitation of the landlords to alight and refresh himself in the neat country towns. Having partaken of a copious breakfast, with fish and rice and hard eggs, at Southampton, he had so far rallied at Winchester to think a glass of sherry necessary. At Alton he stepped out of the carriage at his servant's request, and imbibed some of the ale for which the place is famous. At Farnham he stopped to view the Bishop's Castle, and to partake of a light dinner of stewed eels, veal cutlets, and French beans, with a bottle of claret. He was cold over Bagshot Heath, where the native chattered more and more, and Jos took some brandy-and-water; in fact, when he drove into town he was as full of wine, beer, meat, pickles, cherry-brandy and tobacco as the steward's cabin of a steam-packet.

Thackeray, *Vanity Fair*

George Borrow (1803–81), traveller and writer, criss-crossing Wales on foot, makes a detour through Anglesey (in the 1850s an impoverished, almost wholly rural area) to find the birthplace of the Welsh poet Gronwy Owen. He stays at the inn at Pentraeth, a few miles inland from the Menai Strait.

I arrived at the hostelry of Mr Pritchard without meeting any adventure worthy of being marked down. I went into the little parlour, and ringing the bell, was presently waited upon by Mrs Pritchard, a nice matronly woman, whom I had not before seen, of whom I inquired what I could have for dinner.

'This is no great place for meat,' said Mrs Pritchard, 'that is fresh meat, for sometimes a fortnight passes without anything being killed in the neighbourhood. I am afraid at present there is not a bit of fresh meat to be had. What we can get you for dinner I do not know, unless you are willing to make shift with bacon and eggs.'

'I'll tell you what I'll do,' said I, 'I will have the bacon and eggs with tea and bread-and-butter, not forgetting a pint of ale—in a word, I will box Harry.'

'I suppose you are a commercial gent?' said Mrs Pritchard.

'Why do you suppose me a commercial gent?' said I. 'Do I look like one?'

'Can't say you do much,' said Mrs Pritchard; 'you have no rings on your fingers, nor a gilt chain at your waistcoat-pocket, but when you said "box Harry", I naturally took you to be one of the commercial gents, for when I was at Liverpool I was told that that was a word of theirs.'

'I believe the word properly belongs to them,' said I. 'I am not one of them; but I learnt it from them, a great many years ago, when I was much amongst them. Those whose employers were in a small way of business, or allowed them insufficient salaries, frequently used to "box Harry", that is have a beef-steak, or mutton-chop, or perhaps bacon and eggs, as I am going to have, along with tea and ale instead of the regular dinner of a commercial gentleman, namely, fish, hot joint and fowl, pint of sherry, tart, ale and cheese, and bottle of old port, at the end of it all.'

George Borrow, *Wild Wales*, 1862

LIVINGS

I deal with farmers, things like dips and feed.
Every third month I book myself in at
The —Hotel in —ton for three days.
The boots carries my lean old leather case
Up to a single, where I hang my hat.
One beer, and then 'the dinner', at which I read
The *—shire Times* from soup to stewed pears.
Births, deaths. For sale. Police court. Motor spares.

* * *

Later, the square is empty: a big sky
Drains down the estuary like the bed
Of a gold river, and the Customs House
Still has its office lit. I drowse

Between ex-Army sheets, wondering why
I think it's worth while coming. Father's dead:
He used to, but the business is now mine.
It's time for change, in nineteen twenty-nine.

Philip Larkin, 'Livings, I', 1971

IN EUROPE AND THE NEAR EAST

❧ *Lady Mary Wortley Montagu accompanied her husband Edward Wortley Montagu in 1716 when he went on a two-year mission to Turkey as Ambassador at Constantinople. Her fifty-two 'Turkish Letters', written in a slightly mannered, descriptive style, are not in fact genuine letters but an artificial compilation made some time after the event. The retouching of letters and diary-entries, the writing of retrospective narratives in the form of journals, and the fabrication of letter-books containing supposed copies of letters that were never sent, were not unusual in late seventeenth- and eighteenth-century England, and were not regarded as deliberate deception so much as a permissible means of achieving a desirable literary form.*

To her sister Lady Mar, Adrianople, 18 April [*1717*].

I was invited to dine with the Grand Vizier's Lady and 'twas with a great deal of pleasure I prepar'd my selfe for an Entertainment which was never given before to any Christian. I thought I should very little satisfy her Curiosity (which I did not doubt was a considerable Motive to the Invitation) by going in a Dress she was us'd to see, and therefore dress'd my selfe in the Court Habit of Vienna, which is much more magnificent than ours.

* * * * *

She entertain'd me with all kind of Civillity till Dinner came in, which was serv'd one Dish at a time, to a vast Number, all finely dress'd after their manner, which I do not think so bad as you have perhaps heard it represented. I am a very good Judge of their eating, having liv'd 3 weeks in the house of an Effendi at Belgrade who gave us very magnificent Dinners dress'd by his own Cooks, which the first week pleas'd me extremely, but I own I then begun to grow weary of it and desir'd my own Cook might add a dish or 2 after our manner, but I attribute this to Custom. I am very much enclin'd to beleive an Indian that had never tasted of either would prefer their Cookery to ours. Their Sauces are very high, all the roast much done. They use a great deal of rich Spice. The Soop is serv'd for the last dish, and they have at least as great Variety of ragouts as we have. I was very sorry I could not eat of as many as the good Lady would have had me, who was very earnest in serving me of every thing. The Treat concluded with Coffée and perfumes, which is a high mark of respect. 2 slaves kneeling cens'd my Hair, Cloaths, and handkercheif. After this Ceremony she commanded her Slaves to play and dance, which they did with their Guitars in their hands, and she excus'd to me their want of skill, saying she took no care to accomplish them in that art. I return'd her thanks and soon after took my Leave.

The Complete Letters of Lady Mary Wortley Montagu, Volume I, 1708–20

❧ *T. E. Lawrence (1888–1935) became a Near Eastern archaeologist before the First World War, and dug at Carchemish in Syria as a junior colleague of Sir Leonard Woolley. During the war, as an army officer familiar with the Near East, he was recruited by British military intelligence to encourage a revolt by the Arabs of Hejāz (now part of western Saudi Arabia) against the ruling Turks.* The Seven Pillars of Wisdom *(first published privately in 1926) described his part in the campaign and his relations with the Arabs, while living for the most part in bedouin disguise in the desert.*

At last, two men came staggering through the thrilled crowd, carrying the rice and meat on a tinned copper tray or shallow bath, five feet across, set like a great brazier on a foot. In the tribe, there was only this one food-bowl of the size, and an incised inscription ran round it in florid Arabic characters: 'To the glory of God, and in trust of mercy at the last, the property of His poor suppliant, Auda abu Tayi.' It was borrowed by the host who was to entertain us for the time; and, since my urgent brain and body made me wakeful, from my blankets in the first light I would see the dish going across country, and by marking down its goal would know where we were to feed that day.

The bowl was now brim-full, ringed round its edge by white rice in an embankment a foot wide and six inches deep, filled with legs and ribs of mutton till they toppled over. It needed two or three victims to make in the centre a dressed pyramid of meat such as honour prescribed. The centre-pieces were the boiled upturned heads, propped on their severed stumps of neck, so that the ears, brown like old leaves, flapped out on the rice surface. The jaws gaped emptily upward, pulled open to show the hollow throat with the tongue, still pink, clinging to the lower teeth; and the long incisors whitely crowned the pile, prominent above the nostrils' pricking hair and the lips which sneered away blackly from them.

This load was set down on the soil of a cleared space between us, where it steamed hotly, while a procession of minor helpers bore small cauldrons and copper vats in which the cooking had been done. From them, with much-bruised bowls of enamelled iron, they ladled out over the main dish all the inside and outside of the sheep; little bits of yellow intestine, the white tail-cushion of fat, brown muscles and meat and bristly skin, all swimming in the liquid butter and grease of the seething. The bystanders watched anxiously, muttering satisfaction when a very juicy scrap plopped out.

* * * * *

Two raised each smaller cauldron and tilted it, letting the liquid splash down upon the meat till the rice-crater was full, and the loose grains at the edge swam in the abundance; and yet they poured, till, amid cries of astonishment from us, it was running over, and a little pool congealing in the dust. That was the final touch of splendour; and the host called us to come and eat.

* * * * *

The first dip, for me, at least, was always cautious, since the liquid fat was so hot that my unaccustomed fingers could seldom bear it: and so I would toy with an exposed and cooling lump of meat till others' excavations had drained my rice-segment. We would knead between the fingers (not soiling the palm), neat balls of rice and fat and liver and meat cemented by gentle pressure, and project them by leverage of the thumb from the crooked fore-finger into the mouth. With the right trick and the right construction the little lump held together and came clean off the hand; but when surplus butter and odd fragments clung, cooling, to the fingers, they had to be licked carefully to make the next effort slip easier away.

* * * * *

Our host stood by the circle, encouraging the appetite with pious ejaculations. At top speed we twisted, tore, cut and stuffed: never speaking, since conversation would insult a meal's quality; though it was proper to smile thanks when an intimate guest passed a select fragment, or when Mohammed el Dheilan gravely handed over a huge barren bone with a blessing. On such occasions I would return the compliment with a hideous impossible lump of guts, a flippancy which rejoiced the Howeitat, but which the gracious, aristocratic Nasir saw with disapproval.

T. E. Lawrence, *The Seven Pillars of Wisdom: A Triumph*, 1935

❧ *(Sir) Horace Mann was British envoy at Florence from 1737 until his death in 1786. His enormous correspondence with the dilettante Horace Walpole covered most of this period.*

Horace Mann to Horace Walpole, Florence, 31 January 1747.

Twenty English that are now here . . . embarrass me much. It is vastly the mode to entertain; they have separate lodgings and French cooks, and one is tormented to death. Some indeed, entertain vastly well, and have their *hors d'œuvres* and *entremets* in great order. Others, who won't give ten zecchins a month to a cook, do not succeed quite so well, but yet will imitate the fine way. Lord Hobart and I were ready to burst with laughter t'other day at a noble table, when ten people were set down to a first course of a soup and two *hors d'œuvres*, literally consisting of a mustard pot in a small dish, and opposite to it a plate of the vile white radishes. The mustard was to serve for the *bouilli* which was to relieve the soup.

The Yale Edition of Horace Walpole's Correspondence, edited by W. S. Lewis, Volume XIX, 1955

Ten zecchins: about £5 in mid-18th-century English money; *hors d'œuvres*: small dishes introduced between the courses at banquets; *entremets*: lesser dishes placed between the main dishes when a course was laid out symmetrically on the table; *bouilli*: a dish of boiled meat, fish, or fowl; *relieve* (*or remove*): to be substituted for a dish which is no longer wanted, while the rest of the course remains in place.

❧ *Elizabeth Barrett (1806–61), confined to an invalid's couch by a spinal injury received in adolescence, fell in love with her fellow-poet Robert Browning in 1845. They eloped to Italy together the following year, taking Wilson, her maid.*

To her sister Henrietta, Collegio Fernando, Pisa, 19 December 1846.

Will you take us in some day, Henrietta, and 'include the cooking and housekeeping'? and 'see us properly done for'? Robert and I are just alike in every fancy about those kind of things—he turns away from beef and mutton, and loathes the idea of a Saturday hash! A little chicken and plenty of cayenne, and above all things pudding, will satisfy us both when most we are satisfied; and to order just what is wanted, from the 'traiteur', apart from economical consideration of what is 'in the house', and should be eaten, is our 'ideal' in this way. My appetite is certainly improved. I finish one egg, for instance, in the morning. Then at dinner we have Chianti which is an excellent kind of claret; and fancy me (and Wilson) drinking claret out of tumblers! Ask Arabel if she wishes Robert to make me *drunk* (I write the broad word that she may have room to consider it) as well as—*replete with fish*, to try by reaction to move delicate physiology. . . . A few days ago, our lady of the house sent me a gift of an enormous dish of oranges—for the 'Signora'—great oranges just gathered from her own garden—two hanging on a stalk—and the green leaves glittering round them—twelve or thirteen great oranges they were—and excellent oranges. We have one every day after dinner; and the sight of the green crowding orange leaves is very pretty, and keeps us from thinking too much of the cold.

Elizabeth Barrett Browning: Letters to her Sister, 1846–1859, edited by Leonard Huxley, 1929

SPITTED ORTOLANS

Pray, Reader, have you eaten ortolans
  Ever in Italy?
Recall how cooks there cook them: for my plan's
  To—Lyre with Spit ally.
They pluck the birds,—some dozen luscious lumps,
  Or more or fewer,—
Then roast them, heads by heads and rumps by rumps,
  Stuck on a skewer.
But first—and here's the point I fain would press,—
  Don't think I'm tattling!
They interpose, to curb its lusciousness,
  —What, 'twixt each fatling?

First comes plain bread, crisp, brown, a toasted square:
 Then, a strong sage-leaf;
(So we find books with flowers dried here and there
 Lest leaf engage leaf.)
First, food—then, piquancy—and last of all
 Follows the thirdling:
Through wholesome hard, sharp soft, your tooth must bite
 Ere reach the birdling.
Now, were there only crust to crunch, you'd wince:
 Unpalatable!
Sage-leaf is bitter-pungent—so's a quince:
 Eat each who's able!
But through all three bite boldly—lo, the gust!
 Flavour—no fixture—
Flies, permeating flesh and leaf and crust
 In fine admixture.
So with your meal, my poem: masticate
 Sense, sight and song there!
Digest these, and I praise your peptics' state,
 Nothing found wrong there!

Robert Browning, Prologue to *Ferishtah's Fancies*, 1884

❧ *The novelist Tobias Smollett (1721–71) travelled abroad in 1763 for the sake of his health. The querulous tone of his* Travels *earned him the nickname from Laurence Sterne, a contemporary traveller, of 'Smelfungus'.*

If there were five hundred dishes at table, a Frenchman will eat all of them, and then complain he has no appetite. This I have several times remarked. A friend of mine gained a considerable wager upon an experiment of this kind: the *petit maître* ate of fourteen different *plats*, beside the desert; then disparaged the cook, declaring he was no better than a *marmiton*, or turnspit.

* * * * *

In our journey hither [from Lyons to Montpellier] we generally set out in a morning at eight o'clock, and travelled 'till noon, when the mules were put up and rested a couple of hours. . . . In this country I was almost poisoned with garlic, which they mix in their ragouts, and all their sauces; nay, the smell of it perfumes the very chambers, as well as every person you approach. I was also very sick of *becaficas, grieves*, or *thrushes*, and other little birds, which are served up twice a day at all ordinaries on the road. They make their appearance in vine-leaves, and are always half raw, in which condition the French choose to eat them, rather than run the risque of losing the juice by over-roasting.

* * * * *

At Brignolles, where we dined, I was obliged to quarrel with the landlady, and threaten to leave her house, before she would indulge us with any sort of flesh-meat. It was meagre day, and she had made her provision accordingly. She even hinted some dissatisfaction at having heretics in her house: but, as I was not disposed to eat stinking fish, with ragouts of eggs and onions, I insisted upon a leg of mutton, and a brace of fine partridges, which I found in the larder.

Tobias Smollett, *Travels Through France and Italy*, 1766, Letters VII, IX, XII

Beccafico: blackcap, garden warbler; *grieve* (*grive*): thrush; *meagre day*: fast day.

❧ *Laurence Sterne made a six-month tour of France and Italy in 1765–6, having lived in the south of France for his health's sake during much of the previous three years. His scathing characterization of Smollett as 'Smelfungus,' the perennially discontented traveller, occurs at the beginning of the* Sentimental Journey, *and indicates his own determination to be good-humoured and appreciative.*

A shoe coming loose from the fore-foot of the thill-horse, at the beginning of the ascent of mount Taurira, the postilion dismounted, twisted the shoe off, and put it in his pocket. . . . Coming to a flinty piece of road, the poor devil lost a second shoe, and from off his other fore-foot; I then got out of the chaise in good earnest; and seeing a house about a quarter of a mile to the left-hand . . . I prevailed upon the postilion to turn up to it. The look of the house, and of every thing about it, as we drew nearer, soon reconciled me to the disaster.—It was a little farm-house surrounded with about twenty acres of vineyard, about as much corn—and close to the house, on one side, was a potagerie of an acre and a half, full of every thing, which could make plenty in a French peasant's house—and on the other side was a little wood which furnished wherewithal to dress it. It was about eight in the evening when I got to the house—so I left the postilion to manage his point as he could—and for mine, I walk'd directly into the house.

The family consisted of an old grey-headed man and his wife, with five or six sons and sons-in-law and their several wives, and a joyous genealogy out of 'em.

They were all sitting down together to their lentil-soup; a large wheaten loaf was in the middle of the table; and a flaggon of wine at each end promised joy through the stages of the repast—'twas a feast of love.

The old man rose up to meet me, and with a respectful cordiality would have me sit down at the table; my heart was sat down the moment I enter'd the room; so I sat down at once like a son of the family; and to invest myself in the character as speedily as I could, I instantly borrowed the old man's knife, and taking up the loaf cut myself a hearty luncheon; and as I did it I saw a testimony in every eye, not only of an honest welcome, but of a welcome mix'd with thanks that I had not seem'd to doubt it.

Was it this; or tell me, Nature, what else it was which made this morsel so sweet—and to what magick I owe it, that the draught I took of their flaggon was so delicious with it, that they remain upon my palate to this hour?

Laurence Sterne, *A Sentimental Journey Through France and Italy*, 1768

thill-horse: horse between the shafts of a chaise; ***mount Taurira***: perhaps Tarare, north-west of Lyons; ***luncheon***: hunch, doorstep.

❧ *After Napoleon's final defeat in 1815, English and other visitors began to flock to France, which had been closed to them by war, with one short intermission of just over a year, since 1793. To most of them France meant the social and political glamour of Paris, with an optional extra in the form of a pilgrimage to the battlefield of Waterloo. Tom Moore (1779–1852), the satirical Irish poet, visited France in the autumn of 1816 and caricatured what he saw in the epistolary poem* The Fudge Family in Paris, *a portrait of a parvenu Irish family abroad for the first time. Letter III, from which this extract is taken, was supposedly written by Bob Fudge, a young dandy and gourmet.*

After dreaming some hours of the land of Cocaigne,
That Elysium of all things *friand* and nice,
Where for hail they have *bon-bons*, and claret for rain,
And the skaiters in winter show off on *cream*-ice;
Where so ready all nature its cookery yields,
Macaroni au parmesan grows in the fields;
Little birds fly about with the true pheasant taint,
And the geese are all born with a liver complaint!

* * *

I strut to the old Café Hardy, which yet
Beats the field at a *déjeuner à la fourchette*.
There, Dick, what a breakfast! oh, not like your ghost
Of a breakfast in England, your curst tea and toast;
But a side-board, you dog, where one's eye roves about,
Like a Turk's in a Haram, and thence singles out
One's *paté* of larks, just to tune up the throat,
One's small limbs of chickens, done *en papilotte*,
One's erudite cutlets, drest all ways but plain,
Or one's kidneys—imagine, Dick—done with champagne!
Then, some glasses of *Beaune*, to dilute—or, mayhap,
Chambertin, which you know's the pet tipple of Nap,
And which Dad, by the by, that legitimate stickler,
Much scruples to taste, but I'm not so partic'lar.—
Your coffee comes next, by prescription: and then, Dick, 's
The coffee's ne'er failing and glorious appendix,

* * *

A neat glass of *parfait-amour*, which one sips
Just as if bottled velvet tipped over one's lips.

Thomas Moore, *The Fudge Family in Paris*, 1818, Letter III

JORROCKS IN FRANCE

At length the diligence got its slow length dragged not only to Abbeville, but to the sign of the 'Fidèle Berger'—or 'Fiddle Burgur,' as Mr Jorrocks pronounced it—where they were to dine. The diligence being a *leetle* behind time as usual, the soup was on the table when they entered. The passengers quickly ranged themselves round, and, with his mouth watering as the female garçon lifted the cover from the tureen, Mr Jorrocks sat in the expectation of seeing the rich contents ladled into the plates. His countenance fell fifty per cent. as the first spoonful [of macaroni soup] passed before his eyes.—'My vig, why it's water!' exclaimed he—'water, I do declare, with worms in it—I can't eat such stuff as that—it's not man's meat—oh dear, oh dear, I fear I've made a terrible mistake in coming to France! Never saw such stuff as this at Bleaden's, or Birch's, or anywhere in the city.' 'I've travelled three hundred thousand miles,' said the fat man, sending his plate from him in disgust, 'and never tasted such a mess as this before.' 'I'll show them up in The Times,' cried Mr Jorrocks; 'and look, what stuff is here—beef boiled to rags!—well, I never, *no never*, saw anything like this before. Oh, I wish I was in Great Coram Street again! . . . Oh dear, oh dear, I shall die of hunger, I see—I shall die of *absolute* famine—my stomach thinks my throat's cut already!' At the height of his distress in came two turkeys and a couple of fowls, and his countenance shone forth like an April sun after a shower. 'I'll trouble you, sir, for a leg and a wing, and a bit of the breast, for I'm really famished—oh hang! the fellow's a Frenchman, and I shall lose half the day in looking it out in my dictionary. . . .' Here the Countess Benvolio, who had been playing a good knife and fork herself, pricked up her ears, and guessing at Jorrocks's wants, interceded with her countryman and got him a plateful of fowl. It was soon disposed of, however, and half a dish of hashed hare or cat, that was placed within reach of him shortly after, was quickly transferred into his plate. A French dinner is admirably calculated for leading the appetite on by easy stages to the grand consummation of satiety. It begins meagrely, as we have shown, and proceeds gradually through the various gradations of lights, savories, solids, and substantials. Presently there was a large dish of stewed eels put on. 'What's that?' asked Jorrocks of the man.—'Poisson,' was the reply. '*Poison*! why, you infidel, have you no conscience?' '*Fishe*,' said the Countess. 'Oh, ay, I smell—eels—just like what we have at the Eel-pye house at Twickenham. . . .' Some wild ducks and *fricandeau de veau*, which followed, were cut up and handed round, Jorrocks helping himself plentifully to both as also to *pommes de terre à la maître d'hôtel*, and bread at discretion. 'Faith, but this is not a bad dinner, after all's said and done, when one gets fairly into it.' 'Fear it will be expensive,' observed the fat man. Just when Jorrocks began to think he had satisfied nature, in came a roast leg of mutton, a beef-steak, 'à la G-d-dam,' and a dish of larks and snipes. 'Must have another tumbler of wine before I can grapple with these chaps,' said he, eyeing them. . . . Just as he was taking breath, a garçon entered with some custards and an enormous *omelette soufflé*, whose puffy brown sides bagged over the tin dish that contained it. 'There's a tart!' cried Mr Jorrocks; 'oh my eyes, what a swell!—Well, I suppose I must have a shy at it.—"In for a penny, in for a pound!" as we say at the Lord Mayor's feed. Know I shall be sick, but, however, here goes,' sending his plate across the table to the garçon, who was going to help it. The first dive of the spoon undeceived him as he heard it sound at the bottom of the dish. 'Oh, lauk, what a go! All puff, by Jove!—a regular humbug—a balloon pudding, in short! I won't eat such stuff—give it to Mouncheer there,' rejecting the offer of a piece. 'I like the solids—will trouble you for some of that cheese, sir, and don't let it taste of the knife. . . .' 'You shall take some desert,' said the Countess, handing him over some peaches and biscuits. 'Well, I'll try my hand at it, if it will ob*le*ge your ladyship, but I really have had *almost* enough.' 'And some abricot,' said she, helping him to a couple of fine juicy ones. 'Oh, thank you, my lady, thank you, my lady, I'm *nearly* satisfied.' 'Vous ne mangez pas,' said she, giving him half a plate of grapes. 'Oh, my lady, you don't understand me—I *can't* eat any more—I am regularly high and dry—chock full—*bursting, in fact*.' Here she handed him a plate of sponge cakes, mixed with bon-bons and macaroons, saying, 'Vous êtes un pauvre mangeur—vous ne mangez *rien*, Monsieur.' 'Oh dear, she does not understand me, I see.—Indeed, my lady, *I can not* eat any more. Ge *would*-era, se ge *could*-era, mais ge ne *can*-ne-ra pas!' 'Well, now, I've travelled three hundred thousand miles, and never heard such a bit of French as that before,' said the fat man, chuckling.

Surtees, *Jorrocks's Jaunts and Jollities*

❧ *Written in France in September 1920, on a train journey to Mentone.*

A man poked his head in at the door and said tea was served.

'Tea! Dear me!' she fussed at once. 'Would you care to go? . . . Shall we, do you think? On the other hand, I have some tea here. I'm afraid it will not be very good. Tea that is not fresh . . . and then there is that odd taste—what it is I do not know, but . . . Shall we care to try it?'

'Might as well.'

'In that case, dear, perhaps you would not mind lifting down my suit-case? I am sorry to say the tea is in there. Such a bother! These racks are so very high. I think they are decidedly higher than the English racks. Mind! Do take care! Oh!'

He: 'Ugh!'

Finally, she spread out a piece of paper, put on it a little cup and an odd saucer, the top of the thermos flask, a medicine bottle of milk, and some sugar in a lozenge-tin. 'I am very much afraid . . .' said she. 'Would you like me to try it first?'

He looked over the top of his paper and said drily: 'Pour it out!'

She poured it out, and gave him the cup and saucer, of course, while she gave the most uncomfortable little dripping cup in the world to herself and sipped, anxiously watching him. 'It is so very . . .?'

'Might be worse!'

Fidgeting in her hand-bag, first she pulled out a powder-puff, then a nice substantial handkerchief, and then a paper parcel that held a very large wedge of cake—of the kind known as Dundee.

This she cut with a penknife, while he watched with some emotion.

'This is the last of our precious Dundee,' said she, shaking her head over it, and cutting it so tenderly that it almost seemed an act of cannibalism.

'That's one thing I have learned,' said he, 'and that is never to come abroad without one of Buszard's Dundees.'

Oh, how she agreed!

And each taking a large wedge, they bit into it and ate solemnly with round astonished eyes like little children in a confectioner's shop who are allowed to eat sitting up to the counter.

'More tea, dear?'

'No thanks.'

She: '?' A glance. (I sympathise with her glance for reply.)

'I think I will just have a cup,' said she gaily, so relieved to have a cup after all.

Another dive into the bag and chocolate was produced.

Chocolate! I had not realised before that chocolate is offered playfully. It is not a solemn food. It's as though one thought it rather absurd. But then—who knows? Perhaps . . .

'What?' said he, and peered over the paper. 'No, no!' dismissing the chocolate.

She had thought as much.

And having torn up little shreds of paper and wiped the cup and saucer and the knife clean, she packed it all tight again. But a final rummage in the bag produced an oval-shaped paper, which unwrapped was an egg! This sight seemed to fill her with amazement. But she must have known the egg was there. She did not look as though she had. Bright-eyed, her head on one side, she stared; and I fancied I heard an interrogatory clucking.

The Scrapbook of Katherine Mansfield, edited by John Middleton Murry, 1939

❧ *William Eden (1744–1814), diplomat and politician with a particular expertise in making commercial treaties, was posted from Paris to Madrid in 1788, and became 1st Baron Auckland in the Irish peerage on his return home from Spain the following year. Accompanied by his wife and their large family of young children (the eighth of whom was born in Madrid), he kept a regular letter-diary of their exploits which he sent off at intervals to his mother. From the capital, the Edens moved with the court up to San Ildefonso, in the mountains, in mid-July, 1788.*

11 [July].

I received your letter to-day, in which, by the advice of the Marquis del Campo [the Spanish Ambassador in London], you caution us against eating much meat, because it is so rich and so succulent. It is pleasant to see how prejudiced all people are as to what relates to their own country. It is easy to eat well and even luxuriously in Spain, because the fish, the turkeys, the venison, the vegetables, the fruit, the rabbits, and the hares and partridges, and ducks, are all excellent, and the rest is sometimes good; but the beef and mutton are lean and hard, and dry, and tasteless, and we hardly ever touch either the one or the other.

27th [July].

I must not forget to mention that we find here two excellent articles for the table—good bread, and as fine potatoes as I ever saw. We were much disappointed by the bread at Madrid; the whole city is supplied by a royal privilege, under which the good and bad flour are mixed, and the whole heats itself in large stores. In other places the Spanish bread is remarkably good.

4th [August].

I was told before I came to this country that it was advisable to be careful in eating at the Spanish tables, because of the frequent use either of copper vessels, or of tin linings mixed with lead. Three days ago, some of the ambassadors who dined at Madrid, and a whole company of fourteen people, were dangerously ill on the day following, but they are all recovering. All my kitchen furniture was bought in London.

7th [August].

As I think it likely that you may sometimes pass a summer in this country, I ought to apprise you, among other matters, that the green-gage plums are as good as in England, and much more plentiful; the grapes hitherto are sweet, but they have no other merit. I have already told you that the potatoes are excellent—I never saw better, even from Liverpool. We have red currant tarts here every day, and it is, I believe, the only place in Spain where red currants are found in any plenty, and the confectioner is at this moment occupied in making black currant jelly, provisionally against colds.

Journal and Correspondence of William, Lord Auckland, with a Preface and Introduction by the Right Honourable and Right Reverend the Bishop of Bath and Wells, 1862, Volume II

In September 1798, William and Dorothy Wordsworth, Samuel Taylor Coleridge, and Coleridge's friend John Chester left England for Hamburg. Here they spent a fortnight together, lodging in separate hotels, before the party split up and the Wordsworths went on alone to winter in Goslar in the Harz Mountains of Saxony. Dorothy, an intermittent diarist, had begun a journal of their experiences, which included the voyage to Hamburg and their stay there, but apparently did not survive beyond the journey to Goslar. The high point of the Hamburg visit, for Coleridge as well as the Wordsworths, was a meeting with the aged Romantic poet Gottlieb Friedrich Klopstock (1724–1803), who had retired to Hamburg and in 1791 had married a niece of his late first wife.

[Wednesday, 19 September 1798.]

The first impression that an Englishman receives on entering a Hamburgh inn is that of filth and filthy smells. I sate down for a few moments while the company went to look at the apartments. The landlord, landlady and a party of waiters were preparing plumbs for preserving or bottling. He looked like an English landlord living on the good things of the house. She, about forty, had her hair full-dressed, spread out and powdered, without cap. . . . On enquiry we found that we could have no dinner, for dinner was over. I went upstairs to dress, a *manservant* brought up napkin, water etc. . . . When I returned below I found the party eating cold beef—no cloth spread—no vegetables, but some bad cucumbers pickled without vinegar. Very good wine at one mark 4 sous the bottle. We had afterwards tea and coffee; the bread good, halfpenny rolls, butter not fresh.

Friday [September 21].

Dined at the ordinary. The price a mark. About twenty at each table. Every man had his half or quarter pint of wine at 10d the bottle, or a bottle of beer or porter—a napkin and a glass. Soup, boiled meat and stewed vegetables, roasted meat or fowls, sallad, fowls with stewed plumbs, veal with stewed pears, beef with apple sauce.

Sunday [September 23].

I was unable to go to the Churches, being unwell. We dined at the ordinary at 12 o'clock. An addition of plumb tart, I suppose because it was Sunday.

Wednesday [September 26].

Dined with Mr Klopstock. Had the pleasure of meeting his brother the poet, a venerable old man, retaining the liveliness and alertness of youth, though his legs are swelled immensely and he evidently cannot be very far from the grave. . . . Mr Klopstock, the merchant, very polite and kind; his wife, who cannot speak a word of either English or French, appears a very interesting woman; they have a little girl of 7 years old. She was dressed in a coloured frock, and her neck covered up with a thick handkerchief (N.B. Mrs Klopstock, the poet's lady, much exposed.) The child seemed indulged. The teeth of all the family very bad, their complexions fair. The rest of the party consisted of a young German who spoke a little English, a niece of Mr Klopstock, Wm and myself. . . . We sate round the table without order; Mrs Klopstock on one side, her husband at the foot of the table. Mrs K. distributed all the dishes in succession. Soup 1st, 2nd, stewed veal without vegetables, 3rd sausages with cabbage, 4th oysters with spinnach, 5th fowls with sallad and currant jelly, dessert—grapes, biscuits, pears, plumbs, walnuts; afterwards coffee. A woman servant in the Hanoverian cap waited at table. She seemed more at her ease and more familiar than an English servant, she laughed and talked with the little girl. We withdrew into the next room and had tea. Mr K's niece brought in the candles and washed up the tea things in a sort of passage or lobby . . . The poet and his lady were obliged to depart soon after six. He sustained an animated conversation with William during the whole afternoon. I could not look upon him, the benefactor of his country, the father of German poetry, without the most sensible emotion. We returned home at a little after seven. I had a bad headach and went to bed at 9.

Sunday [September 30].

William called at Mons. de Loutre's from whom he learned that the price of 10 small loaves was 4d. The day before a baker had refused to give him more than two for twopence. The bread was baked this morning; yesterday we had *old* bread, I suppose that yesterday there was no baking in honour of the Saint. It seems there is no imposition of either law or custom which prevents people from making Sunday as much a day of labour as any other if their avarice, or it may be their industry, but alas! I fear the former motive is the moving spring of the Hamburgher's mind! gets the better of their love of pleasure.

Journals of Dorothy Wordsworth, edited by E. de Selincourt, 1941, Volume I

The Saint: Michaelmas (29 September) had been celebrated as a religious holiday in Hamburg.

Wordsworth recorded this humiliating incident in Dorothy's diary a few days before describing it again in a letter.

To Thomas Poole, Hamburg, 3 October [*1798*].

The other day I went into a Bakers shop. Put into his hand two pieces of money for [each of] which I ought to have had five loaves but I thought the pieces had only been worth two loaves each. I took up four loaves. The baker would not permit this, upon which I took from his hand one of the pieces, and pointed to two loaves, and then re-offering to him the piece I took up two others: he dashed the loaves from my hand into the basket in the most brutal manner. I begged him to return the other piece of money, which he refused to do, nor would he let me have any bread into the bargain.

So I left the shop empty-handed and he retained the money. Is there any baker in England who would have done this to a foreigner? I am afraid we must say, yes. Money, money is here the god of universal worship. And rapacity and extortion among the lower classes and the classes immediately above them, are just sufficiently common to be a matter of glory and exultation.

Letters of William and Dorothy Wordsworth, edited by E. de Selincourt, 1967, Volume I

IN AMERICA

Following abortive attempts by Sir Walter Ralegh and others to colonize the coast of the present North Carolina in the 1580s, an expedition embarked under the auspices of the London Virginia Company in December 1606 and landed at Jamestown, Virginia, in May 1607. Reduced to 38 settlers by the end of that year, the expedition was augmented by 120 more from two shiploads which formed the 'First Supply' of January and April 1608. Captain John Smith, one of the original colonists (having been spared execution by Powhatan through the intervention of his daughter Pocahontas), was elected President on returning from an exploration of the Chesapeake Bay in the summer of 1608, and remained in command of the colony until September 1609. During the winter of his presidency the colonists ran seriously short of food, although less so than they did the following winter, which became known as the 'starving time'.

[1609]. In searching our casked corne, we found it halfe rotten, and the rest so consumed with the many thousand rats, increased first from the ships, that we knewe not how to keepe that little wee had. This did drive us all to our wits ende; for there was nothing in the countrie but what nature afforded.

Untill this time *Kemps* and *Tassore* were fettered prisoners and daily wrought [worked]; and taught us how to order and plant our fields: whom now, for want of victual, we set at libertie; but so wel were they used, that they little desired it.

And to express their loves, for 16 days continuance, the Countrie [people] brought us (when least) 100 a daie of squirrils, Turkies, Deare, and other wilde beastes. But this want of corne occasioned the end of all our workes, it being worke sufficient to provide victuall.

60 or 80 with Ensign *Laxon* were sent downe the river to live

upon oysters: and 20 with leiftenant *Percie* to try for fishing at point Comfort, but in 6 weekes, they would not agree once to cast out their net. *Master West*, with as many, went up to the falles; but nothing could bee found but a fewe berries and acornes. Of that in the store, every one had their equall proportion.

Till this present, by the hazard and endeavour of some 30 or 40, this whole number had ever been fed. Wee had more Sturgeon then could be devoured by dogge and man; of which, the industrious by drying and pounding, mingled with caviare, sorrel and other wholsom hearbs, would make bread and good meate. Others would gather as much *Tockwough* roots in a day as would make them bread a weeke. So that of those wild fruites, fish and berries these lived very well, in regard of such a diet.

But such was the most strange condition of some 150, that had they not been forced nolens volens perforce to gather and prepare their victuall, they would all have starved, and have eaten one another. Of those wild fruites, the Salvages often brought us: and for that the President [John Smith] would not fulfil the unreasonable desire of those distracted lubberly gluttons, to sell not only our kettles, howes, tools, and Iron, nay swords, peeces [guns], and the very ordenance and houses (might they have prevailed but to have been but idle) for those salvage fruits, they would have imparted all to the Salvages.

W.S., *The Proceedings of the English Colonie in Virginia since their first Beginning from England in the Yeare of our Lord 1606, till this Present 1612, with all their Accidents that befell them in their Iournies and Discoveries,* in Captain John Smith, *Works, 1608–1631*, 1884

Tockwough roots: Tuckahoe roots, a term used by Virginian Indians for various edible roots, but later restricted to one, *Lycoperdon solidum*, probably a tuberous formation on the mycelium of a fungus attached to tree-roots. Also known as 'Indian bread', 'Indian truffle', etc. (*OED*).

Benjamin Franklin, apprenticed as a printer to his elder brother in Boston, quarrelled with him and left home at the age of 17. After sailing to New York, he received a promise of work in Philadelphia, and made his way there partly on foot, partly by boat down the Delaware River.

The next morning [I] reached Burlington, but had the mortification to find that the regular boats [to Philadelphia] were gone a little before and no other expected to go before Tuesday, this being

Saturday. Wherefore, I returned to an old woman in the town of whom I had bought some gingerbread to eat on the water and asked her advice; she invited me to lodge at her house till a passage by water should offer; and being tired with my foot travelling, I accepted the invitation. . . . She was very hospitable, gave me a dinner of ox cheek with great goodwill, accepting only of a pot of ale in return. And I thought myself fixed till Tuesday should come. However, walking in the evening by the side of the river, a boat came by, which I found was going towards Philadelphia with several people in her. They took me in, and as there was no wind, we rowed all the way; and about midnight, not having seen the city, some of the company were confident we must have passed it and would row no farther; the others knew not where we were, so we put towards the shore, got into a creek, landed near an old fence, with the rails of which we made a fire, the night being cold in October, and there we remained till daylight. Then one of the company knew the place to be Cooper's Creek, a little above Philadelphia, which we saw as soon as we got out of the creek, and arrived there about eight or nine o'clock, on the Sunday morning, and landed at the Market Street wharf.

* * * * *

I walked towards the top of the street, gazing about till near Market Street, where I met a boy with bread. I have often made a meal of dry bread, and inquiring where he had bought it, I went immediately to the baker's he directed me to. I asked for biscuit, such as we had in Boston, but that sort, it seems, was not made in Philadelphia. I then asked for a threepenny loaf and was told they had none such. Not knowing the different prices nor the names of the different sorts of bread, I told him to give me three pennyworth of any sort. He gave me accordingly three great puffy rolls. I was surprized at the quantity but took it, and having no room in my pockets, walked off with a roll under each arm and eating the other. Thus I went up Market Street as far as Fourth Street, passing the door of Mr Read, my future wife's father, when she, standing at the door, saw me, and thought I made—as I certainly did—a most awkward, ridiculous appearance. Then I turned and went down Chestnut Street and part of Walnut Street, eating my roll all the way, and coming round, found myself again at Market Street wharf near the boat I came in, to which I went for a draught of the river water, and being filled with one of my rolls, gave the other two to a woman and her child that came down the river in the boat with us and were waiting to go farther. Thus refreshed, I walked again up the street, which by this time had many cleanly dressed people in it who were all walking the same way; I joined them, and thereby was led into the great meetinghouse of the Quakers near the market. I sat down among them, and after looking round awhile and hearing nothing said, being very drowsy through labour and want of rest the preceding night, I fell fast asleep.

Franklin, *Autobiography*

❧ *Charles Dickens made a six-month tour of the United States between January and June 1842. Already famous at 30, and aware that he had a long journalistic career ahead of him, he conscientiously investigated prisons and slavery, and institutions such as a school for blind children at Boston, in addition to promoting his books. The mildly jaundiced tone of his* American Notes *can be blamed partly on his constant travelling by uncomfortable means and his insistence on treating the tour as one of unmitigated work.*

[Harrisburg to Pittsburgh by canal boat.] As it continued to rain most perseveringly, we all remained below; the damp gentlemen round the stove, gradually becoming mildewed by the action of the fire; and the dry gentlemen lying at full length upon the seats, or slumbering uneasily with their faces on the tables, or walking up and down the cabin, which it was barely possible for a man of the middle height to do, without making bald places on his head by scraping it against the roof. At about six o'clock, all the small tables were put together to form one long table, and everybody sat down to tea, coffee, bread, butter, salmon, shad, liver, steaks, potatoes, pickles, ham, chops, black-puddings and sausages.

'Will you try,' said my opposite neighbour, handing me a dish of potatoes, broken up in milk and butter—'will you try some of these fixings?'

* * * * *

At eight o'clock [in the morning], the shelves [i.e. bunks] being taken down and put away and the tables joined together, everybody sat down to the tea, coffee, bread, butter, salmon, shad, liver, steak, potatoes, pickles, ham, chops, black-puddings, and sausages, all over again. Some were fond of compounding this variety, and having it all on their plates at once. As each gentleman got through his own personal amount of tea, coffee, bread, butter, salmon, shad, liver, steak, potatoes, pickles, ham, chops, black-puddings, and sausages, he rose and walked off. When everybody had done with everything, the fragments were cleared away; and one of the waiters appearing anew in the character of a barber, shaved such of the company as desired to be shaved; while the remainder looked on, or yawned over their newspapers. Dinner was breakfast again, without the tea and coffee; and supper and breakfast were identical.

* * * * *

[Pittsburgh to Cincinnati, by paddle-steamer on the Ohio River.] We are to be on board the *Messenger* three days. . . . There are three meals a day. Breakfast at seven, dinner at half-past twelve, supper about six. At each, there are a great many small dishes and plates upon the table, with very little in them; so that although there is every appearance of a mighty 'spread,' there is seldom really more than a joint; except for those who fancy slices of beet-root, shreds of dried beef, complicated entanglements of yellow pickle; maize, Indian corn, apple-sauce, and pumpkin.

Some people fancy all these little dainties together (and sweet preserves beside), by way of relish to their roast pig. They are generally those dyspeptic ladies and gentlemen who eat unheard-of quantities of hot corn bread (almost as good for the digestion as a kneaded pincushion), for breakfast and for supper. Those who do not observe this custom, and who help themselves several times instead, usually suck their knives and forks meditatively, until they have decided what to take next; then pull them out of their mouths; put them in the dish; help themselves; and fall to work again. At dinner, there is nothing to drink upon the table, but great jugs full of cold water. Nobody says anything at any meal, to anybody. All the passengers are very dismal, and seem to have tremendous secrets weighing on their minds.

Charles Dickens, *American Notes*, 1842

Ishmael and his companion Queequeg have arrived at Nantucket, a whaling port in Massachusetts.

It was quite late in the evening when the little *Moss* came snugly to anchor, and Queequeg and I went ashore; so we could attend to no business that day, at least none but supper and a bed. The landlord of the Spouter-Inn had recommended to us his cousin Hosea Hussey of the Twy Pots, whom he asserted to be the proprietor of one of the best kept hotels in Nantucket, and moreover he had assured us that Cousin Hosea, as he called him, was famous for his chowders.

* * * * *

And so it turned out; Mr Hosea Hussey being from home, but leaving Mrs Hussey entirely competent to attend to all his affairs. Upon making known our desires for a supper and a bed, Mrs Hussey . . . ushered us into a little room, and seating us at a table spread with the remains of a recently concluded repast, turned round to us and said—'Clam or Cod?'

'What's that about Cods, ma'am?' said I with much politeness.

'Clam or Cod?' she repeated.

'A clam for supper? a cold clam; is *that* what you mean, Mrs Hussey?' says I, 'but that's a rather cold and clammy reception in the winter time, ain't it, Mrs Hussey?'

But being in a great hurry . . . and seeming to hear nothing but the word 'clam,' Mrs Hussey hurried towards an open door leading to the kitchen, and bawling out 'clam for two,' disappeared.

'Queequeg,' said I, 'do you think that we can make a supper for us both on one clam?'

However, a warm savoury steam from the kitchen served to belie the apparently cheerless prospect before us. But when that smoking chowder came in, the mystery was delightfully explained. Oh, sweet friends! hearken to me. It was made of small juicy clams, scarcely bigger than hazel nuts, mixed with pounded ship biscuit, and salted pork cut up into little flakes; the whole enriched with butter, and plentifully seasoned with pepper and salt. Our appetites being sharpened by the frosty voyage, and in particular, Queequeg seeing his favourite fishy food before him, and the chowder being surpassingly excellent, we despatched it with great expedition; when leaning back a moment and bethinking me of Mrs Hussey's calm cool announcement, I thought I would try a little experiment. Stepping to the kitchen door, I uttered the word 'cod' with great emphasis, and resumed my seat. In a few moments the savoury steam came forth again, but with a different flavour, and in good time a fine cod-chowder was placed before us.

We resumed business, and while plying our spoons in the bowl, thinks I to myself, 'I wonder now if this has any effect on the head? What's that stultifying saying about chowder-headed people?' 'But look, Queequeg, ain't that a live eel in your bowl? Where's your harpoon?'

Fishiest of all fishy places was the Twy Pots, which well deserved its name; for the pots there were always boiling chowders. Chowder for breakfast, and chowder for dinner, and chowder for supper, until you began to look for fishbones coming through your clothes. The area before the house was paved with clam-shells. Mrs Hussey wore a polished necklace of cod vertebrae; and Hosea Hussey had his account-books bound in superior old shark-skin. There was a fishy flavour to the milk, too, which I could not at all account for, until one morning happening to take a stroll along the beach among some fishermen's boats, I saw Hosea's brindled cow feeding on fish remnants, and marching along the sand with each foot in a cod's decapitated head, looking very slipshod, I assure ye.

Supper concluded, we received a lamp, and directions from Mrs Hussey concerning the nearest way to bed; but, as Queequeg was about to precede me up the stairs, the lady stretched forth her arms and demanded his harpoon; she allowed no harpoon in her chambers. 'Why not?' said I; 'every true whaleman sleeps with his harpoon—but why not!' 'Because it's dangerous,' says she. 'Ever since young Stiggs coming from that unfortunate v'y'ge of his when he was gone four years and a half, with only three barrels of *ile*, was found dead in my first floor back, with his harpoon in his side; ever since then I allow no boarders to take sich dangerous weapons in their rooms a-night. So, Mr Queequeg' (for she had learned his name), 'I will just take this here iron, and keep it for you till morning. But the chowder; clam or cod to-morrow for breakfast, men?'

'Both,' says I, 'and let's have a couple of smoked herring by way of variety.'

Herman Melville, *Moby Dick, or the White Whale*, 1851

❧ *Ellen Montgomery, a young girl from New York, is travelling alone to stay with relations upstate. Tired by the journey, she is rescued by Miss Timmins.*

In great indignation, down stairs went Miss Timmins; and at the foot of the stairs she met a rosy-cheeked, pleasant-faced girl coming up.

'Are you the chambermaid?' said Timmins. . . . 'Well, I am a stranger here . . . and I want you to help me, and I am sure you will. I have got a dear little girl upstairs that I want some supper for; she is a sweet child, and she is under the care of some proud folks here in the tea-room that think it is too much trouble to look at her. . . .'

'James!' said the girl in a loud whisper to one of the waiters who was crossing the hall. He instantly stopped and came towards them, tray in hand, and making several extra polite bows as he drew near. 'What is on the supper table, James?' said the smiling damsel.

'Everything that ought to be there, Miss Johns,' said the man with another flourish.

'Come, stop your nonsense,' said the girl, 'and tell me quick—I am in a hurry.'

'It is a pleasure to perform your commands, Miss Johns. I will give you the whole bill of fare. There's a very fine beef-steak, fricasseed chickens, stewed oysters, sliced ham, cheese, preserved quinces—with the usual complement of bread and toast and muffins, and doughnuts, and new-year cake and plenty of butter; likewise salt and pepper; likewise tea and coffee, and sugar; likewise—'

'Hush!' said the girl. 'Do stop, will you?' and then laughing, and turning to Miss Timmins, she added, 'What will you have?'

'I guess I will have some of the chickens and oysters,' said Timmins, 'that will be the nicest for her, and a muffin or two.'

Wetherall, *The Wide, Wide World*, Volume I

We in America have the raw material of provision in greater abundance than any other nation. There is no country where an ample, well-furnished table is more easily spread, and for that reason, perhaps, none where the bounties of providence are more generally neglected. I do not mean to say that the traveller through the length and breadth of our land could not, on the whole, find an average of comfortable subsistence; yet, considering that our resources are greater than those of any other civilised people, our results are comparatively poorer.

* * * * *

I recollect how I was once struck with our national plenteousness, on returning from a Continental tour, and going directly from the ship to a New York hotel, in the bounteous season of autumn. For months I had been habituated to my neat little bits of chop or poultry garnished with the inevitable cauliflower or potato, which seemed to be the sole possibility once the reign of green peas was over; now I sat down at once to a carnival of vegetables: ripe, juicy tomatoes, raw or cooked; cucumber in brittle slices; rich, yellow sweet potatoes; broad Lima beans, and beans of other and various names; tempting ears of Indian corn steaming in enormous piles, and great smoking tureens of the savoury succotash, an Indian gift to the table for which civilisation need not blush; sliced egg plant in delicate fritters; and marrow squashes, of creamy pulp and sweetness: a rich variety, embarrassing to the appetite, and perplexing to the choice. Verily, the thought has often impressed itself on my mind that the vegetarian doctrine preached in America left a man quite as much as he had capacity to eat or enjoy, and that in the midst of such tantalizing abundance he really lost the apology which elsewhere bears him out in preying upon his less gifted and accomplished animal neighbours.

But with all this, the American table, taken as a whole, is inferior to that of England or France. It presents a fine abundance of material, carelessly and poorly treated. The management of food is nowhere in the world, perhaps, more slovenly and wasteful. Everything betokens that want of care that waits on abundance; there are great capabilities and poor execution.

A tourist through England can seldom fail, at the quietest country inn, of finding himself served with the essentials of English table-comfort—his mutton-chop done to a turn, his steaming little private apparatus for concocting his own tea, his choice pot of marmalade or slice of cold ham, and his delicate rolls and creamy butter, all served with care and neatness. In France, one never asks in vain for delicious *café-au-lait*, good bread and butter, a nice omelet, or some savoury little portion of meat with a French name. But to a tourist taking like chance in American country-fare, what is the prospect? What is the coffee? what the tea? and the meat? and above all the butter?

Crowfield (Harriet Beecher Stowe), *House and Home Papers*

❧ *Thomas Wolfe's novel is set in 1929, the year of the Wall Street Crash. In downtown Manhattan, George Webber, a writer, contemplates the lives of truck-drivers.*

At night, too, five times a week, the mighty vans would line up at the kerb in an immense and waiting caravan. They were covered now in great tarpaulins, small green lamps were burning on each side, and the drivers, their faces faintly lit with the glowing points of cigarettes, would be talking quietly in the shadows of their huge machines. Once George had asked one of the drivers the destination of these nightly journeys, and the man told him that they went to Philadelphia, and would return again by morning.

* * * * *

He knew the joys and labours of such men as these. He could see the shadowy procession of their vans lumbering through the sleeping towns, and feel the darkness, the cool fragrance of the country, on his face. He could see the drivers hunched behind the wheels, their senses all alert in the lilac dark, their eyes fixed hard upon the road to curtain off the loneliness of the land at night. And he knew the places where they stopped to eat, the little all-night lunch-rooms warm with greasy light, now empty save for the dozing authority of the aproned Greek behind the counter, and now filled with the heavy shuffle of the drivers' feet, the hard and casual intrusions of their voices.

They came in, flung themselves upon the row of stools, and gave their orders. And as they waited, their hunger drawn into sharp focus by the male smells of boiling coffee, frying eggs and onions, and sizzling hamburgers, they took the pungent, priceless and uncostly solace of a cigarette, lit between cupped hand and strong-seamed mouth, drawn deep and then exhaled in slow fumes from the nostrils. They poured great gobs and gluts of thick tomato ketchup on their hamburgers, tore with blackened fingers at the slabs of fragrant bread, and ate with jungle lust, thrusting at plate and cup with quick and savage gulpings.

Thomas Wolfe, *You Can't Go Home Again*, 1947

It is the summer of 1988. Rhoda, bored, 53, and alone after several divorces, has arranged to travel to Mexico with her brother and a cousin, both similarly unattached. In New Orleans she meets her cousin, a doctor, before flying with him to San Antonio where they will meet her brother and continue the journey together.

'How do I look?' she asked.

'Wonderful,' Saint John said. 'Let's go.' She took his arm and they walked down Royal Street to Bourbon and over to Galatoire's. Their cousin Bunky Biggs was standing outside the restaurant with two of his law partners. 'Saint John,' he called out. 'Cousin Rhoda, what are you doing in town?'

'She's taking me to Mexico,' Saint John said. 'With Dudley.'

'Oh, my Lord,' Bunky said. 'That will be a trip. I wish I was going.'

'He's taking me,' Rhoda said, very softly. It was all working beautifully, the universe was co-operating for a change. Now it would be all over New Orleans that she and Saint John were off on a glorious adventure. Bunky could be depended upon to spread the word.

* * * * *

At that moment a delivery truck pulled up across the street and a tall black man emerged from the back of the truck carrying a huge silver fish. The man was six and a half feet tall. He hoisted the fish in his arms and carried it across the narrow crowded street. A small Japanese car squeaked to a stop. An older black man wearing a tall white hat opened a door and held it open and the fish and its bearer disappeared into the wall. We live in symbiosis with this mystery, Rhoda thought. No one understands it. Everything we think we know is wrong. Except their beauty. They are beautiful and we know it and I think they know it but I am far away from it now and get tired of trying to figure it out. Forget it.

The maître d' appeared and escorted them inside.

The restaurant was crowded with people. The Friday afternoon professional crowd was out in force. Women Rhoda had known years before were seated at tables near the door, the same tables they might have occupied on the day she left town with the poet. People waved, waiters moved between the crowded tables carrying fabulous crabmeat salads and trout meunière and trout amandine and pompano en papillote and oysters Bienville and oysters Rockefeller and turtle soup and fetuccini and martinis and whiskey sours and beautiful French desserts and bread pudding and flàn.

'I should never have left,' Rhoda exclaimed. 'God, I miss this town.'

Ellen Gilchrist, 'Mexico', in *Light Can Be Both Wave and Particle*, 1990

IN INDIA

❧ *Elizabeth Gwillim (1763–1807) was the wife of Sir Henry Gwillim, Puisne Judge of the Supreme Court at Madras, 1801–9. Her response to India, on arriving there with her husband and unmarried sister, was one of curiosity, tolerance, and delight: an unusual combination in an Englishwoman, as she herself was well aware. Avoiding the close, resentful society of the other English wives at Madras, she enjoyed venturing out alone to the sea-shore or market in her palanquin (a kind of horizontal sedan chair, in which the passenger lay down).*

To her sister, Mrs Hetty James, 7 February 1802.

I frequently make the men set down the Palankeen which they like well enough to do for they are fond of the sea. If a Cattymaran comes to shore which they generally do we buy fish of them & by this means I have seen a great variety of fish that I shou'd never otherwise have seen for they never bring from the markets any but a few particular kinds—all the rest go by the name of Palankeen boys fish, which is indeed all the name I can get for any of them. Many of them are very nice and more to my taste than the other kinds; but they are smaller sorts of fish very like little trout and lasprings [young salmon] & there is a small kind the same as whitebait [sketch] about a penny a plateful. These they dress very nicely; they stick them on bents through the head & then fry them quite stiff & they look excessively pretty & eat the same as whitebait. There is another kind more like an anchovy than our sprats are & I think they are anchovies. Besides these there are many curious fish such as the Ink fish & others—which I shou'd not like to eat but I buy for about 8 pence or 10 pence as many as I like for myself & a day's provision for the nine Palankeen boys who are ready enough to run with me along the Beach to S[an] Thomé and back for such a treat.

Mr Gwillim has not failled to eat fish above one day in twenty since he came here. We have no lobster here but we have Prawns as large as the tail of a middling lobster & exactly the same but there is no inside to them, but we mix some crab with it & it makes very fine lobster-like sauce. We have shrimps all sizes & another thing very unlike any creature I ever saw: the first I saw at table I thought they had been made in sweetmeat & varnished. . . . These things look very pretty [sketch] in a dish & make a fine soup or curry. Mr Gwillim enjoys it exceedingly when we get any new fish or vegetable which by going about I bring home. We talk a great deal to the servants some of whom are very good & intelligent, indeed they are the only people to enquire of for few of the white people care for any thing but having it all as like home as possible & have no pleasure in enquiring into the customs of the people or the Production of the places unless they are likely to turn [these] to account. The men like money & the women like visiting.

To her mother, 23 January 1802.

French beans are here all the year & are very good, of our kind: but their hedges are all full of a wild sort . . . little inferiour to ours, & tho' to be had all the year are now more abundant. They climb up every tree & bower over the hedges which are covered with the profusion of their flowers—sometimes white but more frequently pink or laylock [lilac] & very beautiful. These beans are some of them shelled & boilled as broad beans & are not bad—others are used as we use ours but they are as broad as two fingers. . . . I have eaten Asparagus several times but they are miserable small straws. They are very sweet & wou'd no doubt as they occasionally do grow to a good size, but they have been but lately introduced.

MS. Gwillim Letters

❧ *Mary Symonds, Elizabeth Gwillim's unmarried sister, accompanied her to India in 1801.*

Mary Symonds to her mother [*1801*].

These people are very excellent cooks but they have a very odd way of cooking; all their utensils are very simple but elegant in their forms. The kitchen is a long narrow room with large arches in the wall formed like the mouth of an oven about two feet deep. On this place they light a fire of sticks for roasting and the spits are turned by boys who are apprentices to the cook. The boiling is generally done over Charcoal fires which are lighted in earthen pots and stand out in the garden on any convenient places. They boil and stew everything in earthen vessels which they have of all sizes and various pretty shapes. These cooks are also very good confectioners and make all sorts of mixtures of eggs milk and sugar as good as possible, custards, trifles &c &c. The milk is remarkably rich here and eggs are very plentifull. . . . The largest size turkeys here are the most monstrous things you ever conceive and look like mountains on the table: provisions are in general very cheap and so are the servants wages but the quantity of food you are obliged to put on your table and the number of servants you are obliged to keep make house-keeping quite dear enough.

MS. Gwillim Letters

During the eighteenth and early nineteenth centuries, British residents and sojourners in India were notorious for their heavy consumption of red meat, wine, and spirits. Gradually, however, the recognition spread that in a tropical climate this kind of diet could damage health, and may in many cases have led to premature death. Victorians in India (who included many wives, children, and unmarried female relations of army officers and government officials, such as Emma Roberts) ate more lightly than their predecessors, although not all of them managed to overcome thier prejudices against anything resembling 'native food'. At the same time, the new fashion for service à la Russe, *or a number of courses of one or two dishes each brought to table in succession by the servants, spread from England to India to replace the older fashion for one or two very large courses consisting of many different dishes.*

Anglo-Indians, for the most part, have left England too young to have lost their school-relish for ample fare. . . . The receipt for an Indian dinner appears to be, to slaughter a bullock and a sheep, and place all the joints before the guests at once, with poultry, &c to match. The natives are excellent cooks, and might easily be taught the most delicate arts of the *cuisine*; but as their own recipes differ exceedingly from ours, they can only acquire a knowledge of the European style from the instructions of their employers; their hashes, stews, and haricots, are excellent, but a prejudice exists against these preparations amidst the greater number of Anglo-Indians, who fancy that 'black fellows' cannot do anything beyond their own *pillaus*, and are always in dread of some abomination in the mixture: a vain and foolish alarm, where the servants are cleanly, and where no one ever objects to curry.

For these, or some other equally absurd reasons, made dishes form a very small portion of the entertainment given to a large party, which is usually composed of, in the first instance, an overgrown turkey (the fatter the better) in the centre, which is the place of honour; an enormous ham for its *vis-à-vis*; at the top of the table appears a sirloin or round of beef; at the bottom a saddle of mutton; legs of the same, boiled and roasted, figure down the sides, together with fowls, three in a dish, geese, ducks, tongues, humps, pigeon-pies, curry and rice of course, mutton-chops and chicken-cutlets. Fish is of little account, except for breakfast, and can only maintain its post as a side-dish.

In the hot season, fish caught early in the morning would be much deteriorated before the dinner-hour, and is therefore eaten principally at breakfast. There are no *entremets*, no removes; the whole course is put on the table at once, and when the guests are seated, the soup is brought in. The reason of the delay of a part of the entertainment which invariably takes the precedence in England, is rather curious. All the guests are attended by their own servants, who congregate round the cook-room, and assist to carry in the dinner; were the soup to enter first, these worthies would rush to their masters' chairs, and leave the discomfited *khansamah* at the head of his dishes, without a chance of getting them conveyed to table by his *mussaulchees* under an hour, at least. The second course is nearly as substantial as the first, and makes as formidable an appearance: beef-steaks figure amongst the delicacies, and smaller articles, such as quails or ortolans, are piled up in hecatombs. At the tables of old Indians, the fruit makes a part of the second course; but regular desserts are coming, though slowly, into fashion.

Emma Roberts, *Scenes and Characteristics of Hindostan, with Sketches of Anglo-Indian Society*, 1835, Volume I

❧ *Reginald Heber (1783–1826), scholar and hymn-writer ('From Greenland's icy mountains'; 'Holy, Holy, Holy!') sailed to India in 1823 as Bishop-elect of Calcutta, and died there, prematurely, only three years later.*

[Lucknow.] There was a long table in the middle of the room, set out with breakfast, and some fine French and English china. . . . The king began by putting a large hot roll on the resident's plate, and another on mine, then sent similar rolls to the young Nawab his grandson, who sate on the other side of me, to the prime-minister, and one or two others. Coffee, tea, butter, eggs, and fish were then carried round by the servants, and things proceeded much as at a public breakfast in England. The king had some mess of his own in a beautiful covered French cup, but the other Mussalmans ate as the Europeans did. There was a pillaw, which the king recommended to me, and which, therefore, I was bound to taste, though with much secret reluctance, as remembering the greasy delicacies of the Nawab of Dacca. I was surprised, however, to find that this was really an excellent thing, with neither ghee nor garlic, and with no fault except, perhaps, that it was too dry and too exclusively fowl, rice and spices. Mr Ricketts told me afterwards, that the high-bred Mussalmans of this part of India affect to dislike exceedingly, as vulgar, the greasy and fragrant dishes of the Bengalees and Hindoos, and that the merit of their cookery is to be dry, stimulant, and aromatic.

Heber, *Journey through the Upper Provinces of India*, Volume I

❧ *The semi-independent kingdom of Oudh, in upper Bengal, had been ruled from Lucknow since 1775 by a succession of Muslim kings, who to a great extent owed their security to the administrators of the East India Company, direct rulers of the Presidency of Bengal with its capital in Calcutta. Most British officials, from the Governor-General of India downwards, who travelled up the Ganges or crossed Northern India from Calcutta to Bombay, made a point of visiting Lucknow and claiming entertainment at the Court there. In addition there was a British Residency in Lucknow, later ruined in the protracted siege which took place during the Mutiny of 1857–8.*

It is exceedingly difficult to make native servants comprehend the propriety of serving up tea while it is hot; such a thing may be compassed in private families, but never at a public entertainment, where, in order to be ready, every thing is prepared a long time before it is wanted. Old campaigners usually contrive to bring a supply of such things as are essential to their own comfort. The writer, at a very large assembly of the kind, had the good fortune to find the only vacant seat at table next a gentleman who had provided himself with a tripod of charcoal, and other means and appliances for a comfortable breakfast. The tea-kettle was singing merrily outside the door and the careful *khidmutgar* had ensconced the tea-pot under his master's chair. The neighbours came in for a portion of the beverage which 'cheers but not inebriates,' and which afforded a very requisite refreshment after an encounter with the dust and fatigue attendant upon a native spectacle.

* * * * *

Bishop Heber has borne honourable testimony to the culinary powers of the *maître d'hôtel* who officiated during his sojourn; and the writer can never forget a certain fowl, prepared by the hands of the king's especial attendant . . . which a Ude or a Carême might view with envy. It was roasted, and served up whole, but so spiced and saturated with curry-powder, as to form no bad representation of a salamander. It may not be unimportant to add, that the preparation, though excellent in its kind, which goes under the name of the king of Oude's sauce, does not bear any resemblance to the zests and relishes of various descriptions which are served up at the king's table; the chetney's and sweet pickles, for which Lucknow is famous, and which, especially the latter, London oilmen would do well to import or imitate.

Roberts, *Scenes of Hindostan*, Volume II

'*a salamander*': (loosely) anything capable of withstanding fire or great heat, or used in fire (possibly, in this instance, a form of tandoori chicken); '*king of Oude's sauce . . . imitate*': many oilmen or Italian warehousemen in London stocked a range of bottled sauces and pickles, most of which included oriental seasonings such as tamarind, ginger, and chillies. Such, for example, was the 'Mogul or Real Chetna sauce' stocked by Burgess & Son, of 107 Strand, in the early nineteenth century. Emma Roberts may have been comparing these bottled sauces unfavourably with the freshly made relishes and chutneys at the king of Oudh's table, none of which could have been kept for long enough to sell them; but at the same time acknowledging the superior quality of his longer-lasting pickles and preserves.

❧ *Emily Eden (1797–1869) was the sister of George Eden, 2nd Baron Auckland (1784–1849), whom she accompanied during his period as Governor-General of India between 1836 and 1842. (Neither Emily nor George, nor their younger sister Fanny who was also with them, ever married.) The Edens travelled with their own French chef, and therefore suffered little gastronomic inconvenience except when separated from him. This letter was dated 30 October 1839, soon after the beginning of a journey back from the hot-weather residence at Simla to Government House at Calcutta. At this stage in the journey Emily was carried in a litter* (jonpaun), *looked after by Wright and Rosina, her English and Indian maids.*

More than three hours of a jonpaun knocks me up, and the last three days I have unluckily been ailing. I should not have set off yesterday afternoon, only that my bed and sofa and every atom of clothes had gone on in the morning and three hours of any pain can be borne. So in spite of a desperate headache, I started for Syree, with Dr D., Giles [a servant] and Wright, meaning to get into bed the moment I arrived. But I had the sad spectacle of my bed set down half-way, and the coolies smoking and cooking their dinner round it. However, Rosina had made me up a bed on a native charpoy that did to lie and excruciate my head upon, till the bed came up, and the doctor made me a composing draught; but such a night as I had! I had not tasted anything for thirty-six hours, and about ten an insane desire for a sandwich seized me; so, though I had heard the cooks with all their chattels set off for this place two hours before, I called to the hirkaru who was sleeping at the door, and told him to tell Giles I wanted a sandwich. Hirkarus are good for carrying a note, or a parcel, but are never trusted with a message. After making me repeat sandwich six times, and evidently thinking it meant a friend from England, or some new medicine, I heard him repeating as he walked off round the bungalow, 'Lady Sahib sant vich muncta' (muncta meaning '*wants*', and the only word that we have all learnt, showing what *wanting* creatures we are). Giles made up a mixture of leg of chicken and dust, which was satisfying under the circumstances, but still my head raved; and having heard the jackals (which do not exist at Simla) tearing up a dog, I had a vague idea that the sandwich was made of the remains of Chance [her spaniel], which gave it an unpleasant flavour.

Emily Eden, *Up the Country*, 1866

❧ *Matty Robinson, aged 29, the eldest child of the impoverished Rector of Dyrham in Gloucestershire, and granddaughter of Sir George Abercrombie Robinson (1758–1832), formerly military auditor-general for Bengal, has just arrived in Bombay at the time of the Mutiny as the bride of her cousin Douglas Robinson, a British Army officer. Despite her membership of a strongly Anglo-Indian family (all four of her brothers have, or shortly will have, careers in India in either the army or the civil service), Matty loathes and fears India and cannot wait to leave.*

Matty Robinson to her sister Fanny, Bombay, 19 January 1858.

We found Mr Wight when we came back & had a very pleasant evening sitting up till 11. He persuaded me to try a plantain but I was obliged to get a glass of sherry directly; it tasted just as I should fancy an old pear shut up in the pantry closet for *months* would. I cant touch the Indian fruits or the fish which they say is so delicious & as to the curries it makes me sick to think of them; give me an *English one*! I cannot even eat dry bread for it is made of Indian Corn & so nasty & full of grits. I should be so glad of a good wholesome Ships biscuit now.

* * * * *

They could not understand Douglas & myself (the 'Capt Sahib' they called him) at the hotel, because we would *not* dine at the table D'hote and had nothing but beef or mutton and shut ourselves up at night!

MS Robinson Papers

❧ *Adela Quested, a thoughtful and impressionable young woman, has travelled out to India to join her fiancé, Ronny Heaslop, a City Magistrate and an upholder of the British Raj. Her first reactions to the culture and behaviour of his colleagues and their womenfolk are, on the whole, uneasy.*

And sure enough they did drive away from the club in a few minutes, and they did dress, and to dinner came Miss Derek and the McBrydes, and the menu was: Julienne soup full of bullety bottled peas, pseudo-cottage bread, fish full of branching bones, pretending to be plaice, more bottled peas with the cutlets, trifle, sardines on toast: the menu of Anglo-India. A dish might be added or subtracted as one rose or fell in the official scale, the peas might rattle less or more, the sardines and the vermouth be imported by a different firm, but the tradition remained; the food of exiles, cooked by servants who did not understand it. Adela thought of the young men and women who had come out before her, P. & O. full after P. & O. full, and had been set down to the same food and the same ideas, and had been snubbed in the same good-humoured way until they kept to the accredited themes and began to snub others. 'I should never get like that,' she thought, for she was young herself; all the same she knew that she had come up against something that was both insidious and tough, and that she should need allies.

E. M. Forster, *A Passage to India*, 1924

❧ *V. S. Naipaul, on a visit to India, is staying in Srinagar, Kashmir. After visiting the temple at Awantipur he and his wife attempt to flag down a returning bus to Srinagar. One stops for them, a little hesitantly.*

We sat in the back among some sensationally unwashed people, their cotton dhotis brown with dirt, and many Dalda tins. The man next to me was stretched out on the seat, clearly unwell, his eyes without expression, the pestilential Indian flies undisturbed on his lips and cheeks; from time to time he gave a theatrical groan, to which no one in the chattering bus paid the slightest attention. We saw that we were in a bus of 'lower-income' tourists and that we were sitting with their servants.

* * * * *

[After stopping at the ruins] we were all back in the bus and about to start when the leader suggested food. The conductor threw open the door again and an especially grimy manservant, old and toothless, came to life. Briskly, proprietorially, he shoved the Dalda tins along the dusty floor and lifted them out on the verge. I began to protest at the delay . . . [then] I realised that we had fallen among a family, that the bus was chartered, that we had been offered a lift out of charity. The bus again emptied. We remained helpless in our seats, while Srinagar-bound passenger buses, visibly holding spare seats, went past.

They were a brahmin family and their vegetarian food was served according to established form. No one was allowed to touch it except the dirty old servant who, at the mention of food, had been kindled into such important activity. With the very fingers that a moment before had been rolling a crinkled cigarette and had then seized the dusty Dalda tins from off the dusty bus floor, he now—using only the right hand, of course—distributed puris from one tin, scooped out curried potatoes from another, and from a third secured dripping fingerfuls of chutney. He was of the right caste; nothing served by the fingers of his right hand could be unclean; and the eaters ate with relish. The verge had been deserted; now, in the twinkling of an eye, the eaters were surrounded by villagers and long-haired Kashmiri dogs. The dogs kept their distance; they stood still, their tails low and alert, the fields stretching out behind them to the mountains. The villagers, men and children, stood right over the squatting eaters who, like celebrities in the midst of an admiring crowd, slightly adjusted their behaviour. They ate with noisier relish; just perceptibly they raised their voices, heightened and lengthened out their laughter. The servant, busier than ever, frowned as if made impatient by his responsibilities. His lips disappeared between his toothless gums.

The leader spoke to the servant, and the servant came to where we were. Busily, like a man with little time to waste, he slapped two puris into our hands, plastered the puris with potatoes, leaked chutney on the potatoes, and withdrew, hugging his tins, leaving us with committed right hands.

A family spokesman came to the door of the bus. 'Just *taste* our food.'

We tasted. We felt the eyes of the villagers on us. We felt the eyes of the family on us. We smiled, and ate.

Naipaul, *An Area of Darkness*

Dalda: a commercial substitute for *ghee* or clarified butter, used in cooking; '*using only the right hand*': Hindu protocol demands that the left hand, used for various bodily functions, should never be involved in eating or handling food.

ON SHIPBOARD

Travelling alone on the six-month voyage, with the intention of joining her brother somewhere in Bengal, Judith Weston was unusual in her courage and independence at a time when few European women set foot in India, even as the wives of senior officials. Of the handful of camp-followers who sailed there with the deliberate intention of finding English husbands, few can have been as articulate as she was in describing their adventures.

In the year 1727 I left the Downs . . . for Fort William in Bengal. There was four women passengers beside myself. . . . For three weeks . . . extream sickness was suffered by all the women except my self. . . . For one fortnight we never pulled off our clothes or Lay in a Bed; we could neither set Lye or stand one minute in a place. The chief difficulty to me was to satisfie hunger for as the sea air agreed perfectly with me I had a constant appetite & while my companions were Groaning with sickness & calling for proper Utensels I was striving to get to a Hamper in which was a fine cold Buttock of Beef which the captain had placed there for our relief till the Weather would admit of a regular meal. After many efforts to no other purpose than many a roll back again I at last attained the desired hamper which was well lashed to the Ground. The difficulty now was how to keep my Hold & yet cut sufficient to satisfie my hunger. Here two pair of hands would have been of wonderful service but I made my knees act their parts by pressing them as hard as I could into the Matt while with all my might I held the Hamper with one Hand and cut with the other till I was weary. A delicious repast it was & was well washed down with some warm Flip which as the weather was wet & cold was not disagreeable.

MS Autobiographical Narrative of Judith Weston

The first mate . . . went upon deck immediately . . . desiring me to clean myself as soon as possible, for he intended to regale himself with a dish of salmagundy and a pipe. . . . This affair being ended, the descendant of Caractacus returned, and ordering the boy to bring a piece of salt beef from the brine, cut off a slice and mixed it with an equal quantity of onions, which seasoning with a moderate proportion of pepper and salt, he brought into a consistence with oil and vinegar.—Then tasting the dish, assured us, it was the best salmagundie, that ever he made, and recommended it to our palate with such heartiness that I could not help doing honour to his preparation. But I had no sooner swallowed a mouthful, than I thought my entrails were scorched, and endeavoured with a deluge of small beer, to allay the heat it occasioned.

Tobias Smollett, *The Adventures of Roderick Random*, 1748

❧ *Don Juan, discovered having a love-affair with a married woman, Donna Julia, has been banished from Spain by his mother to go on the Grand Tour. When his ship is wrecked in the Mediterranean, thirty people crowd into a long-boat: among them Juan and his tutor Pedrillo, with Juan's father's old spaniel. By the end of the third day, all the provisions in the boat have been eaten and all the wine drunk.*

The fourth day came, but not a breath of air,
And Ocean slumber'd like an unwean'd child:
The fifth day, and their boat lay floating there,

The sea and sky were blue, and clear, and mild—
With their one oar (I wish they had a pair)
What could they do? and hunger's rage grew wild:
So Juan's spaniel, spite of his entreating,
Was kill'd, and portion'd out for present eating.

On the sixth day they fed upon his hide,
And Juan, who had still refused, because
The creature was his father's dog that died,
Now feeling all the vulture in his jaws,
With some remorse received (though first denied)
As a great favour one of the fore-paws,
Which he divided with Pedrillo, who
Devour'd it, longing for the other too.

The seventh day, and no wind—the burning sun
Blister'd and scorch'd, and, stagnant on the sea,
They lay like carcasses; and hope was none,
Save in the breeze that came not: savagely
They glared upon each other—all was done,
Water, and wine, and food,—and you might see
The longings of the cannibal arise
(Although they spoke not) in their wolfish eyes.

At length one whisper'd his companion, who
Whisper'd another, and thus it went round,
And then into a hoarser murmur grew,
An ominous, and wild, and desperate sound;
And when his comrade's thought each sufferer knew,
'Twas but his own, suppress'd till now, he found:
And out they spoke for lots of flesh and blood,
And who should die to be his fellow's food.

But ere they came to this, they that day shared
Some leathern caps, and what remain'd of shoes;
And then they look'd around them, and despair'd,
And none to be the sacrifice would choose;
At length the lots were torn up, and prepared,
But of materials that must shock the muse—
Having no paper, for the want of better,
They took by force from Juan Julia's [farewell] letter.

Then lots were made, and mark'd, and mix'd, and handed
In silent horror, and their distribution

Lull'd even the savage hunger which demanded,
Like the Promethean vulture, this pollution;
None in particular had sought or plann'd it,
'Twas Nature gnawed them to this resolution,
By which none were permitted to be neuter—
And the lot fell on Juan's luckless tutor.

He but requested to be bled to death:
The surgeon had his instruments, and bled
Pedrillo, and so gently ebb'd his breath,
You hardly could perceive when he was dead.
He died as born, a Catholic in faith,
Like most in the belief in which they're bred,
And first a little crucifix he kiss'd,
And then held out his jugular and wrist.

The surgeon, as there was no other fee,
Had his first choice of morsels for his pains;
But being thirstiest at the moment, he
Preferr'd a draught from the fast-flowing veins:
Part was divided, part thrown in the sea,
And such things as the entrails and the brains
Regaled two sharks, who followed o'er the billow—
The sailors ate the rest of poor Pedrillo.

George Gordon Noel Byron, Lord Byron, *Don Juan*, 1819–24

LITTLE BILLEE

There were three sailors in Bristol city
Who took a boat and went to sea,

But first with beef and captain's biscuit
And pickled pork they loaded she.

There was guzzling Jack and gorging Jimmy,
And the youngest he was little Billee.

Now very soon they were so greedy
They didn't leave not one split pea.

Says guzzling Jack to gorging Jimmy,
'I am extremely hungaree.'

Says gorging Jim to guzzling Jacky,
'We have no provisions, so we must eat we.'

Says guzzling Jack to gorging Jimmy,
'O gorging Jim, what a fool you be.

There's little Bill is young and tender,
We're old and tough, so let's eat he.'

'O Bill, we're going to kill and eat you,
So undo the collar of your chemie.'

When Bill received this information
He used his pocket-handkerchie.

'O let me say my catechism,
As my poor mammy taught to me.'

'Make haste, make haste,' says guzzling Jacky,
While Jim pulled out his snickersnee.

So Bill went up to the main-top-gallant mast,
Where down he fell on his bended knee.

He scarce had got to the Twelfth Commandment,
When up he jumps. 'There's land I see.

There's Jerusalem and Madagascar,
And North and South Amerikee.

There's the British fleet a-riding at anchor,
With Admiral Nelson, K.C.B.'

So when they came to the Admiral's vessel
He hanged fat Jack and flogged Jimmee.

But as for little Bill, he made him
The captain of a seventy-three.

William Makepeace Thackeray, 'Little Billee', 1849

❧ *Stubb, the second mate of the* Pequod *under Captain Ahab, has been responsible for catching a whale.*

Very soon you would have thought from the sound on the *Pequod's* decks, that all hands were preparing to cast anchor in the deep; for heavy chains are being dragged along the deck, and thrust rattling out of the port-holes. But by those clanking links, the vast corpse itself, not the ship, is to be moored. Tied by the head to the stern, and by the tail to the bows, the whale now lies with its black hull to the vessel's, and seen through the darkness of the night, which obscured the spars and rigging aloft, the two—ship and whale—seemed yoked together like colossal bullocks, whereof one reclines while the other is left standing.

If moody Ahab was now all quiescence, at least so far as could be known on deck, Stubb, his second mate, flushed with conquest, betrayed an unusual but still good-natured excitement. Such an unwonted bustle was he in, that the staid Starbuck, his official superior, quietly resigned to him for the time the sole management of affairs. One small, helping cause of all this liveliness in Stubb was soon made strangely manifest. Stubb was a high liver; he was somewhat intemperately fond of the whale as a flavourish thing to his palate.

'A steak, a steak, ere I sleep. You, Daggoo! Overboard you go, and cut me a steak from his small!'

Here it be known, that though these wild fishermen do not, as a general thing, and according to the great military maxim, make the enemy defray the current expenses of the war (at least before realizing the proceeds of the voyage), yet now and then you find some of these Nantucketers who have a genuine relish for that particular part of the Sperm Whale designated by Stubb; comprising the tapering extremity of the body.

About midnight the steak was cut and cooked; and lighted by two lanterns of Sperm oil, Stubb stoutly stood up to his spermaceti supper at the capstan-head, as if that capstan were a sideboard. Nor was Stubb the only banqueter on whale's flesh that night. Mingling their mumblings with his own mastications, thousands on thousands of sharks, swarming round the dead leviathan, smackingly feasted on its fatness. The few sleepers below in their bunks were often startled by the sharp slapping of their tails against the hull, within a few inches of the sleepers' hearts. Peering over the side you could just see them (as before you heard them) wallowing in the sullen, black waters, and turning over on their backs as they scooped out huge globular pieces of the whale of the bigness of a human head. This particular feast of the shark seemed all but miraculous. How, at such an apparently unassailable surface, they contrive to gouge out such symmetrical mouthfuls, remains a part of the universal problem of all things. The mark they thus leave on the whale may best be likened to the hollow made by a carpenter in countersinking for a screw.

Melville, *Moby Dick*

❧ *Hugh Firmin, a left-wing newspaperman, Cambridge graduate, and veteran of the Spanish Civil War, reminisces uncomfortably to himself about the romantic exhibitionism of his late teens, which included a period 'running away to sea' on a cargo-boat bound for Japan.*

For instance . . . the forecastle was not called the 'fo'c'sle' but the 'men's quarters', and was not forward where it should be, but aft, under the poop. . . . The deckhead of the poop roofed what all too patently were 'men's quarters', as they were styled, separate cabins just like on the Isle of Man boat, with two bunks in each running along an alleyway broken by the messroom. But Hugh was not grateful for these hard-won 'better' conditions. To him a fo'c'sle—and where else should the crew of a ship live?—meant inescapably a single evil-smelling room forward with bunks around a table, under a swinging kerosene lamp, where men fought, whored, drank and murdered. On board the *Philoctetes* men neither fought, whored, nor murdered. . . . Tea, too, was the subject of another matter that bothered him. Every afternoon, on the stroke of six and eight bells respectively, it was at first Hugh's duty, his mate being sick, to run in from the galley, at first to the bosun's mess and afterwards to the crew, what the bosun called, with unction, 'afternoon tea'. With tabnabs. The tabnabs were delicate and delicious little cakes made by the second cook. Hugh ate them with scorn. Imagine the Sea Wolf sitting down to afternoon tea with tabnabs! And this was not the worst. An even more important item was the food itself. The food on board the *Philoctetes*, a common British cargo steamer, contrary to a tradition so strong Hugh had hardly dared contradict it till this moment even in his dreams, was excellent; compared with that of his public school, where he had lived under catering conditions no merchant seaman would tolerate for five minutes, it was a gourmet's fantasy. There were never fewer than five courses for breakfast in the P.O.'s mess, to which at the outset he was more strictly committed; but it proved almost as satisfying in the 'men's quarters'. American dry hash, kippers, poached eggs and bacon, porridge, steaks, rolls, all at one meal, even on one plate; Hugh never remembered having seen so much food in his life. All the more surprising then was it for him to discover it his duty each day to heave vast quantities of this miraculous food over the side. This chow the crew hadn't eaten went into the Indian Ocean, into any ocean, rather, as the saying is, than 'let it go back to the office'. Hugh was not grateful for these hard-won better conditions either. Nor, mysteriously, seemed anyone else to be. For the wretchedness of the food was the great topic of conversation. 'Never mind, chaps, soon we'll be home where a fellow can have some tiddley chow he can eat, instead of all this bloody kind of stuff, bits of paint, I don't know what it is at all.' And Hugh, a loyal soul at bottom, grumbled with the rest.

Malcolm Lowry, *Under the Volcano*, 1947

EATING OUT

❧ *Taking the waters, in the eighteenth century, was often an excuse for systematic socializing as much as an opportunity for pursuing a cure. This novel, set in Harrogate in 1731, explains the routine of a pleasant, temporary society, evidently little in need of a good night's rest.*

As to the company at these wells, I found it very good, and was pleased with the manner of living there. In the day-time we drank the waters, walked or rid about, and lived in separate parties; lodging in one or other of the three inns that are on the edge of the common: but at night, the company meet at one of the *public-houses* (the *inns* having the benefit of the meeting in their turn) and sup together between eight and nine o'clock on the best substantial things, such as hot shoulders of mutton, rump-stakes, hot pigeon pies, veal cutlets and the like. For this supper, ladies and gentlemen pay eightpence each, and after sitting an hour, and drinking what wine, punch, and ale, every one chuses, all who please get up to country-dances, which generally last till one in the morning; those that dance, and those who do not, drinking as they will. The ladies pay nothing for what liquor is brought in, either at supper or after, and it costs the gentlemen five or six shillings a man. At one the ladies withdraw, some to their houses in the neighbourhood, and some to their beds in the inns. The men who are temperate, do then likewise go to rest.

Thomas Amory, *The Life of John Buncle Esq*, 1766, Volume II

❧ *Nathaniel Hawthorne and his wife and family had arrived in England from the United States in 1853, and stayed for five years. The Crystal Palace had been moved from Hyde Park after the Great Exhibition of 1851 and re-erected on a hilltop at Sydenham in south-east London, where it became a favourite place of resort.*

The train of carriages stops within the domain of the palace, where there is a long ascending corridor up into the edifice. There was a very pleasant odour of heliotrope diffused through the air; and indeed, the whole atmosphere of the Crystal Palace is sweet with various flower-scents, and mild and balmy, though sufficiently fresh and cool. It would be a delightful climate for invalids to spend the winter in; and if all England could be roofed over with glass, it would be a great improvement on its present condition. The first thing we did, before fairly getting into the palace, was to sit down in a large ante-hall, and get some bread and butter and a pint of Bass's pale ale, together with a cup of coffee for S[ophia]. This was the best refreshment we could find at that spot; but farther within we found abundance of refreshment-rooms, and John Bull and his wife and family at fifty little round tables, busily engaged with cold fowl, cold beef, ham, tongue, and bottles of ale and stout, and half-pint decanters of sherry. The English probably eat with more simple enjoyment than any other people; not ravenously, as we [Americans] often do, and not exquisitely and artificially, like the French, but deliberately and vigorously, and with due absorption in the business, so that nothing good is lost upon them. . . . It is remarkable how large a feature the refreshment-rooms make in the arrangements of the Crystal Palace.

> *Passages from The English Note-Books of Nathaniel Hawthorne*, Volume I

❧ *Little Dorrit (Amy) has gone to find her sister Fanny, who is a chorus-girl in a theatre, and her uncle, who plays a clarinet in the orchestra there. Fanny wishes to speak to Little Dorrit in private.*

'My dear child, when we have got rid of Uncle, you shall know all about it. We'll drop him at the cook's shop where he is going to dine.'

They walked on with him until they came to a dirty shop-window in a dirty street, which was made almost opaque by the steam of hot meats, vegetables, and puddings. But glimpses were to be caught of a roast leg of pork bursting into tears of sage and onion in a metal reservoir full of gravy, of an unctuous piece of roast beef and blisterous Yorkshire pudding, bubbling hot in a similar receptacle, of a stuffed fillet of veal in rapid cut, of a ham in a perspiration with the pace it was going at, of a shallow tank of baked potatoes glued together by their own richness, of a truss or two of boiled greens, and other substantial delicacies. Within, were a few wooden partitions, behind which such customers as found it more convenient to take away their dinners in stomachs than in their hands, packed their purchases in solitude. Fanny opening her reticule, as they surveyed these things, produced from that repository a shilling and handed it to Uncle. Uncle, after not looking at it a little while, divined its object, and muttering 'Dinner? Ha! Yes, yes, yes!' slowly vanished from them into the mist.

Charles Dickens, *Little Dorrit*, 1855–7, Book I

❧ *The eating house described here, in the City of London at the end of Victoria's reign, was of a vanishing type, often referred to in later times as 'Dickensian'. The clientele was exclusively masculine; the food plain, unadorned, and filling. Although lunch had become a regular institution for City businessmen only during the later Victorian period, places such as French's had existed previously to satisfy their need for a mid-afternoon or early evening dinner.*

'One mockturtle, clear; one oxtail; two glasses of port.'

In the upper room at French's, where a Forsyte could still get heavy English food, James and his son were sitting down to lunch.

Of all eating-places James liked best to come here; there was something unpretentious, well-flavoured, and filling about it, and though he had been to a certain extent corrupted by the necessity for being fashionable, and the trend of habits keeping pace with an income that *would* increase, he still hankered in quiet City moments after the tasty flesh-pots of his earlier days. Here you were served by hairy English waiters in aprons; there was sawdust on the floor, and three round gilt looking-glasses hung just above the line of sight. They had only recently done away with the cubicles, too, in which you could have your chop, prime chump, with a floury potato, without seeing your neighbours, like a gentleman.

He tucked the top corner of his napkin behind the third button of his waistcoat, a practice he had been obliged to abandon years ago in the West End. He felt that he should relish his soup—the entire morning had been given to winding up the estate of an old friend.

* * * * *

The waiter brought two glasses of port, but Soames stopped him. 'That's not the way to serve port,' he said; 'take them away and bring the whole bottle.'

Galsworthy, *The Man of Property*, Part II

❧ *Margaret Schlegel and her younger sister Helen, progressive young women of independent means, have befriended the middle-aged businessman Henry Wilcox, a recent widower with several grown-up children. The two families are cultural opposites: the Schlegels imaginative, liberal, sceptical, and devoted to the arts; the Wilcoxes conventional, literal-minded and materialistic. Margaret, nevertheless, finds herself attracted towards Henry Wilcox and romantically attached to his Hertfordshire country house, Howards End, which she already knows about from an earlier friendship with his late wife. Her response to Henry's protectiveness, in the carnivorous, masculine atmosphere of Simpson's, represents a preliminary surrender to his family's values: a surrender which her sister Helen has already avoided in her brief, frustrated passion for the Wilcoxes' son Paul.*

Once [Margaret] had humorously lamented that she had never been to Simpson's restaurant in the Strand. Now a note arrived from Miss Wilcox, asking her to lunch there. Mr Cahill was coming, and the three would have such a jolly chat, and perhaps end up at the Hippodrome. Margaret had no strong regard for Evie, and no desire to meet her fiancé, and she was surprised that Helen, who had been far funnier about Simpson's, had not been asked instead. But the invitation touched her by its intimate tone . . . and declaring that she 'simply must,' she accepted.

But when she saw Evie at the entrance of the restaurant, staring fiercely at nothing after the fashion of athletic women, her heart failed her anew. . . . Depressed at her isolation, she saw not only houses and furniture, but the vessel of life itself slipping past her, with people like Evie and Mr Cahill on board.

There are moments when virtue and wisdom fail us, and one of them came to her at Simpson's in the Strand. As she trod the staircase, narrow, but carpeted thickly, as she entered the eating-room, where saddles of mutton were being trundled up to expectant clergymen, she had a strong, if erroneous conviction of her own futility and wished she had never come out of her backwater, where nothing ever happened except art and literature, and no one ever got married or succeeded in remaining engaged. Then came a little surprise. 'Father might be of the party—yes, father was.' With a smile of pleasure she moved forward to greet him, and her feeling of loneliness vanished.

'I thought I'd get round it if I could,' said he. 'Evie told me of her little plan, so I just slipped in and secured a table. Always secure a table first. Evie, don't pretend you want to sit by your old father, because you don't. Miss Schlegel, come in my side, out of pity. My goodness, but you look tired! Been worrying round after your young clerks?'

'No, after houses,' said Margaret, edging past him into the box. 'I'm hungry, not tired; I want to eat heaps.'

'That's good. What'll you have?'

'Fish pie,' said she, with a glance at the menu.

'Fish pie! Fancy coming for fish pie to Simpson's. It's not a bit the thing to go for here.'

'Go for something for me, then,' said Margaret, pulling off her gloves. . . .

'Saddle of mutton,' said he after profound reflection; 'and cider to drink. That's the type of thing. I like this place, for a joke, once in a way. It is so thoroughly Old English. Don't you agree?'

'Yes,' said Margaret, who didn't. The order was given, the joint rolled up, and the carver, under Mr Wilcox's direction, cut the meat where it was succulent, and piled their plates high.

* * * * *

'Next time,' she said to Mr Wilcox, 'you shall come to lunch with me at Mr Eustace Miles's.'

'With pleasure.'

'No, you'd hate it,' she said, pushing her glass towards him for some more cider.

'It's all proteids and body buildings, and people coming up to you and beg pardon, but you have such a beautiful aura.'

'A what?'

'Never heard of an aura? Oh, happy, happy man. I scrub at mine for hours. Nor of an astral plane?'

He had heard of astral planes, and duly censured them.

'Just so. Luckily it was Helen's aura, not mine, and she had to chaperone it and do the politenesses. I just sat with my handkerchief in my mouth till the man went.'

'Funny experiences seem to come to you two girls. No-one's ever asked me about my—what d'ye call it? Perhaps I've not got one.'

'You're bound to have one, but it may be such a terrible colour that no one dares mention it.'

'Tell me, though, Miss Schlegel, do you really believe in the supernatural and all that?'

'Too difficult a question.'

'Why's that? Gruyère or Stilton.'

'Gruyère, please.'

'Better have Stilton.'

'Stilton. Because, though I don't believe in auras, and think Theosophy's only a halfway-house—'

'—Yet there may be something in it all the same,' he concluded, with a frown.

'Not even that. It may be halfway in the wrong direction. I can't explain. I don't believe in all these fads, and yet I don't like saying that I don't believe in them.'

* * * * *

She did not forget his promise to sample Eustace Miles, and asked him as soon as she could secure Tibby as his chaperon. He came, and partook of body-building dishes with humility.

E. M. Forster, *Howards End*, 1910

Eustace Miles: a well-known vegetarian restaurant, opened in Chandos Street, London, in 1906, and a favourite resort of progressives, the austerely unconventional, and women unaccompanied by men.

ONE FISH BALL

A man went walking up and down
To find a place where he could dine in town.

He found himself an expensive place,
And entered in with modest face.

He took his purse his pocket hence,
But all he had was fifteen cents.

He looked the menu through and through,
To see what fifteen cents would do.

The cheapest item of them all
Was thirty cents for two fish balls.

The waiter, he, on him did call,
He softly whispered, 'One fish ball.'

The waiter bellowed down the hall,
'This creep here wants just one fish ball!'

The guests, they turned, both one and all,
To see who wanted one fish ball.

The man then said, quite ill at ease,
'And a piece of bread, Sir, if you please.'

The waiter bellowed down the hall,
'You get no bread with one fish ball!'

There is a moral to this all.
You get no bread with one fish ball.

Who would have bread with one fish ball,
Must get it first, or not at all.

Who would fish balls with fixin's eat,
Must get some friend to stand a treat.

Anon. (Traditional American.)

In some versions, 'one meat ball'.

❧ *Marcel, the narrator of Proust's long, semi-autobiographical novel, leaves Paris to visit his friend Robert, Marquis de Saint-Loup, an army officer, at Doncières, the garrison town where he is stationed. Living as he does within the confines of a highly developed aesthetic imagination, Marcel transforms his visit to Saint-Loup into a series of romantic episodes of which inhabiting a painting by Brueghel is only one.*

At seven o'clock I dressed myself and went out again to dine with Saint-Loup at the hotel where he took his meals. I liked to go there on foot. It was by now pitch dark, and after the third day of my visit there began to blow, as soon as night had fallen, an icy wind which seemed a harbinger of snow. . . . I returned to the main street and jumped on board the little tramway-car on which, from its platform, an officer, without apparently seeing them, was acknowledging the salutes of the loutish soldiers who trudged past along the pavement, their faces daubed crimson by the cold, reminding me, in this little town which the sudden leap from autumn into early winter seemed to have transported farther north, of the rubicund faces which Brueghel gives to his merry, junketing, forestbound peasants.

And sure enough at the hotel where I was to meet Saint-Loup and his friends and to which the fair now beginning had attracted a number of people from near and far, I found, as I hurried across the courtyard with its glimpses of glowing kitchens in which chickens were turning on spits, pigs were roasting, lobsters being flung, alive, into what the landlord called the 'everlasting fire', an influx (worthy of some *Numbering of the People before Bethlehem* such as the old Flemish masters used to paint) of new arrivals who assembled there in groups, asking the landlord or one of his staff (who, if he did not like the look of them, would recommend lodgings elsewhere in the town) whether they could have dinner and beds, while a scullion hurried past holding a struggling fowl by the neck. And similarly, in the big dining-room which I crossed the first day before coming to the smaller room in which my friend was waiting for me, it was of some feast in the Gospels portrayed with a mediaeval simplicity and an exaggeration typically Flemish that one was reminded by the quantity of fish, pullets, grouse, woodcock, pigeons, brought in dressed and garnished and piping hot by breathless waiters who slid over the polished floor to gain speed and set them down on the huge carving table where they were at once cut up but where—for most of the people had nearly finished dinner when I arrived—they accumulated untouched, as though their profusion and the haste of those who brought them in were due not so much to the requirements of the diners as to respect for the sacred text, scrupulously followed in the letter but quaintly illustrated by real details borrowed from local custom, and to an aesthetic and religious scruple for making evident to the eye the solemnity of the feast by the profusion of the victuals and the assiduity of the servers. One of these stood lost in thought at the far end of the room by a sideboard; and to find out from him, who alone appeared calm enough to be capable of answering me, in which room our table had been laid, making my way forward among the chafing-dishes that had been lighted here and there to keep the late comers' plates from growing cold (which did not, however, prevent the dessert, in the centre of the room, from being piled on the outstretched hands of a huge mannikin, sometimes supported on the wings of a duck, apparently of crystal, but really of ice, carved afresh every day with a hot iron by a sculptor-cook, quite in the Flemish manner), I went straight—at the risk of being knocked down by his colleagues—towards this servitor, in whom I felt that I recognised a character who is traditionally present in all these sacred subjects, for he reproduced with scrupulous accuracy the blunt features, fatuous and ill-drawn, the musing expression, already half aware of the miracle of a divine presence which the others have not yet begun to suspect. I should add that, in view probably of the coming fair, this presentation was strengthened by a celestial contingent, recruited in mass, of cherubim and seraphim. A young angel musician, whose fair hair enclosed a fourteen-year-old face, was not, it was true, playing on any instrument, but stood musing before a gong or a pile of plates, while other less infantile angels flew swiftly across the boundless expanse of the room, beating the air with the ceaseless fluttering of the napkins which fell along the lines of their bodies like the wings in 'primitive' paintings, with pointed ends. Fleeing those ill-defined regions, screened by a hedge of palms through which the angelic servitors looked, from a distance, as though they had floated down out of the empyrean, I explored my way to the smaller room in which Saint-Loup's table was laid.

Marcel Proust, *Remembrance of Things Past*, Volume V: *The Guermantes Way*, Part I, 1920, translated by C. K. Scott-Moncrieff

THE GRAND BABYLON HOTEL

At eight o'clock precisely dinner was served in the immense salle à manger, that chaste yet splendid apartment of white and gold. At a small table near one of the windows a young lady sat alone. Her frock said Paris, but her face unmistakably said New York. It was a self-possessed and bewitching face, the face of a woman thoroughly accustomed to doing exactly what she liked, when she liked, how she liked; the face of a woman who had taught hundreds of gilded young men the true art of fetching and carrying, and who, by twenty years or so of parental spoiling, had come to regard herself as the feminine equivalent of the Tsar of All the Russias. Such women are only made in America, and they only come to their full bloom in Europe, which they imagine to be a continent created by Providence for their diversion.

* * * * *

'*Consommé Britannia*,' she began to read out from the menu [to her father], '*Saumon d'Écosse, Sauce Génoise, Aspics de Homard*. Oh, heavens! Who wants these horrid messes on a night like this?'

'But, Nella, this is the best cooking in Europe,' he protested. . . .

'. . . Let's have filleted steak and a bottle of Bass for dinner tonight. It will be simply exquisite. I shall love it.'

'But, my dear Nella,' he exclaimed, 'steak and beer at Félix's! It's impossible. Moreover, young women still under twenty-three cannot be permitted to drink Bass.'

'I said steak and Bass, and as for being twenty-three, I shall be going in twenty-four tomorrow.'

Miss Racksole set her small white teeth.

There was a gentle cough. Jules stood over them. It must have been out of a pure spirit of adventure that he had selected this table for his own services. Usually Jules did not personally wait at dinner. He merely hovered observant, like a captain on the bridge during the mate's watch. Regular frequenters of the hotel felt themselves honoured when Jules attached himself to their tables.

Theodore Racksole hesitated one second, and then issued the order with a fine air of carelessness:

'Filleted steak for two, and a bottle of Bass.' It was the bravest act of Theodore Racksole's life, and yet at more than one previous crisis a high courage had not been lacking to him.

'It's not in the menu, sir,' said Jules the imperturbable.

'Never mind. Get it. We want it.'

'Very good, sir.'

Jules walked to the service-door, and, merely affecting to look behind, came immediately back again.

'Mr Rocco's compliments, sir, and he regrets to be unable to serve steak and Bass tonight, sir.'

'Mr Rocco?' questioned Racksole lightly.

'Mr Rocco,' repeated Jules with firmness.

'And who is Mr Rocco?'

'Mr Rocco is our chef, sir.' Jules had the expression of a man who is asked to explain who Shakespeare was.

The two men looked at each other. . . .

As for Nella, knowing her father, she foresaw interesting events, and waited confidently for the steak. She did not feel hungry, and she could afford to wait.

* * * * *

[*Racksole obtains an audience with Félix Babylon, the hotel-owner, and purchases the hotel from him for £400,000. He then demands to see the chef.*]

'Rocco,' said Félix Babylon, 'let me introduce Mr Theodore Racksole of New York.'

'Sharmed,' said Rocco, bowing. 'Ze—ze, vat you call it, millionaire?'

'Exactly,' Racksole put in, and continued quickly: 'Mr Rocco, I wish to acquaint you before any other person with the fact that I have purchased the Grand Babylon Hotel. . . . And now, Mr Rocco, will you oblige me very much by ordering a plain beefsteak and a bottle of Bass to be served by Jules—I particularly desire Jules—at table No. 17 in the dining-room, in ten minutes from now? And will you do me the honour of lunching with me tomorrow?'

Arnold Bennett, *The Grand Babylon Hotel*, 1902

❧ *After his initial, modest success as a novelist in England, Arnold Bennett moved to Paris, where he lived alone, then with his French wife Marguerite, between 1903 and 1913. In his earliest years he invariably ate out in restaurants, observing the clientele and (as with* The Old Wives' Tale, *the first idea for which came to him in a cheap Duval restaurant) gaining inspiration for his huge output of published work.*

Wednesday, 27 April [1904].

Yesterday when I was in Paillard's, it occurred to me that the difference between the most excessively *chic* restaurant and an ordinary good one is very slight. Paillard's has the reputation of being the best, or one of the three best in Paris, and therefore in the world. Yet it is small, and not in the least luxurious, and the waiting is no better than it is elsewhere. The *monde* has no special appearance of smartness. The food was very good, and so was the wine. But scarcely appreciably better than at Sylvain's, Maire's, or Noel and Peters. And the prices were about 25 per cent dearer than at those other places—not more. In the evening, at a Boulant, I had for 6d. a bifteck and soufflé potatoes better than which could not possibly be obtained anywhere, at no matter what price. When you have thoroughly good, well-flavoured, tender meat, perfectly cooked—you cannot surpass that.

The Journals of Arnold Bennett, edited by Newman Flower, 1932, Volume I, 1896–1910

❧ *Charles Ryder, the narrator of Evelyn Waugh's novel, is living as an artist in Paris in the mid-1920s. He is visited by Rex Mottram, an ambitious, Canadian-born politician, who hopes to marry the aristocratic Julia Flyte, the sister of Charles's former Oxford friend Sebastian.*

'I say [said Rex], I've got a lot to talk about, and I promised a chap at the Travellers' I'd give him his revenge this afternoon. Won't you dine with me?'

'Yes. Where?'

'I usually go to Ciro's.'

'Why not Paillard's?'

'Never heard of it. I'm paying you know.'

'I know you are. Let me order dinner.'

* * * * *

I was there twenty minutes before Rex. If I had to spend an evening with him, it should, at any rate, be in my own way. I remember the dinner well—soup of *oseille*, a sole quite simply cooked in a white-wine sauce, a *caneton à la presse*, a lemon soufflé. At the last minute, fearing that the whole thing was too simple for Rex, I added *caviar aux blinis*. And for wine I let him give me a bottle of 1906 Montrachet, then at its prime, and, with the duck, a Clos de Bèze of 1904.

Living was easy in France then; with the exchange as it was, my allowance went a long way and I did not live frugally. It was very seldom, however, that I had a dinner like this, and I felt well disposed to Rex, when at last he arrived and gave up his hat and coat with the air of one not expecting to see them again. He looked round the sombre little place with suspicion as though hoping to see apaches or a drinking party of students. All he saw was four senators with napkins tucked under their beards eating in absolute silence. I could imagine him telling his commercial friends later: '. . . interesting fellow I know; an art student living in Paris. Took me to a funny little restaurant—sort of place you'd pass without looking at it—where there was some of the best food I ever ate. There were half a dozen senators there, too, which shows you it was the right place. Wasn't at all cheap either.'

* * * * *

The sole was so simple and unobtrusive that Rex failed to notice it. We ate to the music of the press—the crunch of the bones, the drip of blood and marrow, the tap of the spoon basting the thin slices of breast. There was a pause here of a quarter of an hour, while I drank the first glass of the Clos de Bèze and Rex smoked his first cigarette. He leaned back, blew a cloud of smoke across the table, and remarked, 'You know, the food here isn't half bad; someone ought to take this place up and make something of it.'

* * * * *

I rejoiced in the Burgundy. It seemed a reminder that the world was an older and better place than Rex knew, that mankind in its long passion had learned another wisdom than his. By chance I met this same wine again, lunching with my wine merchant in St James's Street, in the first autumn of the war; it had softened and faded in the intervening years, but it still spoke in the pure, authentic accent of its prime, the same words of hope.

* * * * *

After the duck came a salad of watercress and chicory in a faint mist of chives. I tried to think only of the salad. I succeeded for a time in thinking only of the soufflé. Then came the cognac and the proper hour for . . . confidences.

* * * * *

The cognac was not to Rex's taste. It was clear and pale and it came to us in a bottle free from grime and Napoleonic cyphers. It was only a year or two older than Rex and lately bottled. They gave it to us in very thin tulip-shaped glasses of modest size.

'Brandy's one of the things I do know a bit about,' said Rex. 'This is a bad colour. What's more, I can't taste it in this thimble.'

They brought him a balloon the size of his head. He made them warm it over the spirit lamp. Then he rolled the splendid spirit round, buried his face in the fumes, and pronounced it the sort of stuff he put soda in at home.

So, shamefacedly, they wheeled out of its hiding place the vast and mouldy bottle they kept for people of Rex's sort.

'That's the stuff,' he said, tilting the treacly concoction till it left dark rings round the side of his glass. 'They've always got some tucked away, but they won't bring it out unless you make a fuss. Have some.'

'I'm quite happy with this.'

'Well, it's a crime to drink it, if you don't really appreciate it.'

He lit his cigar and sat back at peace with the world; I, too, was at peace in another world than his. We both were happy. He talked of Julia and I heard his voice, unintelligible at a great distance, like a dog's barking miles away on a still night.

Waugh, *Brideshead Revisited*

PICNICS

THE GARDEN OF EDEN

So hand in hand they pass'd, the loveliest pair
That ever since in loves imbraces met,
Adam the goodliest man of men since born
His Sons, the fairest of her Daughters *Eve*.
Under a tuft of shade that on a green
Stood whispering soft, by a fresh Fountain side
They sat them down, and after no more toil
Of their sweet Gardning labour then suffic'd
To recommend cool *Zephyr*, and made ease
More easie, wholsom thirst and appetite
More grateful, to thir Supper Fruits they fell,
Nectarine Fruits which the compliant boughs
Yeilded them, side-long as they sat recline
On the soft downie Bank damaskt with flowrs:
The savourie pulp they chew, and in the rind
Still as they thirsted scoop the brimming stream.

Milton, *Paradise Lost*, 1667, Book IV

Zephyr: the west wind; *nectarine fruits*: not nectarines in the modern sense (i.e. a variety of thin-skinned, downless peach), but an unspecified fruit of nectar-like sweetness with a hard rind, such as a melon.

AUDLEY COURT

'The Bull, the Fleece are cramm'd, and not a room
For love or money. Let us picnic there
At Audley Court.'
I spoke, while Audley feast
Humm'd like a hive all round the narrow quay,
To Francis, with a basket on his arm,
To Francis, just alighted from the boat,
And breathing of the sea. 'With all my heart,'
Said Francis. Then we shoulder'd thro' the swarm,
And rounded by the stillness of the beach
To where the bay runs up its latest horn.

We left the dying ebb that faintly lipp'd
The flat red granite; so by many a sweep
Of meadow smooth from aftermath we reach'd
The griffin-guarded gates, and pass'd thro' all
The pillar'd dusk of sounding sycamores,
And cross'd the garden to the gardener's lodge,
With all its casements bedded, and its walls
And chimneys muffled in the leafy vine.

There, on a slope of orchard, Francis laid
A damask napkin wrought with horse and hound,
Brought out a dusky loaf that smelt of home,
And, half-cut-down, a pasty costly-made,
Where quail and pigeon, lark and leveret lay,
Like fossils of the rock, with golden yolks
Imbedded and injellied; last, with these,
A flask of cider from his father's vats,
Prime, which I knew; and so we sat and eat
And talk'd old matters over; who was dead,
Who married, who was like to be, and how
The races went, and who would rent the hall:
Then touch'd upon the game, how scarce it was
This season; glancing thence, discuss'd the farm,
The four-field system, and the price of grain;
And struck upon the corn-laws, where we split,
And came again together on the king
With heated faces; till he laugh'd aloud,
And, while the blackbird on the pippin hung
To hear him, clapt his hand in mine and sang. . . .

Alfred Tennyson, 'Audley Court', 1838

❧ *Elizabeth, Countess von Arnim, an Englishwoman living in Prussia in the 1890s, achieved success with her volume of autobiographical sketches,* Elizabeth and her German Garden, *published anonymously in 1898, and went on to write gently satirical novels about English upper- and middle-class life. Irais, in this extract, is a German house-guest; Minora an acquaintance from England. The picnic takes place on the shore of the Baltic.*

It was a hoar-frost day, and the forest was an enchanted forest leading into fairyland, and though Irais and I have been there often before, and always thought it beautiful, yet yesterday we stood under the final arch of frosted trees, struck silent by the sheer loveliness of the place. For a long way out the sea was frozen, and then there was a deep blue line, and a cluster of motionless orange sails; at our feet a narrow strip of pale yellow sand; right and left the line of sparkling forest; and we ourselves standing in a world of white and diamond traceries. The stillness of an eternal Sunday lay on the place like a benediction.

* * * * *

We sat in the sleigh and picknicked. . . . I warmed soup in a little apparatus I have for such occasions, which helped to take the chilliness off the sandwiches,—this is the only unpleasant part of a winter picnic, the clamminess of the provisions just when you most long for something very hot. Minora let her nose very carefully out of its wrappings, took a mouthful and covered it up quickly again. She was nervous lest it should be frost-nipped, and truth compels me to add that her nose is not a bad nose, and might even be pretty on anybody else.

* * * * *

It is the most difficult thing in the world to eat sandwiches with immense fur and woollen gloves on, and I think we ate almost as much fur as anything, and choked exceedingly during the process. Minora was angry at this, and at last pulled off her glove, but quickly put it on again.

'How very unpleasant,' she remarked after swallowing a large piece of fur.

'It will wrap round your pipes, and keep them warm,' said Irais.

'Pipes!' echoed Minora, greatly disgusted by such vulgarity.

'I'm afraid I can't help you,' I said, as she continued to choke and splutter; 'we are all in the same case, and I don't know how to alter it.'

'There are such things as forks, I suppose,' snapped Minora.

'That's true,' said I, crushed by the obviousness of the remedy; but of what use are forks if they are fifteen miles off? So Minora had to continue to eat her gloves.

Countess von Arnim, *Elizabeth and Her German Garden*, 1898

❧ *Eric Newby, having escaped from an Italian-run prisoner-of-war camp ten days earlier, is on the run in Northern Italy in September 1943, and has been left in a forest hide-out near the River Po, waiting for the first in a succession of helpers who will see him, eventually, into the remotest regions of the Apennines. He has recently been hospitalized with a broken ankle, but takes a swim in the river near his hiding-place before falling asleep under the trees.*

I was awakened by someone tugging at my arm. Standing over me there was a man with a big brown moustache, and with a thick head of hair which was just beginning to go grey above the ears.

'You sleep too strongly,' he said. 'I have been whistling for ten minutes and I am tired of it. I am called Giovanni. I have brought you a picnic,' he said. He called it *una merenda*. 'We shall eat it by the river. Then later we shall go to my house.'

He was dressed in an old suit of snuff-coloured velveteen and over his shoulder he had a sack which presumably contained the *merenda*. He was a powerful-looking man, about five feet eight but with a chest like a barrel and a long scar down one side of his nose. He walked with a limp. We went back towards the river, more or less by the route which I had followed before. My ankle now hurt abominably, but at least it stood up to being used just as well without the plaster.

Eventually we reached the bank of the dry backwater that I had already crossed, but further upstream. . . . On the far side there was a path through the dwarf trees, and after following it for a bit we came out in a small clearing behind the hut I had seen earlier which stood high above the embankment on a little forest of piles.

'My house in the country,' Giovanni said. He went up a ladder to it and unlocked the door. Inside there was a room about eight feet square with a bunk on one side, some cooking pots, a fishing rod, a pair of decayed rubber waders, and that was about all.

'*L'e ura d'mangar.*' 'Time to eat,' he said. He spoke the dialect which here, on the river bank, sounded even deeper and more mysterious than it had at the farm on the first night that I was free. I told him I couldn't understand it and he said that, in future, he would speak Italian, and very slowly.

We sat outside in the shade and ate a delicious meal, the best of its kind that I could remember. Everything was home-made.

'*È nostrano*,' he said, whenever he offered me anything. No wonder he had brought a sack. We ate a delicious, thick soup, full of vegetables and *pasta* that was made in the shape of sea shells which he ladled from a pot; and we ate *polenta*, a sort of solidified yellow porridge made from maize, which he sliced with a piece of wire; wonderful hard white bread, made from something called *pasta dura* and with it slices of *culatello*, a kind of unsmoked ham from part of the pig's behind that was cut so thinly that it was almost transparent which, he said, was a local speciality; and there was another sort called *spalla*, made from the shoulder which he said was the sort Verdi preferred; but I thought the *culatello* was the best.

'It's good, the *culatello*,' he said, relapsing into the dialect and offering me more.

We drank *lambrusco* from a black bottle which held two litres. The cork was similar to a champagne cork but without the metal cap with the maker's name on it, and it was prevented from blowing out of the mouth of the bottle by strong thread which was lashed down over the top of it and round the lip. The Italian word for cork was *turacciolo* but he called it *bouchon* in the dialect which seemed to have a lot of French words in it. The wine was deep purple and it seethed in the glasses with its own natural gas. The same wine the farmer had given me on that first night. And then we ate cheese that had been maturing for two years in one of his barns.

Eric Newby, *Love and War in the Apennines*, 1971

IV

LAVISHNESS

CEREMONIAL FOOD

❧ *In the Trojan War, Achilles, deprived by the Greek commander-in-chief Agamemnon of his favourite slave-girl Briseis, retires to sulk in his tent. Anxious to regain his help in the fighting, Agamemnon sends Patroclus, Ulysses, and other messengers to feast with Achilles and try to persuade him to rejoin them. This attempt, however, fails.*

With that, the Chiefs beneath his Roof he lead,
And plac'd in Seats with purple Carpets spread.
Then thus—*Patroclus*, crown a larger Bowl,
Mix purer Wine, and open ev'ry Soul.
Of all the Warriors yonder Host can send,
Thy Friend most honours these, and these thy Friend
He said; *Patroclus* o'er the blazing Fire
Heaps in a Brazen Vase three Chines entire:
The Brazen Vase Automedon sustains,
Which Flesh of Porket, Sheep, and Goat contains:
Achilles at the genial Feast presides,
The Parts transfixes, and with Skill divides.
Mean while *Patroclus* sweats the Fire to raise;
The Tent is brightened with the rising Blaze:
Then, when the languid Flames at length subside,
He strows a Bed of glowing Embers wide,
Above the Coals the smoaking Fragments turns,
And sprinkles sacred Salt from lifted Urns;

With Bread the glitt'ring Canisters they load,
Which round the Board *Menaetius*' Son bestow'd.
Himself oppos'd t'*Ulysses* full in sight,
Each Portion parts, and orders ev'ry Rite.
The first fat Off'rings, to th'Immortals due,
Amidst the greedy Flames *Patroclus* threw;
Then each, indulging in the social Feast,
His Thirst and Hunger soberly represt.

Alexander Pope, *The Iliad of Homer*, Book IX, 1717

Menaetius' Son: Patroclus.

TARTAR OFFERINGS

It is to be understood that his majesty [Kublai Khan] keeps up a stud of about ten thousand horses and mares, which are white as snow; and of the milk of these mares no person can presume to drink who is not of the family descended from Jengiz-khan, with the exception only of one other family, named Boriat, to whom that monarch gave the honourable privilege, in reward of valorous achievements in battle, performed in his own presence. So great, indeed, is the respect shown to these horses that, even when they are at pasture in the royal meadows or forests, no one dares to place himself before them, or otherwise to impede their movements. The astrologers whom he entertains in his service, and who are deeply versed in the diabolical art of magic, having pronounced it to be his duty, annually, on the twenty-eighth day of the moon in August, to scatter in the wind the milk taken from these mares, as a libation to all the spirits and idols whom they adore, for the purpose of propitiating them and ensuring their protection of the people, male and female, of the cattle, the fowls, the grain and other fruits of the earth; on this account it is that his majesty adheres to the rule that has been mentioned, and on that particular day proceeds to the spot where, with his own hands, he is to make the offering of milk. On such occasions these astrologers, or magicians as they may be termed, sometimes display their skill in a wonderful manner; for if it should happen that the sky becomes cloudy and threatens rain, they ascend the roof of the palace where the grand khan resides at the time, and by the force of their incantations they prevent the rain from falling and stay the tempest; so that whilst, in the surrounding country, storms of rain, wind and thunder are experienced, the palace itself remains unaffected by the elements.

The Travels of Marco Polo the Venetian, translated by Sir Henry Yule, 1871

FIRST-FRUITS

At the present day in Lithuania, when new potatoes or loaves made from the new corn are being eaten, all the people at table pull one another's hair. The meaning of this last custom is obscure, but a similar custom was certainly observed by the heathen Lithuanians at their solemn sacrifices. Many of the Esthonians of the island of Oesel will not eat bread baked of the new corn until they have first taken a bite of a piece of iron. The iron is here plainly a charm, intended to render harmless the spirit that is in the corn. In Sutherlandshire at the present day, when the new potatoes are dug all the family must taste them, otherwise 'the spirits in them [the potatoes] take offence and the potatoes would not keep.' In one part of Yorkshire it is still customary for the clergyman to cut the first corn; and my informant believes that the corn so cut is used to make the communion bread. If the latter part of the custom is correctly reported (and analogy is all in its favour), it shows how the Christian communion has absorbed within itself a sacrament which is doubtless far older than Christianity.

Among the heathen Cheremiss on the left bank of the Volga, when the first bread baked from the new corn is to be eaten, the villagers assemble in the house of the oldest inhabitant, the eastern door is opened, and all pray with their faces towards it. Then the sorcerer or priest gives to each of them a mug of beer, which they drain; next he cuts and hands to every person a morsel of the loaf, which they partake of. Finally, the young people go to the elders and bowing down to the earth before them say, 'We pray God that you may live, and that God may let us pray next year for new corn.' The rest of the day is passed in mirth and dancing. The whole ceremony, observes the writer who has described it, looks almost like a caricature of the Eucharist. According to another account, each Cheremiss householder on this occasion, after bathing, places some of each kind of grain, together with malt, cakes, and drink, in a vessel, which he holds up to the sun, at the same time thanking the gods for the good things which they have bestowed upon him. But this part of the ceremony is a sacrifice rather than a sacrament of the new corn.

J. G. Frazer, *The Golden Bough*, 1900, Volume II

❧ *Richard Chancellor (d. 1556), the navigator, commanded a ship on Sir Hugh Willoughby's expedition of 1553 to find the North-East Passage to India and China. Willoughby perished, and Chancellor's was the only one of seven ships to arrive at the rendezvous in the White Sea. From Archangel, Chancellor made his way overland to Moscow, where the Tsar Ivan IV (1530–84), 'Ivan the Terrible', had occupied the throne since the age of 17. Encouraged by the welcome which he received from the Tsar, Chancellor returned home to form the Muscovy Company, but died in a shipwreck off the Scottish coast on his return from a second Russian voyage. The Russian method of serving dishes consecutively, rather than laying them all out together in one or two large, elaborate courses, eventually spread to England from France in the nineteenth century as* service à la Russe.

I came into the dining chamber, where the Duke [of Muscovy, i.e. the Tsar] himselfe sate at this table without cloth of estate, in a gowne of silver, with a crowne emperiall upon his head, he sate in a chaire somewhat hie; There sate none neare him by a great way. There were long tables set round about the chamber, which were full set with such as the Duke had at dinner: they were all in white. Also the places where the tables stoode were higher by two steppes then the rest of the house. In the middest of the chamber stoode a table or cupbord to set plate on; which stoode full of cuppes of gold: and amongst all the rest there stood foure marveilous great pottes or crudences as they call them, of gold and silver: I thinke they were a good yarde and a halfe hie. By the cupborde stoode two gentlemen with napkins on their shoulders, and in their handes each of them had a cuppe of gold set with pearles and precious stones, which were the Dukes owne drinking cups: when he was disposed, he drunke them off at a draught. And for his service at meate it came in without order, yet it was very rich service: for all were served in gold, not onely he himselfe, but also all the rest of us, and it was very massie: the cups also were of golde and very massie. The number that dined there that day was two hundred persons, and all were served in golden vessell. The gentlemen that waited were all in cloth of gold, and they served him with caps on their heads. Before the service came in, the Duke sent to every man a great shiver of bread, and the bearer called the party so sent by his name aloude, and sayd, John Basilivich Emperour of Russia and great Duke of Moscovia doth reward thee with bread: then must all men stand up, and doe at all times when those wordes are spoken. And then last of all he giveth the Marshall bread, whereof he eateth before the Dukes Grace, and so doth reverence and departeth. Then commeth the Dukes service of the Swannes all in pieces, and every one in a severall dish: the which the Duke sendeth as he did the bread, and the bearer sayth the same wordes as he sayd before. And as I sayd before, the service of his meate is in no order, but commeth in dish by dish: and then after that the Duke sendeth drinke, with the like saying as before is tolde.

'The Booke of the Great and Mighty Emperor of Russia, and Duke of Moscovia, and of the Dominions Orders and Commodities Thereunto Belonging: Drawen by Richard Chancelour', in Richard Hakluyt, *The Principal Navigations, Voyages, Traffiques & Discoveries of the English Nation*, 1589–99

The menus given here, for two royal banquets of the late fourteenth century, are taken from a published version of two fifteenth-century MS cookery books inscribed on vellum rolls: Harleian MS 279 and Harleian MS 4016, both in the British Library.

(*a*) King Richard II's Dinner, 1387

This is the purviance made for Kinge Richard, beinge with Þe Duc of lancastre at the Bishoppes place of Durham at Londone, the xxiii day of September, the yere of the kinge forsaid, xij [1387].

First beginning for a-chatry	*Items purchased* [*a-catery*]
Xiiij oxen̄ lying in salte	14 salted oxen
IJ oxen ffresysh	2 fresh oxen
VI^{XX} hedes of shepe fressh̄	120 [6 score] fresh sheeps' heads
VI^{XX} carcase of shepe fressh̄	120 [6 score] fresh sheep carcasses
Xij bores	12 boars

Xiiij Calvys	14 calves
Cxl pigges	140 pigs
CCC maribones	300 marrowbones
Of larde and grece, ynogh̄	Sufficient lard and fat
IIJ ton̄ of salt veneson̄	3 tons of salt venison
IIJ does of fressh̄ veneson̄	3 [ditto?] fresh venison
The pultry	*The poultry*
L Swannes	50 swans
CCx Gees	210 geese
L capons of hie grece	50 larded capons
Viii dussen̄ oþer capons	96 [8 dozen] other capons
Lx dd Hennes	720 [60 dozen] hens
CC copull̄ Conyngg[e]s	200 pairs of grown rabbits
IIIJ Fesauntes	4 pheasants
V Herons and Bitores	5 herons and bitterns
Vi kiddes	6 kids
V duson̄ pullayn̄ for Gely	60 [5 dozen] chickens for jelly
Xij dd to roste	144 [12 dozen] to roast
C dd peions	1200 [100 dozen] pigeons
Xij dd partrych̄	144 [12 dozen] partridges
Viij dd Rabettes	96 [8 dozen] young rabbits
X dosen̄ Curlewes	120 [10 dozen] curlews
Xij dosen̄ Brewes	144 [12 dozen] whimbrels
Xij Cranes	12 cranes
Wilde fowle ynogh̄	Sufficient wild fowl
VJ^{XX} galons melke	120 [6 score] gallons milk
Xij galons Creme	12 gallons cream
Xl galons of Cruddes	40 gallons of curds
IIj bushels of Appelles	3 bushels of apples
xj thousand egges	11,000 eggs.
The first course	
Veneson̄ with̄ Furmenty	Venison with frumenty [wheat hulled, boiled in milk, sweetened and spiced]
A potage called viandbruse	Meat broth
Hedes of Bores	Boars' heads
Grete Flessh̄	Roasted haunches of meat
Swannes rosted	Roast swan
Pigges rosted	Roast pork

Crustade lumbard in paste	A pie containing custard, bone-marrow, parsley, dates, prunes, etc.
And a Sotelte	A decorative device [made of edible or semi-edible material, e.g. pastry, sugar, wax, or marzipan]

The seconde course

A potage called Gele	Jellied chicken broth
A potage de Blandesore	A white soup incorporating almond milk, capon's flesh, almonds, and red colouring
Pigges rosted	Roast pork
Cranes rosted	Roast cranes
Fesauntes rosted	Roast pheasants
Herons rosted	Roast herons
Breme	Bream
Chekens endored	Gilded chickens [coloured with a paste of flour, egg yolks, ginger, and saffron]
Tartes	Tarts
Broke braune	Chopped brawn
Conyngg[e]s rosted	Roast (grown) rabbits
And a sotelte	A decorative device

The thirde course

Potage bruet of Almondes	A cream soup made with curds, honey, and butter
Stwde lumbarde	Lombard-style stew or soup
Venyson̄ rosted	Roast venison
Chekenes rosted	Roast chicken
Rabettes rosted	Roast (young) rabbits
Partrich̄ rosted	Roast partridge
Peions rosted	Roast pigeon
Quailes rosted	Roast quail
Larkes rosted	Roast lark
Payne puff	Little pies of sweetened, spiced pastry, enclosing egg, bone-marrow, currants, sugar, and ginger

A Dissh̄ of Gely	A dish of jelly
Longe Fruto[u]rs	Long fritters [Strips of refried pancake. See recipe]
And a sotelte	A decorative device

Longe Frutours. Take Mulke And make faire croddes there-of in maner of chese al tendur, and take out Þe way clene; then̄ put hit in a faire boll̄, And take yolkes of egges, and white, and menge floure, and caste thereto a good quantite, and drawe hit Þorgh a streynoure into a faire vessell̄; then̄ put hit in a faire pan̄, and fry hit a litull̄ in faire grece, but lete not boyle; then̄ take it oute, and ley on̄ a faire borde, and kutte it in faire smale peces as thou list, And putte hem ayen̄ into the panne til thei be browne; And then̄ caste Sugur on hem, and serve hem forth̄.

Take milk and make curds of it, as you would when making soft cheese, and drain off the whey. Put the curds into a bowl and mix them with egg yolks, [*well-beaten?*] *egg whites and a good quantity of flour. Strain into a jug, then pour into a clean pan and fry lightly in good fat, but do not overcook. Remove, lay on a clean board and cut into neat, small pieces as you wish. Brown these in the pan, dredge with sugar, and serve.*

(*b*) Conuiuium domini Henrici Regis quarti, In coronacione sua apud Westmonasterium

(*The Coronation Banquet of the Lord King Henry IV at Westminster* [*1399*])

Le primer cours	*The first course*
Braun en peuerarde	Brawn in a pottage of wine, spices, onions, vinegar, etc.
Viaund Ryal	A white soup of almond milk, rice flour and milk *or* wine, honey, rice flour, and spices
Teste de senglere enarme	Boar's head and tusks
Graund chare	Roasted haunches of meat
Syngnettys	Cygnets
Capoun de haut grece	Larded capons
Fesaunte	Pheasant
Heroun	Heron
Crustade lumbarde	Pie (*see above*)

Storeioun, graunt luc[es]	Sturgeon, large pike
A sotelte	A decorative device
Le .ij. cours	*The second course*
Venyson en furmenty	Venison with frumenty (*see above*)
Gely	Aspic
Porcelle farce enforce	Stuffed sucking-pig
Pokokkys	Peacocks
Cranys	Cranes
Venyson Roste	Roast venison
Conyng	Grown rabbit
Byttore	Bittern
Pull[e] endore	Gilded chickens (*see above*)
Graunt tartez	Great tarts [of suet crust, containing capons, hens, mallard, rabbits, game, egg yolks, marrow, dates, spices, etc.]
Braun fryez	Chopped brawn cooked in a sweetened, spiced batter
Leche lumbarde	A paste of dates cooked in wine, ground, spiced, and sliced
A sotelte	A decorative device
Le .iij. cours	*The third course*
Blaundesorye	White soup (*see potage de Blandesore, above*)
Quyncys in comfyte	Preserved quinces
Egretez	Egrets
Curlewys	Curlews
Pertryche	Partridge
Pyionys	Pigeons
Quaylys	Quails
Snytys	[Snipe?]
Smal byrdys	Little birds
Rabettys	Young rabbits
Pome dorreng	Rissoles of pork or beef, spit-roasted and cooked again in a sweetened golden batter coloured with parsley or egg yolk
Braun blanke leche	Brawn cooked with almond milk and sugar, sliced cold

Eyroun engele	Eggs in jelly
Frytourys	Pancakes
Doucettys	Cheesecakes
Pety pernaux	Little pies (*see payne puff, above*)
Egle	[?]
Pottys of lylye	[?]
A sotetle	A decorative device

Two Fifteenth-Century Cookery Books, Harleian MS 279 (about 1430) and Harleian MS 4016 (about 1450) . . . , edited by Thomas Austin, Early English Texts Society, 1888

TWELFTH NIGHT

Now, now the mirth comes
With the cake full of plums,
Where Beane's the *King* of the sport here;
Beside we must know
The Pea also
Must revell, as *Queene*, in the Court here.

Begin then to chuse
(This night as ye use)
Who shall for the present delight here,
Be a *King* by the lot,
And who shall not
Be Twelfe-day *Queene* for the night here.

Which knowne, let us make
Joy-sops with the cake;
And let not a man then be seen here,
Who unurg'd will not drinke
To the base from the brink
A health to the King and the Queene here.

Next crowne the bowl full
With gentle lambs-wooll;
Add sugar, nutmeg and ginger,
With store of ale too
And thus ye must doe
To make the wassaile a swinger.

Give then to the King
And Queene wassailing;

And though with ale ye be whet here;
Yet part ye from hence.
As free from offence,
As when ye innocent met here.

Robert Herrick, 'Twelfe night, or *King* and *Queene*', 1648

The austere English Christmas of the period between the Reformation and the early years of Victoria's reign culminated in riotous festivities on Twelfth Night. This was a time for mummers, wassailing, and consuming the ceremonial Twelfth Cake, which contained a bean and a pea for the King and Queen of the revels. Whoever drew the slice with the bean in it was King for the evening; whoever drew the pea was his Queen (or so tradition tells us). Shakespeare's comedy suggests that sexual roles may sometimes have been reversed on this one evening of the year when disguises ruled and conventions went by the board. *Lamb's wool*: a drink of warm spiced ale, the traditional drink for toasts, consumed out of the communal wassail bowl.

❧ *King James II, unpopular since succeeding to the throne in 1685 on account of his open profession of Roman Catholicism, visited Oxford between 3 and 5 September 1687 after dissolving Parliament on 4 July. Anthony Wood (1632–95), an Oxford diarist, noted that the King 'shewed himself extreame curteous and affable to all (they say to gaine and beg favour, to get votes to take off the Test [disenfranchising Roman Catholics])'. Wood was away from Oxford at the time of James's visit; but he collected details of everything that took place, including an abortive feast laid out for the King on his last morning, when he visited the Bodleian Library.*

Monday, 5 Sept., in the morning, about 8 of the clock, [the king] went into the cathedrall and touched againe for the evill. Which don, he took coach and went to the Schooles [then underneath the Bodleian Library], where entering in at the great east dore, the Doctors in the quadrangle were ready to receive him.

The king's entertainment in Bodley's Librarie

[The king] came up into the library between 10 and eleven, attended by the vicechancellor and Drs, besides severall of the lords . . . He found a banquet ready prepared for him at the south end of the library, with a seat of state at the south end of the table; none did eat but he, for he spake to nobody to eat.

[*Part of the following is taken from a note written to Wood by Dr Thomas Hyde, Bodley's Librarian.*]

An account of the dishes wherewith the king was treated at the public Library

Dry sweetmeats and fruits, 20 large dishes, piled high, like so many ricks of hay.

Wet sweetmeats, 24 little flat plates, like trencher plates, not piled; placed among the greater dishes scatteringly in vacant places to fill up the vacances.

28 large dishes of cold fish and cold flesh, as Westphalia hamms, &c: some whole, others cut into slices and piled pretty high.

3 hot dishes, viz., shoulder of mutton, phesant, partridg and quailes; of these the king did eat, not medling with any thing else, except only that he took one little piece of dry sweetmeat.

36 plates of sallating, piled high and copped [rising to a peak], viz., oranges, lemmons, olives, samphire, &c., pears, plums, &c.

The king not bidding the courtiers eat, nobody did eat; but all was in a scramble carryed away by the rabble, which scramble the king stood to look upon about 2 or 3 minutes, and then went away . . .

This ambigue or banquet cost the University 160*li*. He liked the wine well; whereupon they sent some after him.

After the king had don his breakfast, they began to scramble (the scholars some say did begin) insomuch that the king not being able to pass away for the crowd, stayed there awhile, and talked with some by him. Dr [Samuel] Derham, a physitian of Magdalen Hall, was noted here for a scrambler, being in his scarlet, so notorious that they flung things in his face.

The Life and Times of Anthony Wood, Antiquary, of Oxford, 1632–1695, Described by Himself, Collected from his Diaries and Other Papers by Andrew Clark, M.A., Volume III, 1682–94, Oxford Historical Society, 1894

❧ *Emily Eden, in her early thirties when this letter was written, lived with her bachelor elder brother, George Eden, 2nd Baron Auckland, a Whig politician who in 1830–4 was President of the Board of Trade. Her jokingly condemnatory style was very characteristic of the self-consciousness and distrust of enthusiasm among her particular social group.*

To Theresa Lister [*late November, 1830*].

I shall take it as a great compliment being asked to dinner anywhere by anybody, but as a matter of choice I should prefer dining with the Lord Mayor habitually—not from any gourmandise, I beg to mention, for in my days I never saw such uneatable food. The soup had been saved, I imagine, from the day that the King did *not* dine at the Guildhall, and consequently a little salt had been thrown in every day just to preserve it. The preservation had been effected, but how many pounds of salt had been used it is difficult to guess. Nobody offered me anything else but a slice of half-cold peacock, whose tail feathers were still spread and growing. However, though as a mere dinner it was a failure, the flow of soul was prodigious. We were so unanimous, so fond of each other. . . . The Lady Mayoress receives all her guests without stirring from her chair, though it is obvious from her old habit of attending to her shop that she is dying to get up to *serve* them all. The Lord Mayor walks in to dinner before all his visitors, leaving the Duke of Sussex, etc., to take care of themselves, and then he and his wife sit by each other without the relief of a third person.

* * * * *

I am disappointed in the magnificence of the city. The whole set-out is *mesquin* to a degree. Nothing but common blue plates and only one silver fork apiece, which those who were learned in public dinners carefully preserved. I lost mine in the first five minutes. The city ladies are so ill-dressed too; such old gowns with black shoes, etc.

Miss Eden's Letters, edited by Violet Dickinson, 1919

Nathaniel Hawthorne was American Consul at Liverpool between 1853 and 1858. His readiness to be impressed by most of the details of a Mansion House dinner contrasts with the blasé sophistication shown by Emily Eden.

At a given signal we all found our way into an immense room, called the Egyptian Hall, I know not why except that the architecture was classic, and as different as possible from the ponderous style of Memphis and the pyramids. A powerful band played inspiringly as we entered, and a brilliant profusion of light shone down on two tables, extending the whole length of the hall, and a cross-table between them occupying nearly its entire breadth. Glass gleamed and silver glistened on an acre or two of snowy damask, over which were set out all the accompaniments of a stately feast. We found our places without too much difficulty, and the Lord Mayor's chaplain implored a blessing on the food,—a ceremony which the English never omit, at a great dinner or a small one, yet consider, I fear, not so much a religious rite as a sort of preliminary relish before the soup.

The soup, of course, on this occasion, was turtle, of which, in accordance with immemorial custom, each guest was allowed two platefuls, in spite of the otherwise immitigable law of table-decorum. Indeed, judging from the proceedings of the gentlemen near me, I surmised that there was no practical limit, except the appetite of the guests and the capacity of the soup tureens. Not being fond of this civic dainty, I partook of it but once, and then only in accordance with the wise maxim, always to taste a fruit, a wine, or a celebrated dish, at its indigenous site; and the very fountain-head of turtle soup, I suppose, is the Lord Mayor's dinner pot. It is one of those orthodox customs which people follow for half a century without knowing why, to drink a sip of rum punch, in a very small tumbler, after the soup. It was excellently well-brewed, and it seemed to me almost worth while to sup the soup for the sake of supping the punch. The rest of the dinner was catalogued in a bill of fare printed on delicate white paper within an arabesque border of green and gold.

It looked very good, not only in the English and French names of the ceremonial dishes, but also in the positive reality of the dishes themselves, which were all set on the table to be carved and distributed by the guests. This ancient and honest method is attended with a good deal of trouble, and a lavish effusion of gravy, yet by no means bestowed or dispersed in vain, because you have thereby the absolute assurance of a banquet actually before your eyes, instead of a shadowy promise in the bill of fare, and such meagre fulfilment as a guest can contrive to get upon his individual plate. I wonder that Englishmen, who are fond of looking at prize-oxen in the shape of butcher's meat, do not generally better estimate the aesthetic gormandism of devouring the whole dinner with their eyesight, before proceeding to nibble the comparatively few morsels which, after all, the most heroic appetite and widest stomachic capacity of mere mortals can enable even an alderman really to eat. There fell to my lot three delectable things enough . . . —a red mullet, a plate of mushrooms, exquisitely stewed, and part of a ptarmigan, a bird of the same family as the grouse, but feeding high up towards the summit of the Scotch mountains, whence it gets a wild delicacy of flavour very superior to that of the artificially nurtured English game fowl.

Nathaniel Hawthorne, *Our Old Home*, 1863, Volume II

PARTIES

❧ *Richard Ligon describes a typical entertainment on an inland plantation in Barbados, where the host provided a Gargantuan succession of meat dishes rather than the alternating courses of fish and meat served on plantations nearer the sea.*

First then (because beefe being the great rarity in the Island, especially such as this is) I will begin with it, and of that sort there are these dishes at either messe, a Rompe boyl'd, a Chine roasted, a large piece of the brest roasted, the Cheeks bak'd, of which is a dish to either messe, the tongue and part of the tripes minc't for Pyes, season'd with sweet Herbs finely minc't, suet, Spice and Currans; the legges, pallets and other ingredients for an Ollo Podrido to either messe, a dish of Marrow bones, so here are fourteen dishes at the Table and all of beef: and this he intends as the great Regalio, to which he invites his fellow planters; who having well eaten of it, the dishes are taken away, and another Course brought in, which is a Potato pudding, a dish of Scots Collips of a legge of Porke, as good as any in the world, a fricacy of the same, a dish of boyl'd Chickens, a shoulder of a young Goate drest with his blood and thyme, a Kid with a pudding in his belly, a sucking pig, which is there the fattest whitest and sweetest in the world, with the poignant sauce of the brains, salt, sage and Nutmeg done with Claret wine, a shoulder of mutton which is there a rare dish, a Pasty of the side of a young Goate, and a side of a fat young Shot upon it, well season'd with pepper and salt, and with some Nutmeg, a loyne of Veale, to which there wants no sauce being so well furnisht with Oranges, Lymons, and Lymes, three young Turkies in a dish, two Capons, of which sort I have seen some extreame large and very fat, two hens with egges in a dish, four Ducklings, eight Turtle doves, and three Rabbets; and for cold bak't meats, two Muscovie Ducks larded, and season'd well with pepper and salt: and these being taken off the Table, another course is set on, and this is of *Westphalia* or Spanish bacon, dried Neats Tongues, Botargo, pickled Oysters, Caviare, Anchovies, Olives, and (intermixt with these) Custards, Creams, some alone, some with preserves of Plantines, Bonano, Gnavers, put in, and those preserv'd alone by themselves, Cheese-cakes, Puffes, which are to be made with English flower, and bread; for the Cassavie will not serve for this kind of cookerie; sometimes Tansies, sometimes Froizes, or Amulets, and for fruite, Plantines, Bonanoes, Gnavers, Milions, prickled Peare, Anchovie Peare, prickled Apple, Custard Apple, water Milions, and Pines worth all that went before. To this meat you seldome faile of this drink, Mobbie, Beveridge, Brandy, kill-Divell, Drink of the Plantine, Claret wine, White wine, and Rhenish wine, Sherry, Canary, Red sack, wine of Fiall, with all Spirits that come from *England*; and with all this, you shall finde as cheerfull a look, and as hearty a welcome, as any man can give to his best friends. And so much for a Feast of an inland Plantation.

Ligon, *History of the Island of Barbados*

Ollo podrido: a highly spiced stew; *shot*: shoat, a young weaned hog (Ligon claimed to have introduced the planters to this method of cooking, and to other refinements such as making fricassees); *botargo*: a paste of mullet roes, eaten as a relish; *plantines, bonano, gnavers*: plantains, banana, guavas; *milions*: melons; *cassavie*: bread made from cassava (manioc); *tansies, froizes, amulets*: light savoury dishes; *tansy*: a savoury custard, in England flavoured with the juice of the herb tansy; *froize, fraise*: a kind of pancake, flavoured with nutmeg and ginger or (sometimes) stuffed with bacon; *amulet*: ?omelette; *mobbie*: potato wine; *beveridge*: a drink made with spring water, white sugar, and the juice of oranges; *Fiall*: wine from Fayal (Azores).

Tatyana Larina, a young girl, has declared her love by letter to the dandy, Eugene Onegin. Encountering her a few days later he has gently repulsed her, giving rise to a nightmare in which she feels herself overpowered by him. It is now Tatyana's name-day (the feast-day of her patron saint, treated like a birthday in Russia). The Larins are holding a dinner and ball, to which Onegin has been invited with his friend Lensky, the official suitor of Tatyana's best friend Olga. After dinner, impatient at Tatyana's gloomily nervous behaviour, Onegin monopolizes the attentions of Olga, provoking Lensky to challenge him to the duel in which Onegin accidentally kills him. The translation quoted here, by Oliver Elton, was first published in 1937 to commemorate the centenary of Pushkin's death in a duel in 1837.

Husht for a moment is the tattle,
And folk are munching. All around
Plates, knives, forks, *et cetera* rattle;
The glasses jingle and resound.
Soon, slowly are the guests beginning
To raise a general tumult; dinning,
While no one listens as they shriek
And shout and wrangle, laugh and squeak.
The doors fly wide for Lensky, drifting
In with Onegin suddenly.
'Great Heaven, at last!' is Madame's cry.
The guests all crush together, shifting
Forks, knives and stools, and call the pair
And get them seated—ay, but where?

—Seated, with Tanya fairly facing!
Pale as the moon in daylight's rags,
Timorous as doe whom hounds are chasing,
She keeps her overclouded gaze
Still lowered: burning wildly, seething
With passion, sick with stifled breathing.
The greetings Tanya never hears
From the two friends; and now her tears,
Poor child, are like to fall; and nearly
She faints, and drops. And yet her will
And inner strength of reason still
Prevail at last. Two words she merely
Can murmur, through her teeth, at best;
Then sits at table with the rest.

But nerves and tragic revelations
And girls that weep and faint away
Had tried, of old, Evgeny's patience;
Familiar inflictions they!
And our queer fellow, wroth at lighting
On that prodigious feast, and sighting
Poor Tanya, languorous and seized
With tremors, dropt his eyes, displeased.

* * *

And others, too, could well have noted
Tanya's dismay; but every eye
And all attention was devoted
To judging of a fat, rich pie
(Which was too salt, and we regret it.)
They bring Caucasian wine, and set it
In tar-rimmed bottles, as is meet,
After the roast, before the sweet;—
Then rows of glasses, long and slender;
Just like thy waist, Zizi, they seem,
Thou crystal of my soul, thou theme
Of verses innocent and tender,
Thou phial of love, and lure to me,
Intoxicated—once—with thee!

They shift the clattering chairs; and shoving
Into the parlour streams the crowd.
So swarms a beehive honey-loving
Into the fields and buzzes loud.
Now, with that festal dinner mellow,
Each neighbour wheezes to his fellow;
Dames by the fireplace sit in ring,
Girls are in corners whispering.

* * *

Eight lengthy rubbers terminated,
The champions of whist have now
Eight times their places alternated;
And tea is served,—I like, I vow,
To measure out my days by dining—
Tea—supper, thus the hours defining,
We country folk the moment know
Unworried—for our stomachs go
Right like a watch (I take occasion
To note that in my lines I treat
Of banquets, sundry things to eat,
And corks, with no less iteration
Than thine, O godlike Homer, lord
By thirty centuries adored!)

The tea is served; the girls decorous
Just touch their plates; beyond the door

Swiftly bassoon and flute sonorous
Ring out, on the long ballroom floor.

* * *

Alexander Pushkin, *Eugene Onegin*, 1823–30, Book V, translated by Oliver Elton, 1937

Pie: pirog, the traditional Russian meat and cabbage pie, served by old-fashioned families on important occasions. The over-saltedness suggests that their cook may have been unused to making this on the scale demanded by Tatyana's party; *Caucasian wine*: in the original, 'Tsimlyanskoe', an estate-bottled sparkling wine from the Don valley. The appearance of this domestic champagne, in its tar-sealed bottles, is another sign of the Larins' old-fashioned frugality and relative lack of sophistication; *sweet*: in the original, 'blan[c]-mangé', a simple almond-milk jelly, possibly artificially coloured; *Zizi*: a private, joking reference to the plump Zizi Wulf, one of a family of girls with whom Pushkin flirted.

'The last old-Polish banquet', celebrating the betrothal of the hero, Tadeusz, and the reconciliation of two hostile families of neighbouring gentry, forms the culmination of Mickiewicz's epic poem of life in rural Lithuania on the eve of Napoleon's Russian campaign of 1812.

The guests, as in the castle hall they awaited the bringing in of the food, gazed with amazement at the great centrepiece, the metal and the workmanship of which were equally precious. There is a tradition that Prince Radziwill the Orphan had this set made to order in Venice, and had it decorated in Polish style according to his own ideas. The centrepiece had later been carried off in the time of the Swedish wars, and had found its way in some mysterious manner into this country gentleman's mansion; to-day it had been brought forth from the treasury and it now occupied the middle of the table, forming an immense circle, like a coach wheel.

The centrepiece, which was coated from rim to rim with froth and sugar white as snow, counterfeited marvellously well a winter landscape. In the centre a huge grove of confections showed dark; on the sides were houses which seemed to form peasant villages and hamlets of gentry, and which were coated, not with hoar frost, but with sugary froth; the edges were decorated with little porcelain figures in Polish costumes: like actors on a stage, they were evidently representing some striking event; their gestures were artistically reproduced, the colours were individual; they lacked only voice—for the rest they seemed to be alive.

* * * * *

Here the Seneschal . . . gave a sign with his wand; immediately lackeys began to enter in pairs, bringing the different dishes: the beet soup called royal, and the old-Polish broth, artistically prepared, into which the Seneschal in marvellous and mysterious wise had thrown several pearls and a piece of money; such broth purifies the blood and fortifies the health; after it came other dishes—but who could describe them all! Who would even comprehend those dishes of *kontuz*, *arkas*, and *blemas*, no longer known in our times, with their ingredients of cod, stuffing, civet, musk, caramel, pine nuts, damson plums! And those fish! Dry salmon from the Danube, sturgeon, Venetian and Turkish caviare, pikes and pickerel a cubit long, flounders, and capon carp, and noble carp! Finally a culinary mystery: an uncut fish, fried at the head, baked in the middle, and with its tail in a ragout with sauce.

The guests did not ask the names of the dishes, nor were they halted by that curious mystery; they ate everything rapidly with a soldier's appetite, filling their glasses with the generous Hungarian wine.

But meanwhile the great centrepiece had changed its colour, and, stripped of its snow, had already turned green; for the light froth of sugared ice, slowly warmed by the summer heat, had melted and disclosed a foundation hitherto hidden from the eye: so the landscape now represented a new time of year, shining with a green, many-coloured spring. Various grains came forth, as if yeast were making them grow; gilded ears of saffron wheat were seen in rich profusion, also rye, clad in leaves of picturesque silver, and buckwheat, made artistically of chocolate, and orchards blooming with pears and apples.

The guests had scant time to enjoy the fruits of summer; in vain they begged the Seneschal to prolong them. Already the centrepiece, like a planet in its appointed revolution, was changing the season of the year; already the grain, painted with gold, had gathered warmth from the room, and was slowly melting; already the grasses were growing yellow and the leaves were turning crimson and were falling; you might have said that an autumn wind was blowing; finally those trees, gorgeous an instant before, now stood naked, as if they had been stripped by the winds and the frost; they were sticks of cinnamon, or twigs of laurel that counterfeited pines, being clad in caraway seeds instead of needles.

The guests, as they drank their wine, began to tear off the branches, stumps, and roots, and to chew them as a relish. The Seneschal walked about the centrepiece, and, full of joy, turned triumphant eyes on the guests.

Mickiewicz, *Pan Tadeusz*, 1834, translated by George Rapall Noyes, 1930

Radziwill the Orphan: Mikolaj Krzystof Radziwill, a sixteenth-century convert from Calvinism to Catholicism, who in 1582–4 made a pilgrimage to the Holy Land and Egypt; *kontuz*: a kind of sausage; *arkas*: a custard of milk, cream, and egg yolks; *blemas*: almond jelly (see *blancmange* in the previous passage).

Charles Bovary, a doctor in a small town in Normandy, is marrying a farmer's daughter, Emma Rouault. This famous passage from Flaubert's Madame Bovary, *describing the bucolically vulgar celebrations, conveys, in its dispassionate flatness, a sense of the disastrous miscalculations underlying the whole occasion, the ineptitude of which is summed up in the over-elaboration of the triumphantly misjudged wedding cake.*

The guests arrived early, in carriages, one-horse traps, two-wheeled wagonettes, old cabs minus their hoods, or spring-vans with leather curtains. The young people from the neighbouring villages came in farm-carts, standing up in rows, with their hands on the rails to prevent themselves from falling: trotting along and getting severely shaken up. Some people came from thirty miles away, from Goderville, Normanville and Cany. All the relatives on both sides had been invited. Old estrangements had been patched up and letters sent to long-forgotten acquaintances.

* * * * *

The wedding-feast had been laid in the cart-shed. On the table were four sirloins, six dishes of hashed chicken, some stewed veal, three legs of mutton, and in the middle a nice roast sucking-pig flanked by four pork sausages with sorrel. Flasks of brandy stood at the corners. A rich foam had frothed out round the corks of the cider-bottles. Every glass had already been filled to the brim with wine. Yellow custard stood in big dishes, shaking at the slightest jog of the table, with the initials of the newly wedded couple traced on its smooth surface in arabesques of sugared almond. For the tarts and confectioneries they had hired a pastry-cook from Yvetot. He was new to the district, and so had taken great pains with his work. At dessert he brought in with his own hands a tiered cake that made them all cry out. It started off at the base with a square of blue cardboard representing a temple with porticoes and colonnades, with stucco statuettes all round it in recesses studded with gilt paper stars; on the second layer was a castle-keep in Savoy cake, surrounded by tiny fortifications in angelica, almonds, raisins and quarters of orange; and finally, on the uppermost platform, which was a green meadow with rocks, pools of jam and boats of nutshell, stood a little Cupid, poised on a chocolate swing whose uprights had two real rose-buds for knobs at the top.

The meal went on till dusk. When they got tired of sitting, they went for a stroll round the farm, or played a game of 'corks' in the granary, after which they returned to their seats. Towards the end some of the guests were asleep and snoring. But with the coffee there was a general revival. They struck up a song, performed party-tricks, lifted weights, went 'under your thumb', tried hoisting the carts up on their shoulders, joked broadly and kissed the ladies. The horses, gorged to the nostrils with oats, could hardly be got into the shafts to go home at night. They kicked and reared and broke their harness, their masters swore or laughed; and all through the night by the light of the moon there were runaway carriages galloping along country roads, plunging into ditches, careering over stone-heaps, bumping into the banks, while women leaned out of the doors trying to catch hold of the reins.

Gustave Flaubert, *Madame Bovary*, 1857, translated by Alan Russell, 1950

Charles and Emma Bovary, still childless and leading a dull, modest, small-town existence, have been invited to stay for a ball at La Vaubyessard, the home of a grateful patient, the Marquis d'Andervilliers. It is Emma's first taste of aristocratic luxury, presented here like an animated still-life.

Dinner was at seven. The men, who were in the majority, sat down at the first table in the hall, the ladies at the second, in the dining-room, with their host and hostess.

As she went in, Emma felt herself plunged into a warm atmosphere compounded of the scent of flowers and of fine linen, the savour of meat and the scent of truffles. The candles in the chandeliers glowed on the silver dish-covers with elongated flames. The pieces of cut glass had steamed over, and reflected a dull glimmer from one to the other. Bunches of flowers were set in a row down the whole length of the table, and on the wide-rimmed plates stood serviettes folded in the form of a bishop's mitre, each with an oval-shaped roll inside the fold. The red claws of the lobsters lay over the edge of the dishes. Luscious fruits were piled on moss in open baskets. The quails still had their feathers on them. The fumes rose. Solemn as a judge in his silk stockings and knee-breeches, his white cravat and frilled shirt, the major-domo handed the dishes, ready carved, between the guests' shoulders, and flicked the piece you chose on to your plate with his spoon. On the big porcelain stove with its copper rod, a statue of a woman draped to the chin stared fixedly at the roomful of people.

Madame Bovary noticed that several of the women had not put their gloves in their glasses.

* * * * *

Iced champagne was served. Emma shivered all over at the cold taste of it in her mouth. She had never seen pomegranates before, or tasted a pineapple. Even the caster sugar looked finer and whiter than elsewhere.

After dinner the ladies went upstairs to get ready for the ball.

* * * * *

It was stuffy in the ballroom. The lamps were dimming. There was a general movement into the billiard-room. A servant climbing up on a chair broke a couple of window-panes; at the sound of the glass smashing, Madame Bovary turned and caught sight of some peasants outside, with their faces pressed to the window. It reminded her of Les Bertaux: she saw the farmhouse and the muddy pond, her father in his smock beneath the apple-trees, and herself back in the dairy again, skimming cream off the milk with her fingers. But her past life, till now so clear in her mind, had begun to slip right away from her amid the splendours of the present moment; she could not be quite sure it had ever happened. Here she was, at the ball. Outside, over everything else, hung a dark veil. She was eating a maraschino ice, holding the silver-gilt shell in her hand, half-closing her eyes as she put the spoon to her lips.

* * * * *

After supper—at which Spanish wines and Rhine wines flowed freely, accompanied by shell-fish soup and milk-of-almond soup, Trafalgar puddings, and every variety of cold meat, in trembling aspic—the carriages began to move off in ones and twos. If you drew aside the edge of the muslin curtain you could see the lamps gliding away into the darkness. The settees emptied; but some of the card-players still sat on. The musicians moistened the tips of their fingers on their tongues. Charles leaned against a door, half-asleep.

Flaubert, *Madame Bovary*, translated by Alan Russell

❧ *Bob Loveday, a merchant seaman in the Napoleonic War, is the son of a widowed Dorset miller and brother of the trumpet-major John. At home on leave, he has hastily proposed to a Southampton woman, Matilda Johnson, who is shortly due to arrive at his father's house and to settle there permanently in advance of the wedding. A neighbouring widow, Mrs Garland, who lives with her daughter in an adjacent part of the mill house, supervises a drastic turn-out and house-cleaning in the unknown woman's honour.*

The cooking for the wedding festivities was on a proportionate scale of thoroughness. They killed the four supernumerary chickens that had just begun to crow, and the little curly-tailed barrow pig, in preference to the sow; not having been put up fattening for more than five weeks it was excellent small meat, and therefore more delicate and likely to suit a town-bred lady's taste than the large one, which, having reached the weight of fourteen score, might have been a little gross to a cultured palate. There were also provided a cold chine, stuffed veal, and two pigeon pies. Also thirty rings of black-pot, a dozen of white-pot, and ten knots of tender and well-washed chitterlings, cooked plain, in case she should like a change.

As additional reserves there were sweetbreads, and five milts, sewed up at one side in the form of a chrysalis, and stuffed with thyme, sage, parsley, mint, groats, rice, milk, chopped egg, and other ingredients. They were afterwards to be roasted before a slow fire, and eaten hot.

The business of chopping so many herbs for the various stuffings was found to be aching work for women; and David [the miller's servant], the miller, the grinder, and the grinder's boy being fully occupied in their proper branches, and Bob being very busy painting the gig and touching up the harness, Loveday called in a friendly dragoon of John's regiment who was passing by, and he, being a muscular man, willingly chopped all the afternoon for a quart of strong, judiciously administered, and all other victuals found, taking off his jacket and gloves, rolling up his shirt-sleeves and unfastening his stock in an honourable and energetic way.

All windfalls and maggot-cored codlins were excluded from the apple pies; and as there was no known dish large enough for the purpose, the puddings were stirred up in the milking-pail, and boiled in the three-legged bell-metal crock, of great weight and antiquity, which every travelling tinker for the previous thirty years had tapped with his stick, coveted, made a bid for, and often attempted to steal.

Thomas Hardy, *The Trumpet-Major*, 1880

Barrow pig: a castrated boar; *black-pot*: herb and oatmeal sausages coloured black with pig's blood; black puddings; *white-pot*: (usually) a baked, sweet pudding, made with milk or cream, flour or breadcrumbs, suet, sugar, and spices; but in this context probably white puddings, or oatmeal sausages, uncoloured. White puddings are traditional in the West Country; *chitterlings*: pigs' innards, sometimes stuffed and fried, but in this case left plain; *milts*: (pigs') spleen.

The culmination of Lampedusa's famous novel The Leopard, *set in Sicily.*

[Don Fabrizio] waited a moment for the two young people to draw away, then he too went into the supper room. A long narrow table was set at the end, lit by the famous twelve silver-gilt candelabra given to Diego's grandfather by the Court of Madrid at the end of his embassy in Spain.

* * * * *

Beneath the candelabra, beneath the five tiers bearing towards the distant ceiling pyramids of home-made cakes that were never touched, spread the monotonous opulence of buffets at big balls: coraline lobsters boiled alive, waxy *chaud-froids* of veal, steely-tinted fish immersed in sauce, turkeys gilded by the oven's heat, rosy *foie-gras* under gelatine armour, boned woodcocks reclining on amber toast decorated with their own chopped guts, and a dozen other cruel, coloured delights. At the end of the table two monumental silver tureens held limpid soup, the colour of burnt amber. To prepare this supper the cooks must have sweated away in the vast kitchens from the night before.

'Dear me, what an amount! Donna Margherita knows how to do things well. But it's not for me!'

Scorning the table of drinks, glittering with crystal and silver on the right, he moved left towards that of the sweetmeats. Huge blond *babas*, *Mont Blancs* snowy with whipped cream, cakes speckled with white almonds and green pistachio nuts, hillocks of chocolate-covered pastry, brown and rich as the top soil of the Catanian plain from which, in fact, through many a twist and turn they had come, pink ices, champagne ices, coffee ices, all *parfaits* and falling apart with a squelch at a knife cleft, a melody in major of crystallized cherries, acid notes of yellow pineapple, and those cakes called 'Triumphs of Gluttony,' filled with green pistachio paste, and shameless 'Virgin's cakes' shaped like breasts. Don Fabrizio asked for some of these, and as he held them on his plate they looked like a profane caricature of Saint Agatha. 'Why ever didn't the Holy Office forbid these puddings when it had the chance? Saint Agatha's sliced-off breasts sold by convents, devoured at dances. Well! Well!'

Giuseppe Tomasi di Lampedusa, *The Leopard*, 1958, translated by Archibald Colquhoun, 1960

Robert Tressall (otherwise Robert Noonan), a house-painter, died of tuberculosis, leaving this naïve, disorganized, and bitterly autobiographical novel of working life unpublished. 'The beano', a workers' outing at a time when such an annual day out (whether or not subsidized by the employer) was the only kind of holiday known to most manual wage-earners, is the high point of the narrative of events in the lives of a group of thirty-odd men, all employees of Rushton, who owns a firm of builders and decorators, and all variously put upon by Didlum, Grinder, Lettum, and Toonarf, his minions. As Tressall explains in a subsequent passage, the men have each subscribed the considerable sum of five shillings, half of which (2s. 6d.) exactly covers the cost of their dinner, and the remaining 2s. 6d. the cost of their conveyance to the 'Queen Elizabeth' public house by hired brake.

When the eventful day of the beano arrived, the hands were paid at twelve o'clock and rushed off home to have a wash and change.

* * * * *

They reached the long desired 'Queen Elizabeth' at twenty minutes to four, and were immediately ushered into a large room where a round table and two long ones were set for dinner in a manner worthy of the reputation of the house.

The table-cloths and the serviettes, arranged fanwise in the drinking-glasses, were literally as white as snow. About a dozen knives, forks and spoons were laid for each person, and down the centre of the table glasses of delicious yellow custard and cut glasses of glistening red and golden jelly alternated with vases of sweet-smelling flowers.

Rushton, with Didlum and Grinder and his other friends, sat at the round table near the piano. Hunter took the head of the longer of the other two tables and Crass [a foreman] the foot, while on either side of Crass were Bundy and Slyme, who had acted with him as the committee who had arranged the beano. Payne, the foreman carpenter, occupied the head of the other table.

The dinner was all that could be desired. There was soup, roast beef, boiled mutton, roast turkey, roast goose, ham, cabbage, peas, beans and potatoes, plum pudding, custard, jelly, fruit tarts, bread and cheese, and as much beer or lemonade as they liked to pay for, the drinks being an extra.

Everything was cooked to a turn, and although the diners were somewhat bewildered by the multitude of knives and forks, they all, with one or two exceptions, rose to the occasion and enjoyed themselves famously.

The turkeys, the roast beef and the boiled mutton, the peas and beans, and the cabbage, disappeared with astonishing rapidity, which was not to be wondered at, for they were all very hungry from the long drive, and nearly everyone made a point of having at least one helping of everything and some of them went in for two lots of soup.

Crass frequently paused to mop the perspiration from his face and neck with his serviette, an example followed by many others. The beer was of the best, and all the time, amid the rattle of crockery and the knives and forks, the proceedings were enlivened by many jests and flashes of wit which continuously kept the table in a roar.

'Chuck us over another dollop of that there "white stuff," Bob,' shouted the Semi-Drunk to Crass, indicating the blancmange.

Crass reached out his hand and took hold of the dish containing the 'white stuff', but instead of passing it to the Semi-Drunk he proceeded to demolish it himself, gobbling it up quickly from the dish with a spoon.

'Why, you're eating it all yerself, yer swine,' cried the Semi-Drunk indignantly, as soon as he realised what was happening.

'That's all right, matey,' replied Crass, affably, as he deposited the empty dish on the table. 'It doesn't matter, there's plenty more where it came from. Tell the landlord to bring in another lot.'

Upon being applied to the landlord, who was assisted in the waiting by his daughter, two other young women and two young men, brought in several more lots and so the Semi-Drunk was appeased.

As for the plum pudding, it was unanimously voted a fair knock out, just like Christmas; but as Ned Dawson and Bill Bates had drunk all the brandy sauce before the pudding was served, the others all had to have their first helping without any. However, the landlord soon supplied the deficit, so that the incident passed off without unpleasantness.

Robert Tressall, *The Ragged Trousered Philanthropists*, 1914

GREED, EXCESS

❧ *Before his accession, King James I of Scotland had been kept a prisoner in England by Kings Henry IV and Henry V, and had married Jane Beaufort, an English lady. When he returned to Scotland for his coronation in 1424, he took with him a retinue of English gentlemen, many of whom settled permanently in Scotland. Holinshed's* Chronicle *describes the effect that this had on the formerly plain-living Scots.*

Much what about the same time [1430] there was a parlement holden at Perth, in the which Henrie Wardlaw bishop of S. Andrews, in the name of all the three estates there assembled, made a long and pithie oration to this effect: that '. . . there was one wicked usage crept in of late, increasing so fast, that if speedie remedie for it were not had in time, all those commodities brought into the realme by [the king's] comming, should be of small availe, and that was, such superfluous riot in banketing cheere and number of costlie dishes, as were then taken up and used after the English fashion, both to the great hinderance of mans health, and also to the unprofitable wasting of their goods and substance. If the laudable temperance used amongest the Scotishmen in old time were well considered, nothing might appeare more contrarie and repugnant thereto, than that new kind of gluttonie then used, by receiving more excess of meats and drinks than sufficeth to the nourishment of nature, through provocation of such deintie and delicate dishes, confectioned sawces, and devised potions, as were now brought in amongest them. As for such gentlemen as the king had brought with him foorth of England, they were woorthie indeed to be cherished, and had in high favour; neither was this abuse to be so greatlie imputed to them, considering it was appropriate to their nation. But the Scotishmen themselves were chieflie to be blamed, that had so quickly yeelded to so great an inconvenience, the enormitie whereof appeared by the sundrie vices that followed of the same, as excesse, sensuall lust, slouth, reiffe, and wasting of goods . . .'

* * * * *

By these and manie other the like persuasions, bishop Wardlaw used to dissuade the king and his people from all superfluous courses of delicate dishes and surfetting bankets. Insomuch that even then there was order taken, that fewer dishes and more spare diet should be used through the realme, licencing gentlemen onelie, and that on festivall daies, to be served with pies, this use of them not being knowne in Scotland till that season. Nevertheless, such intemperance is risen in process of time following, that the greedie appetite of gluttons in this age may be satisfied with no competent feeding, till their bellies be so stuffed with immoderate gormandise, that they maie scarse fetch breath, through which their noisome surfetting, they fall dailie into sundrie strange and lothsome kinds of diseases, being oftentimes killed by the same in their flourishing youth, as by dailie experience plainlie appeareth.

Raphael Holinshed, *Chronicles of England, Scotland and Ireland*, 1577

reiffe, reif: robbery, spoliation.

THE GLUTTON

Fat, pamper'd *Porus*, eating for Renown,
In Soups and Sauces melts his Manors down;
Regardless of his Heirs, with Mortgag'd Lands,
Buys hecatombs of Fish, and Ortolans;
True Judge of Merit, most disdainful looks
On Chiefs and Patriots when compar'd to Cooks;
With what Delight Pigs whipt to Death he crams
On fattn'd Frogs, or Essences of Hams;
For fifty thousand Tongues of Peacocks sighs

Mix'd with the Brains of Birds of Paradise;
Loud ring the Glasses, powder'd Footmen run,
He eats, drinks, surfeits, still eats, is undone!
See the swoln Glutton in terrific State,
Behind his chair what dire Diseases wait?
There tottering *Gout*, and white-tongu'd *Fever* stand,
Big *Dropsy*, with full Goblets in his Hand,
Asthma, thick-panting for short Gasps of Breath,
And *Apoplexy*, fiercest friend of Death.
Sweeter the lonely Hermit's simple Food,
Who in lone Caves, or near the rushy Flood,
With eager Appetite, at early Hours,
From maple Dish salubrious Herbs devours;
Soft drowsy Dews at Eve his Temples steep,
And happy Dreams attend his easy Sleep;
Wak'd by the Thrush to neighbouring Vale he goes,
To mark how sucks the Bee, how blooms the Rose;
What latent Juice the trodden Herbage yields,
Wild Nature's Physic in the flowery fields.
With Temperance sooth'd each solitary Day,
Free, innocent, and easy, steals away,
Till Age down bends him to the friendly Grave,
No Fashion's Dupe, no powerful Passion's Slave.

Thomas Warton the Elder, *Poems on Several Occasions*, 1747

❧ *Heliogabalus, or Elagabalus, born Varius Avitus Bassianus at Emesa (Homs), Syria* AD *c.200, was a young cousin of the Emperor Caracalla, murdered in 217. A beautiful, voluptuous youth, appointed high priest of the Syrian sun-god Elagabalus, he was rumoured to be the illegitimate son of Caracalla, and was proclaimed emperor by insurrectionary troops in Syria in 218. Three years later, Elagabalus had already so shocked the Roman army and people by his dissipation that, in order to protect himself from outright rebellion, he invested his cousin Alexander Severus with the quasi-imperial rank of Caesar. Severus, however, proved so popular that Elegabalus demoted him in a fit of jealousy, whereupon he and his mother were murdered by mutinous praetorian guards in March 222. His life was written by Aelius Lampridius in* Scriptores Historiae Augustae, *Gibbon's chief source for the lives of the Roman Emperors from Julius Caesar to Alexander Severus (d. 235).*

A rational voluptuary adheres with invariable respect to the temperate dictates of nature, and improves the gratifications of sense by social intercourse, endearing connections, and the soft colouring of taste and the imagination. But Elagabalus (I speak of the emperor of that name), corrupted by his youth, his country, and his fortune, abandoned himself to the grossest pleasures with ungoverned fury, and soon found disgust and satiety in the midst of his enjoyments. The inflammatory powers of art were summoned to his aid: the confused multitude of women, of wines, and of dishes, and the studied variety of attitudes and sauces, served to revive his languid appetites. New terms and new inventions in these sciences, the only ones cultivated and patronised by the monarch,* signalised his reign, and transmitted his infamy to succeeding times. A capricious prodigality supplied the want of taste and elegance; and whilst Elagabalus lavished away the treasures of his people in the wildest extravagance, his own voice and that of his flatterers applauded a spirit and magnificence unknown to the tameness of his predecessors. To confound the order of seasons and climates,† to sport with the passions and prejudices of his subjects, and to subvert every law of nature and decency, were in the number of his most delicious amusements.

* The invention of a new sauce was liberally rewarded; but if it was not relished, the inventor was confined to eat of nothing else, till he had discovered another more agreeable to the Imperial palate. Hist. August. (Lamprid., Heliogab. c. 29), p. 111.

† He never would eat sea-fish except at a great distance from the sea; he then would distribute vast quantities of the rarest sorts, brought at an immense expense, to the peasants of the inland country. Hist. August. (Lamprid., Heliogab. c. 29), p. 109.

Edward Gibbon, *Decline and Fall of the Roman Empire*, 1776–88, Volume I

On Friday, June 25 [1784], I dined with [Johnson] at General Paoli's, where, he says in one of his letters to Mrs Thrale, 'I love to dine.' There was a variety of dishes much to his taste, of all which he seemed to me to eat so much, that I was afraid he might be hurt by it; and I whispered to the General my fear, and begged he might not press him. 'Alas! (said the General) see how very ill he looks; he can live but a very short time. Would you refuse any slight gratifications to a man under sentence of death? There is a humane custom in Italy, by which persons in that melancholy situation are indulged with having whatever they like best to eat and drink, even with expensive delicacies.'

Boswell, *Life of Samuel Johnson*

General Pasquale Paoli: an exiled Corsican patriot, Paoli had lived in England since 1769. Johnson died on 13 December 1785, aged 75.

NATURE'S BALANCE UPSET

Man, nature's guest by invitation sweet,
Receives from her both appetite and treat;
But, if he play the glutton and exceed,
His benefactress blushes at the deed.
For nature, nice, as lib'ral to dispense,
Made nothing but a brute the slave of sense.
Daniel ate pulse by choice—example rare!
Heav'n blessed the youth, and made him fresh and fair.
Gorgonius sits, abdominous and wan,
Like a fat squab upon a Chinese fan:
He snuffs far off th'anticipated joy;
Turtle and venison all his thoughts employ;
Prepares for meals as jockies take a sweat,
Oh, nauseous! an emetic for a whet!
Will Providence o'erlook the wasted good?
Temperance were no virtue if he could.

William Cowper, 'The Progress of Error', 1780

[*John Pintard to his daughter Eliza Davidson, New York, 4 January 1817.*]

A Doctor Magraw a learned physician in this city before the revolution very eminent & facetious always prescribed old Hock to his patients, a Wine to which our palates are unaccustomed. Well did you take plenty of your wine was his usual question. Ah Doctor it is so bad I do not like it & only could swallow one glass. Let me see the Bottle. Why this wine is sound & good, if you do not like it, I must prescribe something else. It is a pity however to lose the wine & so he tossed off the contents. Doctor Romaine our once family physician was famous for a fondness for plum cake, visited all lying in ladies & if he could get in reach of the cake basket would devour the whole. He once annoyed Mama very much. It was a New Years day. A bountiful Cake Tray graced as usual the side board. Mama was dressing. The Doctor raised the Dutch clean napkin & demolished all the Honey & New Years cookies & departed covering over the Tray as before. I dare say it contained some pounds. So you see that every physician has his favourite liquor or food.

Letters from John Pintard to his Daughter

The form . . . of the benediction before eating has its beauty at a poor man's table, or at the simple and unprovocative repasts of children. It is here that the grace becomes exceedingly graceful. The indigent man, who hardly knows whether he shall have a meal the next day or not, sits down to his fare with a present sense of the blessing which can be but feebly acted by the rich, into whose minds the conception of wanting a dinner could never, but by some extreme theory, have entered. The proper end of food—the animal sustenance—is barely contemplated by them. The poor man's bread is his daily bread, literally his bread for the day. Their courses are perennial.

Again, the plainest diet seems the fittest to be preceded by the grace. That which is least stimulative to appetite, leaves the mind most free for foreign considerations. A man may feel thankful, heartily thankful, over a dish of plain mutton with turnips, and have leisure to reflect upon the ordinance and true institution of eating; when he shall confess a perturbation of mind, inconsistent with the purposes of the grace, at the presence of venison or turtle. When I have sate (a *rarus hospes*) at rich men's tables, with the savoury soup and messes steaming up the nostrils, and moistening the lips of the guests with desire and a distracted choice, I have felt the introduction of that ceremony to be unseasonable. With the ravenous orgasm upon you, it seems impertinent to interpose a religious sentiment. It is a confusion of purpose to mutter out praises from a mouth that waters. The heats of epicurism put out the gentle flame of devotion. The incense which rises round is pagan, and the belly-god intercepts it for his own. The very excess of the provision beyond the needs, takes away all sense of proportion between the end and means. The giver is veiled by his gifts. You are startled at the injustice of returning thanks—for what?—for having too much, while so many starve. It is to praise the Gods amiss.

I have observed this awkwardness felt, scarce consciously perhaps, by the good man who says the grace. I have seen it in clergymen and others—a sort of shame—a sense of the co-presence of circumstances which unhallow the blessing. After a devotional tone put on for a few seconds, how rapidly the speaker will fall into his common voice, helping himself or his neighbour as if to get rid of some uneasy sensation of hypocrisy. Not that the good man was a hypocrite, or was not most conscientious in the discharge of the duty; but he felt in his inmost mind the incompatibility of the scene and the viands before him with the exercise of a calm and rational gratitude.

Lamb, 'Grace Before Meat', *Essays of Elia*

❧ Buddenbrooks, *a historical novel comparable in its time-span with* War and Peace, *opens in 1835, with the Buddenbrook family of North German merchants at the height of its prosperity. At this set-piece dinner for family and friends, Herr and Frau Consul Buddenbrook celebrate their move into a new, grandly furnished house, while remembering the comparative economic uncertainty of their early married life during the last years of the Napoleonic War.*

The company had for the most part seated themselves on the chairs and the sofa. They talked with the children or discussed the unseasonable cold and the new house. Herr Hoffstede admired a beautiful Sèvres inkstand, in the shape of a black and white hunting dog, that stood on the secretary. Doctor Grabow, a man of about the Consul's age, with a long, mild face between thin whiskers, was looking at the table, set out with cake and currant bread and salt-cellars in different shapes. This was the 'bread and salt' that had been sent by friends for the house warming; but the 'bread' consisted of rich, heavy pastries, and the salt came in dishes of massive gold, that the senders might not seem to be mean in their gifts.

'There will be work for me here,' said the Doctor, pointing to the sweetmeats and threatening the children with his glance.

* * * * *

The plates were being changed again. An enormous brick-red boiled ham appeared, strewn with crumbs and served with a sour brown onion sauce, and so many vegetables that the company could have satisfied their appetites from that one vegetable-dish. Lebrecht Kröger undertook the carving, and skilfully cut the succulent slices, with his elbows slightly elevated and his two long forefingers laid out along the back of the knife and fork. With the ham went the Frau Consul's celebrated 'Russian jam,' a pungent fruit conserve flavoured with spirits.

* * * * *

And now came, in two great cut-glass dishes, the 'Plettenpudding.' It was made of layers of macaroons, raspberries, lady-fingers, and custard. At the same time, at the other end of the table, appeared the blazing plum-pudding which was the children's favourite sweet.

* * * * *

But where was Dr Grabow? The butter, cheese and fruit had just been handed round; and the Frau Consul rose from her chair and unobtrusively followed the waitress from the room; for the Doctor, Mamsell Jungmann, and Christian were no longer in their places, and a smothered wail was proceeding from the hall. There in the dim light, little Christian was half lying, half crouching on the round settee that encircled the central pillar. He was uttering heart-breaking groans. Ida and the doctor stood beside him . . .

Doctor Grabow felt the lad's pulse. His kindly face grew longer and gentler.

'It's nothing much, Frau Consul,' he reassured her. 'A touch of indigestion.' He prescribed in his best bed-side manner: 'Better put him to bed and give him a Dover powder—perhaps a cup of camomile tea, too, to bring out the perspiration . . . And a rigorous diet, you know, Frau Consul. A little pigeon, a little French bread . . .'.

'I don't want any pigeon,' bellowed Christian angrily. 'I don't want to eat anything ever any more. I'm ill, I tell you, damned ill!' The fervour with which he uttered the bad word seemed to bring him relief.

Doctor Grabow smiled to himself—a thoughtful, almost a melancholy smile. He would soon eat again, this young man. He would do as the rest of the world did—his father, and all their relatives and friends; he would lead a sedentary life and eat four good, rich, satisfying meals a day. Well, God bless us all! He, Friedrich Grabow, was not the man to upset the habits of these prosperous, comfortable tradesmen and their families. He would come when he was sent for, prescribe a few days' diet—a little pigeon, a slice of French bread—yes, yes, and assure the family that it was nothing serious this time. Young as he was, he had held the head of many an honest burgher who had eaten his last joint of smoked meat, his last stuffed turkey, and, whether overtaken unaware in his counting-house or after a brief illness in his solid old four-poster bed, had commended his soul to God. Then it was called paralysis, a 'stroke'; a sudden death. And he, Friedrich Grabow, could have predicted it, on all of these occasions when it was 'nothing serious this time'—or perhaps at the times when he had not even been summoned, when there had only been a slight giddiness after luncheon. Well, God bless us all! He, Friedrich Grabow, was not the man to despise a roast turkey himself. That ham with onion sauce had been delicious, hang it! And the Plettenpudding, when they were already stuffed full—macaroons, raspberries, custard . . . 'A rigorous diet, Frau Consul, as I say. A little pigeon, a little French bread.'

Thomas Mann, *Buddenbrooks*, 1901, Volume I, translated by H. T. Lowe-Porter 1924

❧ *Katherine Mansfield (1890–1923), the New Zealand-born short-story writer, spent the summer and autumn of 1909 in Bavaria, having married and immediately left her first husband, George Bowden, in England, and having become pregnant by her lover, whose baby she lost. While there she began to write short stories, which were first published in 1910 in the* New Age. *This collection,* In a German Pension, *went out of print on its publisher's bankruptcy. In 1914 Katherine Mansfield was invited by other publishers to bring out the collection again; but she refused, regarding the stories as immature and unworthy, and not wishing to have them used as anti-German propaganda. In 1920 she refused a further invitation; and the stories were reissued only after her death by her second husband, John Middleton Murry.*

Bread soup was placed upon the table. 'Ah,' said the Herr Rat, leaning upon the table as he peered into the tureen, 'that is what I need. My "magen" has not been in order for several days. Bread soup, and just the right consistency. I am a good cook myself'—he turned to me.

'How interesting,' I said, attempting to infuse just the right amount of enthusiasm into my voice.

'Oh yes—when one is not married it is necessary. As for me, I have had all I wanted from women without marriage.' He tucked his napkin into his collar and blew upon his soup as he spoke. 'Now at nine o'clock I make myself an English breakfast, but not much. Four slices of bread, two eggs, two slices of cold ham, one plate of soup, two cups of tea—that is nothing to you.'

He asserted the fact so vehemently that I had not the courage to refute it.

All eyes were suddenly turned on me. I felt I was bearing the burden of the nation's preposterous breakfast—I who drank a cup of coffee while buttoning my blouse in the morning.

'Do they really eat so much?' asked Fraülein Stiegelauer. 'Soup and baker's bread and pig's flesh, and tea and coffee and stewed fruit, and honey and eggs, and cold fish and kidneys, and hot fish and liver? All the ladies eat, too, especially the ladies?'

'Certainly. I myself have noticed it, when I was living in a hotel in Leicester Square,' cried the Herr Rat. 'It was a good hotel, but they could not make tea—now—'

'Ah, that's one thing I *can* do,' said I, laughing brightly. 'I can make very good tea. The great secret is to warm the teapot.'

'Warm the teapot,' interrupted the Herr Rat, pushing away his soup plate. 'What do you warm the teapot for? Ha! ha! that's very good. One does not eat the teapot, I suppose?'

He fixed his cold blue eyes upon me with an expression which suggested a thousand premeditated invasions. 'So that is the great secret of your English tea? All you do is to warm the teapot.'

I wanted to say that was only the preliminary canter, but could not translate it, and so was silent.

The servant brought in veal with sauerkraut and potatoes.

* * * * *

'Is it true,' asked the Widow, picking her teeth with a hair-pin as she spoke, 'that you are a vegetarian?'

'Why, yes; I have not eaten meat for three years.'

'Im—possible! Have you any family?'

'No.'

'There now, you see, that's what you're coming to! Who ever heard of having children upon vegetables? It is not possible. But you never have large families in England now. I suppose you are too busy with your suffragetting. Now I have had nine children, and they are all alive, thank God. Fine, healthy babies—though after the first one was born I had to—'

'How *wonderful*,' I cried.

'Wonderful,' said the Widow contemptuously, replacing the hair-pin in the knob which was balanced on the top of her head. 'Not at all! A friend of mine had four at the same time. Her husband was so pleased he gave a supper-party and had them placed upon the table. Of course she was very proud.'

'Germany,' boomed the Traveller, biting round a potato which he had speared with his knife, 'is the home of the Family.'

Followed an appreciative silence.

The dishes were changed for beef, red currants and spinach. They wiped their forks upon black bread and started again.

* * * * *

'What is your husband's favourite meat?' asked the Widow.

'I really do not know,' I answered.

'You really do not know? How long have you been married?'

'Three years.'

'But you cannot be in earnest! You would not have kept house as his wife for a week without knowing that fact.'

'I really never asked him; he is not at all particular about his food.'

A pause. They all looked at me, shaking their heads, their mouths full of cherry stones.

'No wonder there is a repetition in England of that dreadful state of things in Paris,' said the Widow, folding her dinner napkin. 'How can a woman expect to keep her husband if she does not know his favourite food after three years?'

'Mahlzeit!'

'Mahlzeit!'

I closed the door after me.

Katherine Mansfield, 'Germans at Meat', from *In A German Pension*, 1911

❧ *Guy and Harriet Pringle, newly married, are living in Bucharest, where Guy teaches English for a British-run cultural organization. They have been invited to lunch at the home of Emanuel Drucker, a banker and the father of one of Guy's students, where they meet his young second wife, his children, and his three sisters and brothers-in-law, the Hassolels, the Teitelbaums, and the Flöhrs.*

They moved into the living room. As soon as they had sat down, a servant wheeled in a trolley laden with hors d'œuvres and the little grilled garlic sausages made only in Rumania. Harriet, having learnt by now that luncheon might be served any time between two o'clock and three, settled down to drink *tuică* and eat what was offered her.

* * * * *

Luncheon was announced. Doamna Hassolel led the way to the dining-room. Drucker sat at one end of the table, but the other end was taken by Doamna Hassolel, who served from a great silver tureen a rich chicken soup made of sour cream. Doamna Drucker sat half-way down the table between Sasha [Guy's pupil] and Flöhr.

* * * * *

Most of the members of the family had taken two or three plates [of soup]. Doamna Flöhr had excused herself, saying she was slimming. Harriet tried to do the same.

'No, no,' protested Doamna Hassolel, 'it is not possible. If you grow more slim, you will disappear.'

The soup was followed by sturgeon, then an entrée of braised steak with aubergine. The Pringles, supposing the entrée to be the main dish, took two helpings and were dashed by the sight of the enormous roast of beef that followed it.

'I went myself to Dragomir's,' said Doamna Hassolel, 'and ordered it to be cut "sirloin" in the English fashion. We are told how much you eat roast beef. Now you must fill your plate two, three times.'

* * * * *

[*In the afternoon Harriet is left alone with Drucker's sisters, who settle down to interrogate her about her age.*]

Doamna Hassolel rang for the maid and gave an order. The maid brought in some jars of a sort of jam made of whole fruits.

Doamna Teitelbaum murmured her pleasure. 'A little spoonful,' she said, 'I like so much gooseberry.'

Harriet said: 'I really must go.' She started to rise, but the circle of women set firm about her.

'No, no,' said Doamna Hassolel, 'you cannot go. Here already is the "five-o'clock." '

A trolley was wheeled in laden with sandwiches, iced cakes, cream buns, and several large flans made of sliced apples, pears and plums.

Harriet looked from the window. Rain was falling again. The

wind was blowing it in sheets from the soaked trees. Doamna Hassolel watched her calmly as she returned to her chair.

Olivia Manning, *The Great Fortune*, 1960

❧ *Hans Castorp, a healthy young man from Hamburg, on the brink of beginning an engineering career, is visiting his cousin Joachim, an army officer who has contracted tuberculosis and is an inmate at a sanatorium in the Swiss Alps.*

The [midday] meal was as faultlessly prepared as it was abundant. Counting the hearty soup, it consisted of no less than six courses. After the fish followed an excellent meat dish, with garnishings, then a separate vegetable course, then roast fowl, a pudding, not inferior to yesterday evening's, and lastly cheese and fruit. At all seven tables they filled their plates and ate: they ate like wolves; they displayed a voracity which would have been a pleasure to see, had there not been something else about it, an effect almost uncanny, not to say repulsive. It was not only the light-hearted who thus laced into the food—those who chattered as they ate and threw pellets of bread at one another. No, the same appetite was evinced by the silent, gloomy ones as well, those who in the pauses between courses leaned their heads on their hands and stared before them. A half-grown youth at the next table on the left, by his years a schoolboy, with wrists coming out of his jacket-sleeves, and thick, round eye-glasses, cut all the heaped-up food on his plate into a sort of mash, then bent over and gulped it down; he reached with his serviette behind his glasses now and then and dried his eyes—whether it was sweat or tears he dried one could not tell.

* * * * *

At tea all the various beverages were served which it is possible to serve at that meal. Miss Robinson drank again her brew made of rose-hips, the grand-niece spooned up her yoghurt. There were milk, tea, coffee, chocolate, even *bouillon*; and on every hand the guests, newly arisen from some two hours' repose after their heavy luncheon, were busily spreading huge slices of raisin cake with butter.

Hans Castorp chose tea, and dipped *zwieback* in it; he also tasted some marmalade. The raisin cake he contemplated with an interested eye, but literally shuddered at the thought of eating any. Once more he sat here in his place, in this vaulted room with its gay and simple decorations, its seven tables. It was the fourth time. Later, at seven o'clock, he sat there again for the fifth time, and that was supper. In the brief and trifling interval the cousins had taken a turn as far as the bench on the mountain-side, beside the little water-course. The path had been full of patients; Hans Castorp had often to lift his hat. Followed a last period of rest on the balcony, a fugitive and empty interlude of an hour and a half.

He dressed conscientiously for the evening meal, and, sitting in his place between Miss Robinson and the schoolmistress, he ate: julienne soup, baked and roast meats with suitable accompaniments, two pieces of a tart made of macaroons, butter-cream, chocolate, jam and marzipan, and lastly excellent cheese and pumpernickel. As before, he ordered a bottle of Kulmbacher. But, by the time he had half emptied his tall glass, he became clearly and unmistakably aware that bed was the best place for him. His head roared, his eyelids were like lead, his heart went like a set of kettledrums, and he began to torture himself with the suspicion that pretty Marusja, who was bending over her plate covering her face with the hand that wore the ruby ring, was laughing at *him*—though he had taken enormous pains not to give occasion for laughter. Out of the far distance he heard Frau Stöhr telling, or asserting, something which seemed to him such utter nonsense that he was conscious of a despairing doubt as to whether he had heard aright, or whether he had turned her words to nonsense in his addled brain. She was declaring that she knew how to make twenty-eight different sauces to serve with fish.

Thomas Mann, *The Magic Mountain*, 1924, translated by H. T. Lowe-Porter, 1927

❧ *The novelist John Cowper Powys (1872–1963), the eldest of a family of literary brothers, grew up as a clergyman's son at Montacute, Somerset. With his brothers he boarded at Sherborne, a nearby, conventional preparatory and public school, before finishing his education at Corpus Christi College, Cambridge. His* Autobiography *has become a classic of its kind for its frankness, detail, and depth of psychological self-probing.*

We used to receive every Saturday afternoon what was called an 'allowance', fourpence for the older boys and threepence for the younger, and with this in our pockets we would hurry off as soon as possible, for we had full liberty to walk where we liked, to the little bake-shop and sweet-shop kept by the Tuffin family, which was snugly ensconced amid mellow old buildings of Ham Hill stone just opposite the armorial entrance to the school house. A savage greed for sweetmeats quickly became now one of the most important things in my life. It became a vice. It grew so intense—I had almost said so passionate—as to supersede in considerable measure my erotic musings. There does seem to be something in greed as a vice that can mitigate sexual self-indulgence. But as I grew older and the violence of my erotic obsession increased, this lust for sweetmeats completely lost its hold upon me. I remember well, however, what form its final out-cropping took; nothing less, in fact, than a passion for plum-cake when I first went to Corpus! I had, oddly enough, an economic mania in those days, almost amounting to miserliness, though its origin was to please my father. This was certainly a queer tendency in a young collegian and one by no means appreciated by friends. Thus this passion for plum-cake, and it is not a very gracious memory, was confined to devouring it at the expense of others. I never even bought it on those rare occasions when I gave what I regarded as a festive entertainment. After those days, when together with my erotic instincts my tendency to ulcers gave me trouble, plum-cake vanished from among my temptations. I am at the present time, though poetically fastidious in my diet, as free from greediness as a hunting dog.

What I used to like best at Tuffin's was Cadbury's chocolate-cream, which I would buy in great bars, and sucking off the chocolate in a disgusting manner keep the cream till the last. I had a furious fondness too for a sweetmeat called apricot paté, which was always enclosed in silver paper, and for a delicacy known as raspberry 'noyau' which was wrapped in a gauzy edible film. In regard to these precious condiments, into the mastication of which I flung the solemn intensity of my sensual nature, I was selfish to a revolting pitch. It was an unthinkable wrench to part with the least morsel of them. Indeed, I cannot recall, in those Prep. days, one single occasion when I gave away so much as a bite of apricot paté, or so much as a lick of raspberry 'noyau'.

John Cowper Powys, *Autobiography*, 1934

❧ *The story is told by a middle-aged Berlin schoolteacher in the late 1960s. His radical student protégé, Philipp Scherbaum, plans to immolate his pet dachshund in front of Kempinski's, a large, fashionable café, in protest against Western bourgeois greed and the continuation of the Vietnam War. Together, the two are reconnoitring the scene.*

Our appointment had not included the dog but Scherbaum brought the dachshund. The cold, sunny, windless January afternoon permitted us to carry little flags: our breaths. All those who passed us in the opposite direction, overtook us or cut across our path sent up similar smoke signals: We live! We live!

The wide sidewalk at the corner of Kurfürstendamm and Fasanerstrasse presented itself. The pavement was bordered with black rimmed piles of snow, which were marked with dog urine and excited Scherbaum's long-haired dachshund. (Order and merriment.) The terrace of Kempinski's was packed. Under the terrace roof infrared tubes glowed, providing an assembly of opulent stately ladies, who were spooning in pastry, with that upper warmth which makes for cold feet. Amid dwindling cakes, sugar shakers, cream pitchers, coffeepots, filter coffee and—as could be surmised—pots of Sanka stood cheek by jowl. Opulence was accentuated by fashionable clothes, tailor-made, or, when ready-made from the best shops. Furs, mostly Persian lamb, but a good deal of camel's hair, whose café-au-lait color went well with Sachertorte and with chocolate cream puffs, with paper-thin slices of Baumkuchen and the popular walnut layer cake. . . . We stared at the terrace, which may have been interpreted as looking for a friend. Cake dwindled. New pastry was served. I began ironically, in order to divest our scene-of-the-crime investigation of any solemn, definitive quality: 'If we assume that a jelly doughnut contains two hundred calories, it becomes superfluous to ask how many calories are contained in a portion of Schwarzwald Kirsch Torte with whipped cream.'

(Vero Lewand's [Philipp's girl-friend's] estimate had been correct. 'At least three pounds of jewelry apiece. And what do they talk about when they talk? Phew, about weight and dieting. Ugh!')

The ladies in hats glanced, ate, and spoke simultaneously. An unappetizing, much caricatured, yet innocent picture. In view of so much simultaneous and continuous gluttony, an outside observer, Scherbaum for instance with his preconceived opinion, was bound to infer a corresponding process: simultaneous and continuous bowel movements; for this obsessive abundance of apple strudel, almond crescents, cream kisses, and cheesecake could only be counterbalanced by a contrary image, by steaming excrement. I rose to new heights. 'You're right, Philipp. Colossal priggishness . . . Monumentally repulsive . . . And yet, we mustn't forget, it's only a partial aspect.'

Scherbaum said: 'There they sit.'

I said: 'It's worry that makes them stuff.'

Scherbaum: 'I know. They paste cake over everything.'

I: 'As long as they eat cake, they're happy.'

Scherbaum: 'It's got to stop.'

We stared for a while at the mechanism of the loading and unloading cake forks and registered innumerable little bites with detached and uplifted little finger. ('Pastry hour,' they call it.)

I tried to undermine Scherbaum's disgust (and my own): 'When you come right down to it, it's just funny.'

But Scherbaum saw interrelations. 'There you see adults. That's what they wanted and now they've got it. Freedom of choice and second helpings. That's what they mean by democracy.'

Günter Grass, *Local Anaesthetic*, 1969, translated by Ralph Manheim, 1970

Sanka: a brand of decaffeinated coffee; *Baumkuchen*: 'tree cake', a traditional Berlin cake made by spreading layers of dough on a continuously turning plate with a pole in the centre, and covering the completed, baked cylinder with a sugar glaze. Originally, the dough for this cake was moulded round a piece of tree-branch.

V

AUSTERITY

SIMPLE FOOD

Alexander Pope (1688–1744), who had grown up at Binfield in Windsor Forest, took a lease of a house in Twickenham, then a Thames-side country village, at the age of 30, and continued living there until he died. Shares in the South Sea Company, a fashionable speculation (the 'South Sea Bubble'), collapsed in 1720, leaving many of Pope's friends suffering financial damage.

In *South-sea* days not happier, when surmis'd
The Lord of thousands, than if now *Excis'd*;
In Forest planted by a Father's hand,
Than in five acres now of rented land.
Content with nothing, I can piddle here
On Broccoli and mutton round the year;
But ancient friends (tho' poor, or out of play)
That touch my Bell, I cannot turn away.
'Tis true, no Turbots dignify my boards,
But gudgeons, flounders, what my Thames affords.
To Hounslow-heath I point, and Bansted-down,
Thence comes your mutton, and these chicks my own:
From yon old wallnut-tree a show'r shall fall;
And grapes, long-lingring on my only wall,
And figs, from standard and Espalier join:
The devil's in you if you cannot dine.

Then chearful healths (your mistress shall have place)
And, what's more rare, a Poet shall say *Grace*.

Alexander Pope, *The Second Satire of the Second Book of Horace, Paraphrased*, 1734

Piddle: toy with food.

A VISIT TO THE SOLITARY

Following our Guide, we clomb the cottage-stairs
And reached a small apartment dark and low,
Which was no sooner entered than our Host
Said gaily, 'This is my domain, my cell
My hermitage, my cabin, what you will—
I love it better than a snail his house.
But now ye shall be feasted with our best.'

* * *

A napkin, white as foam of that rough brook
By which it had been bleached, o'erspread the board;
And was itself half-covered with a store
Of dainties—oaten bread, curd cheese, and cream;
And cakes of butter curiously embossed,
Butter that had imbibed from meadow-flowers
A golden hue, delicate as their own
Faintly reflected in a lingering stream.
Nor lacked, for more delight on that warm day,
Our table, small parade of garden fruits,
And whortle-berries from the mountain side.

William Wordsworth, *The Excursion*, 1814, Book II

❧ *Thoreau's well-known experiment in simple living near Concord, Massachusetts resulted in the meditative classic,* Walden, or Life in the Woods. *His dislike of Boston, as the ever-encroaching, alienating city, may be compared with William Cobbett's similar attitude towards London, 'the great Wen', in his* Rural Rides (*1830*).

Sometimes, having had a surfeit of human society and gossip, and worn out all my village friends, I rambled still farther westward than I habitually dwell, into yet more unfrequented parts of the town

... or, while the sun was setting, made my supper of huckleberries and blueberries on Fair-Haven Hill, and laid up a store for several days. The fruits do not yield their true flavour to the purchaser of them, nor to him who raises them for the market. There is but one way to obtain it, yet few take that way. If you would know the flavour of huckleberries, ask the cow-boy or the partridge. It is a vulgar error to suppose that you have tasted huckleberries who never plucked them. A huckleberry never reaches Boston; they have not been known there since they grew on her three hills. The ambrosial and essential part of the fruit is lost with the bloom which is rubbed off in the market-cart, and they become mere provender. As long as Eternal Justice reigns, not one innocent huckleberry can be transported thither from the country's hills.

Thoreau, *Walden*

Town: parish, district (US).

CRANKS (URBAN)

Very central in Miss Miniver's universe were the Goopes. The Goopes were the oddest little couple conceivable, following a fruitarian career upon an upper floor in Theobald's Road. They were childless and servantless, and they had reduced simple living to the finest of fine arts. Mr Goopes, Ann Veronica gathered, was a mathematical tutor, and visited schools, and his wife wrote a weekly column in *New Ideas* upon vegetarian cookery, vivisection, degeneration, the lacteal secretion, appendicitis, and the Higher Thought generally, and assisted in the management of a fruit shop in the Tottenham Court Road. Their very furniture had mysteriously a high-browed quality, and Mr Goopes when at home dressed simply in a pyjama-shaped suit of canvas sacking tied with brown ribbons, while his wife wore a purple djibbah with a richly embroidered yoke. He was a small, dark, reserved man, with a large inflexible-looking convex forehead, and his wife was very pink and high-spirited, with one of those chins that pass insensibly into a full, strong neck. Once a week, every Saturday, they had a little gathering from nine till the small hours, just talk and perhaps reading aloud and fruitarian refreshments—chestnut sandwiches buttered with nutter, and so forth—and lemonade and unfermented wine; and to one of these symposia

Miss Miniver, after a good deal of preliminary solicitude, conducted Ann Veronica.

H. G. Wells, *Ann Veronica*, 1909

CRANKS (RURAL)

Felix waited. Tod was getting awfully eccentric, living this queer, out-of-the-way life with a cranky woman year after year; never reading anything, never seeing anyone but tramps and animals and villagers. And yet, sitting there beside his eccentric brother on that fallen tree, he had an extraordinary sense of rest. . . . Tod, who was looking at the sky, said suddenly:

'Are you hungry?'

And Felix remembered that they never had any proper meals, but, when hungry, went to the kitchen where a wood-fire was always burning, and either heated up coffee, and porridge that was already made, with boiled eggs and baked potatoes and apples, or devoured bread, cheese, jam, honey, cream, tomatoes, butter, nuts and fruit, that were always set out there on a wooden table under a muslin awning; he remembered, too, that they washed up their own bowls and spoons and plates, and, having finished, went outside and drew themselves a draught of water. Queer life and deuced uncomfortable—almost Chinese in its reversal of everything that everyone else was doing.

'No,' he said, 'I'm not.'

John Galsworthy, *The Freelands*, 1915

An optimistic view of a middle-class household of 'simple-lifers' in rural Worcestershire before the First World War. Felix Freeland, a successful, urbane writer, lives a conventional life in London; his brother Tod goes bare-headed, dispenses with servants, has an emancipated wife who wears deep-yoked smocks, and supports the rights of the oppressed farm labourer. It is not clear who does the shopping or prepares and keeps fresh the family's constant supply of simple food.

❧ *The author, a prosperous literary man living in the country with his wife and daughter, describes how they voluntarily dispensed with servants in the interests of a simpler, more comfortable life-style.*

There's no doubt about it, the late dinner is unnatural, unscientific, and inimical to health. I will confess to you that when I am in London I do as Londoners do. My duty compels it, and I suffer for it afterwards, dismally. I eat a breakfast for a rowing man; lunch like a prince at the Berkeley; eat a schoolboy's tea; and dine like a king at the Carlton or the Ritz, sometimes—though I blush to own it, going off to supper with Herbert Tree or Harry Irving at midnight.

But in the country I could no more live like this, and survive it, than I could walk across a piece of plough in dancing slippers.

Let me give you a notion of our normal meals.

At *breakfast* we begin with porridge, which has been cooking itself all night in The Hay Box. We then eat two thin rashers of bacon. And we conclude with a piece of toast and some Tiptree marmalade—the best in the world.

Dinner, at 1 p.m., consists of a light dish such as a stew or a ragout—always made of fresh meat, and served with O'Flannigan potatoes and O'Flannigan green food. It concludes with a rice pudding (*unpolished* rice from Savage's in Aldersgate Street) and such a sweet as castle pudding or stewed fruit.

At *tea*, served at five o'clock, we eat eggs, bread-and-butter, Tiptree jams, and home-made cakes.

And at eight o'clock *supper* is served in a tea-cup, taking the shape of cocoa made with milk or lentil soup. A slice of bread-and-butter, with fruit, completes it.

Such is our simple fare, and we find it not merely enough for health but positively all we can eat.

* * * * *

And in the matter of meat; no self-respecting man will desire his wife and daughter to handle unlovely things from the butcher's block. Meat may be necessary or unnecessary, but in the raw it is revolting. You say to your wife after your first visit to the larder, 'Let us have as little of that as possible.' And you presently come to think that a great hulking joint of meat on your table is a horrible sight. You begin to regard a carving knife with repulsion. You say to yourself, 'I am ashamed!'

But some people cannot get along without meat. Try, then, little stews and ragouts. A few small chops from the butcher freshly stewed and served with a touch of onion in the gravy is a brave dish. And then there is the polite-looking chicken, and the not unlovely sole.

In any case, Simplify, simplify, simplify!

Life Without Servants

Miss O'Flannigan: a food reformer who had recently demonstrated the proper methods of cooking vegetables—potatoes with the skins on, leaf vegetables briskly, in little water.

DIETS AND DIETING

THE HARE

Here lies whom hound did ne'er pursue,
Nor swifter greyhound follow,
Whose foot ne'er tainted morning dew,
Nor ear heard huntsman's hallo.

Old Tiney, surliest of his kind,
Who, nurs'd with tender care,
And to domestic bounds confin'd,
Was still a wild Jack-hare.

Though duly from my hand he took
His pittance ev'ry night,
He did it with a jealous look,
And, when he could, would bite.

His diet was of wheaten bread,
And milk, and oats, and straw,
Thistles, or lettuces instead,
With sand to scour his maw.

On twigs of hawthorn he regal'd,
On pippins' russet peel;
And, when his juicy salads fail'd,
Slic'd carrot pleas'd him well.

William Cowper, 'Epitaph on a Hare', 1783

❧ *Sir Thomas Elyot (1499?–1546), lawyer and diplomat, owed much of his advancement to writing* The Book Named the Governor, *a treatise on education and politics. Here he discusses the 'Socratic diet', as vegetarianism continued to be known until the nineteenth century.*

It is right evident to every wise man, who at any time hath haunted affairs whereunto was required contemplation or serious study, that to a man having due concoction and digestion as is expedient, shall in the morning, fasting, or with little refection, not only have his invention quicker, his judgment perfecter, his tongue readier, but also his reason fresher, his ear more attentive, his remembrance more sure, and generally all his powers and wits more effectual and in better estate, than after that he hath eaten abundantly. Which I suppose is the cause why the ancient courts of record in this realm have ever been used to be kept only before noon. And surely the consideration is wonderfully excellent, and to be (as I might say) superstitiously observed; the reasons why be so apparent that they need not here to be rehearsed.

Pythagoras was never seen to eat any fish or flesh, but only herbs or fruits. Semblably did many other who exactly followed his doctrine. Wherefore it was supposed that they rather excelled all other in finding out the secrets and hid knowledge of nature, which to others were impenetrable.

Plato (or rather Socrates, Plato inditing) in his second book of the public weal [*The Republic*], willeth that the people of his city, which he would constitute, should be nourished with barley bread and cakes of wheat, and that the residue of their diet should be salt, olives, cheese, and leeks, and moreover worts that the fields do bring forth, for their pottage. But he addeth too, as it were to make the dinner more delicate, figs, beans, myrtle berries, and beechmast, which they should roast on the coals, and drink to it water moderately. So (saith he) they living restfully and in health unto extreme age, shall leave the same manner of living unto their successors. I know well some readers, for this diet appointed by Socrates, will scorn him, accounting him for a fool, who not only by the answer of Apollo but also by the consent of all excellent writers that followed him, and the universal renown of all people, was approved to be the wisest man of all Greece. Certes I have known men of worship in this realm, which during their youth have drunk for the more part water. Of whom some yet liveth in great authority, whose excellency as well in sharpness of wit as in exquisite learning, is already known through all Christendom.

But here men shall not note me that I write this as who sayeth that noblemen in this realm should live after Socrates' diet, wherein having respect to this time and region, they might perchance find occasion to reprove me. Surely like as the excess of fare is to be justly reproved, so in a nobleman much pinching and niggardship of meat and drink is to be discommended.

Sir Thomas Elyot, *The Book Named the Governor*, 1531, Book III

❧ *The example of Daniel has often been quoted to justify deliberate austerity.*

In the third year of Jehoiakim king of Judah came Nebuchadnezzar king of Babylon unto Jerusalem and besieged it.

And the Lord gave Jehoiakim king of Judah into his hand, with part of the vessels of the house of God: which he carried into the land of Shinar to the house of his god; and he brought the vessels into the treasure house of his god.

And the king spake unto Ashpenaz the master of his eunuchs, that he should bring certain of the children of Israel, and of the king's seed, and of the princes;

Children in whom was no blemish, but well favoured, and skilful in all wisdom, and cunning in knowledge, and understanding science, and such as had ability in them to stand in the king's palace, and whom they might teach the learning and tongue of the Chaldeans.

And the king appointed them a daily provision of the king's meat, and of the wine which he drank: so nourishing them three years, that at the end thereof they might stand before the king.

Now among these were the children of Judah, Daniel, Hananiah, Mishael, and Azariah.

* * * * *

But Daniel purposed in his heart that he would not defile himself with the portion of the king's meat, nor with the wine which he drank: therefore he requested of the prince of the eunuchs that he might not defile himself.

* * * * *

Then said Daniel to Melzar, whom the prince of the eunuchs had set over Daniel, Hananiah, Mishael, and Azariah,

Prove thy servants, I beseech thee, ten days; and let them give us pulse to eat, and water to drink.

Then let our countenances be looked upon before thee, and the countenances of the children that eat of the portion of the king's meat: and as thou seest, deal with thy servants.

So he consented to them in this matter, and proved them ten days.

And at the end of ten days their countenances appeared fairer and fatter in flesh than all the children which did eat the portion of the king's meat.

Thus Melzar took away the portion of their meat, and the wine that they should drink, and gave them pulse.

As for these four children, God gave them knowledge and skill in all learning and wisdom: and Daniel had understanding in all visions and dreams.

1 Daniel: 1–6, 8, 11–17

❧ § *Jonathan Swift (1667–1745), a prebend and (from 1713) Dean of St Patrick's, Dublin, spent long periods frequenting political and literary circles in London. 'Stella' (Esther Johnson), to whom he wrote the playful but emotionally guarded letters which make up the* Journal to Stella, *lived in Dublin.*

17 April 1711

. . . I drink little, miss my glass often, put water in my wine, and go away before the rest, which I take to be a good receipt for sobriety. . . . God be thanked, I am better than I was, though something of a totterer. I ate but little to-day, and of the gentlest meat. I refused ham and pigeons, pease-soup, stewed beef, cold salmon, because they were too strong. I take no snuff at all, but some herb snuff prescribed by Dr Radcliffe.

Jonathan Swift, *Journal to Stella*, 1710–13

Dr Radcliffe: John Radcliffe (1650–1714), London physician to royalty and posthumous benefactor of Oxford University.

❧ § *John Byrom (1692–1763), diarist, hymn-writer, Fellow of the Royal Society and inventor of a system of shorthand, lived in Manchester but, like Swift, usually spent part of each year enjoying the intellectual life of London. While away from home he kept a diary and wrote regularly to his wife, showing great concern with recording the minutiae of his diet. He became a vegetarian in 1735.*

[*To his wife, 15 February 1728.*]

I am fain to keep my bed all day almost for this disorder, which, when I stir, troubles me; I am got to sack whey, nettle broth, &c.

[*To his wife, soon after the death of a daughter, 7 December 1729.*]

Do not children go too bare about the neck for coughs and cold weather? I am sure that herbs, roots and fruits in season, good house-bread, water-porridge, milk fresh, &c., are the properest food for them, and for drink, water and milk, and wine, ale, beer, posset, or any liquor that is in its natural or artificial purity, whenever they have the least occasion for it. Puddings and dumplings are a sort of bread, and so may be very good for 'em if the meal or flour be so; but to take bread and crumble it and sugar it and plum it and boil it, is to take much pains to turn wholesome nourishment into unwholesome, as, if that which disguises it from natural taste, the sugar and sweets, were away, it would soon appear and be rejected as having lost all its proper nourishing sweetness, as much as green gooseberries, apricots, &c. would be rejected as not having yet got their nourishing sweetness if they were not buried in sugar. . . . Thou must excuse me for talking thus ramblingly about their food, &c.; since I have lost one of my young folks it makes me impertinent about the rest.

[*12 April 1735. Having become a vegetarian, he describes a supper eaten with two companions.*]

[We] supped . . . upon six roasted potatoes, but indifferent, and I ate two and a half of them and some apple tart and drank a glass or two of sherry.

[*To his wife, 15 April 1735.*]

Dr Vernon came by and asked me to dinner, so I went with him and ate the sprouts that he had to his veal and bacon, and tart and cheese, and drank a glass or two of his beer (which I fancied I had better have let alone). . . . Thou wonderest how I keep to my vegetable diet, but I am obliged to do it, or I should suffer; I avoid dining with folks, &c., and take the liberty on occasion when I do, as with Dr Vernon whom I dined with today. . . . I have just had some milk porridge to supper, and am going to bed.

The Private Journal and Literary Remains of John Byrom, Volume I, edited by Richard Parkinson, DD, FSA, Chetham Society, 1855

§ *William Stukeley (1687–1765), doctor, clergyman, antiquarian, and scientific amateur, was a friend or associate of Byrom and, like him, a part-time Londoner until he moved from Lincolnshire in 1747 to become Rector of St George's, Bloomsbury.*

18 February 1738.

My settled course of living now [as a recent widower, and incumbent of All Saints', Stamford] is to drink a cup of milk in the morning, warm from the cow, before breakfast. I eat plentifully at dinner of any thing and drink only toast and water, and at night I have only boild milk and bread for supper. Very rarely touch any strong drink.

William Stukeley, MS Journals

THE SPLEEN

I always choose the plainest food
To mend viscidity of blood.
Hail! water-gruel, healing power,
Of easy access to the poor;
Thy help love's confessors implore,
And doctors secretly adore;
To thee I fly, by thee dilute—
Through veins my blood doth quicker shoot,
And, by swift currents throws off clean
Prolific particles of spleen.

Matthew Green (1696–1737), 'The Spleen. An Epistle to Mr Cuthbert Jackson', in *A Complete Edition of the Poets of Great Britain. Volume the Tenth*, 1794

Sun. 8 Feb. [1756].

As I by experience find out how much more conducive it is to my health, as well as pleasantness and serenity to my mind, to live in a low, moderate rate of diet, and as I know I shall never be able to comply therewith in so strict a manner as I should choose . . . I think it therefore [right] . . . to draw up rules of proper regimen, which I do in manner and form following. . . . First, be it either in the summer or the winter, to rise as early as I possibly can; that is, always to allow myself between 7 and 8 hours' sleep, or fully 8, unless prevented on any particular or emergent occasion. 2ndly, to go to breakfast between the hours of 7 and 8 from Lady Day to St Michael, and from St Michael to Lady Day between the hours of 8 and 9. 3rdly, my breakfast to be always tea or coffee and never to exceed 4 dishes. If neither of those, half a pint of water or water gruel; and for eatables bread and cheese, bread and butter, light biscuit, buttered toast, or dry bread, and one morn in every week, dry bread only. 4thly, nothing more before dinner, and always to dine between the hours of 12 and 1 o'clock if at home. 5thly, my dinner to be meat, pudding, or any other thing of the like nature, but always to have regard, if there is nothing but salt provision, to eat sparingly; and to eat plenty of any sort of garden stuff there is at table, together with plenty of bread and acids, if any, at table; and always to have the greatest regard to give white or fresh meats and pudding the preference before any sort of highly seasoned, salt, or very strong meat; and always one day in every respective week to eat no meat. 6thly, my drink at dinner, to be always boiled water with a toast in it, or small beer, but water if I can have it, and never to drink anything stronger until after dinner. 7thly, if I drink tea at home or abroad, to be small, green tea and not more than 4 dishes; and if I eat anything, not more than two ounces. 8thly, my supper never to be meat but weak broth, water gruel, milk pottage, bread and cheese, bread and butter, apple-pie or some other sort of fruit pie, or some such light diet; my drink, water or small beer, and one night at the least in every week to go to bed without any supper. 9thly, never to drink any sort of drams or spirituous liquors of what name or kind soever.

The Diary of Thomas Turner

January 8, 1778.

In all ages the leprosy has made dreadful havoc among mankind. . . . Some centuries ago this horrible distemper prevailed all Europe over; and our forefathers were by no means exempt, as appears by the large provision made for objects labouring under this calamity. . . . It must therefore, in these days, be, to an humane and thinking person, a matter of equal wonder and satisfaction, when he contemplates how nearly this pest is eradicated, and observes that a leper now is a rare sight. He will, moreover, when engaged in such a train of thought, naturally enquire for the reason. This happy change may perhaps have originated and been continued from the much smaller quantity of salted meat and fish now eaten in these kingdoms; from the use of linen next the skin; from the plenty of better bread; and from the profusion of fruits, roots, legumes, and greens, so common in every family. Three or four centuries ago, before there were any enclosures, sown-grasses, field-turnips, or field-carrots, or hay, all the cattle which had grown fat in summer, and were not killed for winter-use, were turned out soon after Michaelmas to shift as they could through the dead months; so that no fresh meat could be had in winter or spring. Hence the marvellous account of the vast stores of salted flesh found in the larder of the eldest Spencer* in the days of Edward the Second, even so late in the spring as the third of May. It was from magazines like these that the turbulent barons supported in idleness their riotous swarms of retainers ready for any disorder or mischief. But agriculture is now arrived at such a pitch of perfection, that our best and fattest meats are killed in the winter; and no man need eat salted flesh, unless he prefers it, that has money to buy fresh.

One cause of this distemper might be, no doubt, the quantity of wretched fresh and salt fish consumed by the commonalty at all seasons as well as in Lent; which our poor now would hardly be persuaded to touch.

* * * * *

The plenty of good wheaten bread that now is found among all ranks of people in the south, instead of that miserable sort which used in old days to be made of barley or beans, may contribute not a little to the sweetening their blood and correcting their juices; for the inhabitants of mountainous districts, to this day, are still liable to the itch and other cutaneous disorders, from a wretchedness and poverty of diet.

As to the produce of a garden, every middle-aged person of observation may perceive, within his own memory, both in town and country, how vastly the consumption of vegetables is increased. Green-stalls in cities now support multitudes in a comfortable state, while gardeners get fortunes. Every decent labourer now has his garden, which is half his support, as well as his delight; and common farmers provide plenty of beans, peas, and greens, for their hinds to eat with their bacon; and those few that do not are despised for their sordid parsimony, and looked upon as regardless of the welfare of their dependants. Potatoes have prevailed in this little district, by means of premiums, within these twenty years only; and are much esteemed here now by the poor, who would scarce have ventured to taste them in the last reign.

Gilbert White, Letter XXXVII, *The Natural History of Selborne*, 1789

The eldest Spencer: Hugh Le Despenser (1262–1326), Earl of Winchester, a prominent supporter of Edward II, banished with his son Hugh Le Despenser, 1321; returned and made Earl of Winchester, 1322; captured and executed by the king's enemies, 1326. White's footnote to the text reads: '*Viz*: Six hundred bacons, eighty carcasses of beef, and six hundred muttons'.

THOREAU

I have found repeatedly, of late years, that I cannot fish without falling a little in self-respect. . . . There is something essentially unclean about this diet and all flesh, and I began to see where housework commences, and whence the endeavour, which costs so much, to wear a tidy and respectable appearance each day, to keep the house sweet and free from all ill odours and sights. Having been my own butcher, and scullion, and cook, as well as the gentleman for whom the dishes were served up, I can speak from an unusually complete experience. The practical objection to animal food in my case was its uncleanliness; and besides, when I had caught, and cleaned, and cooked, and eaten my fish, they seemed not to have fed me essentially. It was insignificant and unnecessary, and cost more than it came to. A little bread or a few potatoes would have done as well, with less trouble and filth. Like many of my contemporaries, I had rarely for years used animal food, or tea, or coffee, &c.; not so much because of any ill effects which I had traced to them, as because they were not agreeable to my imagination. The repugnance to animal food is not the effect of experience, but is an instinct. It appeared more beautiful to live low and fare hard in many respects; and though I never did so, I went far enough to please my imagination.

* * * * *

It is hard to provide and cook so simple a diet as will not offend the imagination; but this, I think, is to be fed when we feed the body; they should both sit down at the same table. Yet perhaps this may be done. The fruits eaten temperately need not make us ashamed of our appetites, nor interrupt the worthiest pursuits. But put an extra condiment into your dish, and it will poison you. It is not worth the while to live by rich cookery. Most men would feel shame if caught preparing with their own hands precisely such a dinner, whether of animal or vegetable food, as is every day prepared for them by others. Yet till this is otherwise we are not civilised, and, if gentlemen and ladies, are not true men and women. . . . Whatever my own practice may be, I have no doubt that it is a part of the destiny of the human race, in its gradual improvement, to leave off eating animals, as surely as the savage tribes have left off eating each other when they came into contact with the more civilised.

* * * * *

No man ever followed his genius till it misled him. Though the result were bodily weakness, yet perhaps no one can say that the consequences were to be regretted, for these were a life of conformity to higher principles. If the day and night are such that you greet them with joy, and life emits a fragrance like flowers and sweet-scented herbs, is more elastic, more starry, more immortal,—that is your success. All nature is your congratulation, and you have cause momentarily to bless yourself.

Thoreau, *Walden*

I became a vegetarian in 1880 or 81. It was at that period that vegetarian restaurants began to crop up here and there, and to make vegetarianism practically possible for a man too poor to be specially catered for. My attention had been called to the subject, first by Shelley (I am an out-and-out Shelleyan), and later on by a lecturer. But of course the enormity of eating the scorched corpses of animals—cannibalism with its heroic dish omitted—becomes impossible the moment it becomes conscious instead of thoughtlessly habitual. I am also a teetotaller, my family having paid the Shaw debt to the distilling industry so munificently as to leave me no obligations in that direction. I flatly declare that a man fed on whiskey and dead bodies cannot do the finest work of which he is capable.

George Bernard Shaw, *Nine Answers*, 1923

❧ *Pacifism, vegetarianism, feminism, fresh-air worship, and the pursuit of the simple life all flourished in England during the twenty years before the outbreak of the First World War. Tolstoy and Gurdjieff provided the philosophical inspiration for this movement; Eustace Miles, a dedicated self-publicist who opened his vegetarian restaurant in Chandos Street, Charing Cross in 1906, the food. Wells's character Miss Miniver, although frumpishly unattractive, is therefore very much a creature of her time, initiating the younger and more commonsensical Ann Veronica into a network of progressive causes none of which can prevent her from falling conventionally and carnally in love with her biology lecturer, Capes.*

'We do not want the men,' said Miss Miniver, 'we do not want them with their sneers and loud laughter. Empty, silly, coarse brutes. They are the brute still with us! Science some day may teach us a way to do without them. It is only the women matter. It is not every sort of creature needs—these males. Some have no males.'

* * * * *

Ann Veronica readjusted her chin on her hand. 'I wonder which of us is right,' she said. 'I haven't a scrap of—this sort of aversion.'

'Tolstoy is so good about this,' said Miss Miniver, regarding her friend's attitude. 'He sees through it all. The Higher Life and the Lower. He sees men defiled by coarse thoughts, coarse ways of living, cruelties. Simply because they are hardened by—by bestiality, and poisoned by the juices of meat slain in anger and fermented drinks—fancy! drinks that have been swarmed in by thousands and thousands of horrible little bacteria.'

'It's yeast,' said Ann Veronica—'a vegetable.'

'It's all the same,' said Miss Miniver. 'And then they are swollen up and inflamed and drunken with matter. They are blinded to all fine and subtle things; they look at life with bloodshot eyes and dilated nostrils. They are arbitrary and unjust and dogmatic and brutish and lustful.'

'But do you really think men's minds are altered by the food they eat?'

'I know it,' said Miss Miniver. '*Experte credo*. When I am leading a true life, a pure and simple life, free of all stimulants and excitements, I think—I think—oh! with *pellucid* clearness; but if I so much as take a mouthful of meat—or anything—the mirror is all blurred.'

Wells, *Ann Veronica*

❧ *The novelist John Cowper Powys (1872–1963) earned his living from 1904 to 1934 as an itinerant lecturer on English Literature in the United States. A sufferer from nervous dyspepsia since his twenties, he did not find this eased by incessant travel in America, or by the broken routines of a life which (from 1910 to 1928) he spent partly in England with his wife and family. After the collapse of his marriage, Powys settled with the American writer Phyllis Playter in New York State.*

During all this travelling I suffered at intervals, not constantly, but at pretty frequent intervals, from my accursed ulcers and from that evil acid dyspepsia which stirred them up. I never touched meat—for I was a vegetarian on principle now—but for the bulk of these fifteen travelling years I did not by any means always eat vegetables. This I think was partly for the sake of economy; for I was so extravagant in my tips to waiters and so fastidious about the hotels I went to, that I should certainly have wasted my substance *en route* if I had not been so extremely parsimonious over my diet. My gastric trouble, or so I conceived, dictated this economy, while a vein of almost rustic miserliness, encouraged it; but, in addition to these motives, this simplicity in diet *suited my taste*. At one time when my ulcers were at the worst I lived entirely on 'hominy', which is a species of cereal, on ice-cream, on raw eggs, and on milk. But as a rule for every meal I would have the same things, tea, dry toast, fried eggs, and guava jelly. Mr Blake, when at the Prep. he had us in to dessert, used to give us guava jelly.

I was still very greedy over what I liked; and just as I had devoured apricot-paté bought at 'Tuffins' and new, brown bread-and-butter at Wildman's, eagerly masticating these things, as a water-rat does, with my front teeth, so now I rolled against my palate three times a day what were called 'individual' jars of guava jelly. If this greediness of mine makes your gorge rise, reader, I must hasten to swear to you, across my heart, that *for the last five years*, since I have lived upon milk in these New York hills, I have lost completely all trace of this furious vice. I get a faint satisfaction from taking *thin* bread-and-butter to my tea, and I enjoy the feeling of drinking milk. But that is all! If I could outgrow my other vices as I have outgrown this one, I would yet approach, before I died, that mediaeval, or, if you prefer it, Tibetan ideal of life, which all my days has beckoned and allured me.

Powys, *Autobiography*

❧ *This extract comes from one of George Orwell's best-known works of journalistic social observation. Like his contemporaries in the Mass Observation movement, Tom Harrisson, Charles Madge, and Humphrey Jennings, who began their project in 1937 with investigations of working-class life in Bolton, Blackpool, and the East End of London, Orwell set out alone to experience the effects of the Depression in the industrial Lancashire slums. The result was* The Road to Wigan Pier, *considered by some to be his least successful book, but one which is in many ways still relevant, especially in its nutritional comments, nearly sixty years later.*

When I was a small boy at school a lecturer used to come once a term and deliver excellent lectures on famous battles of the past, such as Blenheim, Austerlitz etc. He was fond of quoting Napoleon's maxim 'An army marches on its stomach,' and at the end of his lecture he would suddenly turn to us and demand, 'What's the most important thing in the world?' We were expected to shout 'Food!' and if we did not do so he was disappointed.

Obviously he was right in a way. A human being is primarily a bag for putting food into; the other functions and faculties may be more godlike, but in point of time they come afterwards. A man dies and is buried, and all his words and actions are forgotten, but the food he has eaten lives after him in the sound or rotten bones of his children. I think it could be plausibly argued that changes of diet are more important than changes of dynasty or even of religion. The Great War, for instance, could never have happened if tinned food had not been invented. And the history of the past four hundred years in England would have been immensely different if it had not been for the introduction of root-crops and other vegetables at the end of the Middle Ages, and a little later the introduction of non-alcoholic drinks (tea, coffee, cocoa) and also of distilled liquors to which the beer-drinking English were not accustomed. Yet it is curious how seldom the all-importance of food is recognised. You see statues everywhere to politicians, poets, bishops, but none to cooks or bacon-curers or market-gardeners. The Emperor Charles V is said to have erected a statue to the inventor of bloaters, but that is the only case I can think of at the moment.

So perhaps the really important thing about the unemployed, the really basic thing if you look to the future, is the diet they are living on. . . . I have here a budget which was made out for me by an unemployed miner and his wife. . . . This man's allowance was thirty-two shillings a week, and besides his wife he had two children, one aged two years and five months and the other ten months.

* * * * *

The miner's family spend only tenpence a week on green vegetables and tenpence halfpenny on milk . . . and nothing on fruit; but they spend one and nine on sugar (about eight pounds of sugar, that is) and a shilling on tea. The half crown spent on meat *might* represent a small joint and the materials for a stew; probably as often as not it would represent four or five tins of bully beef. The basis of their diet, therefore, is white bread-and-margarine, corned beef, sugared tea and potatoes—an appalling diet. Would it not be better if they spent more money on wholesome things like oranges and wholemeal bread or if they even . . . saved on fuel and ate their carrots raw? Yes, it would, but the point is that no ordinary human being is ever going to do such a thing. The ordinary human being would sooner starve than live on brown bread and raw carrots. And the peculiar evil is this, that the less money you have, the less inclined you feel to spend it on wholesome food. A millionaire may enjoy breakfasting off orange juice and Ryvita biscuits, an unemployed man doesn't. . . . When you are unemployed, which is to say when you are underfed, harassed, bored and miserable, you don't *want* to eat dull wholesome food. . . . You want something a little bit 'tasty'. There is always some cheaply pleasant thing to tempt you. Let's have three pennorth of chips! Run out and buy us a twopenny ice-cream! Put the kettle on and we'll all have a nice cup of tea! . . . White bread and marg and sugared tea don't nourish you to any extent, but they are *nicer* (at least most people think so) than brown bread-and-dripping and cold water. Unemployment is an endless misery that has got to be constantly palliated, and especially with tea, the Englishman's opium. A cup of tea or even an aspirin is much better as a temporary stimulant than a crust of brown bread.

George Orwell, *The Road to Wigan Pier*, 1937

DEPRIVATION

❧ *Juvenal addresses the hapless guest of Virro (probably a rich homosexual).*

If you claim your mind is made up, still, Trebius; if you remain
Unashamed of the life you propose, and count it the highest
Good to scrape crumbs from another man's board; if you swear
You can swallow iniquities such as the lowest wits and jesters
Of Augustus's court would have gagged on, I'll doubt your word
Even on oath. True, I know nothing more cheaply
Satisfied than a belly. Yet suppose the bare subsistence
Needed to fill its void is lacking—are there no sidewalks,
Or bridges, no quarter-share in a beggar's mat
For you to make your pitch from? Is your hunger quite
So all-devouring? Is dinner worth every insult
With which you pay for it? Wouldn't your self-respect

Be better served if you stuck it out where you are,
Shivering cold, on a diet of mouldy dog's bread?
  Get one thing clear from the start: a dinner-invitation
Settles the score in full for all your earlier
Services. This great 'friendship' produces—food. Each meal,
However infrequent, your patron reckons against you
To square his account. So if, after two months' neglect,
With the bottom place to be filled at the lowest table,
He says, 'Be my guest' to you, his forgotten retainer,
You're beside yourself with joy . . .

Yet—heavens!—what a dinner!

* * *

Just get the size of that crayfish: it marks out a platter
Reserved for my lord. See the asparagus garnish
Heaped high around it, the peacocking tail that looks down
On the other guests as it's brought in, borne aloft
By some strapping waiter. But *you* get half an egg
Stuffed with one prawn, dished up in a little saucer
Like a funeral offering. Himself souses his fish
With the finest oil, but *your* colourless boiled cabbage
Will stink of the lamp; the stuff you use as a dressing
Came to town in some native felucca. One good sniff,
And you know why Africans always get plenty of clearance
At the public baths. Rub it on as a prophylactic
Against venomous snakes—they won't come anywhere near you.
  My lord will have his mullet, imported from Corsica or from
The rocks below Taormina: home waters are all fished out
To fill such ravening maws, our local breeding-grounds
Are trawled without cease, the market never lets up—
We kill off the fry now, close seasons go by the board,
Today we import from abroad for domestic consumption: these
Are the luxury fish which legacy-hunters purchase,
And which their spinster quarries sell back to the retailer.
Virro is served with a lamprey: no finer specimen
Ever came from Sicilian waters. When the south wind lies low,
Drying damp wings in his cell, the hardy fishermen
Will dare the wrath of the Straits. But what's in store for you?
An eel perhaps (though it looks like a water-snake), or
A grey-mottled river-pike, born and bred in the Tiber,

Bloated with sewage, a regular visitor to
The cesspools underlying the slums of the Subura.

* * *

You imagine Virro's a chiseller? Hardly. He does it to
Make you suffer, for kicks. What farce or pantomime
Could be a bigger joke than your empty rumbling belly?
So—in case you didn't get it—his whole idea's to reduce you
To tears of rage, an endless grinding of teeth.
You see yourself as a free man, guest at the magnate's banquet;
But *he* assumes you've been hooked by his kitchen's delectable
Odours—and not far wrong. No self-respecting person,
Whether born to purple or homespun, however down-and-out,
Would endure *that* twice. It's the hope of a good dinner
That lures you on. 'Surely he'll give us a picked-over
Hare, some scraps from the boar's haunch? Surely a chicken's
Carcase will come our way?' So you sit there, dumb
And expectant, all of you, clutching untasted rolls.
He's no fool to abuse you like this. If you can swallow
The whole treatment—why, you deserve no better. Some day
You'll find yourself meekly bending your shaven pate to be cuffed,
Like a public buffoon, well inured to the whip, a worthy
Companion for such a feast—and for such a friend.

Juvenal, Fifth Satire, from *The Sixteen Satires*, translated by Peter Green, 1967

SKINFLINTS (AND GLUTTONS)

'Tis yet in vain, I own, to keep a pother
About one Vice, and fall into the other:
Between Excess and Famine lies a mean,
Plain, but not sordid, tho' not splendid, clean.
Avidien and his wife (no matter which,
For him you'll call a dog, and her a bitch)
Sell their presented Partridges, and Fruits,
And humbly live on rabbits and on roots:
One half-pint bottle serves them both to dine,
And is at once their vinegar and wine.
But on some lucky day (as when they found
A lost Bank-bill, or heard their Son was drown'd)

At such a feast old vinegar to spare
Is what their souls so gen'rous cannot bear;
Oyl, tho' it stink, they drop by drop impart,
But souse the cabbage with a bounteous heart.
  He knows to live, who keeps the middle state,
And neither leans on this side nor on that:
Nor stops, for one bad Cork, his Butler's pay,
Swears, like Albutius, a good Cook away;
Nor lets, like Naevius, ev'ry error pass,
The musty wine, foul cloth, or greasy glass.
Now hear what blessings Temperance can bring:
(Thus said our Friend, and what he said I sing.)
First Health: The stomach (cram'd from ev'ry dish,
A Tomb of boil'd, and roast, and flesh, and fish,
Where Bile, and wind, and phlegm, and acid jar,
And all the Man is one intestine war)
Remembers oft the school-boy's simple fare,
The temp'rate sleeps, and spirits light as air!

Pope, *Second Satire*

Avidien and his wife: said to be a reference to the (unhappily married) Edward and Lady Mary Wortley Montagu, who separated in 1739.

An early episode from the life of a spinster, whose mother, having spoilt her chances of marrying early, disowns her when she takes a second husband.

Now, when she married, I from home was sent,
With grandmamma to keep perpetual Lent;
For she would take me on conditions cheap,
For what we scarcely could a parrot keep:
A trifle added to the daily fare
Would feed a maiden who must learn to spare.

With grandmamma I lived in perfect ease;
Consent to starve, and I was sure to please.
Full well I knew the painful shifts we made,
Expenses all to lessen or evade,
And tradesmen's flinty hearts to soften or persuade.

Poor grandmamma among the gentry dwelt
Of a small town, and all the honour felt;
Shrinking from all approaches to disgrace
That might be mark'd in so genteel a place;
Where every daily deed, as soon as done,
Ran through the town as fast as it could run—
At dinners what appear'd—at cards who lost or won.

Our good appearance through the town was known
Hunger and thirst were matters of our own;
And you would judge that she in scandal dealt
Who told on what we fed, or how we felt.

* * *

The good old lady often thought me vain,
And of my dress would tenderly complain;
But liked my taste in food of every kind,
As from all grossness, like her own, refined:
Yet, when she hinted that on herbs and bread
Girls of my age and spirit should be fed,
Whate'er my age had borne, my flesh and blood,
Spirit and strength, the interdict withstood;
But though I might the frugal soul offend
Of the good matron, now my only friend,
And though her purse suggested rules so strict,
Her love could not the punishment inflict:
She sometimes watch'd the morsel with a frown
And sigh'd to see, but let it still go down.

Our butcher's bill, to me a monstrous sum,
Was such, that, summon'd, he forebore to come:
Proud man was he; and when the bill was paid,
He put the money in his bag and play'd,
Jerking it up, and catching it again,
And poising in his hand in pure disdain;
While the good lady, awed by man so proud,
And yet dispos'd to have her claims allow'd,
Balanced between humility and pride,
Stood a fall'n empress at the butcher's side,
Praising his meat as delicate and nice—
'Yes, madam, yes! if people pay the price.'

George Crabbe, 'The Maid's Story', from *Tales of the Hall*, 1819

❧ *William Cobbett habitually looked back from the 1820s to a golden age in English rural life, roughly coincidental with his own childhood in the 1760s and 1770s, when the labouring classes almost everywhere in England had had enough bread and meat to eat and beer to drink, and had lived securely, protected rather than exploited by the farmers for whom they worked. The change, he perceived, had come at the time of the French Revolutionary War of the 1790s: a period of general economic upheaval, with high taxation, increases in agricultural enclosures, rural unemployment, industrialization, and the alienating day-labouring system, all of which contributed towards eroding the feeling of responsibility which farmers and landowners had once felt for their employees. The end of communal eating at the old-fashioned farm kitchen table, and its replacement by the gentrified, farmer's mahogany, symbolized this change ten years into the period of post-war economic divisiveness and working-class misery.*

REIGATE, Thursday Evening, 20 October 1825.

Having done my business . . . today . . . I went to a sale at a farm, which the farmer is quitting. Here I had a view of what has long been going on all over the country. The farm, which belongs to *Christ's Hospital*, has been held by a man of the name of Charington, in whose family the lease has been, I hear, a number of years.

* * * * *

Every thing about this farm-house was formerly the scene of *plain manners* and *plentiful living*. Oak clothes-chests, oak bed-steads, oak chests of drawers, and oak tables to eat on, long, strong, and well supplied with joint stools. Some of the things were many hundreds of years old. But all appeared to be in a state of decay and nearly of *disuse*. There appeared to have been hardly any *family* in that house, where formerly there were, in all probability, from ten to fifteen men, boys and maids: and what was the worst of all, there was a *parlour*! Aye, and a *carpet* and *bell-pull* too! One end of the front of this once plain and substantial house had been moulded into a '*parlour*;' and there was the mahogany table, and the fine chairs, and the fine glass, and all as bare-faced upstart as any stock-jobber in the kingdom can boast of. And there were the decanters, the glasses, the 'dinner set' of crockery ware, and all just in the true stock-jobber style. And I dare say it has been *'Squire* Charington and the *Miss* Charingtons; and not plain Master Charington, and his son Hodge, and his daughter Betty Charington, all of whom this accursed system has, in all likelihood, transmuted into a species of mock gentlefolks, while it has ground the labourers down into real slaves. Why do not farmers now *feed* and *lodge* their work-people, as they did formerly? Because they cannot keep them *upon so little* as they give them in wages. This is the real cause of the change. There needs no more to prove that the lot of the working classes has become worse than it formerly was. . . . All the world knows that a number of people, boarded in the same house, and at the same table, can, with as good food, be boarded much cheaper than those persons divided into twos, threes, or fours, can be boarded. This is a well-known truth: therefore, if the farmer now shuts his pantry against his labourers, and pays them wholly in money, is it not clear that he does it because he thereby gives them a living *cheaper* to him; that is to say, a *worse* living than formerly . . . ?

The land produces, on an average, what it always produced, but there is a new distribution of the produce. This 'Squire Charington's father used, I dare say, to sit at the head of the oak-table along with his men, say grace to them, and cut up the meat and the pudding. He might take a cup of *strong beer* to himself, when they had none; but that was pretty near all the difference in their manner of living. So that *all* lived well. But, the '*Squire* had many *wine-decanters* and *wine-glasses* and 'a *dinner set*,' and a '*breakfast set*,' and '*desert knives*;' and these evidently imply carryings on and a consumption that must of necessity have greatly robbed the long oak table if it had remained fully tenanted. That long table could not share in the work of the decanters and the dinner set. Therefore, it became almost untenanted; the labourers retreated to hovels, called cottages; and instead of board and lodging, they got money; so little of it as to enable the employer to drink wine; but, then, so that he might not reduce them to *quite starvation*, they were enabled to come to him, in the *king's name*, and demand food *as paupers*. And now, mind, that which a man receives in the *king's name*, he knows well he has *by force*; and it is not in nature that he should *thank* any body for it. . . . Is it, in short, surprising, if he resort to *theft* and *robbery*?

Cobbett, *Rural Rides*

❧ *Between the 1820s and the 1840s, economic conditions for the English labouring class worsened. The Corn Laws, with their tariffs on imported corn, kept the farmers in comfort in years of bad harvests by inflating the price of corn until workers on subsistence wages, already unable to buy meat, could barely afford the cheapest and nastiest form of bread. In 1846, thanks largely to the efforts of the Liberal Member of Parliament Richard Cobden (the son of a small farmer at Midhurst, Sussex), the Prime Minister, Sir Robert Peel, reluctantly placed a resolution before Parliament effectively ending the tariff on imported grains. The act embodying this resolution, passed the same year, came too late to avert the Irish famine, and (as the second of these extracts shows) alleviated but did not immediately end the misery of the English rural working class.*

[*Charles Astridge, ex-postman for Midhurst, Sussex.*]
For nearly fifty years I was postman for Midhurst and the district. For twelve year I walked eight mile a day, out to one of the farms, and got three-and-sixpence a week. . . . 'Twas hard living in those times. We had to pay 7d. for a half-quartern loaf; and many a time I remember lookin' in at the butcher's shop at the shoulders of mutton, but I never 'ad the money to buy 'en. The farmers in those parts used to pay their men 9s. a week.

* * * * *

Often on a Saturday I'd see Jonathan Heath, what was the son of a wheelwright who lived in the Petersfield Road and had a large family, comin' along with a penny bag of crammin's—that's what they give the pigs nowadays—to make the Sunday puddin' with. We mostly lived on bread, but 'twasn't bread like 'ee get now; 'twas that heavy and doughy 'ee could pull long strings of it out of your mouth. But 'twas fine compared with the porridge we made out of bruised beans; that made your inside feel as if 'twas on fire, an' sort of choked 'ee. In those days 'ee'd see children from Duck Lane come out in the streets of Midhurst an' pick up a bit of bread, and even potato peelings; y'ee'd see them do that.

We can laugh at these things now, but it was no laughin' matter then.

[*A. J. M., Northampton.*]
My recollection takes me back into the eighteen-fifties when, if bread was but slightly taxed, many other things were heavily burdened. Physically and intellectually we dwelt next door to destitution. The principal course at the morning meal would be a small basin of bread soaked in water, and seasoned with salt, occasionally a little skimmed milk added, and a small piece of bread tinged with lard in winter. During the summer season we might at rare intervals get some dripping from the Hall. For dinner we might get plain pudding—flour and water—or pork dumpling, sometimes both, with

potatoes and onions added to fill the crust. The last course, except the dessert of potato soup, &c., might be potatoes and meat—pork, you should have seen the joint! We might get 2 lbs per week. 'Tea', such as we called it, bread and potted butter. I never remember grumbling about this being sparingly spread, it was at times so rancid. 'Supper?' Well . . . I might get something very much like a small piece of bread and a little piece of pork rubbed over it. Sunday was a high day, of course. We might get a penny black pudding for breakfast, suet pudding, and a pig's foot for five of us to feast thereon. Beef? Yes, we might get a small piece at our feast and a bullock's heart at Xmas. We did occasionally get a pennyworth of bullock's liver if we happened to be going to town—about 3 miles—for the doctor during the week. Beverage? Well, yes, we used to have as much as 4 oz of tea and 2 of coffee for 3 weeks, 1 lb of sugar per week. . . . As an additional drink we had mint-tea for summer, and we might get toast and water, especially when ailing, in winter.

The Hungry Forties. Life Under the Bread Tax. Descriptive Letters and other Testaments from Contemporary Witnesses, with an introduction by Mrs Cobden Unwin, 1904

❧ *Israel Zangwill's story*, A Child of the Ghetto, *is set in Venice.*

There were many fasts in the Ghetto calendar, most of them twelve hours long, but some twenty-four. Not a morsel of food nor a drop of water must pass the lips from the sunset of one day to nightfall on the next. The child had only been allowed to keep a few fasts, and those only partially, but now it was for his own soul to settle how long and how often it would afflict itself, and it determined to do so at every opportunity. And the great opportunity came soon. Not the Black Fast when the congregation sat shoeless on the floor of the synagogue, weeping and wailing for the destruction of Jerusalem, but the great White Fast, the terrible Day of Atonement commanded in the Bible.

* * * * *

'Twas the tenth day, and an awful sense of sacred doom hung over the Ghetto. In every house a gigantic wax taper had burnt, white and solemn, all through the night, and fowls or coins had been waved round the heads of the people in atonement for their iniquities. The morning dawned grey and cold, but with the dawn the population was astir, for the services began at six in the morning and lasted without intermission till seven at night. Many of the male worshippers were clad in their grave-clothes, and the extreme zealots remained standing all day long, swaying to and fro and beating their breasts at the confessions of sin. For a long time the boy wished to stand too, but the crowded synagogue reeked of heavy odours, and at last, towards mid-day, faint and feeble, he had to sit. But to fast till night-fall he was resolved. Hitherto he had always broken his fast at some point in the services, going home round the corner to delicious bread-and-fish. When he was seven or eight this breakfast came at mid-day, but the older he grew the longer he fasted, and it became a point of honour to beat his record every successive year. Last time he had brought his breakfast down to late afternoon, and now it would be unforgivable if he could not see the fast out and go home, proud and sinless, to drink wine with the men. He turned so pale, as the afternoon service dragged itself along, that his father begged him again and again to go home and eat. But the boy was set on a full penance. And every now and again he forgot his head-ache and the gnawing at his stomach in the fervour of passionate prayer and in the fascination of the ghostly figures weeping and wailing in the gloomy synagogue, and once in imagination he saw the heavens opened overhead and God sitting on the judgement throne, invisible by excess of dazzling light. . . . Then a great awe brooded over the synagogue, and the vast forces of the universe seemed concentrated about it, as if all creation was waiting in tense silence for the terrible words of judgment. And then he felt some cool, sweet scent sprinkled on his forehead, and, as if from the ends of the world, he heard a voice that sounded like his father's asking if he felt better. He opened his eyes and smiled faintly, and said nothing was the matter, but now his father insisted that he must go home to eat. . . . He walked towards the tall house with the nine stories, then a great shame came over him. Surely he had given in too early. He was already better, the air had revived him. No, he would *not* break his fast; he would while away a little time by walking, and then he would go back to the synagogue.

Israel Zangwill, *Dreamers of the Ghetto*, 1898

❧ *Augustus Hare, born in 1834 just as the High-Church Tractarian Movement began to make converts among the English middle and upper classes, was subjected to a lonely, austere childhood at the hands of various relatives and tutors, all with strongly religious inclinations and an apparently infinite capacity for joylessness. His 'mother' was not, in fact, his real mother;*

she, known to him as 'Italima' (a contraction of 'Italian mamma'), had been converted to Roman Catholicism and lived mainly abroad.

As an example of the severe discipline which was maintained with regard to me, I remember that one day when we went to visit the curate, a lady very innocently gave me a lollypop, which I ate. This crime was discovered when we came home by the smell of peppermint, and a large dose of rhubarb and soda was at once administered with a forcing-spoon, though I was in robust health at the time, to teach me to avoid such carnal indulgences as lollypops for the future. For two years, also, I was obliged to swallow a dose of rhubarb every morning and every evening because—according to old-fashioned ideas—it was supposed to 'strengthen the stomach!' I am sure it did me a great deal of harm, and had much to do with accounting for my after sickliness.

At a very early age I was made to go to church—once, which very soon grew into twice, on a Sunday. Uncle Julius's endless sermons were my detestation. I remember someone speaking of him to an old man in the parish, and being surprised by the statement that he was 'not a good winter parson,' which was explained to mean that he kept the people so long with his sermons, that they could not go home before dark.

I was not six years old before my mother—under the influence of the Maurices—began to follow out a code of penance with regard to me which was worthy of the ascetics of the desert. Hitherto I had never been allowed anything but roast-mutton and rice-pudding for dinner. Now all was changed. The most delicious puddings were talked of—*dilated* on—until I became, not greedy, but exceedingly curious about them. At length *le grand moment* arrived. They were put on the table before me, and then, just as I was going to eat some of them, they were snatched away, and I was told to get up and carry them off to some poor person in the village. I remember that, though I did not really in the least care about the dainties, I cared excessively about Lea's wrath at the fate of her nice puddings, of which, after all, I was most innocent. We used at this time to read a great deal about the saints, and the names of Polycarp, Athanasius, &c., became as familiar to me as those of our own household. Perhaps my mother, through Esther Maurice's influence, was just a little High Church at this time, and always fasted to a certain extent on Wednesdays and Fridays, on which days I was never allowed to eat butter or to have any pudding.

Augustus Hare, *The Story of My Life*, 1896, Volume I

❧ *Jane Eyre has fled from Thornfield Hall, the home of her former employer and fiancé, Mr Rochester, after an intruder has disrupted their marriage-service by revealing that her future husband's first wife is still living. Determined to see no more of Mr Rochester, she spends all her money on travelling by coach as far away from Thornfield as she can. Now penniless and on foot, she has reached a village.*

About two o'clock p.m. I entered the village. At the bottom of its one street there was a little shop with some cakes of bread in the window. I coveted a cake of bread. With that refreshment I could perhaps regain a degree of energy; without it, it would be difficult to proceed. The wish to have some strength and some vigour returned to me as soon as I was amongst my fellow-beings. I felt it would be degrading to faint with hunger on the causeway of a hamlet. Had I nothing about me I could exchange for one of these rolls? I considered. I had a small silk handkerchief tied round my throat; I had my gloves. I could hardly tell how men and women in extremities of destitution proceeded. I did not know whether either of these articles would be accepted: probably they would not; but I must try.

I entered the shop: a woman was there. Seeing a respectably-dressed person, a lady as she supposed, she came forward with civility. How could she serve me? I was seized with shame: my tongue would not utter the request I had prepared. I dared not offer her the half-worn gloves, the creased handkerchief: besides, I felt it would be absurd. I only begged permission to sit down a moment, as I was tired. Disappointed in the expectation of a customer, she coolly acceded to my request. She pointed to a seat; I sank into it. I felt sorely urged to weep; but conscious how unseasonable such a manifestation would be, I restrained it.

* * * * *

[*After further wandering, and calling at houses in fruitless attempts to find work as a servant, Jane is still hungry.*]

Once more I took off my handkerchief—once more I thought of the cakes of bread in the little shop. Oh, for but a crust! for but one mouthful to allay the pang of famine! Instinctively I turned my face again to the village; I found the shop again and I went in; and though others were there besides the woman I ventured the request—'Would she give me a roll for this handkerchief?'

She looked at me with evident suspicion: 'Nay, she never sold stuff i' that way.'

Almost desperate, I asked for half a cake; she again refused. 'How could she tell where I had got the handkerchief?' she asked.

'Would she take my gloves?'

'No! what could she do with them?'

Reader, it is not pleasant to dwell on these details. Some say there is enjoyment in looking back to painful experience past; but at this day I can scarcely bear to review the times to which I allude: the moral degradation, blent with the physical suffering, form too distressing a recollection ever to be willingly dwelt on. I blamed none of those who repulsed me. I felt it was what was to be expected, and what could not be helped: an ordinary beggar is frequently an object of suspicion; a well-dressed beggar inevitably so. To be sure, what I begged was employment; but whose business was it to provide me with employment? Not, certainly, that of persons who saw me then for the first time, and who knew nothing about my character. And as to the woman who would not take my handkerchief in exchange for her bread, why, she was right, if the offer appeared to her sinister or the exchange unprofitable. Let me condense now. I am sick of the subject.

A little before dark I passed a farmhouse, at the open door of which the farmer was sitting, eating his supper of bread and cheese. I stopped and said—

'Will you give me a piece of bread? for I am very hungry.' He cast on me a glance of surprise; but without answering, he cut a thick slice from his loaf, and gave it to me. I imagine he did not think I was a beggar, but only an eccentric sort of lady, who had taken a fancy to his brown loaf. As soon as I was out of sight of his house, I sat down and ate it.

I could not hope to get a lodging under a roof, and sought it in the wood I have before alluded to. But my night was wretched, my rest broken: the ground was damp, the air cold; besides, intruders passed near me more than once, and I had again and again to change my quarters: no sense of safety or tranquillity befriended me. Towards morning it rained; the whole of the following day was wet. Do not ask me, reader, to give a minute account of that day; as before, I sought work; as before, I was repulsed; as before, I starved; but once did food pass my lips. At the door of a cottage I saw a little girl about to throw a mess of cold porridge into a pig trough. 'Will you give me that?' I asked.

She stared at me. 'Mother!' she exclaimed, 'there is a woman wants me to give her these porridge.'

'Well, lass,' replied a voice within, 'give it her if she's a beggar. T'pig doesn't want it.'

The girl emptied the stiffened mould into my hands and I devoured it ravenously.

Charlotte Brontë, *Jane Eyre*, 1847

❧ Hunger (Sult), *which describes the ordeal of a starving writer surviving on the streets of Christiania (Oslo), was the Norwegian Knut Hamsun's first novel.*

I was terribly hungry, and I did not know what to do with myself and my shameless appetite. I writhed from side to side on the seat, and bowed my chest right down to my knees; I was almost distracted. When it got dark I jogged along to the Town Hall—God knows how I got there—and sat on the edge of the balustrade. I tore a pocket out of my coat and took to chewing it; not with any defined object, but with dour mien and unseeing eyes, staring straight into space. I could hear a group of little children playing around near me, and perceive, in an instinctive sort of way, some pedestrians pass me by; otherwise, I observed nothing.

All at once, it enters my head to go to one of the meat bazaars underneath me, and beg a piece of raw meat. I go straight along the balustrade to the other side of the bazaar buildings, and descend the steps. When I had nearly reached the stalls on the ground floor, I called up the archway leading to the stairs, and made a threatening backward gesture, as if I were talking to a dog up there, and boldly addressed the first butcher I met.

'Ah, will you be kind enough to give me a bone for my dog?' I said; 'only a bone. There needn't be anything on it; it's just to give him something to carry in his mouth.'

I got the bone, a capital little bone, on which there still remained a morsel of meat, and hid it under my coat. I thanked the man so heartily that he looked at me in amazement.

'Oh, no need of thanks,' said he.

'Oh yes; don't say that,' I mumbled; 'it is kindly done of you,' and I ascended the steps again.

My heart was throbbing violently in my breast. I sneaked into one of the passages, where the forges are, as far in as I could go, and stopped outside a dilapidated door leading to a back-yard. There was no light to be seen anywhere, only blessed darkness all around me; and I began to gnaw at the bone.

It had no taste; a rank smell of blood oozed from it, and I was forced to vomit almost immediately. I tried anew. If I could only keep it down it would, in spite of all, have some effect. It was simply a matter of forcing it to remain down there. But I vomited again. I grew wild, bit angrily into the meat, tore off a morsel, and gulped it down by sheer strength of will; and yet it was of no use. Just as soon as the little fragments of meat became warm in my stomach up they came again, worse luck. I clenched my hands in frenzy, burst into tears from sheer helplessness, and gnawed away as one possessed. I cried, so that the bone got wet and dirty with my tears, vomited, cursed and groaned again, cried as if my heart would break, and vomited anew. I consigned all the powers that be to the lowermost torture in the loudest voice.

Knut Hamsun, *Hunger*, 1888, translated from the Norwegian by George Egerton, 1899

❧ *Ivan Denisovich Shukhov begins his day as a prisoner in a Soviet Labour camp in the early 1950s. It is breakfast-time in the mess.*

The air was as thick as in a bath-house. An icy wave blew in through the door and met the steam rising from the skilly. The teams sat at tables or crowded the aisles in between, waiting for places to be freed. Shouting to each other through the crush, two or three men from each team carried bowls of skilly and porridge on wooden trays and tried to find room for them on the tables. Look at that bloody stiff-backed fool. He doesn't hear, he's jolted a tray. Splash, splash! You've a hand free, swipe him on the back of the neck. That's the way. Don't stand there blocking the aisle, looking for something to filch!

There at the table, before dipping his spoon in, a young man crossed himself. A West Ukrainian, that meant, and a new arrival too.

As for the Russians, they'd forgotten which hand to cross themselves with.

They sat in the cold mess-hall, most of them eating with their hats on, eating slowly, picking out putrid little fish from under leaves of boiled black cabbage and spitting the bones out on the table. When the bones formed a heap and it was the turn of another team, someone would sweep them off and they'd be trodden into a mush on the floor. But it was considered bad manners to spit the fishbones straight out on the floor.

* * * * *

The skilly was the same every day. Its composition depended on the kind of vegetable provided that winter. Nothing but salted carrots last year, which meant that from September to June the skilly was plain carrot. This year it was black cabbage. The most nourishing time of the year was June: then all vegetables came to an end and were replaced by groats. The worst time was July: then they shredded nettles into the pot.

The little fish were more bone than flesh; the flesh had been boiled off the bone and had disintegrated, leaving a few remnants on head and tail. Without neglecting a single fish-scale or particle of flesh on the brittle skeleton, Shukhov went on champing his teeth and sucking the bones, spitting the remains on the table. He ate everything—the gills, the tail, the eyes when they were still in their sockets but not when they'd been boiled out and floated in the bowl separately—great fish-eyes! Not then. The others laughed at him for that.

This morning Shukhov economised. As he hadn't returned to the hut he hadn't drawn his rations, so he ate his breakfast without bread. He'd eat the bread later. Might be even better that way.

After the skilly there was magara porridge. It had grown cold too, and had set into a solid lump. Shukhov broke it up into pieces. It wasn't only that the porridge was cold—it was tasteless when hot, and left you no sense of having filled your belly. Just grass, except that it was yellow, and looked like millet. They'd got the idea of serving it instead of cereals from the Chinese, it was said. When boiled, a bowlful of it weighed nearly a pound. Not much of a porridge but that was what it passed for.

* * * * *

[*Later, at work*] Shukhov . . . felt something pressing against the left side of his chest, near his heart. It was the edge of the hunk of bread in his little inner pocket—that half of his morning ration which he'd taken with him for dinner. He always brought the same amount with him to work and never touched it till dinner-time. But usually he ate the other half at breakfast. This morning he hadn't. But he realized he had gained nothing by economising: his belly called out to him to eat the bread at once, in the warmth. Dinner was five hours off—and time dragged.

And that nagging pain had now moved down to his legs, which felt quite weak. Oh, if he could only get to the stove!

He laid his mittens on his knees, unbuttoned his coat, untied the tapes of his face-cloth, stiff with cold, folded it several times over and put it in his knee-pocket. Then he reached for the hunk of bread, wrapped in a piece of clean cloth, and, holding the cloth at chest level so that not a crumb should fall to the ground, began to nibble and chew at the bread. The bread, which he had carried under two garments, had been warmed by his body. The frost hadn't caught it at all.

More than once during his life in the camps, Shukhov had recalled the way they used to eat in his village: whole saucepans of potatoes, pots of porridge, and, in the early days, big chunks of meat. And milk enough to split their guts. That wasn't the way to eat, he learned in camp. You had to eat with all your mind on the food—like now, nibbling the bread bit by bit, working the crumbs up into a paste with your tongue and sucking it into your cheeks. And how good it tasted, that soggy black bread! What had he eaten for eight, no, more than eight years? Next to nothing. But how much work had he done? Ah!

Alexander Solzhenitsyn, *One Day in the Life of Ivan Denisovich*, 1962, translated by Ralph Parker, 1963

INSTITUTIONAL FOOD

❧ *Extracts from the diary for 1728 of John Baptist Grano, a musician imprisoned in the Marshalsea for debt. In the early eighteenth century, debtors' prisons did not have the grimly deterrent character which they acquired later. Prisoners who could afford to do so were encouraged to send out for food and entertain one another, and were treated virtually as equals by the prison governor.*

Sunday Morn June the 2d got up about 6 ate some raw milk & Bread for Breakfast, by which time I came to know ye Names of the unfortunate People in ye Room with me as also their several Grievances; my chum or Bedfellows name is Blunt; ye other two Gentlemen are Mr Sandford and Blundel: my Chum originally was a

Clothier Mr Sandford a young Fellow, the son of a Rich Man but under the displeasure of his Father and Mr Blundel an unfortunate Jeweler. I joyn'd with the above Gentlemen for Dinner and had a few Mackerell, and some of ye usual Drink.

* * * * *

Sunday 11th of August . . . sent for a Fowl Bacon and Cabbidge for Dinner.

* * * * *

Friday Morn the 29th of November arose between 6 and 7. perform'd a Religious Exercise went up to Mac Donnell's drank Coffee for Breakfast, order'd a Fire in my own Room, came back into our Room where Mr Grange being so kind to offer me a Dram in a handsome manner (tho' not being accustom'd to it) I accepted the same: when my Fire was well lighted and the rubbidge taken out of the Room, I went in to it and order'd some boyl'd Onions for Dinner; waiting for which, I wrote and read; but before I settled to my Study my dear Governour sending to know if I would play at Shuttle-Cock with him I sent for a pair of new ones and had the pleasure of playing with Him being releiv'd now and then by Mr Blunt: 'twas about 4 a Clock before I went to Dinner and Mr Blunt did me the favour of eating with me; I had a Rabbit to entertain him with, but ate none of it my selfe.

John Baptist Grano, MS Diary, 1728–9

❧ *Two men, strangers to one another, the Swiss Rigaud and the Italian John Baptist Cavaletto, are in prison together in Marseilles. The jailer comes with his small daughter to bring their daily ration of food from outside, which they receive through the bars of their cell.*

'Look at the birds, my pretty.'

'Poor birds!' said the child.

The fair little face, touched with divine compassion, as it peeped shrinkingly through the grate, was like an angel's in the prison. John Baptist rose and moved towards it, as if it had a good attraction for him. The other bird remained as before, except for an impatient glance at the basket.

'Stay!' said the jailer, putting his little daughter on the outer ledge of the grate, 'we shall feed the birds. This big loaf is for Signor John

Baptist. We must break it to get it through into the cage. So, there's a tame bird to kiss the little hand! This sausage in a vine leaf is for Monsieur Rigaud. Again—this veal in savoury jelly is for Monsieur Rigaud. Again—these three little white loaves are for Monsieur Rigaud. Again, this cheese—again, this wine—again, this tobacco—all for Monsieur Rigaud. Lucky bird!'

The child put all these things between the bars into the soft, smooth, well-shaped hand, with evident dread—more than once drawing back her own and looking at the man with her fair brow roughened into an expression half of fright and half of anger. Whereas she had put the lump of coarse bread into the swart, scaled, knotted hands of John Baptist (who had scarcely as much nail on his eight fingers and two thumbs as would have made out one for Monsieur Rigaud), with ready confidence; and, when he kissed her hand, had herself passed it caressingly over his face. Monsieur Rigaud, indifferent to this distinction, propitiated the father by laughing and nodding at the daughter as often as she gave him anything; and, so soon as he had all his viands about him in convenient nooks of the ledge on which he rested, began to eat with an appetite.

When Monsieur Rigaud laughed, a change took place in his face, that was more remarkable than prepossessing. His moustache went up under his nose, and his nose came down over his moustache, in a very sinister and cruel manner.

'There!' said the jailer, turning his basket upside down to beat the crumbs out, 'I have expended all the money I received; here is the note of it, and *that's* a thing accomplished. Monsieur Rigaud, as I expected yesterday, the President will look for the pleasure of your society at an hour after mid-day, today.'

'To try me, eh?' said Rigaud, pausing, knife in hand and morsel in mouth.

'You have said it. To try you.'

'There is no news for me?' asked John Baptist, who had begun contentedly to munch his bread.

The jailer shrugged his shoulders.

* * * * *

[*The jailer and his daughter depart, the child singing the* Marseillaise.]

Monsieur Rigaud, finding the listening John Baptist in his way before the echoes had ceased (even the echoes were the weaker for imprisonment, and seemed to lag) reminded him with a push of his foot that he had better resume his own darker place. The little man sat down again upon the pavement, and placing three hunks of coarse bread before himself, and falling to upon a fourth, began contentedly to work his way through them, as if to clear them off were a sort of game.

Perhaps he glanced at the Lyons sausage, and perhaps he glanced at the veal in savoury jelly, but they were not there long, to make his mouth water; Monsieur Rigaud soon dispatched them, in spite of the president and tribunal, and proceeded to suck his fingers as clean as he could, and to wipe them on his vine leaves. Then, as he paused in his drink to contemplate his fellow-prisoner, his moustache went up, and his nose came down.

'How do you find the bread?'

'A little dry, but I have my old sauce here,' returned John Baptist, holding up his knife.

'How sauce?'

'I can cut my bread so—like a melon. Or so—like an omelette. Or so—like a fried fish. Or so—like Lyons sausage,' said John Baptist, demonstrating the various cuts on the bread he held, and soberly chewing what he had in his mouth.

'Here!' cried Monsieur Rigaud. 'You may drink. You may finish this.'

It was no great gift, for there was mighty little wine left; but Signor Cavaletto, jumping to his feet, received the bottle gratefully, turned it upside down at his mouth, and smacked his lips.

Dickens, *Little Dorrit*, Book I

❧ *The essayist Charles Lamb (1775–1835) was born in Crown Office Row in the Inner Temple, London, and was a schoolboy at Christ's Hospital, in Newgate Street north of St Paul's Cathedral. At school Lamb befriended the poet Samuel Taylor Coleridge, two or three years his senior, who had been sent there as an unwilling boarder after the death of his father, the Vicar of Ottery St Mary, Devon. In this essay, written in 1820, Lamb projects himself into the person of Coleridge, a 'poor friendless boy' from 'far away', and tries to depict the extent of his sufferings in comparison with his own.*

In Mr Lamb's *Works*, published a year or two since, I find a magnificent eulogy on my old school, such as it was, or now appears to him to have been, between the years 1782 and 1789.

* * * * *

I remember L. at school; and can well recollect that he had some peculiar advantages, which I and others of his schoolfellows had not. His friends lived in town, and were near at hand; and he had the privilege of going to see them, almost as often as he wished, through some invidious distinction, which was denied to us. . . . He had his tea and hot rolls in a morning, while we were battening upon our quarter of a penny loaf—our *crug*—moistened with attenuated small beer, in wooden piggins, smacking of the pitched leathern jack it was poured from. Our Monday's milk porritch, blue and tasteless, and the pease soup of Saturday, coarse and choking, were enriched for him with a slice of 'extraordinary bread and butter', from the hot-loaf of the Temple. The Wednesday's mess of millet, somewhat less repugnant (we had three banyan to four meat days in the week)—was endeared to his palate with a lump of double-refined, and a smack of ginger (to make it go down the more glibly) or the fragrant cinnamon. In lieu of our *half-pickled* Sundays, or *quite fresh* boiled beef on Thursdays (strong as *caro equina*), with detestable marigolds floating in the pail to poison the broth—our scanty mutton scrags on Fridays—and rather more savoury, but grudging, portions of the same flesh, rotten-roasted or rare, on the Tuesdays (the only dish which excited our appetites, and disappointed our stomachs, in almost equal proportion)—he had his hot plate of roast veal, or the more tempting griskin (exotics unknown to our palates), cooked in the paternal kitchen (a great thing), and brought him daily by his maid or aunt! I remember the good old relative (in whom love forbade pride) squatting down upon some odd stone in a by-nook of the cloisters, disclosing the viands (of higher regale than those cates which the ravens ministered to the Tishbite); and the contending passions of L. at the unfolding. There was love for the bringer; shame for the thing brought, and the manner of its bringing; sympathy for those who were too many to share in it; and, at top of all, hunger (eldest, strongest of the passions!) predominant, breaking down the stony fences of shame, and awkwardness, and a troubling over-consciousness.

Lamb, 'Christ's Hospital Five-and-Thirty Years Ago', *Essays of Elia*

Small beer: a weak brew considered suitable for invalids or children, in this case further weakened by watering down; *hot-loaf of the Temple*: Lamb's father was clerk for nearly forty years to Samuel Salt, a bencher at the Inner Temple from 1782 and treasurer there from 1788 until his death in 1792; *banyan* (*banian*): a Hindu (hence, a vegetarian); *double refined*: sugar (then an expensive delicacy, treated like a spice); *caro equina*: horse-flesh; *griskin*: 'the lean part of the loin of a bacon pig' (*OED*); *Tishbite*: the prophet Elijah, whom God ordered to hide himself by the brook Cherith, where ravens fed him twice daily on bread and flesh (1 Kings 17: 2–6).

❧ *Jane Eyre is experiencing her first breakfast as a pupil at Lowood, a severe, almost sadistically austere boarding-school in the north of England. The reference to 'rotten potatoes' in this passage is painfully topical.* Jane Eyre *was written at the time of the Irish potato famine, in the 'hungry forties' when not only English boarding-school children but many agricultural labourers and their families lived in permanent want.*

The refectory was a great, low-ceiled, gloomy room; on two long tables smoked basins of something hot, which, however, to my dismay, sent forth an odour far from inviting. I saw a universal manifestation of discontent when the fumes of the repast met the nostrils of those destined to swallow it: from the van of the procession, the tall girls of the first class, rose the whispered words, 'Disgusting! The porridge is burned again!'

'Silence!' ejaculated a voice; not that of Miss Miller, but one of the upper teachers, a little and dark personage, smartly dressed, but of somewhat nervous aspect, who installed herself at the top of our table, while a more buxom lady presided at the other. . . . A long grace was said, and a hymn sung; then a servant brought in some tea for the teachers, and the meal began.

Ravenous, and now very faint, I devoured a spoonful or two of my portion without thinking of its taste; but, the first edge of hunger blunted, I perceived I had got in hand a nauseous mess: burned porridge is almost as bad as rotten potatoes; famine itself soon sickens over it. The spoons were moved slowly; I saw each girl taste her food and try to swallow it; but in most cases the effort was soon relinquished. Breakfast was over, and none had breakfasted. Thanks being returned for what we had not got, and a second hymn chanted, the refectory was evacuated for the school-room. I was one of the last to go out, and in passing the tables, I saw one teacher take a basin of the porridge and taste it; she looked at the others; all their countenances expressed displeasure, and one of them, the stout one, whispered, 'Abominable stuff! How shameful!'

Brontë, *Jane Eyre*

❧ *Augustus Hare was removed from his public school, Harrow, at the age of 14 because of supposedly delicate health, and was sent to board with a clerical tutor at Lyncombe, near Bath. Here, although persistently underfed and under-occupied, he remained for over two years.*

My only consolation, and that a most dismal and solitary one, was in the long expeditions which I made; but I look back upon those as times of acute suffering from poverty and *hunger*, as I never had any allowance and was always sent back to my tutor's with only five shillings in my pocket. Thus, though I walked sometimes twenty-four miles in a day, and was out for eight or ten hours, I never had a penny with which to buy even a piece of bread, and many a time sank down by the wayside from the faintness of sheer starvation, often most gratefully accepting some of their food from the common working-people I met. If I went out with my companions, the utmost mortification was added to the actual suffering of hunger, because, when they went into the village inns to have a good well-earned luncheon, I was always left starving outside, as I never had the means of paying for any food. I believe my companions were very sorry for me, but they never allowed their pity to be any expense to them, and then 'È meglio essere odiato che compatito' [it is better to be hated than pitied] is an Italian proverb which means a great deal, especially to a boy. After a time, too, the food at Lyncombe itself became extremely stinted and of the very worst quality—a suet dumpling filled with coarse odds and ends of meat being our dinner on at least five days out of the seven, which of course was very bad for an extremely delicate rapidly-growing youth—and, if I was ill from want of food, which was frequently the case, I was given nothing but rice.

* * * * *

[In 1850] I . . . wrote to my mother—

'We are in the last extremities as regards food. I will give you a perfectly correct account of the last few days. Saturday dinner, boiled beef. Sunday, breakfast, ditto cold with bread and butter. Luncheon a very small portion of ditto with dry bread and part of the rind of a decayed cheese. Dinner, a little of ditto with a doughy plum-tart. Monday, breakfast, ditto with two very small square pieces of bread. Luncheon, ditto with bread and . . . butter. Dinner, ditto and a rice-pudding. Tuesday, breakfast, ditto; luncheon, a very small fragment of ditto and one potato apiece doled round. Dinner, ditto. Wednesday, breakfast, scraps of ditto; luncheon, fat and parings of ditto. We all have to sit and do our work now by the light of a single bed-candle. Oh! I am more thankful every day that you will at last let me leave this place.'

Hare, *Story of My Life*, Volume I

❧ *The novelist Henry James (1843–1916) was born and brought up in New York. With his elder brother William, the future philosopher, he attended a succession of small private day-schools in the Greenwich Village area. This extract from James's biography of William (in fact a joint biography and autobiography) describes their third school.*

At 'Forest's', or in other words at the more numerous establishment of Messrs Forest and Quackenboss, where we spent the winter of 1854, reality, in the form of multitudinous mates . . . swarmed about me increasingly: at Forest's the prolonged roll-call in the morning, as I sit in the vast bright crowded smelly smoky room, in which rusty black stove-shafts were the nearest hint of architecture, bristles with names, Hoes and Havemeyers, Stokeses, Phelpses, Colgates and others, of a subsequently great New York salience. It was sociable and gay, it was sordidly spectacular, one was then, by an inch or two, a bigger boy.

* * * * *

Fresher even than yesterday, fadelessly fresh for me at this hour, is the cutting remark . . . of another boy . . . : 'Oh, oh, oh, I should think you'd be too proud—!' So fine was the force of the suggestion that I have never in all the years made certain returns upon my spirit without again feeling the pang from the cool little voice of the Fourteenth Street yard. Such was the moral exercise it at least allowed us room for. It also allowed us room, to be just, for an inordinate consumption of hot waffles retailed by a benevolent black 'auntie' who presided, with her husband's aid as I remember, at a portable stove set up in a passage or recess opening from the court; to which we flocked and pushed, in a merciless squeeze, with all our coppers, and the products of which, the oblong farinaceous compound, faintly yet richly brown, stamped and smoking, not crisp nor brittle, but softly absorbent of the syrup dabbed upon it for a finish, revealed to me for a long time, even for a very long time supposed, the highest pleasure of sense. We stamped about, we freely conversed, we ate sticky waffles by the hundred—I recall no worse acts of violence unless I count as such our intermissional rushes to Pynsent's of the Avenue, a few doors off, in the particular interest of a confection that ran the waffle close, as the phrase is, for popularity, while even surpassing it for stickiness. Pynsent's was higher up in the row in which Forest's had its front—other and dearer names have dropped from me, but Pynsent's adheres with all the force of the strong saccharine principle. This principle, at its highest, we conceived, was embodied in small amber-coloured mounds of chopped cocoanut or whatever other substance, if a finer there be; profusely, lusciously endued and distributed on small tin trays in the manner of haycocks in a field. We acquired, we appropriated, we transported, we enjoyed them, they fairly formed perhaps, after all, our highest enjoyment; but with consequences to our pockets—and I speak of those other than financial, with an intimacy, a reciprocity of contact at any, or every, personal point, that I lose myself in the thought of.

Henry James, *A Small Boy and Others*, 1913

SHERBORNE IN THE 1880S

By the time I was in Mr King's form Littleton and I had a study of our own. . . . We bought a rubber pipe and a little iron tripod; and with this apparatus, by the aid of a gas jet, we used to heat up Epp's, or Van Houten's, cocoa; and sweeten it with condensed milk out of a tin. Every night as we worked at preparing the next day's lesson we used to enjoy cups of cocoa for our refreshment; and as a rule we had a pot of home-made rhubarb jam to go with it, which we used to spread with a spoon upon Osborne biscuits. Hampers from Montacute would arrive in the rainy autumn term, full of walnuts from the tree in our field and a variety of apples from our orchard. These edibles with an occasional sponge-cake, we kept in our study, where their sweet fragrance sustained us; and we shared them most scrupulously; not forgetting, when we used to meet the melancholy figure of the little Theodore, who was by this time in the Prep., waiting for us at the end of the lane, where later they built Richmond Villa, to fill our pockets for his benefit.

I recollect perfectly how one night after some quarrel with Littleton, and when, too, I was burning with an erotic fever that none of the treasures in my gold and ebony chest could assuage, I tried to overcome the two most formidable of human passions—anger and desire—by abandonment to the vice of pure gluttony. In that one night I ravenously devoured a whole sponge cake.

Powys, *Autobiography*

Littleton, Theodore (*the future novelist T. F. Powys*): two of the writer's younger brothers. In defiance of the prevailing public-school cult of undemonstrative manliness, the Powys brothers were openly home-loving and affectionate towards one another.

❧ *Evelyn Waugh (1903–66) was a schoolboy at Lancing College, a high Anglican public school in Sussex. The end of rationing, some time after the Armistice of November 1918, brought to an end a period of near-starvation for pupils in boarding-schools.*

The food in Hall would have provoked mutiny in a mid-Victorian poor-house and it grew steadily worse until the end of the War. In happier times it was supplemented from the Grub Shop and by hampers from home. In 1917–18 it afforded a bare subsistence without any pretence to please. There was, I recall, a horrible substance named 'Honey-Sugar', a sort of sweetened cheeselike matter, the by-product of heaven knows what chemical ingenuity, which appeared twice a week at supper in cardboard pots. There was milkless cocoa and small pots of margarine and limitless bread. At midday dinner there was usually a stew consisting chiefly of swedes and potatoes in their skins. Perhaps the table manners were an unconscious protest against this prison diet. Clean cloths were laid on Sunday; by Tuesday they were filthy. Boys from perfectly civilised homes seemed to glory in savagery and it was this more than the wretched stuff they slopped about which disgusted me. Exceptionally accomplished boys were able to flick pats of margarine from their knives to the high oak rafters overhead, where they stuck all the winter until released by the summer heat they fell, plomp, on to the tables below.

* * * * *

[In 1919] gluttony, the master-passion of boyhood, reasserted its sway. No subsequent experiences of the *haute cuisine* or the vintage can rival the gross, innocent delight in the commonplace confections that now began to appear. The Grub Shop, which hitherto had offered an irregular and meagre supply of fruit and oat-cakes, was now replete with 'whipped-cream walnuts', 'cream slices', ices and every kind of bun and chocolate. Our appetites were bounded only by our purses. Most Lower boys had £1 a term pocket-money and it was soon exhausted. While it lasted, we gorged. For two-thirds of the school the 'Grubber' and the 'play-boxes' where we kept food sent from home were the only sources of gourmandising. For the upper third of the school there was a variety of entertainment. The lowest was the 'settle-tea' on Sundays for the seniors of the House Room. These were provided by each member in turn, with ostentatious rivalry. They began with crumpets, eight or more a head, dripping with butter. From there we swiftly passed to cake, pastry, and, in season, strawberries and cream, until at six we tottered into chapel taut and stupefied with eating. The House-captains had tea daily in their own room served by fags; as became their dignity they were more moderate. Between these were 'the pits', the half-dozen or so boys with private studies. There we had some pretensions to be epicures. Little pots of *foie gras* and caviar occasionally came from London and we were as nice in the brewing of tea as a circle of maiden ladies. There was then a shop on the north side of Piccadilly which offered a dozen or more varieties of China tea. We subscribed for quarter-pound packets and tasted them with reverence, discoursing on their qualities as later we were to talk of wine. We were scrupulous about filling the pot with steam and allowing the leaf to open before adding boiling water. We eschewed milk and sugar. But when the rites had been performed and the delicacies consumed we fell back on stuffing ourselves with the same fare as the Settle. Fullness was all.

Evelyn Waugh, *A Little Learning: The First Volume of an Autobiography*, 1964

The Settle: 'the top eight boys in the House Room who enjoyed certain privileges and authority, above whom were "the pits", and the six House Captains'. (Waugh's remarks refer only to his particular house, Head's, within the school.)

Christ Church, Oxford, the grandest of the Oxford colleges since the late eighteenth or early nineteenth century, received its share of complaints from undergraduates about the quality of the food. Here are some of the letters addressed to the Steward in 1888–90.

From T. Clarence E. Goff, 28 November 1888.

Dear Sir,

I am very sorry that you were not in Hall tonight so that I could have sent you up a plate of soup, which was given to me, so that you could have seen a specimen of the sort of soup we have in Hall. It was called 'Cressy Soup,' & I should say the ingredients were poison, because up to now 10.30 P.M. although I had only a mouthful I have failed to eradicate the taste yet!

I have to complain also of the Potatoes which are simply old ones warmed up & boiled in fat so one of the servants told me. I do really think sir that it is part of your duty to look into these things & see that we don't have such things served up.

Annotated: not true: very difficult this year to get good potatoes.

From Mr Fox-Tarratt, 20 January 1889.
Mr Fox-Tarratt

Begs to mention that he received a partridge the other [evening] so high as to be absolutely uneatable, and hopes that this will not happen again.

From G. Gathorne-Hardy, 23 January 1889.
Sir,

I wish to mention that I have twice been sent rhubarb tart when I have ordered apple, as I have a particular objection to Rhubarb tart I hope it may not occur again. I also wish to mention that the food in Hall is not what it should be.

From B. Chinnery-Haldane, 3 June 1890.
Dear Sir,

I am sorry to have to make a serious complaint about the butter, with which I am supplied from the Buttery. There is no other word for it but '*Rancid*'. The butter has been bad as often as good nearly the whole of this term, and my only reason for not complaining before now was, that I knew that numerous complaints had been made to you. . . . Yesterday the butter I had for my lunch was simply 'rancid', and had I had any strangers lunching with me I should have been ashamed to put such butter before them.

From W. G. Mackintosh, [*November 1890*].
Dear Sir,

I am sorry to have to trouble you with a complaint of the porridge, but it has been so bad for the last week or more, that I am forced to do so. They *never* send really good porridge out from the Kitchen but lately it has not been fit for human food.

As far as I can see, the meal has been reduced to a sickly white pulp by over boiling or steaping.

In my opinion it is always overdone but I am only now complaining of the gruel which has lately been sent out under the name of porridge.

Annotated: asked him to dine Nov 14 90. / Had some porridge made differently. That apparently satisfied the complainant.

Steward's Memorandum Book, 1888–95, Christ Church, Oxford

❧ *Virginia Woolf (1882–1941), who had not herself attended university, visited Girton College, Cambridge in the autumn term of 1928. On 27 October, she wrote in her diary: 'Starved but valiant young women—that's my impression. Intelligent, eager, poor, and destined to become schoolmistresses in shoals. I blandly told them to drink wine and have a room of their own.' Virginia Woolf's description of the peculiarly female austerities of Girton might well have been written of any of the seven or eight women's colleges at Oxford and Cambridge during the following fifty years.*

Here was my soup. Dinner was being served in the great dining-hall. . . . It was an evening in October. Everybody was assembled in the big dining-room. Dinner was ready. Here was the soup. It was a plain gravy soup. There was nothing to stir the fancy in that. One could have seen through the transparent liquid any pattern that there might have been on the plate itself. But there was no pattern. The plate was plain. Next came beef with its attendant greens and potatoes—a homely trinity, suggesting the rumps of cattle in a muddy market, and sprouts curled and yellowed at the edge, and bargaining and cheapening, and women with string bags on a Monday morning. There was no reason to complain of human nature's daily food, seeing that the supply was sufficient and coal-miners doubtless were sitting down to less. Prunes and custard followed. And if anyone complains that prunes, even when mitigated by custard, are an uncharitable vegetable (fruit they are not), stringy as a miser's heart and exuding a fluid such as might run in misers' veins who have denied themselves wine and warmth for eighty years and yet not given to the poor, he should reflect that there are people whose charity embraces even the prune. Biscuits and cheese came next, and here the water-jug was liberally passed round, for it is the nature of biscuits to be dry, and these were biscuits to the core. That was all. The meal was over. Everybody scraped their chairs back; the swing doors swung violently to and fro; soon the hall was emptied of every sign of food and made ready no doubt for breakfast next morning. Down corridors and up staircases the women of England went banging and singing. . . . Happily my friend, who taught science, had a cupboard where there was a squat bottle and little glasses—(but there should have been sole and partridge to begin with)—so that we were able to draw up to the fire and repair some of the damage of the day's living.

Virginia Woolf, *A Room of One's Own*, 1931

UNPLEASANT FOOD

❧ *Abraham Pryme, or de la Pryme, was a member of an Anglo-Flemish family living in south-eastern Yorkshire. He began his diary as an adolescent in the 1680s, and filled it mainly with local or national news culled at second- or third-hand. Louth, in Lincolnshire, between the Wolds and an area of coastal marshland, was not far from Pryme's home in the Yorkshire Levels, where Commissioners of Drainage, or Sewers, regularly oversaw the drainage of flooded land. Tansy was a savoury custard, usually flavoured with the bitter herb tansy* (tanacetum vulgare) *and eaten for cleansing purposes in spring.*

[*April 1697.*]

There was a commission [of drainage] lately at Louth; amongst other dishes of meat that was brought up, there was towards the latter end thereof a tansey. After they had eaten of this tansey all the commissioners fell sick. Immediately some vomited, some purged, some fainted, others were so gryp'd they did not know what to do, yet put as good face on everything as they could. After dinner their servants were call'd in, and being asked what sort of liquor they had drunk, and what sort of meat they had eaten, they told them the very same that came from their table, only they did not eat any tansey because there was meat enough besides, and they sayd they were very well. Upon this they sent for their hostess up, and asked her where shee got so much tansey grass this cold and backward year, to make her tansey so green as it was. Shee told them shee knew what they meant, and begging their pardons, told them that truly shee could not get any [thing] to make her tansey green, and that therefore, going into the garden, shee got a great handful of daffadilly leaves and stalks, and having brused them and squeezd the juse out, it was with them that shee had coloured it green. So they concluded that it was them alone that had wrought such effects upon them.

The Diary of Abraham de la Pryme, The Yorkshire Antiquary, Surtees Society, 1870

THE BOARDING-SCHOOL MISS

To Farmer *Moss*, in Langar Vale, came down,
His only Daughter, from her school in town;
A tender, timid maid! who knew not how

To pass a pig-sty, or to face a cow:
Smiling she came, with petty talents graced,
A fair complexion, and a slender waist.

Used to spare meals, disposed in manner pure,
Her father's kitchen she could ill endure:
Where by the steaming beef he hungry sat,
And laid at once a pound upon his plate;
Hot from the field, her eager brother seized
An equal part, and hunger's rage appeased;
The air surcharg'd with moisture, flagg'd around,
And the offended damsel sigh'd and frown'd;
The swelling fat in lumps conglomerate laid,
And fancy's sickness seized the loathing maid:
But when the men beside their stations took,
The maidens with them, and with these the cook;
When one huge wooden bowl before them stood,
Fill'd with huge balls of farinaceous food;
With bacon, mass saline, where never lean
Beneath the brown and bristly rind was seen;
When from a single horn the party drew
Their copious draughts of heavy ale and new;
When the coarse cloth she saw, with many a stain
Soil'd by rude hinds who cut and came again—
She could not breathe; but with a heavy sigh,
Rein'd the fair neck, and shut th'offended eye;
She minced the sanguine flesh in frustums fine
And wonder'd much to see the creatures dine.

George Crabbe, *The Widow's Tale*, 1812

❧ *It is Jubilee Day in the summer of 1887, fifty years after Queen Victoria's accession. The town of Bursley is celebrating in the traditional way with an ox-roast in the market-place. Edwin Clayhanger and his employee, Big James, leave their printing-office to inspect the scene.*

No breeze moved, and the heat was tremendous. And there at the foot of the Town Hall tower, and in its scanty shadow, a dead ox, slung by its legs from an iron construction, was frizzling over a great primitive fire. The vast flanks of the animal, all rich yellows and browns, streamed with grease, some of which fell noisily on the almost invisible flames, while the rest was ingeniously caught in a system of runnels. The spectacle was obscene, nauseating to the eye, the nose, and the ear, and it powerfully recalled to Edwin the legends of the Spanish Inquisition. He speculated whether he would ever be able to touch beef again. Above the tortured and insulted corpse the air quivered in huge waves. Mr Doy, the leading butcher of Bursley, and now chief executioner, regarded with anxiety the operation which had been entrusted to him, and occasionally gave instructions to a myrmidon. Round about stood a few privileged persons, whom pride helped to bear the double heat; and farther off on the pavements, a thin scattered crowd. The sublime spectacle of an ox roasted whole had not helped to keep the townsmen in the town. Even the sages who had conceived and commanded this peculiar solemnity for celebrating the Jubilee of a Queen and Empress had not stayed in the borough to see it enacted, though some of them were to return in time to watch the devouring of the animal by the aged poor at a ceremonial feast in the evening.

'It's a grand sight!' said Big James, with simple enthusiasm. 'A grand sight! Real old English! And I wish her well!' He meant the Queen and Empress. Then suddenly, in a different tone, sniffing the air, 'I doubt it's turned! I'll step across and ask Mr Doy.'

He stepped across, and came back with the news that the greater portion of the ox, despite every precaution, had in fact very annoyingly 'turned', and that the remainder of the carcase was in serious danger.

'What'll the old people say?' he demanded sadly. 'But it's a grand sight, turned or not!'

Edwin stared and stared, in a sort of sinister fascination. He thought that he might stare for ever. At length, after ages of ennui, he loosed himself from the spell with an effort. . . . The odour of the shrivelled ox remained with him; it was in his nostrils for several days.

Bennett, *Clayhanger*

❧ *Leopold Bloom is wandering through Dublin on the morning of 16 June, 1904.*

His heart astir he pushed in the door of the Burton restaurant. Stink gripped his trembling breath: pungent meatjuice, slop of greens. See the animals feed.

Men, men, men.

Perched on high stools by the bar, hats shoved back, at the tables calling for more bread no charge, swilling, wolfing gobfuls of sloppy food, their eyes bulging, wiping wetted moustaches. A pallid suetfaced young man polished his tumbler knife fork and spoon with his napkin. New set of microbes. A man with an infant's saucestained napkin tucked round him shovelled gurgling soup down his gullet. A man spitting back on his plate: halfmasticated gristle: no teeth to chewchewchew it. Chump chop from the grill. Bolting to get it over. Sad booser's eyes. Bitten off more than he can chew. Am I like that? See ourselves as others see us. Hungry man is an angry man. Working tooth and jaw. Don't! O! A bone! That last pagan king of Ireland Cormac in the schoolpoem choked himself at Sletty southward of the Boyne. Wonder what he was eating. Something galoptious. Saint Patrick converted him to Christianity. Couldn't swallow it all however.

—Roast beef and cabbage.

—One stew.

Smells of men. His gorge rose. Spaton sawdust, sweetish warmish cigarette smoke, reek of plug, spilt beer, men's beery piss, the stale of ferment.

Couldn't eat a morsel here. Fellow sharpening knife and fork, to eat all before him, old chap picking his tootles. Slight spasm, full, chewing the cud. Before and after. Grace after meals. Look on this picture then on that. Scoffing up stew-gravy with sopping sippets of bread. Lick it off the plate, man! Get out of this.

He gazed round the stooled and tabled eaters, tightening the wings of his nose.

—Two stouts here.

—One corned and cabbage.

That fellow ramming a knifeful of cabbage down as if his life depended on it. Good stroke. Give me the fidgets to look. Safer to eat from his three hands. Tear it limb from limb. Second nature to him. Born with a silver knife in his mouth. That's witty, I think. Or no. Silver means born rich. Born with a knife. But then the allusion is lost.

An illgirt server gathered sticky clattering plates. Rock, the bailiff, standing at the bar blew the foamy crown from his tankard. Well up: it splashed yellow near his boot. A diner, knife and fork upright, elbows on the table, ready for a second helping stared towards the foodlift across his stained square of newspaper. Other chap telling him something with his mouth full. Sympathetic listener. Table talk. I munched hum un thu Unchster Bunk un Munchday. Ha? Did you, faith?

Mr Bloom raised two fingers doubtfully to his lips. His eyes said.

—Not here. Don't see him.

Out. I hate dirty eaters.

He backed towards the door. Get a light snack in Davy Byrne's Stopgap. Keep me going. Had a good breakfast.

—Roast and mashed here.

—Pint of stout.

Every fellow for his own, tooth and nail. Gulp. Grub. Gulp. Gobstuff.

He came out into clearer air and turned back towards Grafton street. Eat or be eaten. Kill! Kill!

Joyce, *Ulysses*

❧ *George Orwell shared lodgings above a tripe-shop in Wigan while investigating working-class life in a run-down industrial area during the Depression of the 1930s.*

The shop was a narrow, cold sort of room. Oh the outside of the window a few white letters, relics of ancient chocolate advertisements, were scattered like stars. Inside there was a slab on which lay the great white folds of tripe, and the grey flocculent stuff known as 'black tripe', and the ghostly translucent feet of pigs, ready boiled. It was the ordinary, 'tripe and pea' shop, and not much else was stocked except bread, cigarettes and tinned stuff. . . . I heard dreadful stories from the other lodgers about the place where the tripe was kept. Blackbeetles were said to swarm there. I do not know how often fresh consignments of tripe were ordered, but it was at long intervals, for Mrs Brooker used to date events by it. 'Let me see now, I've had in three lots of froze (frozen tripe) since that happened,' etc., etc. We lodgers were never given tripe to eat. At the time I imagined that this was because tripe was too expensive; I have since thought that it was merely because we knew too much about it. The Brookers never ate tripe themselves, I noticed.

* * * * *

The meals at the Brookers' house were uniformly disgusting. For breakfast you got two rashers of bacon and a pale fried egg, and bread-and-butter which had often been cut overnight and always had thumb-marks on it. However tactfully I tried, I could never induce Mr Brooker to let me cut my own bread-and-butter; he *would* hand it to me slice by slice, each slice gripped firmly under that broad black thumb. For dinner there were generally those threepenny steak puddings which are sold ready-made in tins—these were part of the stock of the shop, I think—and boiled potatoes and rice pudding. For tea there was more bread-and-butter and frayed-looking sweet cakes which were probably bought as 'stales' from the baker. For supper there was the pale flabby Lancashire cheese and biscuits. The Brookers never called these biscuits biscuits. They always referred to them reverentially as 'cream crackers'—'Have another cream cracker, Mr Reilly. You'll like a cream cracker with your cheese'—thus glozing over the fact that there was only cheese for supper. Several bottles of Worcester Sauce and a half-full jar of marmalade lived permanently on the table. It was usual to souse everything, even a piece of cheese, with Worcester Sauce, but I never saw anyone brave the marmalade jar, which was an unspeakable mass of stickiness and dust.

Orwell, *The Road to Wigan Pier*

VI

FOOD AND THE EMOTIONS

FOOD AND DISTRESS

The suicide of Vatel, steward of the household to the Prince de Condé at Chantilly, during a visit by Louis XIV and his entourage, is well known for its circumstances of tragic futility. Here it is recounted by Mme de Sévigné in a letter to her daughter.

To Madame de Grignan, Paris, Sunday, 26 April [*1671*].

It is Sunday 26 April; this letter will not go until Wednesday. It is not a letter, however, so much as an account, which Moreuil has just given me for your sake, of what happened to Vatel at Chantilly. I wrote on Friday telling you that he had stabbed himself: here are the details of the business. The King arrived on Thursday evening. Everything went as smoothly as possible: the hunt, the lanterns, the moonlight, the promenade, the picnic in a jonquil-carpeted glade. At supper, several tables did not get any roast meat because a number of unexpected guests had turned up. Vatel was put out by this, and repeated several times: 'My reputation is ruined. I shall never cope with this disgrace.' He said to Gourville, 'I feel giddy; I haven't slept for twelve nights. Help me to give orders.' Gourville comforted him as best he could, but he kept on fretting about the roast meat, which after all hadn't failed to turn up on the King's table but only on those of the twenty-fifths. Gourville told Monsieur le Prince about it, and Monsieur le Prince went to him in his room and said 'Vatel, everything's all right; the King's supper went superbly.' Vatel said to him: 'Monseigneur, your kindness is too much for me. I know that there were two tables without any roast meat.—Not at all, said Monsieur le Prince, don't get worked up about it; everything was fine.'

That night the firework display came to nothing; a cloud obscured it; it had cost 16,000 francs. At four in the morning Vatel went out and found everything still shut up for the night. He met a small purveyor who was bringing him just two loads of fresh fish. 'Is that all there is?' Vatel asked. The man said 'Yes, Sir,' not realizing that Vatel had sent to all the seaports for fish. Vatel waited for a bit, but no other purveyors came. His head felt feverish, and he began to believe that no more fresh fish would come. Meeting Gourville, he said 'Sir, I shall not be able to live down this disgrace. I shall lose my reputation and self-respect.' Gourville laughed at him. Then Vatel went up to his room, wedged his sword against the door and ran it through his own heart; but he did so only at the third attempt, the first two failing to kill him. He fell dead. Meanwhile loads of fish were arriving from all directions. Messengers went out to alert Vatel so that he could distribute the fish; tried his room, knocked, broke open the door, found him drowned in his own blood, and ran to tell Monsieur le Prince, who was desolated. Monsieur le Duc [de Condé] was in tears, since he had depended entirely on Vatel to organize his Burgundian expedition. Monsieur le Prince broke the news to the King very sadly. . . . The King said that he had put off returning to Chantilly for five years, since he understood the amount of fuss that this generated. He told Monsieur le Prince that he required only two tables and that he should not bother himself about anything else. He swore that he would not allow Monsieur le Prince to go to such trouble again; but this was too late for poor Vatel. Meanwhile Gourville tried to make up for the loss of Vatel; the guests dined very well, took a collation, supper and a promenade, played and went hunting; everything was enchanted and perfumed with jonquils. Yesterday, Saturday, the same thing happened again; and in the evening the King went to Liancourt, where he had ordered a *medianoche*. He will remain there today. This is what Moreuil told me to pass on to you; and that is all that I know.

Selected Letters of Madame de Sévigné, edited by A. T. Baker, 1918

Moreuil: first gentleman of the household to the Prince de Condé; *Gourville*: a prominent member of the Prince de Condé's household; *Monsieur le Duc*: son of the Prince de Condé, about to preside over a meeting of the States in place of his father; *medianoche*: a midnight meal at the end of a fast-day.

❧ *Thomas Turner lost his first wife, Peggy, in 1761.*

Sun. 21 June [1761].

My friend Mr Tucker and my father[-in-law] Slater came to see us in the forenoon and both dined with us on a piece of veal boiled, a piece of pork, a gooseberry pudding and spinach. They both went home in the even. Dame Durrant and Bett Mepham with my wife all day and also sat up with her all night, who is so bad that it is past description and we do not expect her to live from one minute to the other. Myself lay at Master Durrant's.

Mon. 22 June.

My brother came over in the forenoon and he and Dame Durrant dined with us on part of a neck of veal roasted and green salad. My brother stayed with me till about 4.10. Dame Durrant and Bett Mepham with my wife all day, who is, poor creature, so extreme bad that it would I think even draw tears from the most obdurate heart breathing to see her. Lucy Mepham sat up with my wife. I lodged in at Joseph Durrant's.

Tues. 23 June.

About 1.50 it pleased Almighty God to take from me my beloved wife, who, poor creature, has laboured under a severe though lingering illness for these 38 weeks past, which she bore with the greatest resignation to the Divine will. In her I have lost a sincere friend and virtuous wife, a prudent and good economist in her family and a very valuable companion (and one endued with more than a common share of good sense). I will once more say she was virtuous even in the most strictest sense of the word virtue: she was always decent in her apparel and remarkably sweet and cleanly in her person, and had by nature a cheerful though religious turn of mind. . . . May I endeavour to copy the many excellencies she was undoubtedly possessed of; therefore I may justly say with the incomparable Mr Young: 'Let them who have ever lost an angel pity me.'

We dined on the remains of yesterday's dinner. My friend George Richardson came to advise me in the even, and stayed with me all night, and both of us lodged at Master Durrant's. Dame Durrant and Bett Mepham stayed with my servants.

Weds. 24 June.

In the morn my father[-in-law] Slater came to see me and to condole and sympathize with me in my misfortunes . . .

Thurs. 25 June.

I dined on the remains of yesterday's dinner, with the addition of a hog's cheek boiled and gooseberry pudding. Oh, how melancholy my situation. Not a friend to pour that pleasing balm of consolation into a heart overwhelmed with grief, no, nor one enlivening object gains admittance in my distracted breast.

The Diary of Thomas Turner

❧ *Laurence Sterne first met Eliza Draper in January 1767, when she was nearing the end of a two-year stay in England for the sake of her health. Born in India, she had been orphaned at the age of 4 and married to a businessman, Daniel Draper, at 14. Like Sterne himself, she was no doubt an incorrigible flirt; and his letters to her after their parting at the beginning of April 1767 have a suggestion of theatricality in their mournfulness and self-pity.*

April 16 [1761].

5 in the afternoon—I have just been eating my Chicking, sitting over my repast upon it, with Tears—a bitter Sause—Eliza! but I could eat it with no other—when Molly spread the Table Cloath, my heart fainted within me—one solitary plate—one knife—one fork—one Glass! O Eliza! 'twas painfully distressing—I gave a thousand pensive penetrating Looks at the Arm chair thou so often graced on these quiet sentimental Repasts—and sighed and laid down my knife and fork,—and took out my handkerchiff, clap'd it across my face, and wept like a child—I shall read the same affecting Account of many a sad Dinner which Eliza has had no power to taste of, from the same feelings and recollections, how She and her Bramin have eat their bread in peace and Love together.

Letters of Laurence Sterne

Bramin, Bramine: Sterne's and Eliza's pet names for one another. Sterne's nickname for Eliza, 'the Bramine,' originally alluded to her Anglo-Indian background.

❧ *Bob Loveday, home from the sea during the Napoleonic War, has been cheated of his plan to marry Matilda Johnson, a Southampton woman, when his brother the trumpet-major, recognizing her as a woman of loose morals, sends her packing. Their father the miller has promptly married his next-door neighbour, the widow Garland, using up the food prepared for Bob and Matilda's wedding by inviting the parish poor to be their guests. After the wedding, Bob's father warns him against undue pining for fear that the neighbours should think him unhinged by sorrow.*

On reflection he remembered that since Miss Johnson's departure his appetite had decreased amazingly. He had eaten in meat no more than fourteen or fifteen ounces a day, but one-third of a quartern pudding on an average, in vegetable only a small heap of potatoes and half a York cabbage, and no gravy whatsoever; which considering the usual appetite of a seaman for fresh food at the end of a long voyage, was no small index of the depression of his mind. Then he had waked once every night, and on one occasion twice. While dressing each morning since the gloomy day he had not whistled more than seven bars of a hornpipe without stopping and falling into thought of a most painful kind; and he had told none but absolutely true stories of foreign parts to the neighbouring villagers when they saluted and clustered about him, as usual, for anything he chose to pour forth.

* * * * *

'I'll raze out her image,' he said. 'She shall make a fool of me no more.' And his resolve resulted in conduct which had elements of real greatness.

He went back to his father, whom he found in the mill-loft. ' 'Tis true, father, what you say,' he observed: 'my brains will turn to bilge-water if I think of her much longer. By the oath of a—navigator, I wish I could sigh less and laugh more! She's gone—why can't I let her go, and be happy? But how begin?'

'Take it carelessly, my son,' said the miller, 'and lay yourself out to enjoy snacks and cordials.'

'Ah—that's a thought!' said Bob.

'Baccy is good for't. So is sperrits. Though I don't advise thee to drink neat.'

'Baccy—I'd almost forgot it,' said Captain Loveday.

He went to his room, hastily untied the package of tobacco that he had brought home, and began to make use of it in his own way, calling to David [the servant] for a bottle of the old household mead that had lain in the cellar these eleven years. He was discovered by his father three-quarters of an hour later as a half-invisible object behind a cloud of smoke.

The miller drew a breath of relief. 'Why, Bob,' he said, 'I thought the house was a-fire!'

'I'm smoking rather fast to drown my reflections, father. 'Tis no use to chaw.'

To tempt his attenuated appetite the unhappy mate made David cook an omelet and bake a seed-cake, the latter so richly compounded that it opened to the knife like a freckled buttercup. With the same object he stuck night-lines into the banks of the mill-pond, and drew up next morning a family of fat eels, some of which were skinned and prepared for his breakfast. They were his favourite fish, but such had been his condition that, until the moment of making this effort, he had quite forgotten their existence at his father's back-door.

Hardy, *The Trumpet-Major*

❧ *Dominie Abel Sampson, a preacher of pedantic and fearful disposition, is travelling alone through wild country when he finds himself passing the home of Meg Merrilies, an old gipsy woman.*

Now it must be confessed that our friend Sampson, although a profound scholar and mathematician, had not travelled so far in philosophy as to doubt the reality of witchcraft or apparitions. . . . With these feelings, and in a thick misty day, which was already drawing to its close, Dominie Sampson did not pass the Kaim of Derncleugh without some feelings of tacit horror.

What, then, was his astonishment, when, on passing the door . . . that door, that very door, opened suddenly, and the figure of Meg Merrilies, well known though not seen for many a revolving year, was placed at once before the eyes of the startled Dominie! She stood immediately before him in the footpath, confronting him so absolutely that he could not avoid her except by fairly turning back, which his manhood prevented him from thinking of.

* * * * *

'Sit down there,' she said, pushing the half-throttled preacher with some violence against a broken chair—'sit down there, and gather your wind and your senses, ye black barrow-tram o' the kirk that ye are! Are ye fou or fasting?'

'Fasting—from all but sin,' answered the Dominie, who, recovering his voice . . . thought it best to affect complaisance and submission. . . . But as the Dominie's brain was by no means equal to carry on two trains of ideas at the same time, a word or two of his mental exercise sometimes escaped, and mingled with his uttered speech in a manner ludicrous enough, especially as the poor man shrunk himself together after every escape of the kind, from terror of the effect it might produce upon the irritable feelings of the witch.

Meg, in the meanwhile, went to a great black cauldron that was boiling on a fire on the floor, and, lifting the lid, an odour was diffused through the vault, which, if the vapours of a witch's cauldron could in aught be trusted, promised better things than the hell-broth which such vessels are usually supposed to contain. It was in fact the savour of a goodly stew, composed of fowls, hares, partridges, and moorgame, boiled in a large mess with potatoes, onions, and leeks, and, from the size of the cauldron, appeared to be prepared for half a dozen people at least.

'So ye hae eat naething a' day?' said Meg, heaving a large portion of this mess into a brown dish, and strewing it savourily with salt and pepper.

'Nothing,' answered the Dominie—'*scelestissima*!—that is—gudewife.'

'Hae then,' said she, placing the dish before him, 'there's what will warm your heart.'

'I do not hunger—*malefica*—that is to say—Mrs Merrilies!' for he said unto himself, 'the savour is sweet, but it hath been cooked by a Canidia or an Ericthoe.'

'If ye dinna eat instantly, and put some saul in ye, by the bread and the salt, I'll put it down your throat wi' the cutty spoon, scaulding as it is, and whether ye will or no. Gape, sinner, and swallow!'

Sampson, afraid of eye of newt, and toe of frog, tigers' chaudrons, and so forth, had determined not to venture; but the smell of the stew was fast melting his obstinacy, which flowed from his chops as it were in streams of water, and the witch's threats decided him to feed. Hunger and fear are excellent casuists.

'Saul,' said Hunger, 'feasted with the witch of Endor.'—'And,' quoth Fear, 'the salt which she sprinkled upon the food showeth plainly that it is not a necromantic banquet, in which that seasoning never occurs.'—'And besides,' says Hunger, after the first spoonful, 'It is savoury and refreshing viands.'

Walter Scott, *Guy Mannering*, 1815

Barrow-tram: shaft of a barrow (presumably referring to Sampson's rigid appearance); *scelestissima, malefica*: most wicked, evil-doer (Sampson's use of Latin suggests the ceremony of exorcism); *Canidia*: a Neapolitan courtesan denounced by the poet Horace, her former lover, as a sorceress; *eye of newt . . . tigers' chaudrons*: see *Macbeth*, IV. i; *Saul . . . Endor*: 1 Samuel 28.

FOOD IN DREAMS AND FANTASY

❧ *Sir Epicure Mammon, accompanied by his friend Pertinax Surly, a gambler, visits Subtle, a pretended alchemist, in the hope of finding the magic formula for the way to riches, the philosopher's stone. While claiming that his desire for wealth is purely public-spirited ('I shall employ it all in pious uses, | Founding of colleges and grammar schools, | Marrying young virgins, building hospitals, | And here and there a church'), Mammon cannot resist expressing his real wish for luxury, in the form of a vulgarian's banquet of exotic, sensuously textured foods.*

SIR EPICURE MAMMON (to Surly). . . . We will be brave, Puffe, now we have the med'cine.
My meat shall all come in, in Indian shells,
Dishes of agat set in gold, and studded
With emeralds, sapphires, hyacinths and rubies.
The tongues of carps, dormice, and camels' heels,
Boiled in the spirit of sol, and dissolved pearl,
Apicius' diet, 'gainst the epilepsy:
And I will eat these broths, with spoons of amber,
Headed with diamond and carbuncle.
My foot-boy shall eat pheasants, calvered salmons,
Knots, godwits, lampreys: I myself will have
The beards of barbel served instead of salads;
Oiled mushrooms; and the swelling unctuous paps
Of a fat pregnant sow, newly cut off,
Drest with an exquisite and poignant sauce;
For which, I'll say unto my cook, *There's gold,*
Go forth, and be a knight.

Ben Jonson, *The Alchemist*, 1610, II. i

Brave: in this context, grand, ostentatious; *Apicius*: a gastronomic authority of the first century AD, supposed author of a collection of recipes, *De Re Coquinaria*, of which seven printed editions, in Latin, had appeared in Venice, Milan, Basel, Lyons, and Zürich between *c.*1483 and 1542. Mammon's reference to Apicius implies a certain intellectual cosmopolitanism in Jonson's audiences, at least at second hand; for no London edition of Apicius's work appeared until 1705. The dormouse (*glis*), stuffed and roasted or stewed in broth, was a favourite Mediterranean food in Roman times, and recipes for cooking it appear in Apicius, as do various recipes for sow's womb, udder, and belly. Several of the other ingredients mentioned by Mammon seem to belong to alchemy rather than to Roman cookery.

❧ *The poet Thomas Gray (1716–71) made a Grand Tour in Europe after leaving Cambridge in 1738. In Rome he indulged in a mannered fantasy of dining on Lucullan food, a shade more pedestrian than that of Sir Epicure Mammon.*

Thomas Gray to Mr West, Rome, May 1740.

I am today just returned from Alba, a good deal fatigued; for you know the Appian is somewhat tiresome. We dined at Pompey's; he indeed was gone for a few days to his Tusculan, but, by the care of his Villicus, we made an admirable meal. We had the dugs of a pregnant sow, a peacock, a dish of thrushes, a noble scarus just fresh from the Tyrrhene, and some conchylia of the lake with garum sauce. For my part I never eat better at Lucullus's table. We drank half-a-dozen cyathi apiece of ancient Alban to Pholoe's health, and, after bathing, and playing an hour at ball, we mounted our *essedum* again, and proceeded up the mount to the temple. . . . But quitting my Romanities, to your great joy and mine, let me tell you in plain English, that we come from Albano.

The Poems of Thomas Gray, with a Selection of Letters and Essays, 1912

Villicus: steward; *scarus*: a kind of sea-fish; *conchylia*: mussels, small shellfish (in this context, probably fresh-water mussels); *garum*: a favourite sauce of the ancient Romans. A small fish, *garus*, was puréed, intestines and all, and the sauce fermented; *cyathi*: ladles, measures; *essedum*: war-chariot (of the Gauls and Britons).

❧ *Joseph, Jacob's favourite son, has antagonized his half-brothers by tactlessly telling them certain of his dreams which suggest (according to him) that he ought to be their master. In retaliation they have sold him to the Ishmeelites, who have transported him into Egypt and sold him to Potiphar, an officer in Pharaoh's guard. When Joseph refuses the advances of Potiphar's wife, she accuses him of attempted rape and has him imprisoned. Joseph, however, becomes a 'trusty', who is held responsible for all the other prisoners. These include Pharaoh's chief butler and chief baker, each of whom has dreamt a symbolic dream.*

And the chief butler told his dream to Joseph, and said to him, In my dream, behold, a vine *was* before me;

And in the vine *were* three branches; and it *was* as though it budded, *and* her blossoms shot forth; and the clusters thereof brought forth ripe grapes:

And Pharaoh's cup *was* in my hand: and I took the grapes, and pressed them into Pharaoh's cup, and I gave the cup into Pharaoh's hand.

And Joseph said unto him, This *is* the interpretation of it: The three branches *are* three days:

Yet within three days shall Pharaoh lift up thine head, and restore thee unto thy place: and thou shalt deliver Pharaoh's cup into his hand, after the former manner when thou wast his butler.

But think on me when it shall be well with thee, and shew kindness, I pray thee, unto me, and make mention of me unto Pharaoh, and bring me out of this house:

For indeed I was stolen away out of the land of the Hebrews: and here also have I done nothing that they should put me into the dungeon.

When the chief baker saw that the interpretation was good, he said unto Joseph, I also *was* in my dream, and, behold, *I had* three white baskets on my head:

And in the uppermost basket *there was* of all manner of bakemeats for Pharaoh; and the birds did eat them out of the basket on my head.

And Joseph answered and said, This *is* the interpretation thereof: The three baskets *are* three days:

Yet within three days shall Pharaoh lift thy head from off thee, and shall hang thee on a tree, and the birds shall eat thy flesh from off thee.

And it came to pass the third day, *which was* Pharaoh's birthday, that he made a feast unto all his servants: and he lifted up the head of the chief butler and of the chief baker among his servants.

And he restored the chief butler unto his butlership again; and he gave the cup unto Pharaoh's hand:

But he hanged the chief baker: as Joseph had interpreted to them.

Yet did not the chief butler remember Joseph, but forgat him.

And it came to pass, at the end of two full years, that Pharaoh dreamed: and behold, he stood by the river.

And, behold, there came up out of the river seven well favoured kine and fatfleshed; and they fed in a meadow.

And, behold, seven other kine came up after them out of the river, ill favoured and leanfleshed; and stood by the *other* kine upon the brink of the river.

And the ill favoured and leanfleshed kine did eat up the seven well favoured and fat kine. So Pharaoh awoke.

And he slept and dreamed the second time: and, behold, seven ears of corn came up upon one stalk, rank and good.

And, behold, seven thin ears and blasted with the east wind sprung up after them.

And the seven thin ears devoured the seven rank and full ears. And Pharaoh awoke, and, behold, *it* was a dream.

And it came to pass in the morning that his spirit was troubled; and he sent and called for all the magicians of Egypt, and all the wise men thereof: and Pharaoh told them his dream; but *there was* none that could interpret them unto Pharaoh.

[*Eventually, through the mediation of the chief butler, Joseph is fetched out of prison to interpret Pharaoh's dreams. He explains that they portend seven fat years followed by seven years of famine, and urges Pharaoh to make due preparations by storing up food for the lean years to come. Pharaoh is so impressed that he appoints Joseph ruler over all of Egypt, second in authority only to himself.*]

Genesis, 40: 9–23; 41: 1–8

RUSKIN'S DREAMS

November 12th. Friday [1869].

Dreamed curious dream about man running a race, who was a friend of mine, and called to me to get him a basket of strawberries from a girl walking in front. So I ran on and caught her, and she had four little baskets of strawberries, all stuck together, and the big strawberries tumbled off when I separated them, and I couldn't choose which basket to take; and then it turned into a baker's shop, out of which the racing man wanted some cakes, and there were currant buns and plain ones, and the baker wouldn't let me take them because he said he had better under the dresser; and at last I got the plate in my hand and ran off after the racing man—to the great delight of the public; and then somehow it turned into a little room in a French old-fashioned inn, which I couldn't get out of, or wouldn't, by the regular way, but wanted to get out of quietly by a winding stair, and when I got to the bottom of the stair, its little wicket door was shut, so I woke.

November 13th. Saturday.

Took unwholesome things yesterday and am languid and useless today. Must stop this.

November 14th. Sunday.

Just the same to-day. But how my dreams run in grooves! see last page about the currant buns. Well, last night, I had got a piece of rich cake in my hand and wanted a bit of paper to put it in, and went to a shop where I thought they were under obligations to me, but they hadn't a bit; then I went into a confectioner's next door, where they were under no obligations to me, and they gave me a brown bag directly. Then I thought I must buy something to pay for their civility, so I asked for some pastry, and they gave me some which I said was too rich, but they said they hadn't any but that and some made with 'marrow' or 'marrow fat'. Then I asked them how they had got into such vulgar cookery; and they said they *were* low, but not so low as the working classes in the city. Then I gave them a long lecture upon the virtue of people who worked twelve hours a day. And then things changed, and I was in a railroad train going to Dijon, very fast, and always with little swings down hill. An *octroi* man beckoned from the side of the road to ask if we had anything to 'déclarer'. We flew past him, and I thought all was safe, but a scrupulous passenger declared he had something to *déclarer*; and the train was stopped, and then I found I had something to *déclarer* myself, which was a bottle of magnificent old brandy; and the *octroi* man took the cork out and smelt it and said it was very fine, and he must taste it, and he began pouring it out into a tumbler, and I wondered when he would stop; and he filled the tumbler quite full and more than half emptied the bottle, and I told him he had taken ten shillings' worth at least, and as he had taken that, he might as well take all the bottle, and so I came away very angry; and woke.

The Diaries of John Ruskin, II, 1848–1873, selected and edited by Joan Evans and John Howard Whitehouse, 1958

HOW GARGANTUA DID EAT UP SIX PILGRIMS IN A SALLAD

The story requireth, that we relate that which happened unto six pilgrims, who came from Sebastian near to Nantes: and who for shelter that night, being afraid of the enemy, hid themselves in the garden upon the chichling peas, among the cabbages and lettuces. Gargantua finding himself somewhat dry, asked whether they could get any lettuce to make him a sallad; and hearing that there were the greatest and fairest in the country, for they were as great as plum-trees, or as walnut-trees, he would go thither himself, and brought thence in his hand what he thought good, and withal carried away the six pilgrims, who were in so great fear, that they did not dare to speak nor cough. Washing them, therefore, first at the fountain, the pilgrims said to one another softly, What shall we do? We are almost drowned here amongst these lettuce, shall we speak? But if we speak he will kill us for spies. And, as they were thus deliberating what to do, Gargantua put them with the lettuce into a platter of the house, as large as the huge tun of the White Friars of the Cistertian order; which done, with oil, vinegar, and salt, he ate them up, to refresh himself a little before supper, and had already swallowed up five of the pilgrims, the sixth being in the platter, totally hid under a lettuce, except his bourbon or staff that appeared, and nothing else. Which Grangousier seeing, said to Gargantua, I think that is the horn of a shell snail, do not eat it. Why not, said Gargantua, they are good all this month: which he no sooner said, but, drawing up the staff, and therewith taking up the pilgrim, he ate him very well, then drank a terrible draught of excellent white wine. The pilgrims, thus devoured, made shift to save themselves as well as they could, by drawing their bodies out of the reach of the grinders of his teeth, but could not escape from thinking they had been put in the lowest dungeon of a prison. And when Gargantua whiffed the great draught, they thought to have drowned in his mouth, and the flood of wine had almost carried them away into the gulf of his stomach. Nevertheless, skipping with their bourbons, as St Michael's palmers use to do, they sheltered themselves from the danger of that inundation under the banks of his teeth. But one of them by chance, groping or sounding the country with his staff, to try whether they were in safety or no, struck hard against the cleft of a hollow tooth, and hit the mandibulatory sinew or nerve of the jaw, which put Gargantua to very great pain, so that he began to cry for the rage that he felt. To ease himself therefore of his smarting ache, he called for his tooth-picker, and rubbing towards a young walnut-tree, where they lay skulking, unnestled you my gentlemen pilgrims.

François Rabelais, *Gargantua*, 1535, Book I, translated by Sir Thomas Urquhart, 1653

They roused him with muffins—they roused him with ice—
They roused him with mustard and cress—
They roused him with jam and judicious advice—
They set him conundrums to guess.

Lewis Carroll, 'The Baker's Tale', from *The Hunting of the Snark*, Fit the Third, 1876

I'll tell thee everything I can;
There's little to relate.
I saw an aged aged man
A-sitting on a gate.
'Who are you, aged man?' I said.
'And how is it you live?'
And his answer trickled through my head
Like water through a sieve.

He said, 'I look for butterflies
That sleep among the wheat:
I make them into mutton pies,
And sell them in the street.'

* * *

But I was thinking of a way
To feed oneself on batter,
And so go on from day to day
Getting a little fatter.

* * *

He said, 'I hunt for haddocks' eyes
Among the heather bright,
And work them into waistcoat-buttons
In the silent night.
And these I do not sell for gold
Or coin of silvery shine,

But for a copper halfpenny,
And that will purchase nine.

'I sometimes dig for buttered rolls
Or set limed twigs for crabs;
I sometimes search the grassy knolls
For wheels of Hansom-cabs.
And that's the way' (he gave a wink)
'By which I get my wealth—
And very gladly will I drink
Your Honour's noble health.'

Lewis Carroll, 'The Knight's Song', from *Through the Looking-Glass*, 1872

❧ *Like much of Lewis Carroll's fantasy, Edward Lear's poem 'The New Vestments' betrays a peculiarly mid-Victorian fascination with food. Half-forbidden as a subject of polite conversation, and much used in rewarding and punishing children, it was conveniently regarded as the main, or indeed only, object of a child's appetites, and was often referred to with a certain coyness by adults, especially when discussing sweet treats. To find it dwelt on in a nonsense-poem could therefore be the source of an almost prurient form of pleasure: intensified, here, by masochistic overtones.*

There lived an old man in the Kingdom of Tess,
Who invented a purely original dress;
And when it was perfectly made and complete,
He opened the door and walked into the street.

By way of a hat, he'd a loaf of Brown Bread,
In the middle of which he inserted his head;—
His Shirt was made up of no end of dead Mice,
The warmth of whose skins was quite fluffy and nice;—
His Drawers were of Rabbit-skins; so were his Shoes;—
His stockings were skins—but it is not known whose;—
His Waistcoat and Trowsers were made of Pork Chops;—
His Buttons were Jujubes, and Chocolate Drops;—
His Coat was all Pancakes with Jam for a border,
And a girdle of Biscuits to keep it in order;
And he wore over all, as a screen from bad weather,
A Cloak of green Cabbage-leaves stitched all together.

He had walked a short way, when he heard a great noise,
Of all sorts of Beasticles, Birdlings, and Boys;—
And from every long street and dark lane in the town
Beasts, Birdles, and Boys in a tumult ran down.
Two Cows and a half ate his Cabbage-leaf cloak;—
Four Apes seized his Girdle, which vanished like smoke;—
Three Kids ate up half his Pancaky Coat,—
And the tails were devour'd by an ancient He Goat;—
An army of Dogs in a twinkling tore *up* his
Pork Waistcoat and Trowsers to give to their Puppies;—
And while they were growling, and mumbling the Chops,
Ten boys prigged the Jujubes and Chocolate Drops.—
He tried to run back to his house, but in vain,
For Scores of fat Pigs came again and again;—
They rushed out of stables and hovels and doors,—
They tore off his stockings, his shoes, and his drawers;—
And now from the housetops with screechings descend,
Striped, spotted, white, black, and gray Cats without end,
They jumped on his shoulders and knocked off his hat,—
When Crows, Ducks, and Hens made a mincemeat of that;—
They speedily flew at his sleeves in a trice,
And utterly tore up his Shirt of dead Mice;—
They swallowed the last of his Shirt with a squall,—
Whereon he ran home with no clothes on at all.

And he said to himself as he bolted the door,
'I will not wear a similar dress any more,
'Any more, any more, any more, never more!'

Edward Lear, *Laughable Lyrics*, 1877

(*1*). *To Make Gosky Patties.*

Take a Pig, three or four years of age, and tie him by the off hind leg to a post. Place 5 pounds of currants, 3 of sugar, 2 pecks of peas, 18 roast chestnuts, a candle, and 6 bushels of turnips, within his reach; if he eates [*sic*] these, constantly provide him with more.

Then, procure some cream, some slices of Cheshire cheese, four quires of foolscap paper, and a packet of black pins. Work the whole into a paste, and spread it out to dry on a sheet of clean brown waterproof linen.

When the paste is perfectly dry, but not before, proceed to beat the Pig violently, with the handle of a large broom. If he squeals, beat him again.

Visit the paste and beat the Pig alternately for some days, and ascertain if at the end of that period the whole is about to turn into Gosky Patties.

If it does not then, it never will; and in that case the Pig may be let loose, and the whole process may be considered as finished.

(2). *To Make an Amblongus Pie.*

Take 4 pounds (say 4½ pounds) of fresh Amblongusses, and put them in a small pipkin.

Cover with water and boil them for 8 hours incessantly, after which add 2 pints of new milk, and proceed to boil for 4 hours or more.

When you have ascertained that the Amblongusses are quite soft, take them out and place them in a wide pan, taking care to shake them well previously.

Grate some nutmeg over the surface, and cover them carefully with powdered gingerbread, curry-powder, and a sufficient quantity of Cayenne pepper.

Remove the pan into the next room, and place it on the floor. Bring it back again, and let it simmer for three-quarters of an hour. Shake the pan violently till all the Amblongusses have become of a pale purple colour.

Then, having prepared the paste, insert the whole carefully, adding at the same time a small pigeon, two slices of beef, four cauliflowers, and any number of oysters.

Watch patiently till the crust begins to rise, and add a pinch of salt from time to time.

Serve up on a clean dish, and throw the whole out of the window as fast as possible.

Edward Lear, *Nonsense Botany, and Nonsense Alphabets, etc., etc.,* 1888

FOOD AND HAPPINESS

LILAC-TIME IN A GERMAN GARDEN

My other half being indulgent, and with some faint thought perhaps that it might be as well to look after the place, consented to live in it at any rate for a time; whereupon followed six specially blissful weeks during which I was here alone, supposed to be superintending the painting and papering, but as a matter of fact only going into the house when the workmen had gone out of it. How happy I was! I don't remember any time quite so perfect since the days when I was too little to do lessons and was turned out with sugar on my eleven o'clock bread and butter on to a lawn closely strewn with dandelions and daisies. The sugar on the bread and butter has lost its charm, but I love the dandelions and daisies even more passionately now than then. . . . During those six weeks I lived in a world of dandelions and delights.

* * * * *

There were only the old housekeeper and her handmaiden in the house, so that on the plea of not giving too much trouble I could indulge what my other half calls my *fantaisie déréglée* as regards meals—that is to say, meals so simple that they could be brought out to the lilacs on a tray; and I lived, I remember, on salad and bread and tea the whole time, sometimes a very tiny pigeon appearing at lunch to save me, as the old lady thought, from starvation. Who but a woman could have stood salad for six weeks, even salad sanctified by the presence and scent of the most gorgeous lilac masses? I did, and grew in grace every day, though I have never liked it since. How often now, oppressed by the necessity of assisting at three dining-room meals daily, two of which are conducted by the functionaries held indispensable to a proper maintenance of the family dignity, and all of which are pervaded by joints of meat, how often do I think of my salad days, forty in number, and of the blessedness of being alone as I was then alone!

von Arnim, *Elizabeth and her German Garden*

Katherine Mansfield was living with her husband John Middleton Murry in East Heath Road, Hampstead at the time of this entry in her journal. Athenaeum, the kitten born in early April, was named after the literary magazine of which Murry was editor. Katherine Mansfield's mother had died in New Zealand the previous year.

[*May, 1919*.]
Saturday. This joy of being alone. What is it? I feel so gay and at peace—the whole house takes the air. Lunch is ready. I have a baked

egg, apricots and cream, cheese straws and black coffee. How delicious! A baby meal! Mother shares it with me. Athenaeum is asleep and then awake on the study sofa. He has a silver spoon of cream—then hides under the sofa frill and puts out a paw for my finger. I gather the dried leaves from the plant in the big white bowl, and because I must play with something I take an orange up to my room and throw and catch it as I walk up and down.

The Journal of Katherine Mansfield

❧ *The Ramsay family are on holiday in Scotland with their guests, Paul, Minta, Augustus Carmichael, William Bankes, Lily Briscoe, and Charles Tansley. This famous passage, in which Mrs Ramsay contemplates the dinner and its setting and the lives of the various intellectual, artistic, or ordinary people who are gathered around her to eat it, contains the earliest celebration in fiction of an English family at their own table consuming French peasant-style food.*

Now eight candles were stood down the table, and after the first stoop the flames stood upright and drew with them into visibility the long table entire, and in the middle a yellow and purple dish of fruit. What had she done with it, Mrs Ramsay wondered, for Rose's arrangement of the grapes and pears, of the horny pink-lined shell, of the bananas, made her think of a trophy fetched from the bottom of the sea, of Neptune's banquet, of the bunch that hangs with vine leaves over the shoulder of Bacchus (in some picture), among the leopard skins and the torches lolloping, red and gold. . . . Thus brought up suddenly into the light it seemed possessed of great size and depth, was like a world in which one could take one's staff and climb up hills, she thought, and go down into valleys, and to her pleasure (for it brought them into sympathy momentarily) she saw that Augustus too feasted his eyes on the same plate of fruit, plunged in, broke off a bloom there, a tassel here, and returned, after feasting, to his hive. That was his way of looking, different from hers. But looking together united them.

* * * * *

For herself—'Put it down there,' she said, helping the Swiss girl to place gently before her the huge brown pot in which was the *Bœuf en Daube*—for her own part she liked her boobies. Paul must sit by her. She had kept a place for him. Really, she sometimes thought she liked the boobies best. They did not bother one with their dissertations. . . . There was something, she thought as he sat down, very charming about Paul. His manners were delightful to her, and his sharp cut nose and his bright blue eyes. He was so considerate. Would he tell her—now that they were all talking again—what had happened

'We went back to look for Minta's brooch,' he said, sitting down by her. 'We'—that was enough. She knew from the effort, the rise in his voice to surmount a difficult word that it was the first time he had said 'we'. 'We' did this, 'we' did that. They'll say that all their lives, she thought, and an exquisite scent of olives and oil and juice rose from the great brown dish as Marthe, with a little flourish, took the cover off. The cook had spent three days over that dish. And she must take great care, Mrs Ramsay thought, diving into the soft mass, to choose a specially tender piece for William Bankes. And she peered into the dish, with its shiny walls and its confusion of savoury brown and yellow meats, and its bay leaves and its wine, and thought, This will celebrate the occasion—a curious sense rising in her, at once freakish and tender, of celebrating a festival, as if two emotions were called up in her, one profound—for what could be more serious than the love of man for woman, what more commanding, more impressive, bearing in its bosom the seeds of death; at the same time these lovers, these people entering into illusion glittering eyed, must be danced round with mockery, decorated with garlands.

'It is a triumph,' said Mr Bankes, laying his knife down for a moment. He had eaten attentively. It was rich; it was tender. It was perfectly cooked. How did she manage these things in the depths of the country? he asked her. She was a wonderful woman. All his love, all his reverence had returned; and she knew it.

'It is a French recipe of my grandmother's,' said Mrs Ramsay, speaking with a ring of great pleasure in her voice. Of course it was French. What passes for cookery in England was an abomination (they agreed). It is putting cabbages in water. It is roasting meat till it is like leather. It is cutting off the delicious skins of vegetables. 'In which,' said Mr Bankes, 'all the virtue of the vegetable is contained.' And the waste, said Mrs Ramsay. A whole French family could live on what an English cook throws away. Spurred on by her sense that William's affection had come back to her, and that everything was all right again, and that her suspense was over, and that now she was free both to triumph and to mock, she laughed, she gesticulated, till

Lily thought, How childlike, how absurd she was, sitting up there with all her beauty opened again in her, talking about the skins of vegetables.

Virginia Woolf, *To the Lighthouse*, 1927

A CHILDHOOD IN LEEDS

If you were unable to get out on a particular weekend, and that happened more often than not, you could always sit on the step, the door open as far as seemed decent, so that what wind there was could waft into the living-room, a cushion to soften the stone or brick, a book, and an eye out for whatever might be happening in the street. By late afternoon a cooler breeze usually came up so that you were sorry to be called in to tea. Sometimes you asked to be allowed to take your tea on to the step. On one such day Grandma had been baking and had at the end put 'oven-cakes' in the bottom of the oven, made from the left-over bread dough and looking like large teacakes but with the consistency of ordinary not sweetened bread; they tasted better when fresh, chiefly because they had such crisp crust all round and the white inside was springy and warm; and moist, since the margarine or butter had melted into them.

On this occasion, a Monday during the school holidays, there was a little tinned salmon left over from a Sunday tea at which we had had a couple of family visitors, and Grandma gave me that on a sizeable piece of oven-cake. Not a lot of salmon, but it has a strong taste so a little, spread carefully, can go a long way; the pepper, salt and vinegar mix with the oily juice from the tin and the seasoned mixture seeps into the warm cells of the white inside.

I then had for a few moments a sensation of unpremeditated and unalloyed happiness. A difficult and dangerous phrase to use in English, but it is apt here. Among many reasons why I admire Chekhov is his willingness to try to describe such moments, as in the short story 'After the Theatre' in which he captures a young girl's unaffected sense of pure contentment. I guess it is not an accident but an emanation of the English spirit that when we try to describe such a sensation we slip into 'un' words, as I have done three times in this paragraph. We find it hard to go straight, positively to name the sensation, so we circle round it, saying not this and not that, un-this and un-that, as though our readers will have to infer the still light in the middle.

What I experienced on the step that day was more than a boy's elemental pleasure in a succulent snack, though it was that certainly. It was a brief sense of being wholly at one with the world, at peace. The weather lambent, the house at the time not too much threatened, school no doubt going well and for the time not making demands, Grandma's bright gesture of affection in offering the sandwich, the body presumably in good shape. It would be far too much to claim that 'blood, imagination, intellect' were running together, but in a small and immature way something like that was happening.

Hoggart, *A Local Habitation*

TO A POOR OLD WOMAN

munching a plum on
the street a paper bag
of them in her hand

They taste good to her
They taste good
to her. They taste
good to her

William Carlos Williams, *Selected Poems*, 1969

FOOD, SENSUALITY, LOVE, AND SEX

Thy lips, O *my* spouse, drop as the honeycomb: honey and milk *are* under thy tongue; and the smell of thy garments *is* like the smell of Lebanon.

A garden inclosed *is* my sister, *my* spouse; a spring shut up, a fountain sealed.

Thy plants *are* an orchard of pomegranates, with pleasant fruits; camphire, with spikenard,

Spikenard and saffron; calamus and cinnamon, with all trees of frankincense; myrrh and aloes, with all the chief spices:

A fountain of gardens, a well of living waters, and streams from Lebanon.

Awake, O north wind; and come, thou south; blow upon my

garden, *that* the spices thereof may flow out. Let my beloved come into his garden, and eat his pleasant fruits.

* * * * *

How fair and how pleasant art thou, O love, for delights!

This thy stature is like to a palm tree, and thy breasts to clusters of *grapes*.

I said, I will go up to the palm tree, I will take hold of thy boughs thereof: now also thy breasts shall be as clusters of the vine, and the smell of thy nose like apples;

And the roof of thy mouth like the best wine for my beloved, that goeth *down* sweetly, causing the lips of those that are asleep to speak.

I *am* my beloved's, and his desire *is* toward me.

Come, my beloved, let us go forth into the field; let us lodge in the villages.

Let us get up early to the vineyard; let us see if the vine flourish, *whether* the tender grape appear, *and* the pomegranates bud forth: there will I give thee my loves.

The mandrakes give a smell, and at our gates *are* all manner of pleasant fruits, new and old, *which* I have laid up for thee, O my beloved.

The Song of Solomon, 4: 11–16; 7: 6–13

A LOVE SONNET

I loved a lass, a fair one,
As fair as e'er was seen;
She was indeed a rare one,
Another Sheba Queen:
But, fool as then I was,
I thought she loved me too:
But now, alas! sh'as left me,
Falero, lero, loo!

Her hair like gold did glister,
Each eye was like a star,
She did surpass her sister,
Which passed all others far;
She would me honey call,
She'd—oh, she'd kiss me too!

But now, alas! sh'as left me,
Falero, lero, loo!

In summer time to Medley
My Love and I would go:
The boatmen there stood ready,
My Love and I to row;
For cream there would we call,
For cakes and for prunes too:
But now, alas! sh'as left me,
Falero, lero, loo!

* * *

In summer time or winter
She had her heart's desire;
I still did scorn to stint her
From sugar, sack, or fire:
The world went round about,
No cares we ever knew:
But now, alas! sh'as left me,
Falero, lero, loo!

George Wither, from *A Description of Love*, 1618

Medley: a farm and former hamlet, on the River Thames immediately north-west of Oxford.

❧ *The virgin Madeline has gone to bed fasting on St Agnes' Eve (20 January) in the hope of seeing her lover and receiving 'visions of delight | And soft adorings' from him in a dream. (Belief in this indulgence was evidently a late medieval softening of an older, tougher Roman Catholic tradition, according to which Agnes, martyred as a young girl, has long been venerated as the patron saint of girls who say 'no'.) Porphyro, Madeline's lover, preferring real contact to dreams, has chosen this night to persuade her to elope with him. Entering the house unseen, he has found his way to Madeline's chamber with the help of an elderly servant-woman, and is waiting there for the moment of her vision.*

Then by the bed-side, where the faded moon
Made a dim, silver twilight, soft he set
A table, and, half anguish'd, threw thereon

A cloth of woven crimson, gold, and jet:—
O for some drowsy Morphean amulet!
The boisterous, midnight, festive clarion,
The kettle-drum, and far-heard clarionet,
Affray his ears, though but in dying tone:—
The hall-door shuts again, and all the noise is gone.

And still she slept an azure-lidded sleep,
In blanched linen, smooth, and lavender'd,
While he from forth the closet brought a heap
Of candied apple, quince, and plum, and gourd;
With jellies soother than the creamy curd,
And lucent syrops, tinct with cinnamon;
Manna and dates, in argosy transferr'd
From Fez; and spiced dainties, every one,
From silken Samarcand to cedar'd Lebanon.

These delicacies he heap'd with glowing hand
On golden dishes and in baskets bright
Of wreathed silver: sumptuous they stand
In the retired quiet of the night,
Filling the chilly room with perfume light.—
'And now, my love, my seraph fair, awake!
Thou art my heaven, and I thine eremite:
Open thine eyes, for meek St Agnes' sake,
Or I shall drowse beside thee, so my soul doth ache.'

Thus whispering, his warm unnerved arm
Sank in her pillow. Shaded was her dream
By the dusk curtains:—'twas a midnight charm
Impossible to melt as iced stream:
The lustrous salvers in the moonlight gleam;
Broad golden fringe upon the carpet lies:
It seem'd he never, never could redeem
From such a steadfast spell his lady's eyes;
So mused awhile, entoil'd in woofed phantasies.

[*Madeline dreams, then wakes, and the pair flee at once, leaving Porphyro's feast untasted and disregarded.*]

John Keats, 'The Eve of St Agnes', 1819

APHRODISIACS

With lovers 'twas of old the fashion
By presents to convey their passion;
No matter what the gift they sent,
The Lady saw that love was meant.
Fair *Atalanta*, as a favour,
Took the boar's head her Hero gave her;
Nor could the bristling thing affront her,
'Twas a fit present from a hunter.
When Squires send woodcocks to the dame,
It serves to show their absent flame:
Some by a snip of woven hair,
In posied lockets bribe the fair;
How many mercenary matches
Have sprung from Di'mond-rings and watches!
But hold—a ring, a watch, a locket
Would drain at once a Poet's pocket;
He should send songs that cost him nought,
Nor ev'n be prodigal of thought.
Why then send Lampreys? fye, for shame!
'Twill set a virgin's blood on flame.
This to fifteen a proper gift!
It might lend sixty-five a lift.
I know your maiden Aunt will scold,
And think my present somewhat bold.
I see her lift her hands and eyes.
'What, eat it, Niece? eat *Spanish* flies!
Lamprey's a most immodest diet:
You'll neither wake nor sleep in quiet.
Should I to night eat Sago cream,
'Twould make me blush to tell my dream;
If I eat Lobster, 'tis so warming,
That ev'ry man I see looks charming.
Wherefore had not the filthy fellow
Laid *Rochester* upon your pillow?
I vow and swear, I think the present
Had been as modest and as decent.
'Who has her virtue in her power?
Each day has its unguarded hour;
Always in danger of undoing,

A prawn, a shrimp, may prove our ruin!
  'The shepherdess, who lives on sallad,
To cool her youth, controuls her palate;
Should *Dian's* maids turn liqu'rish livers,
And of huge lampreys rob the rivers,
Then all beside each glade and Visto,
You'd see Nymphs lying like *Calisto*.
  'The man who meant to heat your blood,
Needs not himself such vicious food'—
  In this, I own, your Aunt is clear,
I sent you what I might well spare:
For when I see you (without joking)
Your eyes, lips, breasts, are so provoking,
They set my heart more cock-a-hoop,
Than could whole seas of craw-fish soupe.

John Gay, 'To a Young Lady, with some LAMPREYS', 1720

Atalanta: a celibate beauty, exposed as a child and suckled by a she-bear. Meleager presented her with the head of the Calydonian Boar, which she had been the first to wound, and which he killed; *Spanish flies*: *Cantharides vesicatoria*, a dried beetle, taken as an aphrodisiac or diuretic; *Rochester*: John Wilmot, 2nd Earl of Rochester (1648–80), a notorious libertine, author of love-lyrics; *Dian, Calisto*: Diana (Artemis), the mythical chaste huntress, and her companion the nymph Callisto, beloved of Zeus.

Don Juan, shipwrecked on a voyage from Cadiz to Leghorn, has drifted in an open boat until washed up on a Greek island inhabited by the ravishing Haidée. In the absence of her father, a Mediterranean pirate, Juan and Haidée become lovers. Now her father returns.

Old Lambro passed unseen a private gate,
And stood within his hall at eventide;
Meantime the lady and her lover sate
At wassail in their beauty and their pride:
An ivory inlaid table spread with state
Before them, and fair slaves on every side;
Gems, gold and silver, form'd the service mostly,
Mother of pearl and coral the less costly.

The dinner made about a hundred dishes;
Lamb and pistachio nuts—in short, all meats,
And saffron soups, and sweetbreads; and the fishes

Were of the finest that e'er flounced in nets,
Drest to a Sybarite's most pamper'd wishes;
The beverage was various sherbets
Of raisin, orange, and pomegranate juice,
Squeezed through the rind, which makes it best for use.

These were ranged round, each in its crystal ewer,
And fruits, and date-bread loaves closed the repast,
And Mocha's berry, from Arabia pure,
In small fine China cups, came in at last;
Gold cups of filigree made to secure
The hand from burning underneath them placed;
Cloves, cinnamon, and saffron too were boil'd
Up with the coffee, which (I think) they spoil'd.

Lord Byron, *Don Juan*

The Salina family, with a handsome young cousin, Tancredi Falconeri, have returned from Palermo to their ancestral home of Donnafugata, a mansion in the centre of a small Sicilian country town. After attending ceremonial prayers at the church, the Prince and Princess invite several local worthies to evening dinner at the house. Among these is the awkward, nouveau-riche *mayor, don Calogero Sedara, who brings his newly grown-up daughter Angelica, recently returned home from a Tuscan boarding-school.*

The door opened and in came Angelica. The first impression was one of dazed surprise. The Salina family all stood there with breath taken away; Tancredi could even feel the veins pulsing in his temples. Under the first shock from her beauty men were incapable of noticing or analysing its defects, which were numerous; there were to be many for ever incapable of this critical appraisal. She was tall and well-made, on an ample scale; her skin looked as if it had the flavour of fresh cream which it resembled, her childlike mouth that of strawberries. Under a mass of raven hair, curling in gentle waves, her green eyes gleamed motionless as those of statues, and like them a little cruel. She was moving slowly, making her wide white skirt rotate around her, and emanating from her whole person the invincible calm of a woman sure of her own beauty. Only many months later was it known that at the moment of that victorious entry of hers she had been on the point of fainting from nerves.

She took no notice of the Prince hurrying towards her, she passed by Tancredi grinning at her in a daydream; before the Princess's armchair she bent her superb waist in a slight bow, and this form of homage, unusual in Sicily, gave her for an instant the fascination of exoticism as well as that of local beauty.

* * * * *

The Prince was too experienced to offer Sicilian guests, in a town of the interior, a dinner beginning with soup, and he infringed the rules all the more readily as he disliked it himself. But rumours of the barbaric foreign usage of serving an insipid liquid as first course had reached the citizens of Donnafugata too insistently for them not to quiver with a slight residue of alarm at the start of a solemn dinner like this. So when three lackeys in green, gold and powder entered, each holding a great silver dish containing a towering macaroni pie, only four of the twenty at table avoided showing pleased surprise; the Prince and Princess from fore-knowledge, Angelica from affectation and Concetta [the Salinas' daughter, who was in love] from lack of appetite. All the others (including Tancredi, I regret to say), showed their relief in varying ways, from the fluty and ecstatic grunt of the notary to the sharp squeak of Francesco Paolo [an adolescent son]. But a threatening circular stare from the host soon stifled these improper demonstrations.

Good manners apart, though, the aspect of those monumental dishes of macaroni was worthy of the quivers of admiration they evoked. The burnished gold of the crusts, the fragrance of sugar and cinnamon they exuded, were but preludes to the delights released from the interior, when the knife broke the crust; first came a smoke laden with aromas, then chicken livers, hard boiled eggs, ham, chicken and truffles in masses of piping hot, glistening macaroni, to which the meat juice gave an exquisite hue of suède.

The beginning of the meal, as happens in the provinces, was quiet. The arch-priest made the sign of the Cross and plunged in without a word. The organist absorbed the succulent dish with closed eyes; he was grateful to the Creator that his ability to shoot hare and woodcock could bring him ecstatic pleasures like this, and the thought came to him that he and Teresina [his dog] could exist for a month on the cost of one of these dishes; Angelica, the lovely Angelica, forgot her Tuscan affectations and part of her good manners and devoured her food with the appetite of her seventeen years and the vigour given by grasping her fork half-way up the handle. Tancredi, in an attempt to link gallantry with greed, tried to imagine himself tasting, in the aromatic forkfuls, the kisses of his neighbour Angelica, but he realised at once that the experiment was disgusting and suspended it, with a mental reserve about reviving this fantasy with the pudding; the Prince, although rapt in the contemplation of Angelica sitting opposite him, was the only one at table able to notice that the *demi-glace* was overfilled, and made a mental note to tell the cook so next day; the others ate without thinking of anything, and without realising that the food seemed so delicious because sensuality was circulating in the house.

Lampedusa, *The Leopard*, translated by Archibald Colquhoun

❧ *Two couples have left England together for the Austrian mountains in winter. Gerald and Gudrun are lovers; Gudrun's sister Ursula and Rupert Birkin are newly married. On arrival at their hotel, Gerald and Gudrun retire to their room, where Gudrun silently submits to Gerald's lovemaking.*

The overweening power of his body was too much for her. She relaxed again, and lay loose and soft, panting in a little delirium. And to him, she was so sweet, she was such bliss of release, that he would have suffered a whole eternity of torture rather than forgo one second of this pang of unsurpassable bliss.

'My God,' he said to her, his face drawn and strange, transfigured, 'what next?'

* * * * *

He kissed her, kissed her eyes shut, so that she could not look any more. He wanted something now, some recognition, some sign, some admission. But she only lay silent and childlike and remote, like a child that is overcome and cannot understand, only feels lost. He kissed her again, giving up.

'Shall we go down and have coffee and *Kuchen*?' he asked.

The twilight was falling slate-blue at the window. She closed her eyes, closed away the monotonous level of dead wonder, and opened them again to the real world.

'Yes,' she said briefly, regaining her will with a click. She went again to the window. Blue evening had fallen over the cradle of snow and over the great pallid slopes. But in the heaven the peaks of snow were rosy, glistening like transcendent, radiant spikes of blossom in the heavenly upper world, so lovely and beyond.

Gudrun saw all their loveliness, she *knew* how immortally beautiful they were, great pistils of rose-coloured, snow-fed fire in the blue twilight of the heaven. She could *see* it, she knew it, but she was not of it. She was divorced, debarred, a soul shut out.

* * * * *

They went downstairs, both with a strange other-world look on their faces, and with a glow in their eyes. They saw Birkin and Ursula sitting at the long table in the corner, waiting for them.

'How good and simple they look together,' Gudrun thought jealously. She envied them some spontaneity, a childish sufficiency to which she herself could never approach. They seemed such children to her.

'Such good *Kranzkuchen*!' cried Ursula greedily. 'So good!'

'Right,' said Gudrun. 'Can we have *Kaffee mit Kranzkuchen*?' she added to the waiter.

And she seated herself on the bench beside Gerald. Birkin, looking at them, felt a pain of tenderness for them.

'I think the place is really wonderful, Gerald,' he said; '*prachtvoll* and *wunderbar* and *wunderschön* and *unbeschreiblich* and all the other German adjectives.'

Gerald broke into a slight smile.

'*I* like it,' he said.

The tables, of white scrubbed wood, were placed round three sides of the room, as in a Gasthaus. Birkin and Ursula sat with their backs to the wall, which was of oiled wood, and Gerald and Gudrun sat in the corner next them, near to the stove. It was a fairly large place, with a tiny bar, just like a country inn, but quite simple and bare, and all of oiled wood, ceilings and walls and floor, the only furniture being the tables and benches going round three sides, the great green stove, and the bar and the doors on the fourth side. The windows were double, and quite uncurtained. It was early evening.

The coffee came—hot and good—and a whole ring of cake.

'A whole *Kuchen*!' cried Ursula. 'They give you more than us! I want some of yours.'

D. H. Lawrence, *Women in Love*, 1921

❧ *Moses Herzog, a middle-aged, New York academic, living in the past as he contemplates his childhood and the ruins of his two marriages, and at other times given to philosophical speculation, spends an evening with his mistress Ramona, who hopes to marry him.*

In the dining room she handed him the bottle—Pouilly Fuissé, well chilled—and the French corkscrew. With competent hands and strong purpose, his neck reddening as he exerted himself, he pulled the cork. Ramona had lighted the candles. The table was decorated with spiky red gladiolas in a long dish. On the windowsill the pigeons stirred and grumbled; they fluttered and went to sleep again. 'Let me help you to this rice,' said Ramona. She took the plate, good bone china with a cobalt rim (the steady spread of luxury into all ranks of society since the fifteenth century, noted by the famous Sombart, inter alia). But Herzog was hungry, and the dinner was delicious. (He would become austere hereafter.) Tears of curious, mixed origin came into his eyes as he tasted the shrimp remoulade. 'Awfully good—my God, how good!' he said.

'Haven't you eaten all day?' said Ramona.

'I haven't seen food like this for some time. Prosciutto and Persian melon. What's this? Watercress salad. Good Christ!'

She was pleased. 'Well, eat.'

After the shrimp Arnaud and salad, she offered cheese and cold-water biscuits, rum-flavored ice cream, plums from Georgia, and early green grapes. Then brandy and coffee. In the next room, Mohammed al Bakhar kept singing his winding, nasal, insinuating song to the sound of wire coathangers moved back and forth, and drums, tambourines and mandolines and bagpipes.

Bellow, *Herzog*

❧ *Fourteen-year-old Ivan (Van) Veen has fallen in love with his 12-year-old cousin Ada, having been sent to stay with her family at their country property, Ardis, near Ladore, in a fantastically Russianized version of the north-eastern United States.*

Hammock and honey: eighty years later he could still recall with the young pang of the original joy his falling in love with Ada. Memory met imagination halfway in the hammock of his boyhood's dawns.

At ninety-four he liked retracing that first amorous summer not as a dream he had just had but as a recapitulation of consciousness to sustain him in the small gray hours between shallow sleep and the first pill of the day.

* * * * *

He would fall asleep at the moment he thought he would never sleep again, and his dreams were young. As the first flame of day reached his hammock, he woke up another man—and very much of a man indeed. 'Ada, our ardors and arbors'—a dactylic trimeter that was to remain Van Veen's only contribution to Anglo-American poetry—sang through his brain. . . . He was fourteen and a half; he was burning and bold; he would have her fiercely some day!

One such green resurrection he could particularize when replaying the past. Having drawn on his swimming trunks, having worked in and crammed in all that intricate, reluctant multiple machinery, he had toppled out of his nest and forthwith endeavoured to determine whether her part of the house had come alive. It had. He saw a flash of crystal, a fleck of colour. She was having *sa petite collation du matin* alone on a private balcony. Van found his sandals—with a beetle in one and a petal in the other—and, through the toolroom, entered the cool house.

Children of her type contrive the purest philosophies. Ada had worked out her own little system. Hardly a week had elapsed since Van's arrival when he was found worthy of being initiated in her web of wisdom. An individual's life consisted of certain classified things: 'real things' which were unfrequent and priceless, simply 'things' which formed the routine stuff of life; and 'ghost things', also called 'fogs', such as fever, toothache, dreadful disappointments, and death. Three or more things occurring at the same time formed a 'tower', or if they came in immediate succession, they made a 'bridge'. 'Real towers' and 'real bridges' were the joys of life, and when the towers came in a series, one experienced supreme rapture; it almost never happened, though. In some circumstances, in a certain light, a neutral 'thing' might look or even actually become 'real' or else, conversely, it might coagulate into a fetid 'fog'. When the joy and the joyless happened to be intermixed, simultaneously or along the ramp of duration, one was confronted with 'ruined towers' and 'broken bridges'.

The pictorial and architectural details of her metaphysics made her nights easier than Van's, and that morning—as on most mornings—

he had the sensation of returning from a much more remote and grim country than she and her sunlight had come from.

Her plump, stickily glistening lips smiled.

(When I kiss you *here*, he said to her years later, I always remember that blue morning on the balcony when you were eating a *tartine au miel*; so much better in French.)

The classical beauty of clover honey, smooth, pale, translucent, freely flowing from the spoon and soaking my love's bread and butter in liquid brass. The crumb steeped in nectar.

'Real thing?' he asked.

'Tower,' she answered.

And the wasp.

The wasp was investigating her plate. Its body was throbbing.

'We shall try to eat one later', she observed, 'but it must be *gorged* to taste good. Of course, it can't sting your tongue. No animal will touch a person's tongue. When a lion has finished a traveller, bones and all, he *always* leaves the man's tongue lying like that in the desert' (making a negligent gesture).

'I doubt it'.

'It's a well-known mystery.'

Her hair was well brushed that day and sheened darkly in contrast with the lustreless pallor of her neck and arms. She wore the striped tee shirt which in his lone fantasies he especially liked to peel off her twisting torso. The oilcloth was divided into blue and white squares. A smear of honey stained what remained of the butter in its cool crock.

'All right. And the third Real Thing?'

She considered him. A fiery droplet in the wick of her mouth considered him. A three-coloured velvet violet, of which she had done an aquarelle on the eve, considered him from its fluted crystal. She said nothing. She licked her spread fingers, still looking at him.

Van, getting no answer, left the balcony. Softly her tower crumbled in the sweet silent sun.

Vladimir Nabokov, *Ada*, 1969, Part One

ACKNOWLEDGEMENTS

The editor wishes to thank those friends who have suggested material, lent books, or contributed in other ways, directly or indirectly, to the compilation of this anthology.

For permission to quote from unpublished manuscript material, the publishers wish to make the following acknowledgements. To the Bodleian Library, Oxford, for extracts from the diary of a castaway on Ascension Island (MS. Rawl. C. 871 [unfoliated]), the diary of John Baptist Grano in the Marshalsea (MS. Rawl. D. 34, ff. 5, 65 and 200–1), and the diaries of William Stukeley for 1738 (MS. Eng. misc. d. 719/8, f. 2) and 1741 (MS. Eng. misc. e. 125, f. 36); to the British Library, Oriental and India Office Collections, for extracts from the Gwillim Papers (IOR MS. Eur. C. 204), the Robinson Papers (IOR MS. Eur. F. 142/63), and the narrative of Judith Weston (IOR MS. Eur. B. 162); and to the Governing Body of Christ Church, Oxford, for extracts from the Steward's Memorandum Book, 1888–1895 (Archives, S. xxxi. a. 2, ff. 62, 64, 72, 74, 76 and 222).

All rights in respect of the Authorized King James Version of the Holy Bible are vested in the Crown in the United Kingdom and controlled by Royal Letters Patent.

The editor and publisher are also grateful for permission to include the following copyright material:

Athenaeus, reprinted by permission of the publishers and the Loeb Classical Library from Athenaeus, *The Deipnosophists*, with an English translation by Charles Burton Gulick Ph.D.; Cambridge, Mass: Harvard University Press, 1927–1941.

Sybille Bedford, from *Jigsaw: An Unsentimental Education* (Hamish Hamilton, 1989). Copyright © Sybille Bedford, 1989. Reproduced by permission of Hamish Hamilton Ltd.

Max Beerbohm, from *Zuleika Dobson*. Reprinted by permission of Mrs Eva Reichman.

Saul Bellow, from *Herzog* (Secker & Warburg Ltd, 1961). Reprinted by permission of Reed Consumer Books Ltd.

Gerald Brenan, from *South From Granada* (1957). Reproduced by permission of Margaret Hanbury, 27 Walcot Square, London SE11 4UB.

Willie Elmhirst, from *A Freshman's Diary* (1969). Reprinted by permission of Blackwell Publishers.

J. G. Farrell, from *Troubles* (Jonathan Cape, 1970). Reprinted by permission of Rogers Coleridge & White Ltd and Random House UK Ltd.

Gustave Flaubert, from *Madame Bovary*, trans. Alan Russell (Penguin Classics, 1950), © Alan Russell, 1950. Reprinted by permission of Penguin Books Ltd.

E. M. Forster, from *A Passage to India*. Reprinted by permission of King's College, Cambridge, and the Society of Authors as the literary representatives of the E. M. Forster Estate; from *Howards End*, reprinted by permission of King's College, Cambridge, the Society of Authors as the literary representative of the E. M. Forster Estate, and Alfred A. Knopf Inc.

John Gay, from *John Gay: Poetry and Prose*, ed. Vinton A. Deaning and Charles E. Beckwith (1974). Reprinted by permission of Oxford University Press.

Ellen Gilchrist, from *Light Can Be Both Wave and Particle* (Faber, 1990), © Ellen Gilchrist 1990. Reprinted by permission of Sheil Land Associates Ltd.

Goethe, from *Italian Journey 1786–1788*. Trans. W. H. Auden and Elizabeth Mayer. Reprinted by permission of HarperCollins Publishers.

Maxim Gorky, from *Fragments from My Diary* (1924), trans. Moura Budberg (1940).

Gunter Grass, from *Dog Years*, trans. Ralph Mannheim. Originally published in German as *Hundejahre*. Copyright © 1963 by Herman Lucterhand Verlag Gmbh, English translation © 1965 by Harcourt Brace & Co and Martin Secker & Warburg and renewed 1993 by Harcourt Brace & Co. Reprinted by permission of Harcourt Brace & Co and Reed Consumer Books Ltd. *Local Anaesthetic*, trans. Ralph Mannheim, original German title *Ortlich Betauht*. Reprinted by permission of Reed Consumer Books Ltd and Steidl Verlag.

Joyce Conyngham Green, from *Salmagundi* (1947). Reprinted by permission of J. M. Dent & Sons Ltd. Publishers.

Robert Herrick, from *The Poetical Works of Robert Herrick*, ed. L. C. Martin (Clarendon Press, 1956). Reprinted by permission of Oxford University Press.

Richard Hoggart, from *A Local Habitation* (Chatto & Windus Ltd). Reprinted by permission of Random House UK Ltd.

Samuel Johnson, from *A Journey to the Western Islands of Scotland*, ed. R. W. Chapman (1924). Reprinted by permission of Oxford University Press.

James Joyce, from *Ulysses*, copyright © 1934 and renewed 1962 by Lucia and George Joyce. Reprinted by permission of Random House, Inc. and the Society of Authors as literary representatives of the James Joyce Estate.

Juvenal, extract from Satire V, from *The Sixteen Satires*, trans. Peter Green (Penguin Classics 1967, revised ed. 1974), © Peter Green, 1967, 1974. Reprinted by permission of Penguin Books Ltd.

John Keats, from *The Letters of John Keats*, ed. Maurice Buxton Forman (4th edn., 1952). Reprinted by permission of Oxford University Press.

Guiseppe Tomasi di Lampedusa, from *The Leopard*, trans. Archibald Colquhoun (1960). Reprinted by permission of HarperCollins Publishers Ltd.

Philip Larkin, from 'Livings I' from *Collected Poems*. Copyright © 1988, 1989 by Philip Larkin. Reprinted by permission of Farrar Straus & Giroux Inc and Faber & Faber Ltd.

from *Nella Last's War: A Mother's Diary 1939–45*, ed. Richard Broad and Suzie Fleming (Bristol: Falling Wall Press, 1981).

D. H. Lawrence, from *Women in Love*, copyright 1920, 1922 by D. H. Lawrence, renewed 1948, 1950 by Frieda Lawrence. Extract from *The Boy in the Bush* by D. H. Lawrence and M. L. Skinner, copyright 1924 by Thomas Seltzer, Inc., copyright renewed 1952 by Frieda Lawrence Ravagli. Used by permission of Viking Penguin, a division of Penguin Books USA, Inc.

Grevel Lindop, 'Summer Pudding' – For Carol Reeves' from *Tourists* (1987). Reprinted by permission of Carcanet Press Ltd.

Malcolm Lowry, from *Under the Volcano*, copyright 1947 by Malcolm Lowry. Reprinted by permission of Sterling Lord Literistic Inc.

Ethel Mannin, from *Confessions and Impressions* (1936), © the Estate of Ethel Mannin.

Olivia Manning, from *The Great Fortune* (William Heinemann Ltd). Reprinted by permission of Reed Consumer Books Ltd.

from *The Journal of Katherine Mansfield*, ed. John Middleton Murry (1927). Reprinted by permission of the Society of Authors as literary representatives of the Estate of Katherine Mansfield.

Adam Mickiewicz, from *Pan Tadeusz* (1834), trans. George Rapall Noyes (Everyman's Library, David Campbell Publishers).

from *The Complete Letters of Lady Mary Wortley Montagu*, ed. Robert Halsband, II, 1721–1751 (1966). Reprinted by permission of Oxford University Press.

Iris Murdoch, from *Sea, The Sea* (Chatto & Windus, 1978). Copyright © 1978 by Iris Murdoch. Reprinted by permission of Random House UK Ltd and Viking Penguin, a division of Penguin Books USA Inc.

Vladimir Nabokov, from *Ada, or Ardor, A Family Chronicle* (Weidenfeld, 1969), © the Estate of Vladimir Nabokov. Used with permission.

V. S. Naipaul, from *An Area of Darkness* (1964). Reprinted by permission of Aitken, Stone & Wylie Ltd.

Eric Newby, from *Love and War in the Apennines* (HarperCollins Publishers Ltd).

George Orwell, from *The Road to Wigan Pier*. Reprinted by permission of A. M. Heath on behalf of the Estate of the late Sonia Brownell Orwell and the British publisher, Martin Secker & Warburg Ltd. Published in the US by Harcourt Brace Jovanovich.

Arnold Palmer, from *Movable Feasts. A Reconnaissance of the Origins and Consequences of Fluctuations in Meal-Times With Special Attention to the Introduction of Luncheon and Afternoon Tea* (1952). Reprinted by permission of Oxford University Press.

Letters from John Pintard to his Daughter Eliza Noel Pintard Davidson 1816–1833, ed. Dorothy C. Barck, 4 Volumes, published by The New York Historical Society, 1937–1940. Reprinted by permission of The New York Historical Society.

J. B. Priestley, from *The Good Companions*. Reprinted by permission of the Peters Fraser & Dunlop Group Ltd.

Alexander Pushkin, from *Eugene Onegin*, Book V, trans. Oliver Elton, 1937 (London: Pushkin Press, 1943).

Arthur Ransome, from *The Big Six* (Jonathan Cape, 1940) and *Missee Lee* (Jonathan Cape, 1941). Reprinted by permission of Random House UK Ltd.

Jean Rennie, from *Every Other Sunday: The Autobiography of a Kitchenmaid* (Arthur Barker Ltd., 1955).

A. L. Rowse, from *A Cornishman Abroad* (Jonathan Cape, 1976). Copyright © 1976 by A. L. Rowse. Reprinted by permission of Random House UK Ltd and Curtis Brown, New York.

Howard Ruede, from *Sod-House Days: Letters From a Kansas Homesteader 1877–78*, ed. John Ise (1937), © Columbia University Press, New York. Reprinted with permission of the publisher.

Bernard Shaw, from *Bernard Shaw: Nine Answers*. Reprinted by permission of the Society of Authors on behalf of the Bernard Shaw Estate.

Shorter Oxford English Dictionary, definition of 'Lady', 'Parliament', and 'Tockwough Roots'. Reprinted by permission of Oxford University Press.

Gary Snyder, from *The Black Country*. Copyright © 1968 by Gary Snyder. Reprinted by permission of New Directions Publishing Corp.

Alexander Solzhenitsyn, from *One Day in the Life of Ivan Denisovich* (1962), trans. Ralph Parker. Reprinted by permission of Victor Gollancz Ltd.

Laurence Sterne, from *The Letters of Laurence Sterne*, ed. Lewis Perry Curtis (1935). Reprinted by permission of Oxford University Press.

from *Diary of William Tayler, Footman, 1837*, ed. Dorothy Wise (St Marylebone Society Publications Group, 1962).

Flora Thompson, from *Lark Rise to Candleford* (1939). Reprinted by permission of Oxford University Press.

from letters to *The Times*, 11 May 1989, © J. R. Colclough, © John Champion.

Leo Tolstoy, from *War and Peace*, trans. Rosemary Edmonds (Penguin Classics, 1957), © Rosemary Edmonds, 1957, 1978. Reprinted by permission of Penguin Books Ltd.

from *The Diary of Thomas Turner 1754–1765*, ed. David Vaisey (1984). Reprinted by permission of Oxford University Press.

Evelyn Waugh, from *Brideshead Revisited*, and from *A Little Learning: The First Volume of an Autobiography*. Reprinted by permission of the Peters Fraser & Dunlop Group Ltd.

H. G. Wells, from *Ann Veronica*. Reprinted by permission of A. P. Watt Ltd., on behalf of the Literary Executors of the Estate of H. G. Wells.

Laura Ingalls Wilder, from *The Little House in the Big Woods* (Harper Bros., 1932).

William Carlos Williams, from *The Collected Poems of William Carlos Williams, 1909–1939 Vol. I*. Copyright © 1938 by New Directions Publishing Corp. Reprinted by permission of New Directions Publishing Corp.

Virgil, reprinted by permission of the publishers and the Loeb Classical Library from Virgil, the *Aeneid Book viii*, trans. H. Rushton Fairclough, Cambridge, Mass.: Harvard University Press, 1918.

Virginia Woolf, extracts from *The Waves, A Room of One's Own* and *To the Lighthouse*. Published in the US by Harcourt Brace Jovanovich Inc.

from *The Journals of Dorothy Wordsworth*, ed. Ernest de Selincourt (Macmillan, 1941). Reprinted by permission of Oxford University Press.

While every effort has been made to secure permission, we may have failed in a few cases to trace the copyright holder. We apologize for any apparent negligence.

INDEX OF AUTHORS

INCLUDING TITLES OF ANONYMOUS WORKS QUOTED

For third-person references to authors, see General Index

GENERAL INDEX

Oxford Reference

The Oxford Reference series offers authoritative and up-to-date reference books in paperback across a wide range of topics.

Abbreviations
Art and Artists
Ballet
Biology
Botany
Business
Card Games
Chemistry
Christian Church
Classical Literature
Computing
Dates
Earth Sciences
Ecology
English Christian Names
English Etymology
English Language
English Literature
English Place-Names
Eponyms
Finance
Fly-Fishing
Fowler's Modern English Usage
Geography
Irish Mythology
King's English
Law
Literary Guide to Great Britain and Ireland
Literary Terms
Mathematics
Medical Dictionary
Modern Quotations
Modern Slang
Music
Nursing
Opera
Oxford English
Physics
Popes
Popular Music
Proverbs
Quotations
Sailing Terms
Saints
Science
Ships and the Sea
Sociology
Spelling
Superstitions
Theatre
Twentieth-Century Art
Twentieth-Century History
Twentieth-Century World Biography
Weather Facts
Word Games
World Mythology
Writer's Dictionary
Zoology

OXFORD REFERENCE

THE CONCISE OXFORD COMPANION TO ENGLISH LITERATURE

Edited by Margaret Drabble and Jenny Stringer

Based on the immensely popular fifth edition of the *Oxford Companion to English Literature* this is an indispensable, compact guide to the central matter of English literature.

There are more than 5,000 entries on the lives and works of authors, poets, playwrights, essayists, philosophers, and historians; plot summaries of novels and plays; literary movements; fictional characters; legends; theatres; periodicals; and much more.

The book's sharpened focus on the English literature of the British Isles makes it especially convenient to use, but there is still generous coverage of the literature of other countries and of other disciplines which have influenced or been influenced by English literature.

From reviews of *The Oxford Companion to English Literature*:

'a book which one turns to with constant pleasure . . . a book with much style and little prejudice' Iain Gilchrist, *TLS*

'it is quite difficult to imagine, in this genre, a more useful publication' Frank Kermode, *London Review of Books*

'incarnates a living sense of tradition . . . sensitive not to fashion merely but to the spirit of the age' Christopher Ricks, *Sunday Times*